W9-BWD-435

BECOMING FREE, BECOMING BLACK

How did Africans become "blacks" in the Americas? *Becoming Free, Becoming Black* tells the story of enslaved and free people of color who used the law to claim freedom and citizenship for themselves and their loved ones. Their communities challenged slaveholders' efforts to make blackness synonymous with slavery. Looking closely at three slave societies – Cuba, Virginia, and Louisiana – Alejandro de la Fuente and Ariela J. Gross demonstrate that the law of freedom, not slavery, established the meaning of blackness in law. Contests over freedom determined whether and how it was possible to move from slave to free status, and whether claims to citizenship would be tied to racial identity. Laws regulating the lives and institutions of free people of color created the boundaries between black and white, the rights reserved to white people, and the degradations imposed only on black people. By 1860, different racial regimes had emerged. In Cuba, free people of color remained part of public life, whereas in Virginia and Louisiana, citizenship was bound to whiteness, with lasting legacies.

Alejandro de la Fuente is the Robert Woods Bliss Professor of Latin American History and Economics, Professor of African and African American Studies, and the Director of the Afro-Latin American Research Institute at Harvard University. He is the author of *Diago: The Pasts of This Afro-Cuban Present* (2017); *Havana and the Atlantic in the Sixteenth Century* (2008); and *A Nation for All: Race, Inequality, and Politics in Twentieth-Century Cuba* (2001).

Ariela J. Gross is the John B. and Alice R. Sharp Professor of Law and History and the Co-Director of the Center for Law, History, and Culture at the University of Southern California Gould School of Law. She is the author of *What Blood Won't Tell: A History of Race on Trial in America* (2008) and *Double Character: Slavery and Mastery in the Antebellum Southern Courtroom* (2000).

See the Studies in Legal History series website at
http://studiesinlegalhistory.org/

STUDIES IN LEGAL HISTORY

Editors
Sarah Barringer Gordon, University of Pennsylvania
Holly Brewer, University of Maryland, College Park
Michael Lobban, London School of Economics and Political Science
Reuel Schiller, University of California, Hastings College of the Law

Other books in the series:

Elizabeth Papp Kamali, *Felony and the Guilty Mind in Medieval England*
Michael A. Schoeppner, *Moral Contagion: Black Atlantic Sailors, Citizenship, and Diplomacy in Antebellum America*
Sam Erman, *Almost Citizens: Puerto Rico, the U.S. Constitution, and Empire*
Jessica K. Lowe, *Murder in the Shenandoah: Making Law Sovereign in Revolutionary Virginia*
Martha S. Jones, *Birthright Citizens: A History of Race and Rights in Antebellum America*
Cynthia Nicoletti, *Secession on Trial: The Treason Prosecution of Jefferson Davis*
Edward James Kolla, *Sovereignty, International Law, and the French Revolution*
Assaf Likhovski, *Tax Law and Social Norms in Mandatory Palestine and Israel*
Robert W. Gordon, *Taming the Past: Essays on Law and History and History in Law*
Paul Garfinkel, *Criminal Law in Liberal and Fascist Italy*
Michelle A. McKinley, *Fractional Freedoms: Slavery, Intimacy, and Legal Mobilization in Colonial Lima, 1600–1700*
Mitra Sharafi, *Law and Identity in Colonial South Asia: Parsi Legal Culture, 1772–1947*
Karen M. Tani, *States of Dependency: Welfare, Rights, and American Governance, 1935–1972*
Stefan Jurasinski, *The Old English Penitentials and Anglo-Saxon Law*
Felice Batlan, *Women and Justice for the Poor: A History of Legal Aid, 1863–1945*
Sophia Z. Lee, *The Workplace Constitution from the New Deal to the New Right*
Michael A. Livingston, *The Fascists and the Jews of Italy: Mussolini's Race Laws, 1938–1943*

ALEJANDRO DE LA FUENTE
ARIELA J. GROSS

BECOMING
FREE,
BECOMING
BLACK

RACE, FREEDOM, AND
LAW IN CUBA, VIRGINIA,
AND LOUISIANA

CAMBRIDGE
UNIVERSITY PRESS

CAMBRIDGE
UNIVERSITY PRESS

University Printing House, Cambridge CB2 8BS, United Kingdom

One Liberty Plaza, 20th Floor, New York, NY 10006, USA

477 Williamstown Road, Port Melbourne, VIC 3207, Australia

314–321, 3rd Floor, Plot 3, Splendor Forum, Jasola District Centre, New Delhi – 110025, India

79 Anson Road, #06–04/06, Singapore 079906

Cambridge University Press is part of the University of Cambridge.

It furthers the University's mission by disseminating knowledge in the pursuit of education, learning, and research at the highest international levels of excellence.

www.cambridge.org
Information on this title: www.cambridge.org/9781108480642
DOI: 10.1017/9781108612951

First published 2020

Printed in the United Kingdom by TJ International Ltd. Padstow Cornwall

A catalogue record for this publication is available from the British Library.

ISBN 978-1-108-48064-2 Hardback

Contents

List of Figures and Tables	*page* vi
Preface	ix
List of Abbreviations	xiv

Introduction 1

1 "A Negro and by Consequence an Alien": Local Regulation
   and the Making of Race, 1500s–1700s 13

2 The "Inconvenience" of Black Freedom: Manumission,
   1500s–1700s 39

3 "The Natural Right of All Mankind": Claiming Freedom in
   the Age of Revolution, 1760–1830 79

4 "Rules . . . for Their Expulsion": Foreclosing Freedom,
   1830–1860 132

5 "Not of the Same Blood": Policing Racial Boundaries,
   1830–1860 178

Conclusion: "Home-Born Citizens": The Significance of Free
People of Color 219

Notes 225
Index 270

Figures and Tables

FIGURES

1. *Nanny Pegee v. Hook* . . . . *page* 2
2. *Carte de la Louisiane*, 1755 20
3. Cuba 1707 22
4. John Smith's Virginia 28
5. Anthony Johnson's mark 55
6. Battle of Santo Domingo 81
7. *Carte de la Virginie* 85
8. Map of the city and harbor of Havana 101
9. *Santiago v. Antonio Moreira* freedom suit, 1826 107
10. New Orleans fort map 1763 115
11. Victoria, Francisca, and Luisa request letters of freedom 120
12. Mathew Carey's Louisiana 124
13. David Walker's *Appeal* 136
14. "Horrid Massacre in Virginia" 138
15. *View of the Main Promenade of Havana* 154
16. A legal demand presented on behalf of the enslaved driver Agustin . 172
17. Luisa Vasquez requests a new master 174
18. First African Baptist Church, Richmond, Virginia 192
19. "The Holy King's Day" 194
20. Free woman of color with her daughter 198
21. "Not a negro" certificate of Lavinia Sampson 202
22. A portrait, in the *costumbrista* tradition, of free women of color . . . 210
23. Petition of Ann Riter for reenslavement 223

TABLES

1. Populations by Race and Status, ca. 1770 72
2. Free Population of Color as Percent of Total Population, 1770–1860 . 156

Preface

We each grew up in a society in which a person's life chances – wealth, education, and even possibility of incarceration – are ordered by "race." Although we grew up a thousand miles apart, Alejandro in the bustling and seemingly integrated city of Havana, Cuba, and Ariela in the posh university town of Princeton, New Jersey, in the United States, we both grew up white, and this gave us opportunities people of color in the same places did not have. Both of us grew up aware of this fundamental injustice, and we came to the study of law and of history to gain some purchase on its origins. Although we do not believe there is a straight line from the past we explore in this book to the present day, we do believe that understanding the origins of race, across the New World, requires us to study slavery and the slave trade from their beginnings, as we do here. How did Africans who came to the Americas become "blacks"?

This book started serendipitously. In 2002 we participated in a panel on law and slavery at the annual conference of the American Society of Legal History. It was an improbable place to meet, as these conferences at the time were fairly Anglocentric in emphasis, with very little representation of Latin American topics. Also on the panel were the African American women's historian Martha Jones and historian of slavery Walter Johnson, both of whom had recently begun to write about law, slavery, and freedom. We did not know it at the time, but this comparative panel would lead to a process of collaboration and exchange that, along the way, became a book. And a friendship.

The panel itself was a creation of program committee member Rebecca J. Scott, who was adamant about the need to bring legal historians of race and slavery from across the Americas into a shared conversation. Over the years, our project has benefited enormously from Rebecca's collegiality, enthusiasm, and groundbreaking scholarship. By the mid- to late 2000s there was something of an informal group of scholars interested in comparative questions that met more or less regularly at various universities around the globe and that functioned as an incubator for projects like ours. Participating in these meetings were scholars from whom we have benefited a great deal. In addition to Rebecca and Martha, they include Manuel Barcia, Ada Ferrer, Keila Grinberg, Jean Hébrard, Silvia Hunold Lara, Richard Turits, and Michael Zeuske.

We arrived at the ASLH panel through very different personal and intellectual trajectories. Ariela had written a book about the history of the everyday law of slavery in the U.S. Deep South that emphasized local culture and law, drawing on cases from five state courts but with its deepest evidentiary base in an exhaustive study of trials in one county in Mississippi, including not only the testimony from the trials themselves but also census records, tax records, land records, newspaper articles, personal papers, and other local archival materials. This study had immersed her in the particularities of law on the ground, with little attention to comparative questions. By 2002 she was working on a second book, a far broader study of race and racism in America encompassing two centuries and the entire United States, but also using local case studies and trial records. This project, because it raised theoretical questions about the nature of racial categories and their construction in law and other discourses, brought her back to the comparative questions she had first encountered as a student of George Fredrickson, the great comparative historian of black freedom and white supremacy in the United States and South Africa. She also drew on the insights of her other mentor and teacher, Bob Gordon, whose writings on critical legal histories inspired a generation of legal historians to think about the mutual constitutiveness of law and culture, and whose comparative studies of law and efforts to repair past injustice continue to inform all of her thinking about slavery and race.

Alejandro's work, like that of any scholar of slavery and race in Latin America, was always implicitly comparative. Many of the questions, methods, and frames of reference used to study slavery and race in Latin

America developed in dialogue with scholarship produced in the United States. It is also no coincidence that Alejandro's mentor, Manuel Moreno Fraginals, worked and coauthored papers with American scholars, such as Stanley Engerman and Herbert Klein. Alejandro then went on to work with George Reid Andrews, whose own comparative studies look to the interior of Afro-Latin America. All of these scholars have influenced our work in fundamental ways – in fact, in many more ways than we can acknowledge here.

We may have come from different intellectual traditions, but we share several things that made our collaboration possible, perhaps even plausible. First, there is our common concern about the enduring, ongoing, and devastating impact of racial constructs and ideologies in the Americas. We also share a passion for primary sources and archival research. Working through dusty, barely known, and difficult to read legal files is our definition of a good time. Finally, we share the conviction that the law cannot be reduced, as many previous comparatists have implied, to the illusory certitude of written edicts or statutes. We see the law as a set of claims, counterclaims, and conflicts that produce contentious vernacular understandings of rights and justice, with the participation of different social actors, including slaves. We find slave "agency" not only in enslaved individuals' attempts to use the law to their advantage, but also in their relentless efforts to advance their own understanding of rights and fairness.

Thus, our book examines the development of the legal regimes of slavery and race in Cuba, Virginia, and Louisiana, but it does so from the bottom up, using the initiatives of slaves and free people of color as a guide. It is a synthetic book in the sense that it covers three and a half centuries in three different locations, but is a synthesis based on primary sources and our own archival research. Indeed, what made the project daunting was the need to conduct primary research on places and periods we had not studied before (like colonial Virginia) and on topics that had not been at the center of our previous work. But we knew that to move old comparative debates into new territory, it was necessary to be grounded locally, to recover slaves' lives and actions, and to be attentive to change across time. That could be achieved only through the nitty-gritty of archival research. It became evident to both of us that a project of this scope, based on primary research, required collaborating in ways that historians rarely do.

The local court records and other materials we consulted are mostly to be found on paper in the archives of Cuba, Louisiana, and Virginia. Alejandro collected records from archives in Havana, Seville, and Madrid over many years, sometimes on his own and at other times with the help of assistants, as having access to Cuban archives has been difficult for him since he moved to the United States. Ariela visited the Library of Virginia in Richmond many times to photograph the colonial court records of Accomack and Northampton Counties, as well as the original trial records of freedom suits and "free negro and slave records" from every Virginia county, for the late eighteenth and nineteenth centuries, which the Library of Virginia archivists have aggregated into their own collections. Moreover, all of the Virginia chancery court cases and legislative petitions have been digitized by the library, so she was able to collect hundreds of cases and petitions online. In Louisiana, colonial judicial records are held at the Louisiana Historical Center in New Orleans, where Ariela photographed original copies of freedom suits, as well as at the New Orleans Notarial Archives, where she read and copied all of the records of notary Francisco Broutin, who worked for several decades in New Orleans, as a sample of the many notarial records of manumission from the Spanish period. Orlando Rivero Valdés transcribed and translated the Spanish judicial records and notarial records that she collected. The nineteenth-century trial records of the Louisiana Supreme Court, held at the University of New Orleans, have now been digitized and are all available online, which made it possible for Alejandro to read them as well. Many other sources concerning Louisiana and Virginia are also available online, which is not the case with Cuban materials.

We presented different chapters of the manuscript at numerous conferences and events. Particularly useful were discussions in law and history workshops, where we presented our work together, at the University of Michigan, Princeton University, the University of North Carolina–Chapel Hill, Tulane University, the University of Pennsylvania, New York University, and Stanford University, as well as at our home institutions, the University of Southern California and

Harvard University. Participants in these workshops raised poignant questions, leading us to clarify key arguments. Ariela also benefited from discussions of this work, and about race in a comparative perspective more generally, with Yasuko Takezawa and colleagues at the University of Kyoto and others who participated in the symposium titled A Japan-Based Global Study of Racial Representations, and with Jean-Fred Schaub, Silvia Sebastiani, Eric Fassin, Pap Ndiaye, Johann Michel, Paul Schor, Clément Thibeaud, Federica Morelli, and colleagues at the École des Hautes Études en Sciences Sociales in Paris, over the course of many visits there, as well as with participants in faculty workshops at Tel Aviv University, UC Berkeley, Boston University, DePaul University, the American Bar Foundation, Chicago-Kent Law School, and Vanderbilt University. We finished the manuscript with the generous support of a collaborative research grant from the American Council of Learned Societies. Ariela is also grateful for a fellowship from the Center for Advanced Study in the Behavioral Sciences at Stanford, which gave her the time to finish writing in 2017–2018. We thank the many colleagues who gave us invaluable comments on chapters along the way, including Bob Gordon, Dirk Hartog, Sam Erman, Nomi Stolzenberg, Hilary Schor, Jean Hébrard, and of course Rebecca Scott. And we are particularly indebted to those who read and gave us comments on the full manuscript: George Reid Andrews, Martha Jones, Bianca Premo, Leslie Harris, Renee Romano, Wendy Wall, Alice Yang, Karen Dunn-Haley. We also thank the students in the seminar Comparative Slavery and the Law: Africa, Latin America, and the United States, which Alejandro teaches with Emmanuel Akyeampong at Harvard, for their comments and suggestions, and James Bennett for invaluable research assistance.

Finally, a note to Sally Gordon. Her friendship, her careful, critical reading of the manuscript, and her boundless enthusiasm for this project kept us going. We gratefully acknowledge her generous and numerous suggestions, which made this book better. Debbie Gershenowitz edited with a keen eye, and shepherded the book skillfully and cheerfully through the production process. Our spouses, Jon Goldman and Patricia (Patri) Gonzalez, tolerated our absences and preoccupations with good humor, asking only occasionally whether we were done yet.

Abbreviations

ACAHO	–	Actas Capitulares del Ayuntamiento de la Habana, Originales (Museo de la Ciudad de la Habana)
ACAHT	–	Actas Capitulares del Ayuntamiento de la Habana, Trasuntadas (Museo de la Ciudad de la Habana)
AGI	–	Archivo General de Indias, Seville
AH	–	Academia de la Historia
AHN	–	Archivo Histórico Nacional, Madrid
ANC	–	Archivo Nacional de Cuba, Havana
ER	–	Escribanía Regueira
FNSR	–	Free Negro and Slave Records
GSC	–	Gobierno Superior Civil
LHQ	–	*Louisiana Historical Quarterly*
LSCA, UNO	–	Louisiana Supreme Court Archives, University of New Orleans
LVA	–	Library of Virginia, Richmond
LVA-LPDC	–	Legislative Petitions Digital Collection, Library of Virginia
PNH	–	Protocolos Notariales de la Habana
RC	–	*Real cédula*
SD	–	Santo Domingo

Introduction

I N 1690, HAVANA RESIDENT JUAN JUNCO GONZALEZ ISSUED A
notarized receipt declaring that his twenty-year-old slave Juana had
asked him to "give her freedom," and that he had "agreed to do it" in
exchange for 300 pesos. Juana had already paid half the price, so now,
Gonzalez stated, he was "*obligated by law* to concede her freedom whenever my slave Juana gives me the rest to complete the said 300 pesos."
Although he presented emancipation (also known as manumission) as a
master's concession ("otorgarle la dicha libertad"), the agreement transformed it into a legal obligation that the slaveholder could not evade.
Through what was known as *coartación* (from *cortarse*, to cut up in pieces),
Juana had acquired the legal right to become free whenever she completed the payment. In practice this meant that Juana, a *coartada*, could
be sold, transferred, or mortgaged to someone else only on conditional
terms: the new owners could not refuse to free her if she came up with the
remaining 150 pesos. The contract also specified that Juana, after paying
a portion of her price, now owned a portion of her own labor. Any buyer
"must grant her half of the time that belongs to her and discount it from
her price." Nor could Gonzalez go back on the agreement. A notarized
contract of *coartación* like Juana's and Gonzalez's turned a master's prerogative into a slave's right, one that the slave could exercise even against
the will of the owner.[1]

More than a century after Juana achieved *coartada* status in Cuba,
Nanny Pegee made her own claim for freedom in a Virginia chancery
court. The basis for her claim, however, did not rest on Iberian contract-
ing arrangements but on her Indian ancestry, as Virginia courts had
recently declared that Indians were presumptively free. She brought

1

1. *Nanny Pegee v. Hook.* In this document, Nanny Pegee, along with her five children, sued for "trespass assault Battery and false imprisonment," on the ground that "Nanny is a free person & in no sort liable to be held as a slave." Pegee v. Hook (1808), Franklin County (VA) Judgments (Freedom Suits), Barcode 7573898, LVA.

her suit in 1808, just two years after Virginia's General Assembly had passed legislation decreeing that freed slaves would have to leave the state after their emancipation, but had rejected more stringent limits on enslaved people's freedom suits. In depositions taken in Franklin County, where Pegee brought her claim, Pegee's witnesses portrayed her as appearing Indian or white, and described her hair as long and straight, "hanging loose down her neck and about her ears," although some thought it "dark or black" and others "rather fair." Several of her owner's witnesses described her as "mulatto Nan," while others described her as "too white." One who "never considered [her] any other than a slave" connected his belief to her "exceedingly strong scent – especially when the weather was warm." Although Pegee's owner complained to the chancery court of the Western District of Virginia that she was being aided by Quakers "inimical to slavery," who were "unfriendly" to him, and that the trial had been marked by "unblushing partiality" on the part of the judge, the jury awarded 200 pounds to Pegee and set her free. Pegee won at every level of the state court system, with the Virginia Supreme Court finally deciding that the jury had the right to determine her racial identity and thus her status as free or enslaved. Like Juana, Nanny Pegee made use of the law to win freedom for herself and to carve out a place for herself in the local community of free people of color.[2]

Nearly four decades after Nanny Pegee won her freedom, Eulalie Oliveau was kidnapped from her home in Pointe Coupée Parish, Louisiana, and sold to slave traders Daniel Long and Zachariah Mabry in New Orleans. In 1852, Eulalie sued Long and Mabry, arguing that she should be free "by prescription," because her owner, the widow Magdelaine Oliveau Porche, had allowed her to leave her plantation forty-five years earlier to marry Madame Porche's mixed-race half-brother, Henri Oliveau, and Eulalie had lived as free ever since. Henri was not taken by the kidnappers, and it was he who secured a lawyer to fight Eulalie's case. According to Eulalie's witnesses, Madame Porche had wanted to set all her slaves free at her death but realized "it was useless for her to make any last will in which all her slaves should be set free, because witness knew, that the police Jury [of Pointe Coupée Parish] would never permit its execution." Eulalie's case went all the way to the Louisiana Supreme Court twice, in 1854 and 1856. When it came before the court the second time, Louisiana's legislature had just passed a law requiring that all freed slaves be sent to Liberia. Nevertheless, Eulalie and her children won their freedom based on an

article of the Louisiana Civil Code providing that a slaveholder who
"suffer[ed] a slave to enjoy his liberty for ten years" could not reclaim
possession of the slave. The judges in her case disagreed on whether her
status was actually that of a free woman, or if the law required only that
her owner not be able to recapture her. Either way, Eulalie and her
children became free, and they did not leave for Liberia.[3]

Becoming Free, Becoming Black tells the story of enslaved and free people
of color across the Americas who sought and shaped liminal spaces in the
law through which they could claim freedom for themselves and their
loved ones and create communities that challenged slaveholders' efforts
to align blackness with enslavement. Although "manumission" should be
understood as the prerogative of an enslaver with the power to emancipate those he held in bondage, the cases reveal individuals who were not
mere passive recipients of a gift of freedom. Instead, they entered into
contracts with their owners, and labored and accumulated property to
achieve their ends. Not only did they use the legal tools available to them,
but their initiatives shaped the laws of slavery and freedom. The Cuban
practice of *coartación* had its origins in Iberian custom, but people like
Juana expanded it and gave it meaning, using it to carve out spaces of
relative autonomy for herself even before she became fully free. Eulalie
Oliveau, too, drew on a legal tradition that traced its roots to Roman law
but remained part of the local knowledge of enslaved and free people of
color in Pointe Coupée, Louisiana, after Louisiana became part of the
United States. Nanny Pegee challenged her enslaved status through her
racial identity, building on a very recent precedent suggesting that
Indians could be presumed free. Thus, enslaved people staked their
claims through self-purchase arrangements and other efforts to bargain
for freedom, as well as through the lawsuits they brought when such
arrangements fell through. Enslaved people who found their way to a
notary's office or a courtroom to claim freedom were exceptional in
certain ways. The majority of men and women born in bondage remained
enslaved their entire lives. Yet those who became free were key to the
construction of race in the Americas.

It was not the law of slavery but the law of freedom that was most
crucial for the creation of racial regimes in law. The laws regulating
manumission and freedom suits determined whether it was possible to

move from slave to free status, under what circumstances, and whether race would become the primary basis for claims to freedom. Laws regulating the lives and institutions of free people of color created the boundaries between black and white, the rights that would be reserved to white people, and the degradations imposed only on black people. This book challenges traditional perceptions of a contrast between a racially fluid system in Latin America that recognized the slave as a person, and a harsher binary system in the British colonies that saw the slave only as chattel. People like Nanny Pegee, who contested both her racial identity and her enslaved status in the courtroom, give the lie to this comparison, according to which she should never have existed in starkly black-and-white nineteenth-century Virginia. It was not a society's recognition of slaves' humanity, nor its racial fluidity, that marked the differences among Cuba, Virginia, and Louisiana. It was how successfully the elites of that society drew connections between blackness and enslavement, on the one hand, and whiteness, freedom, and citizenship, on the other.

In all three places, slaveholding elites acted to cement the association between African origin and slavery, linking blackness to social degradation. By the early eighteenth century, the legal regimes in all three jurisdictions constituted blackness as a debased category that was equivalent to enslavement. But despite these similar beginnings, by the mid-nineteenth century the social implications of blackness in each region were fundamentally different. A free man of color in Cuba in the 1850s could marry a white woman, attend public school, and participate in a religious confraternity that gave him opportunities to be part of public life. A free man of color in 1850s Louisiana or Virginia saw his churches and schools being shut down, faced prosecution for marrying across the color line, and ran the risk of being kidnapped, imprisoned and even reenslaved if he remained in the state in which he was born. In Louisiana or Virginia, when a person sought to prove in court that he was not a person of color, he would bring evidence of civic acts, because citizenship and whiteness were so linked in political thought and legal doctrine that it was believed a citizen must be a white man, and only a white man could be a citizen. In Cuba, similar evidence of gentlemanly civic behavior was not necessarily incompatible with blackness.

The key to these divergent trajectories of racial differentiation was the law of freedom. It began with legal traditions: in Cuba, the right to manumission was firmly entrenched in the Iberian law of slavery and was not tied to race, a key difference from the law in both Louisiana and Virginia. But it did not end there. The creation of race through law was a long process with many unpredictable twists and turns, not a linear progression. In some ways a more open society than Cuba in the seventeenth century, Virginia became more inimical to free people of color in the early eighteenth century but then witnessed the creation of new legal avenues for freedom in the Age of Revolution, making Pegee's suit possible. In Louisiana, New Orleans, which had been a mecca for free people of color in the early nineteenth century, was a completely different place by the 1850s. These dramatic shifts in the fortunes of free people of color suggest the power of legal regulation and contestation. What decided Pegee's case had less to do with edicts emanating from the capitol than with a law of freedom created from the bottom up, as families of enslaved people across Virginia learned that they could use the identity of a distant ancestor to emancipate themselves, just as Cuban *coartados* like Juana learned to claim rights that were not formally regulated in any code or statute.

As we explore the effects of local politics and culture, we discover some key differences between Louisiana and Virginia, on the one hand, and Cuba, on the other. The presence of Indians shaped understandings of race, and the legal status of free people of color, in Virginia and Louisiana, whereas in Cuba, indigenous peoples had ceased to be a meaningful presence in early colonial times. In the United States, the "negro race" was defined in contrast to Indian "nations," as lawmakers sought to prevent black-Indian alliances. Furthermore, as growing restrictions were imposed on free blacks, many "negroes" were reclassified as Indian, melting into mixed-race communities that persisted into the nineteenth century and migrating out of Virginia into the Carolinas and beyond.

The divergent trajectories of race in Cuba and the United States were also the result of political and ideological configurations that grew even further apart after U.S. independence. Although racism flourished in all three societies, only in the United States, divided between a North where slavery was dying out and a South increasingly dependent on it, did a racial defense of slavery become inextricably linked politically to "white man's democracy." As slaveholders appealed to nonslaveholders with the promise of broad citizenship rights for all white men, free people of color became increasingly anomalous, and even dangerous, to the polity. To many slaveholders and nonslaveholders alike, the extension of citizenship rights to all white men required the removal of free black people from their midst. That is why colonization efforts that sought to remove free blacks to a distant location in Africa prospered in Virginia and Louisiana but not in Cuba. And that is also why Virginia and Louisiana acted in the nineteenth century, especially in the 1850s, to end the possibility of manumission, self-purchase, or freedom suits.

In the long run, the obstacles that Virginia and Louisiana placed in the way of manumissions, first during the colonial period and again in the antebellum period, produced dramatic results: communities of free people of color attained significant numbers in Cuba, while those in Virginia and Louisiana dwindled. An enslaved person in mid-nineteenth-century Cuba was likely to encounter free people of African descent on a regular basis. Such a prospect was rare in many areas of Virginia and Louisiana. This, in turn, helped to solidify the link between race and enslavement in the United States. Communities of free people of color in Cuba maintained important institutions, such as military units staffed by free black (*moreno*) and mulatto (*pardo*) soldiers and officers, that were important platforms for mobility and social standing. Militias of free men of color never took hold in Virginia and they died out in Louisiana by 1834. Communities of free people of color were also key to the expansion of freedom, as they could provide resources and legal knowledge to enslaved people. Perhaps most important, their members made claims on citizenship that made it difficult to argue that only white people could be citizens.

Gender played a critical role in the demography as well as the politics of racial differentiation. All jurisdictions endorsed the widely observed principle of *partus sequitur ventrem*, which tied the status of children to that of their mother, regardless of the social and racial background of the father. Because of that principle, women were key to the reproduction of slavery, and of freedom. As the case of Nanny Pegee shows, the racial identity of a female ancestor constituted a potent basis for a freedom claim. Manumissions were also gendered, as women were able to obtain freedom at much higher rates than men. And when they did, it meant that their progeny, indeed all their descendants, would be forever free. The predominance of women in manumissions was thus a key factor in the growth of the communities of free people of color across time. Finally, gender and sexuality played a key role in the creation of a racial order, because much of the policing of racial boundaries involved legal prohibitions against interracial marriage and even sex, particularly targeting the sexuality of white women. Numerous bastardy cases in eighteenth-century Virginia involved white female indentured servants who engaged in sexual relations across color lines. In nineteenth-century Cuba, although interracial marriage remained legal, even destitute white women seeking to marry a man of color frequently encountered the opposition of family members and authorities. In all of these ways, the policing of sexuality, and especially the differing treatment of white woman/black man and white man/black woman dyads, contributed to the construction of legal regimes of race.

The history we tell here builds on decades of important work on slavery and race in the Americas. Mid-twentieth-century comparative historians first traced the contrast between a "Latin" American "slave system" based on a well-established body of Iberian law, with Roman and canonical roots, that conferred legal and moral personality on slaves, and an Anglo-American system in which planters were free to treat slaves as chattel.[4] Revisionist historians challenged the sharp contrast between British and Spanish America by deemphasizing the influence of law and religion in favor of demographics and economics. They demonstrated the brutality of Latin American sugar plantations, the persistence of racial hierarchies and inequality in Latin America after emancipation, and the lack of enforcement of paternalist laws about humane treatment of slaves.[5] Finally, a new generation of cultural-legal historians has brought law back to the center of inquiry, but working from the ground up, and in microhistories that traverse jurisdictional lines.[6]

This book returns to early comparativists' broad questions about the development of regimes of race and slavery. But we bring to bear on those questions the tools and approaches of cultural-legal history close to the ground. Instead of starting with static legal traditions to trace their effects in law, we look at the way legal practices, emerging not only from doctrines and traditions but also from participants' own strategies, shaped institutional change. We define "law" broadly, including the codes and royal edicts emanating from the metropole as well as local statutes, trials, and adjudications in which different social actors, including slaves, articulated competing notions of rights. While major codes and royal edicts were steeped in imperial tradition, slaveholders had a hand in drafting local statutes, and multiple local players shaped the outcomes of local adjudications. Slaveholders' interests were often shared across jurisdictions, different legal traditions notwithstanding, although they were also influenced by different political imperatives, such as the need to appeal to nonslaveholding whites. Our approach assumes the "mutual constitutiveness" of law and culture: legal traditions shape society, as local politics and culture, and the actions of ordinary people, in turn shape the operation of the law.

We have chosen three plantation societies for our study: Cuba, Virginia, and Louisiana. Historians have often paired Cuba and Virginia as exemplars of the Spanish and British colonial systems, respectively; we add a third point of comparison, the hybrid legal system of Louisiana, where we examine how slaves took advantage of shifting legal regimes during the eighteenth and nineteenth centuries to obtain their freedom. By the mid-nineteenth century all three locations were mature Atlantic plantation societies based on slave labor. In each of them, race was a key category of difference, stratification, and social worth; white people widely perceived black people to be degraded and inferior, a perception that had solid foundations in local law. Furthermore, all three locations were interconnected through Atlantic networks of trade, culture, and finance. Virginia was a major exporter of slaves to New Orleans, the largest slave market in the American South. Cuba and Louisiana were under shared Spanish control for several decades and intense communication between Havana and New Orleans continued well into the nineteenth century. Many of the free people of color of Louisiana could claim ancestors who, escaping from the violence of revolutionary Saint-Domingue, arrived in New

Orleans by way of Cuba. The ripples of Saint-Domingue, in turn, reached all three societies, where whites constantly feared that a similar insurrection would put an end to their lives and fortunes. Because of these similarities and linkages, comparing the three societies allows us to see the difference that the developing law of freedom made in their divergent trajectories of race.

The first two chapters of the book explore the early colonial period, beginning with the settlement of Cuba in the sixteenth century, then Virginia in the seventeenth, and Louisiana in the eighteenth. Chapter 1 demonstrates that legal and social precedents mattered deeply to the development of these new slave societies, but not in the way traditional comparisons among the competing empires might lead one to believe. By the time Iberians arrived in the New World, they were familiar with the enslavement of sub-Saharan Africans and set about immediately to establish a racially based society in Cuba. In Virginia, by contrast, distinctions of race were not systematized in law until slave status was set in stone decades after the colony's settlement. The French arrived in Louisiana at a much later point in the development of their empire, and they had already written a code for slaves and "noirs." Across all three regions, colonial legislators established a degraded status for people of African descent, but they did so much more quickly in Cuba and Louisiana.

Chapter 2 looks more closely at two aspects of legal regulation in which Cuba diverged from both Virginia and Louisiana: laws regarding manumission, and the regulation of interracial marriage. Although seventeenth-century Virginians set no restrictions on the ability of a person of color to become free, or to marry a white person, that began to change toward the end of the century. By the early eighteenth century, manumission and interracial sex and marriage were restricted in both Virginia and Louisiana, unlike in Cuba. This chapter explores that shift, as well as the important effects of this divergence.

Our long view puts the Age of Revolution, the subject of Chapter 3, in a new perspective. Across the Americas, the chaos of war, ideologies of equality and liberty, and, above all, the specter of slave rebellion in Haiti inspired legal claims-making and created new opportunities for emancipation. Historians have highlighted the ways in which slaves and free people of color seized the moment of upheaval to claim freedom in urban areas as distant from each other (and Haiti) as Baltimore and Rio de Janeiro.[7] Yet what made freedom possible was often the unintended consequence of retrenchment and reform, rather than revolution. Louisiana changed hands from France to Spain. Reforms put in place by the Spanish Bourbons, as well by Virginia legislators, to shore up existing institutions to withstand revolutionary challenges ended up creating openings for enslaved people to make stronger claims. The expansion and legal solidification of customary self-purchase practices, such as *coartación*, in both Havana and Louisiana were not the products of revolution. Instead, they reflected efforts by Bourbon reformers seeking to shore up the monarchy and raise revenue. In Virginia, two kinds of freedom suits became most important: claims of illegal importation and claims based on Indian ancestry. The claims about Indian identity highlight the central irony of the American Revolution: the nation's new Constitution and its language of equality and liberty coincided with the massive expansion of plantation slavery and an increasing emphasis on race as the basis of citizenship and freedom. Thus, some enslaved people became free, but only by claiming they were not "negro." Claims to freedom based on an Indian foremother signaled the salience of race as a marker of legal status.

In Chapters 4 and 5 we explore the growing restrictions on manumission and free people of color in Louisiana and Virginia in the second half of the antebellum era, which stand in contrast to the significant but less successful efforts of Cuban slaveholders to limit the rights of freed people. Chapter 4 compares "colonization" campaigns to "remove" free people of color in all three jurisdictions, as well as the differing trajectories of manumission and freedom suits. Chapter 5 looks most closely at the 1850s, when slaveholders in Louisiana and Virginia sought to shut down the leading institutions of communities of color, churches and schools, and compares trials of racial identity and cases of interracial marriage, in which U.S. courts drew tight connections between whiteness and the possibility of citizenship, whereas Cuban courts held out the possibility that a person of color could also be a respectable gentleman and could marry across the color line.

Like their counterparts in Louisiana and Virginia, Cuban slaveholders sought total dominion over slaves and reduced rights for free people of color. Since early colonial times, they had shared a contempt for people of African descent. But as colonial authorities argued in mid-nineteenth-century Havana, any attempt to curtail African-descended people's "rights or concessions sanctioned by law" was dangerous and politically inadvisable. Such "rights" and "concessions" had deep colonial roots and owed much to the initiatives of enslaved people themselves. In the pages that follow, we will explore those initiatives.

CHAPTER 1

"A Negro and by Consequence an Alien"

Local Regulation and the Making of Race, 1500s–1700s

I N 1561 BEATRIZ NIZARDO, DESCRIBED AS "OF DARK COLOR"
(*de color morena*), approached the town council of Havana to request
an urban lot. Havana was then a small town, inhabited by just forty to sixty
vecinos, or heads of household; a few hundred slaves, mostly of African
origin; and a small but growing community of free blacks, who may have
represented between 10 and 15 percent of the total free population.
Located at a crucial site in the sea-lanes of the Spanish Empire, the
town was on the verge of becoming one of the most important naval
and commercial port cities of the early modern Atlantic, a transformation made possible, to no small degree, by the labor and the abilities of
enslaved and free Africans and their descendants.[1]

Nizardo's request was unusual. According to the minutes of the town
council, only four other free black individuals, all women, had registered
petitions for urban lots in the previous decade. Through these petitions,
free blacks performed rituals of subjecthood and belonging, as they
signaled the will and the means to "populate" the lots, to build houses
in them, and to reside permanently in town. Such requests represented
an important step toward *vecindad*, loosely translated as "citizenship" or
"residency," a social and legal category that implied standing and membership in a local community. Acts like these turned the abstract idea of
"total freedom" promised by formulaic manumission letters into socially
meaningful opportunities for respectability and advancement.[2] Nizardo
married Diego de Rojas, a free black man, and they amassed a small
fortune that included several farms – a *corral* (pig farm) Rio Grande, west
of Havana, among them – as well as urban property. A son of Rojas, Diego
de Salazar, worked in 1599 as a sugar master and operated one of the

many taverns that proliferated in the shadow of Havana's bustling service economy. Nizardo and Rojas do not appear to have owned slaves, but many free blacks did. In 1600, for instance, Cecilia Velazquez declared in her will that she owned six slaves. Another free black man, Anton de Licona, also listed six slaves in his 1628 will, four adult Africans and two children. Sebastian Vazquez, "of Angola nation, free moreno," owned two slaves in 1637, Juan Malemba and Catalina Conga. As they accumulated property and standing, Nizardo and her family helped to create a vibrant and enduring community of free people of color in colonial Havana.³

Nevertheless, the limits of freedom are apparent in the response to Nizardo's own petition. The town council rejected it because the lot was not located "near where the other free blacks are." As early as the mid-sixteenth century, the local authorities of Havana were crafting a social and residential urban layout that identified blackness with certain areas of the emerging city. Indeed, a petition from 1559 had already made reference to the "neighborhood where the other *negras horras* [free black women]" lived. It is possible that similar efforts also shaped the allocation of farmland near Havana, as clusters of agricultural units owned by free blacks are evident in the records going back to the early seventeenth century. In 1600, for instance, the *morena horra* Isabel Perez requested an *estancia* – a small farm in the outskirts of the city – adjacent to those of Matias and Diego Perez, *negros horros*. Likewise, the estancia of Sebastian Vazquez, a "free *moreno*, of the Angola nation," was located near the farms of two other freed Africans, Juan Bañon and Manuel Congo. Distinctions based on race as well as status were already being built into law and custom in early colonial Havana.⁴

Compared with Cuba, seventeenth-century Virginia was a small colonial outpost with few white colonists and even fewer Africans, free or enslaved. Anthony Johnson may have arrived in Virginia in the first shipment of "negars" in 1620, but by midcentury he owned property and slaves in Northampton County, on the Eastern Shore in Virginia. He appears frequently in court records, trading cattle, mares, land, and tobacco with other free people of color and white men. Johnson owned upwards of two hundred fifty acres of land and at least two black servants, as well as several herds of livestock. In 1653 his own servant John Casor sued him for his freedom, claiming that he had been indentured for seven years, whereas Johnson insisted he was a slave for life. Several of Johnson's white neighbors backed Casor's claim, and the following year Johnson took the aggressive approach of suing one of the neighbors, George Parker, for "detaining" Casor on his property. Johnson won, and Casor returned to bondage. Johnson's son John received a patent for land after suing a white resident of Northampton who had tried to take possession of the land illegally. In 1667 Johnson was charged with stealing corn from a Native American man and apparently received the same sentence as his two white partners in the crime. And several years after that he was sued by a white man, Randall Revell, and was allowed to testify against Revell after declaring that he was a Christian and understood the meaning of taking an oath.[5]

Yet by the time Anthony Johnson died, his property could not protect his children from discrimination on the basis of race. His land reverted ("escheated") to the Crown when he died in 1670 because "he was a Negroe and by consequence an alien."[6] In the late seventeenth century, Virginia's colonial legislators began to pass laws constituting blackness as a debased condition. By the early eighteenth century, it would have been impossible for Johnson or his son to appear in court to testify against a white man. Statutes spoke of "negroes and other slaves" as though "negroes" were by definition enslaved – and uniquely appropriate for enslavement.

By marking out areas of public life reserved for white people, and relegating even free people of African descent to a degraded position in colonial society, colonists in both Cuba and Virginia created race through law – as did the French colonists settling Louisiana a century later. Legal race making became a distinctive feature of Atlantic slave societies, reducing Africans and their descendants to "negroes," "negros," "nègres," or "noirs," subjects without history, honor, or genealogy. Blackness obliterated and flattened a multitude of cultures, languages, histories, and experiences into a single legally defined, socially constituted category of degradation.[7] Across linguistic and imperial barriers, the law constituted "blacks" as social outcasts, conflating their social existence with enslavement. Legal prohibitions that applied to "all black men and women, free or enslaved," or defined certain actions by "any black or mulatto" against "whites" as a crime, made blackness, rather than enslavement, the mark of degradation.[8]

Across the Americas, slaveholding elites began the process of legal race making almost as soon as they arrived in the colonies. The Iberians, however, had a head start. Unlike the British and the French, by the sixteenth century the Iberians had already advanced considerably in the creation of a legal doctrine that identified *negros* (and occasionally mixed-race *mulatos* or *pardos* as well) with slaves, and that rendered people of African descent socially degraded and culturally inferior. By the time they arrived in Havana, Spanish colonists could draw on Iberian social and legal precedents that had already settled key questions concerning slaves, such as the heritability of slave status, the compatibility of slavery and baptism, and the indelible social stains associated with enslavement. French colonists arrived in Louisiana in the early eighteenth century with decades of experience enslaving Africans in the Caribbean. By contrast, Virginia's colonists lacked clear legal precedents for slavery, and thus important questions about the relationships among Christianity, African origin, and enslavement remained unsettled and open to interpretation in Virginia. This created opportunities for slaves and free blacks that were absent in the Spanish and French colonies. Although it is true that Iberians arrived in the New World with a slave code, the Siete Partidas, that referred to the slave "as a human being," whereas British planters could define slaves as "chattel," the practical effect of Iberian legal and social precedents was to arrive even more quickly at hardened racial distinctions in the law.[9]

The Spanish colonists in Havana built on their experience of slavery on the Iberian Peninsula. Although the number of "white slaves" (from North Africa or the eastern Mediterranean) in Iberia was far from negligible in the sixteenth century, the proportion of sub-Saharan Africans was growing fast, and they represented the overwhelming majority of the enslaved in the colonies. By as early as the sixteenth century, "negros" were deemed to be people "without honor and faith" and described as ugly, barbarous, and savage. Hell itself was associated with blackness. As a tutor to the prince of Portugal explained in 1535, when he arrived in Portugal he felt he had been "transported to a city in hell; indeed, everywhere [he] looked [he] saw nothing but blacks." The Spanish concept of *limpieza de sangre,* or purity of blood, developed in the fifteenth century to distinguish between "Old Christians" and those of Jewish, Muslim, or heretical origin, also shaped Iberian ideas of difference between Africans and Europeans. When Spaniards traveled to the New World, ideas of purity of blood as applied to Africans contributed to early modern conceptions of race.[10]

Iberian legal ordinances blurred the line between social status and skin color or African ancestry. In early sixteenth-century Lisbon, for instance, a variety of prohibitions applied to black people both free and enslaved. As of 1515, "black women," either slave or free, "could sell their wares only" in certain designated spaces, and by midcentury these black petty traders, again regardless of social condition (and this time, also regardless of gender), were subject to special penalties when they defrauded customers. "Blacks" were also forbidden from holding dances and gatherings. Laws segregated the city's municipal fountain according to race, with separate spouts for whites and for all others, enslaved or free.[11] Slaveholders in Havana and other Spanish colonies ruthlessly and expeditiously built on these precedents to create racially discriminatory legal systems for *los negros.*

Building on local legal precedents and racialized understandings of blood purity, the Iberians pioneered the creation of racist legal regimes in the Americas; by the early eighteenth century, British and French colonies had caught up to them.[12] From their institutional bases of power, in the cabildos (town councils), in the courts, and, later, in consultative bodies such as the Real Consulado de Agricultura y Comercio, slaveholders in Cuba created a racist slave legal regime that prefigured the slave codes of Virginia and Louisiana.[13]

LEGAL BORROWINGS

None of these legal regimes developed in isolation. The Europeans who introduced African slaves and slavery into the New World built on practices and principles that circulated around the Atlantic. Many of the Spanish colonizers came from (or through) cities such as Seville, Lisbon, and Valencia, the slaveholding capitals of sixteenth-century Western Europe. Northern Europeans were less familiar with both slavery and African peoples, but even they knew about the institution. Trade and exchanges with the Iberian Peninsula through the late Middle Ages had spread information about slavery and Africans. By the fifteenth century some basic principles, such as the impropriety of enslaving fellow Christians, were widely shared and respected.[14]

Colonizers and lawmakers in new colonies borrowed slave regulations from other colonial legal regimes. Enslaved people also drew on their experiences in other colonial settings as they made claims on legal institutions, invoking different understandings of law and rights as they moved around the New World. When a slave named Fernando sued his Virginia master in 1667 for wrongful enslavement, for example, he used legal strategies that he probably had acquired in an Iberian colony, "pretending hee was a Christian and . . . present[ing] several papers in Portugell or some other language which the Court could not understand which he alledged were papers From several Governors where hee had lived as a freeman." Many of the first Africans imported into Virginia had spent some time in Caribbean colonies first, not only Barbados but also Spanish holdings, as evidenced by the Spanish names of some early enslaved and free men of color on the Eastern Shore of Virginia. Judicial authorities in Virginia did not have a clear body of slave law to rely on, as the Spanish colonists did, but they appealed to established legal practices elsewhere and drew from the English legislation on vagabonds and other masterless subjects.[15]

Later slave legal regimes had the advantage of hindsight and could build on previous practices and solutions. By the time the English settled Virginia in the early seventeenth century, the enslavement of Africans had already spread across the New World. In adjudicating the status of Africans and their descendants, such as Fernando, the English colonists could follow the lead of the Iberians and conclude that slavery was a permanent condition, and apply the principle of *partus sequitur ventrem*, according to which slave status passed from mother to child. By the time African slaves arrived in Louisiana, the French had already accumulated significant experience with slavery in the Caribbean colonies of Martinique and Guadeloupe. French legislation and legal principles concerning slaves were readily transplanted to Louisiana. Like the English, the French borrowed Iberian legal practices that settled some of the thorniest questions concerning slaves, such as those addressing conversion to Christianity and baptism. As the Dominican friar Jean-Baptiste Du Tertre casually acknowledged, French slaveholders were attentive to how other Christian nations managed their slaves.[16]

The Virginia colonists lacked the direct cultural and legal references available to the Spanish and French. Although it is now well established that the British imported Africans from the first as slaves, Virginia during the early decades of the colony was characterized by a high degree of uncertainty about many of the basic rules regarding slavery. There were no provisions for slavery in English common law because slavery had disappeared there several centuries earlier. Villeinage, the British form of serfdom, was not seen as a suitable precedent for the regulation of slaves. Although apprenticeship, which bound a servant to a master for a period of years, bore some similarities to slavery, and early colonial statutes sometimes lumped together English indentured servants with African slaves, the law of master and servant left open important questions. The first British colony to develop a slave code, Barbados, did so in 1661, decades after the first slaves had set foot in Virginia. The Barbadian code drew on French and Spanish colonial slave laws as well as English master-servant law, but Virginia's lawmakers did not borrow wholesale from Barbados as their fellow colonists in South Carolina did, waiting instead until 1691 to pass their first comprehensive slave code. Thus Africans in early colonial Virginia had an ambiguous legal status that was unthinkable in the Spanish colonial world.[17]

When the French sought a legal basis for slavery in Louisiana a century later, they drew on a different set of legal precedents – the 1685 Code Noir for the French colonies in the Caribbean, as well as local regulations – to draft the Louisiana Code Noir of 1724. Antillean officials had drafted the first Code Noir in 1685, based on the first fifty years of French experience with slavery. Like Spanish law, it established certain protections for slaves, including the right to observe Sundays free from work, and the right to petition in cases of abuse. Masters over the age of twenty had the right to manumit their slaves for any reason and without permission, and freed people gained all "the same rights, privileges, and liberties enjoyed by persons born free," although they were also required to "retain a particular respect for their former masters, their widows, and their children." Any

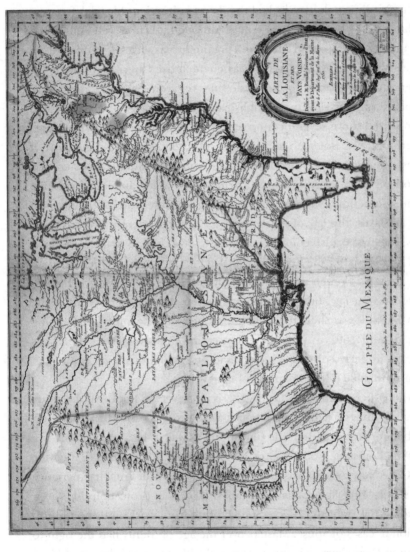

2. *Carte de la Louisiane*, 1755. On this "map of Louisiana and its neighbors," Jacques Nicolas Bellin drew topographic features and also indicated the locations of Indian tribes. Jacques Nicolas Bellin, *Carte de la Louisiane et des pays voisins* (Paris? between 1755 and 1762). Map, Library of Congress, Geography and Map Division, www.loc.gov/item/73693831/.

insult to the former master's family would be "punished more severely tha[n] if it had been done to another person." This code was in force in Saint-Domingue, Martinique, and Guadeloupe for nearly forty years before the colony of Louisiana was established. Thus, the French already had a great deal of practice when it came to the regulation of African and Indian slaves.[18]

Unlike the Spanish colonists in Cuba, who brought legal and social precedents for African slavery with them from Iberia, the colonists in Louisiana and Virginia drew on legal precedents with Atlantic colonial roots and were particularly susceptible to the influence and preferences of slave owners. The systems in both Virginia and Louisiana were based on colonial experience and both owed their creation to the efforts of colonial legislatures populated by slave owners. As in the French Caribbean during the seventeenth century, slavery was "a practice" long before it was "an institution" in Virginia.[19] By contrast, long before slavery was practiced in Cuba, slavery was a well-known and well-defined institution in the Iberian world.

LEGISLATING BLACKNESS IN CUBA

Spanish colonists in Havana acted immediately upon arrival. Efforts to legislate a subordinate place for "negros" regardless of their legal status, can be documented as early as local municipal ordinances become available, in 1550.[20] These efforts built on police regulations and municipal ordinances produced in the slave centers of Mediterranean Spain and Santo Domingo, the first colonial slave society in the Americas. The town council of Santo Domingo produced the first slave code indigenous to the Americas in 1522. It was titled "Ordenanzas de los negros," even though not all slaves on the island were black. The ordinances acknowledged the existence of slaves who were "blancos e canarios" (white and from the Canary Islands), but nonetheless conflated the categories of slave and *negro* in several of its articles. The article dealing with the prohibition on carrying weapons, for instance, made reference to "los dichos negros y esclavos," as if all "negros" were presumed enslaved. Other articles reinforced the connection, making reference to "negros y esclavos" who were drunkards and thieves. The conflation of *negro* and

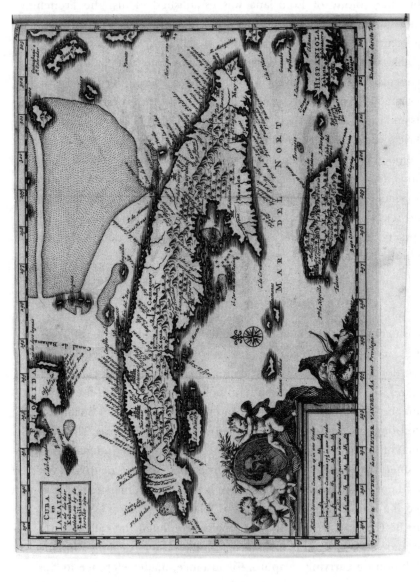

3. Cuba 1707. This map of Cuba and Jamaica with portions of Florida and Hispaniola, "as populated by the Castilians," depicts the centrality of Cuba in the Caribbean. John Carter Brown Library Map Collection, Brown University.

esclavo was reinforced and in fact amplified by subsequent statutes. An ordinance approved in 1535 mentioned the "negro huído" (runaway black), "negros alzados" (insurgent blacks), or simply "negros" and established prohibitions and punishments that sometimes referred to negros and Berber slaves as if "negro" did not require such a qualification. By 1544, when the town council of Santo Domingo approved new regulations concerning slaves, it referred to the laws as "ordenanzas cerca del trato de los negros," or "ordinances concerning the treatment of blacks."[21]

Municipal officials in Havana were therefore traversing familiar territory when they set to the task of creating a legal order that placed negros and slaves, two categories frequently used interchangeably, at the bottom of the social order. To that end, colonial officials often wrote regulations referring only to "negros," even though they clearly targeted slaves. For example, the Havana cabildo, or town council, issued an ordinance on January 28, 1554, after local officials bemoaned that "some blacks, men and women" ("negros y negras") lived in houses "separate from the house of their masters," where suspicious gatherings of blacks "and even Spaniards" took place. The cabildo ordered "that no black man or woman could have his own house to live [in] outside the houses of his master." Another municipal ordinance from 1620 concerning self-employed female slaves spoke of "negras ganadoras."[22] Like the regulation of 1554, it did not directly refer to slaves, but both laws made reference to "masters," which suggests that the regulations dealt primarily with slaves (although, as we shall see, masters were sometimes mentioned with reference to freedmen as well). Regulations of this sort implied that the term "negro" could be used as an unproblematic substitute for "slave," blurring possible distinctions between the two and contributing to the social debasement of blackness.

Other Havana regulations, including municipal ordinances, police regulations, and gubernatorial *bandos* or decrees, targeted "negros," whether free or enslaved, creating legal distinctions based only on race. "In this town," the town council complained in 1553, "some *negras* have lodging houses and serve food and sell wine which is of great damage to this town."[23] In 1561 the council ordered the confiscation of weapons that "many *negros* of this town have in their houses and estancias." The council also forbade wine sales to "blacks . . . given that there is little wine." A 1612 regulation prohibited sales of meat, except at authorized butcher shops, to all persons "of any quality or condition," but stipulated different penalties for Spaniards and for "negras y mulatas." A 1550 ordinance banned *negros* from cutting trees around the town, under penalty of 300 lashes and ten days in jail.[24] In the 1750s, the colonial governor prohibited "gatherings of blacks and other degraded people." A 1765 regulation condemned "los negros" who threw litter from the docks to six months of forced labor in the forts. Another ordinance in 1773 forbade the use of fireworks when "blacks gather for their dances" in their cabildos or brotherhoods, during local festivities, and a 1786 law established a curfew for "las negras" who sold pastries during religious festivals. By 1799, a gubernatorial *bando* established limits on trading and marketing that applied to all "people of color," or "gente de color," regardless of status.[25]

Several ordinances explicitly included free and enslaved blacks under the same legal regime. Unlike the previous set of regulations, which spoke of *negros* (or, later, of "gente de color") without reference to status, these established similar legal treatment for both free and enslaved blacks. In other words, in these regulations race trumped status. One 1556 ordinance, for instance, made reference to "those who have been recently manumitted" as "free slaves." A 1551 ordinance prohibited the sale of crabs and fruits to slaves who hired themselves out "and to any other negro." One in 1565 banned blacks, "slave and freed," from hunting on their own. Another in 1570 forbade black "freedwomen and captives" from selling wine. In 1589, a regulation stipulated that a "person slave or black" selling corn tortillas at unfair prices "should be jailed until her master" paid a penalty. A 1599 ordinance prohibited "negras captives and freed" from going to the estancias to make a living. One in 1621 stipulated that no black man, either "captive or freedman," was allowed to sell meat in the streets, under penalty of 200 lashes. In 1766 Governor Antonio Maria Bucarelli prohibited "all black men and women, free or enslaved" from selling merchandise in the streets. Another gubernatorial decree, this one from 1792, asserted that no "black, free or slave" could carry weapons, and established identical punishments for those who did, regardless of status. All of these laws demonstrated how tenuous the line could be separating freedmen from slaves.[26]

Another group of rules specifically targeted the "negros horros," or free blacks. Theoretically, a freed slave became a vassal of the king and could enjoy all the privileges associated with free status. But in Spanish colonial society, the lowly origin and tainted lineage of free blacks became formidable obstacles for gaining social standing and mobility. Colonial officials and local elites inscribed these differences in social worth and status in the law. For instance, as free men who served in the military and who owned houses and land, free blacks claimed the category of *vecinos*, which indicated that "they were socially and politically members of the local community." Among the privileges linked to *vecindad* was participation in municipal elections and in open town council meetings – the so-called *cabildos abiertos*. Claiming in 1621 that the number of free blacks was too large, and that there was a real danger that a member of this group could end up being elected, colonial officials and the town councilors of Havana created new electoral procedures that effectively barred free black men from municipal office.[27]

This was not an isolated incident. Free black men complained that local colonial officials and members of the elite systematically humiliated them in public and denied them the privileges to which they were entitled as vassals of the king. In the 1670s, the Marquis of Varinas warned that the "ill treatments given in this city [Havana] to the free blacks and mulattoes" were bad policy for a city with such a large free black population. Efforts to mark the social inferiority of free blacks were reflected in a variety of police regulations. One in 1565 prohibited free blacks from hosting slaves in their homes, a prohibition that was renewed in 1632 and again in a gubernatorial decree of 1777. A 1603 ordinance against vagrancy ordered all "mulatto youngsters and freedmen to take on a master in the following month" and settle on farms.[28] This regulation placed "freedmen" and "masters" in the same sentence – another example of the authorities' desire to reduce the distance between slaves and freedmen.[29] The same goal informed a 1611 regulation that ordered all free blacks to register with local authorities and to declare their place of residence, under penalty of becoming royal slaves. Reproducing discriminatory sumptuary laws approved elsewhere in Spanish America, a 1623 ordinance restricted freedwomen's ability to wear gold and silk, symbols of high social status. Free blacks and mulattoes were also barred from entering honorable professions and certain bureaucratic institutions, attending universities, or joining the clergy, all of which required purity of blood, or proof of a "clean" Catholic lineage. The occasional exceptions did not undermine this socioracial order. Some colonial authorities complained, for instance, that clerics were being ordained without observing the necessary formalities concerning lineage, allowing mulattoes to access the clerical orders. One extreme example was that of Juan del Rosario, son of a "negra bozal esclava" (black African female slave who did not speak Spanish), who was described as "not just mulatto, but of such dark color that [it] creates irreverence."[30]

These laws eroded distinctions between Africans and their descendants who were legally free, and those who lived under slavery. Free blacks navigated this restrictive legal regime the best way they could, obtaining specific licenses or permits to perform occupations that were otherwise closed to them. In 1565, for instance, the cabildo acknowledged that Catalina Rodriguez, Juana Garcia, and Angelina Martin, "negras horras" (freedwomen), as well as "Diego negro," had been selling wine lawfully for years and authorized them to do so in the future. Yet, when a few years later Juana Garcia tried to be exempted from a prohibition against selling wine in the neighboring village of Guanabacoa, on the ground that she was free by birth, that she was married to a Spaniard, and that she had "lived well and in favor of this republic," her request was denied.[31] Though the cabildo mostly lacked enforcement power over its regulations – hence their repetition – every new ordinance reinforced the inexorable association of blackness with slavery and dishonor.

These legal initiatives were precocious and systematic. By the late sixteenth century, these regimes were in place in all Spanish colonies, and there were no doubts about the degraded place that *negros* occupied. That is why colonial officials and chroniclers frequently enumerated the categories of Spaniards, *vecinos*, and *negros*, as though they were exclusive, although in practice many *vecinos* were in fact *negros*.[32] Spanish monk and chronicler Antonio Vázquez de Espinosa reported in 1628 that Havana had 1,200 "Spanish vecinos" and "a large number of people of service blacks and mulattoes."[33] Grouping blacks into a single population group without status distinctions reinforced the primacy of race in marking social cleavage.

FLUIDITY AND CODIFICATION IN VIRGINIA

Virginian colonists also created a racial legal regime closely associating blackness with slave status. Its creation was slower and more fitful, however, because the lack of legal precedents in English law concerning slaves and blacks allowed for a degree of ambiguity and uncertainty that was unthinkable and unnecessary in Havana. From the initial decades of colonial settlement through at least the mid-seventeenth century, "negroes" were not legally defined as slaves and at least some of them enjoyed privileges and rights later reserved for Englishmen. Virginia's racial legal regime was built over decades, as colonists grappled with such basic questions as whether enslavement was a permanent and inheritable condition, how slave status would be transmitted to children, and whether Christian baptism was compatible with enslavement. None of these questions had posed serious doctrinal or logistical quandaries to Iberian slave owners. In the last decades of the seventeenth century, legal innovations linked black people to lifelong servitude, making slavery a heritable condition, and reducing black people's privileges and rights. Colonists set moral and religious scruples aside, writing laws that associated enslavement with non-Christian origins, rather than heathenism. By the early eighteenth century, Virginians had codified a legal regime that deprived even free black people of basic civil rights and prevented them from holding any public office.[34]

The early status of Africans in Virginia is difficult to pin down. From the beginning, the legal records include a notation of racial status only for "negroes" or "Indians," mentioning white people by name or nationality but without a racial designation, which suggests a distinction between Europeans and others that slowly made its way into the language of the law. Yet the first statutes and legal decisions to refer to "negroes" were not obviously discriminatory. For example, the first such statute was a 1639 act excluding "Negroes" from a state subsidy for arms and ammunition: "All persons except Negroes are to be provided with arms and ammunition or be fined at the pleasure of the governor and council."

4. John Smith's Virginia. Captain John Smith's map of Virginia, the first detailed map of the colony, was used for most of the seventeenth century. John Smith and William Hole, *Virginia* (London, 1624). Map, Library of Congress, Geography and Map Division, www.loc.gov/item/99446115/.

Some historians have interpreted this act as barring blacks from bearing arms, but the language of the statute does not justify such a conclusion. The act of 1639 directed that "all masters of families . . . use their best endeavours for the f[u]rnishing of themselves and all those of their families which shall be capable of arms (excepting negroes) with arms both offensive and defensive." The statute neither prevented all blacks from bearing arms nor made it illegal for blacks to engage in offensive or defensive warfare, and it appears to have been more focused on the taxation of arms than on keeping arms from the hands of black people. The legislature did not reconsider the question of black people bearing arms for another two decades.[35]

In criminal cases, as well, the written decisions of Virginia's General Court leave unclear the distinctions between European and "negro" offenders. In 1640, three of Hugh Gwyn's servants were punished for running away together. Two Europeans, a "Dutchman and a Scotchman," were each sentenced to additional years of servitude, while "negro . . . John Punch" was sentenced to serve for his natural life. A few weeks later, servants of Captain William Pierce plotted to run away. Christopher Miller, identified as a Dutchman, was sentenced to whipping, branding with the letter R, working with a shackle on his leg for one year, and giving an additional seven years of service; Peter Wilcocke was sentenced to whipping, branding, and giving three years of additional service; Richard Cookson, an additional two and a half years of service; Andrew Noxe, whipping; and John Williams, working seven additional years. The only servant who was named with a racial label, "Emanuel the Negro," was sentenced to whipping, branding, and working with a shackle on his leg for at least one year.[36]

How can we interpret these sentencing decisions? It is certainly plausible to infer that a presumption was already developing that Africans would serve their masters for life while Europeans would serve only for a period of years, but that is not the only possible conclusion. Although it was possible that only Emanuel was already serving Captain Pierce for life, Christopher Miller, the Dutchman, as well as Wilcocke, received sentences similar to Emanuel's. In this case we have clear evidence that people designated as "negroes" as well as those identified by their European nationality or unidentified by race (and

therefore presumably accepted as white) ran away together or con-
spired to run away together, along with ambiguous evidence that
negroes may have been viewed as more appropriately serving their
masters for life rather than for a period of years. This interpretation
grows stronger when read in light of later statutes that make direct
reference to cases in which negroes could not serve additional years
because they were already serving for life.[37] When one compares these
cases to later decisions, however, most striking is how minimally the
"negro" is singled out for differential treatment.

The connections between race and status began to be clarified after
1660, although the first full slave code did not appear until 1691. The new
laws establishing more firmly the debased status of people of African
origin may well have been a response to the rising population of free
people of color, as well as to political pressure. As many as one-third of
the people of color in some Virginia counties in the late seventeenth
century were free, and white elites increasingly feared the formation of
political alliances among white indentured servants, blacks, and
Indians.[38] This fear came to a head in the aftermath of Bacon's
Rebellion, an uprising of servants against elites that involved Indians as
well as Europeans and Africans.

The first direct reference to "negroes" *as slaves* in Virginia legislation
appeared in a 1659 statute imposing reduced import duties on slave
merchants. In 1662, the Virginia General Assembly adopted the rule of
partus sequitur ventrem, already universal in other parts of the Americas,
that a child's slave or free status would follow the condition of the
mother. The assembly members explained, "Whereas some doubts have
arisen whether children got by any Englishman upon a negro woman
should be slave or free, Be it therefore enacted and declared by this
present grand assembly, that all children born in this country shal[l be]
held bond or free only according to the condition of the mother." The
law went on to double the fine for fornication if it occurred between a
"Christian" and a "negro man or woman." The first clear statutory racial
distinction among free people was a 1668 law proclaiming that negro
women were not exempted from the head tax because, though free, they
"ought not in all respects to be admitted to a full fruition of the exemptions and impunities of the English." These first laws engendered racial

difference by designating different consequences for production and reproduction by black and white women.[39]

In 1667 the Virginia legislature severed the link between Christianity and freedom, decreeing that even baptized slaves would not be "exempt . . . from bondage." Three years later, it added the further restriction that "noe negroe or Indian though baptised and enjoyned their owne ffreedome" would be allowed to buy Christians, although they could buy "any of their owne nation." Finally, the legislature clarified that non-Christian servants who arrived in the colony "by shipping" became slaves for life, whereas those who arrived on land – namely, Indians – would be indentured servants.[40]

A 1669 case hints at the multiple dimensions of racial status in early colonial Virginia, yet leaves many questions unanswered: "Hannah Warwick's case extenuated because she was overseen by a negro overseer."[41] From this single-sentence record, we do not even know Hannah Warwick's crime. Because Hannah's racial status was not noted, it is likely that she was white. On the one hand, we observe that it was possible for a white servant to work under a "negro," while on the other hand, the extenuation of her case suggests a belief that a white person working under a "negro" was a violation of the natural racial order. But the sparse record does not allow us to draw firm conclusions.

Several late-seventeenth-century acts reinforced the notion that "negroes" and "slaves" belonged in the same legal category. In 1672 Virginia's first comprehensive act for apprehending and suppressing "runaways, negroes, and slaves" was passed. A 1680 statute complained about "the frequent meetings of considerable numbers of Negro slaves under pretense of feasts and burials" and determined that "no Negro or slave may carry arms." The same statute prescribed severe punishments, even death, for "any Negro [who] lift up his hand against any Christian." A 1691 act referred to troubles caused by "negroes, mulattoes, and other slaves" who "unlawfully absent themselves from their masters and mistresses service," while one of 1692 established expedited proceedings for the prosecution of "negroes and other slaves." These statutes make it clear that there were still "other slaves," namely Indians, and that there were "negroes" who were not slaves, yet also that the legislators viewed African heritage as peculiarly related to enslavement.[42]

By establishing a clear and rigid distinction between "negro" and "Christian," the act of 1680 also exemplified how the legislature navigated the thorny question of slaves' conversion to Christianity and the enslavement of coreligionists. At least some of the black people living in early colonial Virginia were Christians who claimed rights and even freedom on that basis. Slaveholders became reluctant to baptize enslaved children, fearing that they might then demand privileges and rights. The 1667 law put an end to these doubts, severing once and for all the link between Christianity and freedom. The slave code of 1705 reiterated that conversion would not emancipate a slave:

> All servants imported and brought into this country, by sea or land, who were not [C]hristians in their native country, (except Turks and Moors in amity with her majesty, and others that can make due proof of their being free in England, or any other [C]hristian country, before they were shipped, in order to transportation hither) shall be accounted and be slaves, and such be here bought and sold notwithstanding a conversion to [C]hristianity afterwards.[43]

The slave code of 1705 also expanded significantly the rights of "[C]hristian white servants." Through these legal maneuvers, the legislature helped to solidify and naturalize distinctions between whites, especially those of the lower social strata, and blacks, regardless of status. The law made it illegal to "whip a [C]hristian white servant naked" and offered detailed instructions for how to feed, clothe, and care for servants: "That all masters and owners of servants, shall find and provide for their servants, wholesome and competent diet, clothing, and lodging, by the discretion of the county court; and shall not, at any time, give immoderate correction." The law also provided mechanisms for servants to file complaints with justices of the peace, who in turn were instructed "to adjudge, order, and appoint what shall be necessary as to diet, lodging, clothing, and correction." These provisions applied to "all servants (not being slaves)."[44]

By the early eighteenth century, the association in law between negro and slave was clearly established. Initial questions concerning the terms of servitude had been settled, in the case of Africans by rendering them slaves for life. The legislature of Virginia had also clarified that this condition was heritable and transmitted through the maternal line. On this aspect the legislature had turned against traditional English doctrine, which held that the status of the child was determined by the status of the father. Now, like other slave societies, including the Spanish and French, Virginians followed the Roman principle of *partus sequitur ventrem*. Virginia legislators also decided that conversion to Christianity did not imply freedom, an idea well established in the Catholic Mediterranean world, where baptizing slave children was customary and prominent theologians had ruled that baptism affected sin, "but not the circumstances or obligations of men." Once these principles were established in the early eighteenth century, later acts and regulations mostly just reiterated and elaborated them, especially a series of limits on the rights of "free negro[es], mulatto[es], or Indian[s]," including the right to vote, bear arms, or intermarry with white men and women.[45]

Unlike in Cuba, however, racial differentiation took hold only gradually in seventeenth-century Virginia. There were three legal mechanisms for racial formation: regulations of sexual conduct and reproduction; laws distinguishing negroes, regardless of social status, from Indians and white servants; and statutes severing racial status from religious affiliation. Together, such legislation firmly established African slavery and the legal subordination of blacks in the legal system. In the same period, the tobacco economy guaranteed that the institution of slavery would grow. Between 1700 and 1740, the number of slaves grew tenfold, to sixty thousand, and by the time the first census was taken in the new republic in 1790, slaves made up 44 percent of the population of Virginia.[46]

LOUISIANA'S CODE NOIR

In contrast to Virginia, by the time French colonists settled Louisiana in the early eighteenth century, few doubts existed about the place that Africans and their descendants were to occupy in the colony's social structure. There is some debate among scholars concerning the centrality of race in the evolution of Louisiana's slave law, however. Some have argued that the Code Noir of Louisiana did not establish a racial order. Instead, they contend, the extension of equal rights to free blacks undermined the creation of such an order.[47] But there is considerable evidence that Louisiana planters and legislators sought to associate slavery with blackness. Ordinances and police regulations that spoke of "negroes" when referring to slaves, or that imposed specific and harsher punishments on black offenders, illustrate this trend.

The Code Noir's very name suggests the will to connect slavery with race.[48] The code dealt in fact not just with *esclaves nègres* but also with freed and free-born Africans and their descendants. As in Havana and Virginia, some regulations concerning slaves spoke of negroes, as if both words meant the same thing. Article 31 held masters liable for thefts committed by their slaves unless they preferred to surrender ownership of their "negroes." Article 15 forbade "negroes to sell any commodities, provisions, or produce of any kind" without a written authorization from "their masters." According to article 4, "negroes" placed under the care of non-Catholics were liable to confiscation.

The code also marked out a degraded status for freed slaves, thereby building racial distinctions into the law. As was the case in Havana and Virginia, the code stipulated harsher, racially specific punishments for black transgressors and introduced legal handicaps that applied only to free people of African descent. The fines that freedmen or "free-born negroes" paid for hosting a fugitive slave, for example, were three times higher than those paid by "all other free persons, guilty of the same offense." Article 34 of the code also asserted that black persons who could not pay their fines would "be reduced to the conditions of slaves, and be sold as such." The law prohibited all free blacks, regardless of whether they had been born free or enslaved, from receiving any donations or legacies "from the whites." This measure limited black people's opportunities for accumulation and mobility, by inserting a barrier against interactions between "negroes" and "whites." The same concern animated the prohibition against interracial marriage and interracial sex. These prohibitions were not included in the 1685 Code Noir; they came later, in answer to French Caribbean colonists' growing anxiety about the preservation of the racial order. The code's regulation on marriage was couched in specifically racial terms, forbidding "white subjects, of both sexes, to marry with the blacks" and priests and missionaries "to sanction such marriages." Concubinage between "white subjects" and "blacks" was also prohibited, and in cases of interracial sex between a white master and his slave, any children were to be confiscated and could never become free. The situation was different if an unmarried free black man and an enslaved woman had a child together. In such cases, their subsequent marriage could emancipate both mother and child, bestowing legitimacy on the child. This radical divergence in the fortunes of mother and child, depending on whether or not she crossed racial lines, helped to make the Louisiana Code Noir "the most racially exclusive colonial law of the French Empire."[49]

The colonial governor issued a set of police regulations in 1751 that further entrenched racial distinctions.[50] As in Havana and Virginia, these laws often conflated "negros" and slaves, or referred to them inter-changeably. Article 24, for instance, made reference to "any Negro or any slave." It empowered whites to stop them at any time to verify that they were in possession of a written pass to be in the streets of New Orleans or on the "public roads." Another section decreed that "all the negroes and other slaves" should attend an early mass, apparently sepa-rate from whites. The 1751 laws also elaborated on "the respect and submission" that "any negro or other slave" owed "to white people." Any white person who met a black person carrying a stick, or considered the black person insolent in any way, was exhorted to whip the slave, or even to have him branded on his backside with a fleur-de-lis. Like the ordinances of Havana and Virginia, many regulations in the code referred to slaves as "negroes": for example, the law instructing slave-holders to "punish [their] negroes with moderation."[51] Later laws also prescribed special punishments for slaves who committed crimes, using the language of race rather than status.[52] By the time Louisiana changed hands from the French to the Spanish in 1763, racial distinctions had been firmly established in the colony through regulations that limited the reach of manumission, created distinct rules for "negroes" and "freed or free-born negroes," and blurred the lines between "negroes" and slaves.

***

The debasement of all "blacks" in the legal regimes of Cuba, Virginia, and Louisiana revealed itself most dramatically in the draconian system of repression against *cimarrones*, or runaway slaves. Legislators across imperial, cultural, and linguistic lines described slave resistance in racialized terms – most regulations dealing with runaway slaves made reference to "black" *cimarrones*, or runaways. As early as 1534 the governor of Cuba reported on "negros alzados," or insurgent blacks. In the late sixteenth century, when the town council of Havana held hearings on the problem of runaway slaves, it referred to the "large quantity of male and female black runaways" ("negros y negras cimarronas").[53] The first municipal ordinances concerning runaway slaves, approved by the council and ratified by the governor in 1600, were titled "Ordinances for the Reduction of Black Runaways" ("negros cimarrones").[54] Punishments included flogging, mutilation of nose and ears, and death by hanging. Subsequent regulations made reference to "the blacks who have escaped" ("negros que huidos andan") and "black fugitives" ("negros fugitivos"). Similar language was used in a new ordinance "for the capture of black runaways" passed by the town council in 1690 and in 1796, which spoke of *negros* as if a law regarding runaway slaves could encompass free blacks as well.[55]

In Virginia, both an influx of new African slaves and the experience of Bacon's Rebellion, in which slaves and servants revolted against masters, led legislators to take steps against conspiracies and rebellions. In 1680, a new "Act for Preventing Negroes['] Insurrections" established limits on slaves' mobility, their right to carry weapons, and their social gatherings, which were perceived as breeding grounds for insurrectionary plots. County sheriffs were authorized to prosecute "marauding" blacks, to hold them in irons, and whip them if found guilty. In 1692, the colonial assembly passed a new law "for the speedy prosecution of negroes and other slaves," removing procedural obstacles in capital cases. Convicted blacks suffered harsher punishments than whites, including torture, whipping, dismemberment, burning, beheading, and hanging.[56]

The growth of the slave population in Louisiana prompted similar concerns and regulatory efforts. The slave population of the colony multiplied sevenfold between 1721 and 1731, when the French Company of the Indies returned the control of the colony to the French monarchy. By mid-decade, colonial officials were advocating sweeping action against maroons (runaways), "lest soon the community be raided by whole gangs

thereof." As in Havana and, later, Virginia, the officials advocated "stringent" punishments against "ringleaders," including capital punishment.
Article 32 of the Code Noir provided punishments similar to those stipulated by Havana's colonial legislators a century earlier. Slaves who had
been absent for a month would suffer mutilation of the ears and branding
for their first offense, and would be hamstrung and branded again for a
second offense. The punishment for a third time was death. Although in
criminal cases slaves were to be tried using "the same rules, formalities, and
proceedings observed for free persons," the code made an exception in
the case of runaways, who had no recourse to appeal. And "free or free-
born negroes" who harbored fugitive slaves would pay higher fines than
"all other free persons." If free blacks could not pay the fine, they would
"be reduced to the conditions of slaves, and be sold as such."[57]

Virginia stands out, in its early years, as the most experimental and
open with regard to the status of Africans. As late as 1681, a Virginia
slaveholder claimed that slavery's identification with a permanent status
was something of an innovation: "now . . . [that blacks] continue to be
slaves forever."[58] No such doubts existed in sixteenth-century Havana or
in eighteenth-century Louisiana. But by the early eighteenth century, all
three colonies had established firm racial distinctions through legal
regulation. It took longer in Virginia, but by the turn of the eighteenth
century they all sought to make race and status coterminous, drawing the
links between blackness and enslavement.

These discriminatory legal regimes represented formidable obstacles
to social mobility, family reproduction, and community life for the
Africans and their descendants, even if they were free. The essence of
the racist legal regimes built in the Americas during the early colonial
period – in Cuba, in Virginia, and in Louisiana – rested on the assumption that slaves were black, and that black people should be slaves. This
assumption was never fully realized, however. The existence of free
blacks challenged the notion that blackness was synonymous with
enslavement.

The law played a critical role in constituting blackness as a debased
status identified with enslavement, but this conflation also produced
unexpected and undesirable results, at least from the perspective of
white slaveholding elites. By blurring distinctions between blackness

and enslavement, the law contributed to the formation of black communities and solidarities across barriers of status, in the long term facilitating alliances between the enslaved and the free. The cabildo of Havana may have pushed free blacks such as Beatriz Nizardo to special areas of the emerging city, but by doing so it facilitated the formation of free black residential communities that frequently functioned as safe havens for the enslaved. Prohibitions against free blacks hosting slaves in their homes, and against social gatherings of free blacks with slaves, reflected slaveholders' fears about those communities. Indeed, by 1657 the Havana town council acknowledged that black neighborhoods such as Campeche and Ejido – areas that the cabildo had created as part of its racialized layout of the city – provided refuge to numerous slaves "who are ordinarily absent and fugitive from the service of their masters."[59] Not only in Cuba but also in Virginia and Louisiana, these free black communities became an important reservoir of support for the enslaved, an alliance that slaveholders across jurisdictions would come to dread. In other words, by creating a legal category of "black" that came to be a stronger dividing line in society than slave status, white colonists perhaps inadvertently facilitated the creation of black communities that later constituted a threat to slavery.

Yet free black communities did not develop at the same rate across all jurisdictions. Despite key similarities, there were two main differences between the Spanish legal regime, on the one hand, the French and British, on the other. The first was the law of manumission – that is, a master's right to bestow freedom on his slaves, either in exchange for money or services, or in recognition of past services and good conduct. The second concerned interracial unions and the treatment of racially intermediate groups of "*mulatos*," "*mulastres*," or "mulattoes." Such groups came into existence in each colonial territory, as it was impossible to impose a strict regime of sexual segregation among different racial groups. Interracial marriages, and sometimes even interracial sex, were criminally prosecuted in Louisiana and Virginia by the late seventeenth century, but such unions did not trigger the same condemnation in Cuba. The next chapter explores the effects of these key distinctions in the three legal regimes, as well as their profound and lasting consequences.

CHAPTER 2

The "Inconvenience" of Black Freedom

Manumission, 1500s–1700s

DESPITE THE EFFORTS OF WHITE COLONISTS TO INSTANTIATE the link between blackness and enslavement during the earliest years of colonization in the Americas, many people of African descent began making their way to freedom as soon as they landed in the New World. They drew on customary practices as well as legal mechanisms, and they relied on the resources of the communities of color that were created in part by the discriminatory legislation detailed in Chapter 1. Yet the very same legal traditions that made it easier for Spanish colonists to establish racial distinctions in law quickly also made it unthinkable to curtail enslaved people's manumission or suits for freedom. In seventeenth-century Virginia, as in Cuba, an enterprising man of African descent could purchase his freedom with a tobacco crop or a white servant, in a completely unregulated transaction. But by the early eighteenth century, white Virginians, like the French colonists who settled Louisiana at that time, had already begun to restrict this practice. This change had lasting consequences for the ways communities of free people of color shaped regimes of race.

Becoming free was never easy. When François Tiocon, a freedman of the "Senegal nation" and a resident of New Orleans, managed to formalize an agreement to secure the freedom of his wife, Marie Aram, he had to agree to many years of service. He signed the contract on July 15, 1737, to purchase her freedom from the recently created Hôpital des Pauvres de la Charité (Hospital of Saint John). We do not know when Marie Aram had become a slave of the hospital. It is possible that she was bequeathed to the institution by Jean Louis, a French boatbuilder who in 1735 left most of his estate to create the hospital, although the will does not contain a detailed inventory of his possessions. Nor do we know how long before his marriage took place Tiocon had arrived in New Orleans. Tiocon was apparently an *affranchy* (freedman) who had obtained his freedom by fighting against the Indians in the Natchez war.[1]

Tiocon's agreement was fairly onerous. To obtain Aram's freedom, he committed to "work and exert himself for it and do all that he may be ordered and commanded to do at the said hospital for the service of the poor and sick" for six consecutive years, beginning in January 1738, "during which time he [would] work at the said hospital without any remuneration whatever, being fed with provisions of the country and supported as the Inspector wills." The hospital's representatives, in turn, promised at the end of the contract to "give and remit liberty to one Marie Aram, negress slave of the said hospital, wife of the said Tiocon." Despite the many obvious uncertainties involved in an agreement of this sort, Tiocon and Aram succeeded in their endeavor. On March 6, 1744, the hospital's officials certified that the couple had "worked and served the Hospital well and faithfully" and that in consequence it was "just to grant freedom" to Aram as agreed. They also declared that the couple's intention was to remain employed at the hospital. To complete the manumission of Aram, the director of the institution petitioned the governor and members of the council "to confirm and grant freedom to the said Marie Aram, negress, wife of François Tiocon, that in the future she may be free as are all the subjects of His Majesty in France." Issued by the French colonial governor, the commissary of the marine, and the intendant, the official confirmation ratified that "as a recompense of the good services rendered to the hospital," Aram was indeed free and was entitled to "enjoy the privileges of persons born free."[2]

A similar official confirmation was required for Will, a Virginia slave, to be declared free in 1710. Will, described in the records as "a Negro belonging to Robert Ruffin," a resident of the county of Surry, was deemed worthy of becoming a free man for being "signally serviceable in discovering a conspiracy of diverse negroes in the said county, for levying war in this colony." Colonial officials, including the lieutenant governor and the Council of Burgesses of the General Assembly, decided to reward such "fidelity" as encouragement to other slaves in the future. After providing for the owner to be compensated, they certified that "the said Negro Will, is and shall be forever hereafter free from his slavery, and shall be esteemed, deemed and taken, as is hereby declared to be a free man, and shall enjoy and have all the liberties, privileges and immunities of or to a free negro belonging." In addition, the colonial officials stipulated that Will could stay in Virginia if he wished to do so.[3]

The intervention of colonial officials was also required in the case of Cristobal and Jose, two African slaves of the "Mina nation" living in Havana. In 1691 they petitioned the lieutenant governor, Licenciado Francisco Manuel de Loa, to request their freedom. They explained that their former owner, Melchor Borroto, had granted them freedom in his will, but then had died with insufficient assets to cover his debts. Rather than freeing the slaves, the executors had auctioned them to Juan Garcia for 800 pesos. Invoking "the right that assists us" (*el derecho que nos favorece*), Cristobal and Jose "exhibited" 800 pesos, showing that they could pay their own price, and requested that they be declared "free people not subject to captivity and servitude." They also requested a certified copy of their petition and the official's ruling, to confirm their freedom in the future as needed, and asked that another copy be kept in the records of the notary in case the original documents got lost. The lieutenant governor ruled favorably on all of their requests and declared that Cristobal and Jose were thereafter free.[4]

These cases illustrate how enslaved people across the Americas strove from the earliest years of colonization to secure freedom for themselves and their loved ones. The paths to legal freedom could involve considerable personal sacrifice and draconian service agreements, as in the case of Aram and Tiocon; the denunciation and betrayal of other slaves, as in Will's example; or the unusual savings that some enterprising slaves managed to accumulate, as in the case of Cristobal and Jose. Furthermore, across jurisdictions, manumission frequently was not a private matter between master and slave but a public event that required the intervention of colonial officials and the creation of public documents backed by the power and the legitimacy of the colonial state. The very colonial states that were building slavery and racial distinctions into law were also making freedom possible.

Yet by seeking freedom, slaves breached the racial order. Each slave who managed to escape slavery represented a crack in the strict racial hierarchy that colonial legislators and slave owners were carefully constructing in Cuba, Virginia, and Louisiana between the sixteenth and eighteenth centuries. Colonial legislators in each of these settings went to great lengths to create a rigid association between African ancestry and slave status.[5] The presence of free people of color undermined this link and created a problematic intermediate group in what was conceived as a dichotomous order of free white masters and enslaved black servants. Free people of color challenged the racial order in other ways as well. Some free people of color accrued property and social status, and many mixed freely with whites as well as slaves, having sex and even marrying across the color line. "Mulattoes" made up a disproportionate number of the free people of color. Even in Virginia, a jurisdiction that sought to restrict their ability to mix with whites, the court minute books are filled with cases of "fornication" and "bastard bearing" by white women and "negroes" or "mulattoes." Thus, the rate at which enslaved people could become free could have significant consequences.

The formation of sizable communities of free people of color not only subverted the "negro-slave" association but also tempered attempts to turn people of African descent into a class of disenfranchised and socially dead subjects. Many of the enslaved who managed to obtain their freedom, frequently by purchasing it, did so with the assistance and support of kin and other free blacks. The size and economic well-being of the free black community was critical in this regard, as it provided the networks, institutional access, and often the resources the enslaved needed to escape their condition. Furthermore, scholars of Latin American independence frequently explain the elimination of legal caste systems in the region as a by-product of the size and political might of its free communities of color.[6] The connecting thread, we argue, is race. Free people of color undermined and breached the solid line between free whites and enslaved blacks that legislators sought to inscribe in the law.

In Cuba, unlike Virginia and Louisiana, enslaved people continued to claim freedom without restriction throughout the eighteenth century. This should not necessarily be seen as an indicator of friendly attitudes toward slaves, nor of "the mystique of the Portuguese or Spanish soul."[7] There were strong demographic and economic reasons for Iberian masters to free their slaves in greater numbers than did the British or French.

Iberian colonies lacked a steady stream of European migration, so free people of color performed interstitial economic roles that might otherwise have been filled by white immigrants. The boom-and-bust cycles of the Iberian colonial economies provided incentives for manumission, as did the prospect of slaves working hard and paying a high price for self-purchase.[8] Yet the patterns of manumission and regulation that unfolded in these three colonies suggest that something more than economic imperatives was at work. By the early eighteenth century in both Virginia and Louisiana, slaveholders had come to see manumission as something that required regulation, and to see that regulation as linked to the creation of a racial order. In Cuba, manumission was never tied to race but was part of the traditional architecture of slavery.

The growth of free communities of color was greatly facilitated by higher rates of manumission among women, which meant that their progeny would be free. The gendered organization of labor required women to work in service activities and domestic duties that gave them access to financial resources and social networks that could be used to obtain freedom. Since most manumissions involved self-purchase, and since most purchases required collaboration from third parties, it is also possible that family strategies played a role in this process, to make sure that the offspring of these women would be free. Gender conventions also appear to have shaped slaveowners' preferences. Although both male and female owners favored women in manumission, mistresses did so at much higher rates than men, perhaps to reward their closest servants in the household. Through these gendered processes, and thanks to their own initiative, women became a germinal force of black freedom. Their wombs could reproduce enslavement, but they could also become "spaces in which freedom was, literally, conceived."[9]

LEGAL REGIMES OF MANUMISSION

The presence or absence of well-developed legal precedents helped to determine slaves' opportunities to become free. Ironically, the same legal culture that allowed slaveholders in Cuba (and in the Iberian colonial world more generally) to create a discriminatory legal regime against *negros* prevented them from constructing the neat, racially stratified order that they sought to build. Although Iberian legal precedents gave local elites an important resource in their efforts to entrench racial distinctions in law, Cuban colonists also had to contend with a robust institution of manumission, already deeply entrenched in the legal and slaving practices of Mediterranean Spain and Portugal. Most important, racial regulations and ordinances developed apart from the law of freedom, which was grounded on Roman rules and canonical principles. In Iberia, manumission applied to individuals of a variety of origins and ethnicities, was not tied to race-making efforts, and frequently took the form of ransoms paid for the liberation of Christian or Muslim captives who suffered temporary enslavement. Iberian precedents informed the development of both racial regulations and manumission practices in the colonies, but these institutions were neither intertwined nor tied to each other.

By contrast, the French colonizers of Louisiana had already determined, based on their experience in the Caribbean, that manumission and intermarriage should be carefully restricted. As racialized slavery developed in Martinique and Guadeloupe, the French governors of those colonies had passed local restrictions on manumission that were absent in the Code Noir of 1685. The new Code Noir for Louisiana, issued in 1724, contained strict limits.

The lack of legal precedents initially worked in favor of Africans' efforts to gain their freedom in Virginia's colonial society. During most of the seventeenth century in Virginia, as in Cuba, manumission and intermarriage remained unregulated, and a significant community of free people of color developed in the Chesapeake Bay region. But as fears of interracial alliances grew along with the expansion of racial slavery in the late seventeenth and early eighteenth centuries, colonists cracked down on manumission, intermarriage, and the rights of free people of color. As a result, mid-eighteenth-century Virginia looked more like Louisiana, with only a handful of manumissions being granted over several decades.

CUBA. Iberian colonists operated within a legal regime in which a variety of customs had established that slavery was not necessarily a permanent condition.[10] Spaniards were familiar with the widespread practice of *rescate*, or ransom, by which Christians and Muslims liberated coreligionists either through payments or the exchange of enslaved "captives." Although this tradition rarely extended to sub-Saharan slaves, it made freedom purchasing a frequent and unremarkable legal practice that was not tied to race or to race-making efforts. African slaves seized opportunities to free themselves through a variety of well-known and time-honored processes, so that by the mid-sixteenth century the slave centers of Iberia – Seville, Lisbon, Valencia – were home to large communities of free people of African origin.[11]

Manumission in the Iberian colonies was deemed a private matter, a logical extension of the slave owners' right to do with their slaves as they wished. Slaves obtained freedom either through freedom letters or by wills, both of which were issued by slaveholders. Only exceptionally, when a manumission was disputed or litigated, did state authorities intervene to decree the liberation of a slave. Although masters were not compelled legally or morally to grant freedom to their slaves, manumission was considered a pious act, and both freedom letters and testamentary freedoms were couched in the language of religion and piety, as services to God. Although some scholars are skeptical about the importance of religious motives, given the high proportion of self-purchases in all manumissions, profit and piety were not necessarily contradictory.[12] The manumission of a few select slaves in wills suggests that most masters wanted to keep the services of their slaves during their lifetime, but also that they perceived bestowing freedom on a worthy bondsman as a righteous act.

We know of no legislative effort to restrict manumission in the Spanish colonial empire. Although some Mediterranean practices were lost under the weight of Atlantic slavery – such as the careful interrogation of slaves in Valencia to determine if they had been properly enslaved – manumission was neither questioned nor curtailed. On the contrary, from the early decades of colonial expansion, Spanish and colonial legislation treated manumission and self-purchase as ordinary social practices. A *real cédula* (royal cedula) of 1526 asked the governor of Cuba whether it was expedient to give freedom to slaves after they had served some time and paid a given amount. Neither the possibility of "giving freedom" nor the fact that slaves could pay for it were challenged.

Manumission was clearly regulated in the Siete Partidas, and numerous colonial regulations ratified its validity in questions of slave management. For instance, a royal cedula from 1540 ordered that slaves who claimed to be free were to be heard by the *audiencias,* the highest courts in the colonies. This provision built on the traditional doctrine, established in the Siete Partidas, that slaves who claimed to be victims of egregious abuses had the right to be heard in court. Likewise, when Santo Domingo authorities wondered in 1527 if allowing slaves to marry entitled them to freedom, the King's Council replied by invoking "the laws of this Kingdom," particularly Law 1, Title 5, Partida 4, which stated that marriage did not confer freedom on slaves.[13] Thus manumission rules evolved parallel to, but disconnected from, contemporaneous efforts to debase blackness in local law.

Most manumissions took place through self-purchase. Of all manumissions performed in early seventeenth-century Havana, 74 percent involved payments, whereas freedom was conferred gratis – that is, as a reward for past services or owing to other personal considerations – in 17 percent. Most nonpayment manumissions were testamentary and took place only after the death of the owner. The other cases, about 9 percent of the total, were conditional manumissions that typically involved various services and obligations for the slave. Self-purchase rates were lower in sixteenth-century Lima (48 percent) and Mexico (36 percent), but still considerable. In eighteenth-century Havana, self-purchases represented about 80 percent of all manumissions.[14]

More women managed to purchase and obtain their freedom than men. They represented 65 percent of all slaves who obtained their freedom at the turn of the seventeenth century (1585–1610) in Havana, and they continued to outnumber men a century later. The gender gap was particularly noticeable among Africans; enslaved African women represented 75 percent of those who obtained their freedom, despite the fact that among slave imports women were always a minority. The prevalence of women in manumissions throughout the Iberian colonies was linked to several factors. First of all, enslaved women performed tasks in numerous service occupations, as laundresses, wet nurses, cooks, seamstresses, cleaners, and vendors, among others, which gave them access to cash payments and allowed them to accumulate savings at higher rates than men. Second, women were preferred for domestic work, which provided intimate access to owners' families. Female slaveholders particularly favored women in manumissions, probably those who were under their direct supervision in the gendered domestic sphere.[15] Women represented a whopping 92 percent of African slaves manumitted in early colonial Havana (1585–1610) by slaveholding women. Male slaveholders also preferred to manumit women, although at a lower rate (68 percent).

The prevalence of women in manumissions had long-term consequences. Since children followed the social condition of the mother, the progeny of these women would be free. The principle of *partus sequitur ventrem* guaranteed that slaves' children would also be enslaved, but the same doctrine applied to freedwomen's children, even if the fathers were enslaved. Many of the women who managed to obtain freedom were of reproductive age (the average age of women manumitted in Havana between 1585 and 1610 was about fourteen for those born on the island; for Africans, it was thirty-seven and a half), and this led to higher reproduction rates among the free population of color and the early formation of free communities of color in many Iberian colonies.

Other factors contributed to the consolidation of these free communities of color. Most manumissions were in fact freedom purchases, and buying the freedom of children was frequently preferred. Because of family considerations and parents' love for their children, and because manumission prices were considerably lower for children, parents and other relatives targeted them. The manumission price for a five-year-old child was about half of the price that a prime-age woman in her twenties had to pay for her freedom. In early colonial Havana, the average manumission age for *criollos*, slaves born on the island (who represented about half of total manumissions), was only ten years old. Indeed, 68 percent of *criollos* who obtained manumission were ten or younger. These children were born under slavery but spent almost all of their life as free people.[16]

It is possible that many of the children who escaped slavery at such a young age were related to a slaveholder or to members of a slaveholder's social circle. As early as the turn of the seventeenth century, about a quarter of the slaves obtaining freedom in Havana were described as *pardos* or *mulatos*, the offspring of interracial sexual unions. In 28 percent of these cases the manumission price was paid by a white resident who did not acknowledge any family relation to the child, although of course that does not mean that such a link did not exist. Finally, many of the relatively rare manumissions that were given without payment benefited children who were described as racially mixed. Such was the case of Juanica, a one-year-old whom the prominent Havana *vecino* Hernán Manrique de Rojas manumitted gratis in 1602 and who was the daughter of one of his own slaves, Maria, a "*mulata.*" It was also the case of Francisca, "of *pardo* color" (*de color pardo*), manumitted gratis in 1691 in reward for services rendered by her mother. The female slaveholder in this case also acknowledged that Francisca was the "natural daughter" of her unmarried son, Juan Rodriguez. Francisca was her granddaughter.[17]

Enslaved people made use of some customary practices to shape self-purchase in ways favorable to them. As early as the sixteenth century, slaves and masters sometimes agreed on a manumission price that, once established, could not be altered. As we saw in Juana's case in the Introduction, in practice this meant that the owner could not go back on the agreement, and any new buyer would also have to free the slave if she could pay the agreed price. Drawn up and registered by notaries, powerful legal intermediaries in Iberian law, these agreements transformed a master's prerogative (manumission) into a slave's right (self-purchase), one that the slave could invoke even against the will of the owner.[18] By paying half of her price, Juana also achieved the anomalous and hard-to-define social status of a *coartada*, which afforded her the possibility of claiming some additional rights.

Coartados occupied a middle category of uncertain and highly contentious legal and social standing. A good example may be the case of Esteban Barrios, a person described as a "free *pardo*" in 1694. Barrios was legally free, but to complete his payments for freedom he agreed to serve Custodio Hernandez for eighteen months, "doing everything" that Hernandez "commanded and ordered, as if he were his slave" (*como si fuera su esclavo*). The contract stipulated that Barrios would not be paid during this period. While the notarized document listed Barrios as free, the contract explicitly placed him in a situation close to that of a slave.[19]

Conflicts over *coartación*, and manumission more generally, frequently resulted in litigation. Self-purchase often led to disputes over the fair price of a slave when slave and owner had not agreed in advance on the price of freedom. Estate settlements also led to frequent legal contests, as in the petition initiated by Cristobal and Jose Mina in 1691 Havana. The town council of Havana, which functioned as a court of appeals, heard more than twenty manumission-related cases between 1650 and 1700.[20] Such litigation continued in the eighteenth century. A study of 1,320 freedom letters in Havana (dated 1700 to 1770), found that in 102 cases the slaves were forced to litigate their freedom.[21] Outsiders often intervened in this contentious process, and private individuals sometimes provided support for an enslaved person by lending money or serving as guarantors. Colonial officials also played a role, dispensing royal justice, mediating between masters and slaves, and providing paths, however narrow, for slaves to fight legally for freedom.

One exceptional path to freedom was created by slaves who claimed to move between different imperial jurisdictions for religious reasons. Just as some slaves used their past experience in the Iberian colonies and their condition as baptized Christians to demand freedom in seventeenth-century Virginia, slaves who had escaped from the English and the Dutch used religious reasons – being converts to Catholicism – to press freedom claims in Havana. In 1681, for instance, the slave Felipa petitioned the town council of Havana for her freedom "because she ran away from Jamaica from the power of the English, whose slave she was." A royal cedula of 1750 ratified that three slaves who had escaped from Jamaica were free. The royal cedula mentioned that this was the established legal doctrine and that numerous royal regulations prescribed that slaves who found "refuge" in the Spanish territories from "foreign colonies" were to be freed.[22]

Whatever route they took, a significant number of enslaved Africans and their descendants in Cuba found their way to freedom in the seventeenth and eighteenth centuries, so that by 1770, Havana at least had a well-established community of free people of color that represented about 14 percent of the city's total population. Although similar communities developed both in New Orleans and on the Eastern Shore of Virginia, they were small compared with Havana's, in large part because of more restrictive laws in both jurisdictions in the eighteenth century.

LOUISIANA. A few free people of color arrived in the Louisiana Territory among the first immigrants. Marie, a domestic servant, and Jean-Baptiste César, a laborer, arrived in 1719, and several other free people of color appear in the earliest court records in the 1720s: Raphael Bernard, Simon Vanon, and John Mingo. Mingo was a runaway slave who arrived from South Carolina in 1726, and was declared free by Jonathas Darby, who directed the concession of French banker Bernard Cantillon; Mingo then purchased his wife, Thérèse, by installments, using his wages as a plantation manager. However, a much greater number of Africans arrived in New Orleans as slaves, about seven thousand between 1718 and 1735.[23] For them, the paths to freedom were considerably narrower than those in early colonial Cuba. It was possible for slaves to become free in French Louisiana, but such opportunities were rare.

French slaveholders exploited the relative novelty of slavery in French law to introduce innovations in the legal treatment of manumission. Compared with the 1685 version, the Louisiana Code Noir of 1724 was very restrictive concerning manumissions. Whereas the 1685 code authorized any master at least twenty years old to manumit a slave without state interference, by the time the 1724 code was promulgated, the legal regime of manumissions in the French Caribbean colonies had become considerably more restrictive and was consistent with a racial order based on black debasement. Claiming that slaves resorted to illicit means to secure funds for self-purchase, in 1711 the intendant and the governor of Martinique and Guadeloupe ordered that owners could not set slaves free without prior authorization. A royal confirmation followed two years later, nullifying any manumission that was not officially sanctioned and prescribing that illegally freed slaves would be sold for the king's profit. The Louisiana Code Noir followed this restrictive doctrine. It allowed manumission only if the master was at least twenty-five years old and had secured the authorization of the Superior Council. According to article 50 of the code, the council would authorize manumissions only "when the motives for the setting free of said slaves, as specified in the petition of the master, shall appear legitimate to the tribunal." Unauthorized manumissions were "null." In such cases the slaves would be confiscated and sold for the benefit of the Company of the Indies.[24]

As the case of Marie Aram and her husband, François Tiocon, showed at the opening of this chapter, slaves made the best of this restrictive legal regime to secure their freedom. Gwendolyn Midlo Hall's comprehensive database of all surviving records of Africans and African Americans in Louisiana shows 119 manumissions during the French period. Some slaves managed to obtain freedom by performing important public services, particularly in cases involving public order. Slaveholders across imperial lines rewarded a few slaves with freedom when they participated in colonial defense or, as in the case of Will from Virginia, when they denounced or helped quash slave revolts. In 1729, for instance, the governor of Louisiana granted manumission to about a dozen slaves who fought for the French against the Natchez Indians. The former slaves, including Tiocon, fought again alongside whites against several indigenous groups in the 1730s.[25]

For most enslaved people, however, their only hope for escaping slavery legally lay in persuading masters to grant them freedom. This could take the form of an outright manumission, to reward past services, or a freedom purchase. Both forms of manumission were discouraged by the Code Noir, but some did take place. Unlike in Havana, where most manumissions involved freedom purchases, in French colonial New Orleans they were rare. Those records that survive pertain to free husbands purchasing their enslaved wives. Of course, because the law prescribed that freedom should be granted only for "good and faithful services" or "good and agreeable services," it is possible that some of the manumissions that recited such a reason may have in fact involved payments that were not acknowledged openly.

In most cases, to win Superior Council approval, as in the 1735 petition for the "manumission of Marie Charlotte and Louise, her small daughter, by their master, St. Pierre," the master stated that freedom was being offered "for the services rendered him by said slave."[26] In 1762 the Superior Council granted a slaveowner's petition "to free a negress named Jeanneton, in reward for her zeal and fidelity in his service." Similarly, a captain in the colonial troops petitioned the governor and the intendant, "wishing to recognize the faithful services of a negress named Mimi." The first recorded manumission in the colony was granted in 1733 by Governor Bienville himself, who freed an enslaved couple in recognition of their twenty-six years of service.[27]

As in Havana, some manumissions in Louisiana were granted in wills, and some agreements made between masters and slaves during their lifetime took effect only after the owner passed away. For example, in 1739 "Louis Connard, and his wife Catherine, for themselves and their children (all negroes), praying that their freedom, granted by will of . . . their late Master, be confirmed," petitioned the Superior Council for a copy of their late master's will because he had "promised them their liberty." The manumission was confirmed two days later by Governor Bienville and Intendant Salmon, after an examination of the will. In 1747, Pantalon, a "negro slave," petitioned the council for his freedom based on his master's will, although this case involved payment, for the will provided that Pantalon would pay the price "at which he and his family be appraised." They were appraised at "3000 livres." A Mr. Fabry pledged himself as security for the 3,000 livres, and Pantalon, his wife, and children were set free. Other masters petitioned to free their slaves when they were returning to France or otherwise leaving the colony.[28]

Pantalon's case is similar to that of Cristobal and Jose Mina, the African slaves who sought their freedom in 1691 in Havana. In both cases, the slaves had been promised freedom in their master's will. In both cases, they had to petition authorities to enforce the will; both cases also involved cash payments. Pantalon secured the financial support of a third party, a practice that was common in Havana and in the Iberian colonies more generally.

The main difference, however, is that by law all manumissions in Louisiana had to be confirmed and approved by the Superior Council. Owners were forced to state a rationale for their acts. The intervention of authorities was needed even in conditional, future manumissions, such as that of Charlotte, "of Senegal nationality," and her son Louis. The slave owner, Antoine Meuillion, surgeon of the king, declared before the notary of the Superior Council in 1746 that he "granted freedom" to Charlotte and her son, but that their freedom was to take effect only if he left the colony or died: "in such case," he stated, he was "petitioning the Governor and Commissioner Ordonnateur to confirm her manumission."[29]

The social situation of manumitted slaves and free blacks was precarious even with papers, so it was to their advantage to make sure that a change in status was properly inscribed in public documents.[30] Writing was crucial, and an unsanctioned manumission was, by law, no manumission at all. As Rebecca Scott and Jean Hébrard explain, "Words could protect, and words could enslave." Slaves knew this. When Louis and Catharine, acting for several fellow slaves, "beseech[ed] a copy or extract of the will of their late master, Captain De Coustillas, who had promised them their liberty," they recognized the value of such "freedom papers."[31] Although it is possible that there were unrecorded manumissions that swelled the ranks of free people of color, it is doubtful that they were many in number, or that the people thus freed were recognized as truly free.

VIRGINIA. Manumission evolved differently in Virginia, where colonists did not have clear legal precedents to rely on. Unlike Louisiana, which instituted the restrictive Code Noir at the outset of colonial settlement, seventy years passed before the Virginia General Assembly passed any limitations on a master's right to free his slave or a free person of color's right to marry a white person, and effective regulations were not in place until the early eighteenth century. Between 1705 and 1782, however, the Virginia legislature steadily shut down the possibilities for manumission and self-purchase, limited the rights of free people of color, ended intermarriage, and greatly increased the penalties for interracial sex. All these measures complemented legal efforts to build a strict racial regime in the colony. Free people of color had formed significant communities in the small populations on the Eastern Shore in the seventeenth century, but these communities lost status and were dwarfed in size by the influx of slaves from Africa and the Caribbean in the eighteenth century.

Unlike in Cuba, rules of manumission developed in Virginia along with the construction of a racial order. Between the 1640s and 1691, manumissions appear to have been considered a private right of slaveholders, as in the Iberian colonies. The presence of black servants, however, makes it difficult to discern at times if the cases in the General Court of Virginia concerned slaves for life or Africans subject to terms of service. In 1645, for instance, a master emancipated several black individuals in his will and left them some lands as well. It is not clear whether they were servants or slaves. The "negro [s]ervant" John Graweere was "permitted by his said master to keep hogs and make the best benefit thereof," paying half the proceeds to his master and keeping half for himself. Graweere had a child "which he desired should be made a christian," and "by reason whereof" he purchased the child's freedom in 1641. The General Court decreed that the child should be free from Graweere's master as well as his mother's, but the records do not reveal whether Graweere was an indentured servant or a slave for life. In 1668 the court issued a favorable "judgment for a negro for her freedom," and in 1672 "a Negro man," Edward Mozingo, became free after his indenture was completed. At least some of these servants collected freedom dues after their years of service, just as white servants did.[32]

Local court records in Accomack County and Northampton County, on the Eastern Shore, give greater depth to this picture of a free black community with a significant flow of manumissions and freedom suits. A number of free "negro" planters who settled on the Eastern Shore in the mid-seventeenth century became heads of large families and appear often in the records. The first of these men was Anthony Johnson, who owned property and slaves in Northampton County, including John Casor, whom he freed in 1654. Philip Mongom, Domingo Mathews, Bashaw Fernando, Black Jacke, and Nese were others who were given freedom by will or deed in the 1650s, and slaves continued to obtain their freedom throughout the seventeenth century and into the eighteenth.[33]

Some of these manumissions were the result of self-purchases or the efforts of others to secure a slave's freedom; others are less clear in their origins. Philip Mongom and Mingo (or Domingo) Mathews, slaves of William Hawley, won their freedom during the four years they were hired out to planter John Foster, beginning in 1648. Foster complained that "the Negroes which hee had of Capt. William Hawley were very stubborne and would not followe his business." Finally, Foster got Hawley to sign an agreement with the two slaves in which they promised to finish their term of service with Foster, after which "they shalbe free from their servitude and bee free men, and labour for themselves," provided they paid Hawley 1,700 pounds of tobacco or "one man servant,

5. Anthony Johnson's mark. A free man of color, Johnson amassed a substantial fortune in land and slaves in Northampton County, Virginia, and then moved with his family to Somerset County, Maryland, in 1665. This is his mark as it appears in the Somerset County Land Records, recording a lease of 300 acres of land in 1666.

beinge an able hand." However, the two were set free early, in 1650, after giving the Northampton County court information about a local Indian plot to poison English wells.[34]

Extant records of self-purchase agreements suggest a fair amount of autonomy for slaves who purchased themselves, such as Francis Payne, one of the first free people of color in the colony. Philip Taylor had bought "Francisco a Negroe" in 1637, but all later records refer to him as Francis or Frank. After Taylor died, his widow left Payne alone on her old plantation when she remarried. In 1649 she deeded him rights to its crops, authorizing him "to use the best meanes lawfully hee can for the further betteringe of the said cropp," and giving him "the power from tyme to tyme to make use of the ground and plantation," in return for 1,500 pounds of tobacco and six barrels of corn at harvest time. Later that year, they signed a self-purchase agreement in which he promised to pay her "three male servants between 15 and 24 years old, each having six or seven years to serve." Although he was not able to meet the one-year deadline in the contract, he seems to have succeeded in buying his freedom by 1651. A letter from the widow Taylor's new husband, William Eltonhead, suggests that he was actively trying to help Payne fulfill the agreement: "After my love to thee etc. I cannot heare of any servants in Yorke. They are all sould. But if you doe get your tobacco in caske, I question not but to get them, when I come downe againe, and likewise I will bring downe some caske with mee if I can come soone enough, soe I rest your loveinge mayster."[35] Despite the fact that Payne still held the status of slave, the letter reads as one between social equals.

It is worth noting the Iberian names of the slaves Domingo and Francisco. Most of the Africans imported to Virginia in the seventeenth century arrived there by way of the Caribbean, many of them having spent time as slaves in Brazil, Barbados, or one of the Spanish colonies. Those experiences, which led Ira Berlin to describe the first generation of slaves as "Atlantic creoles," allowed the Africans to learn local languages, customs and legal cultures.[36] Enslaved Africans who spent time in Spanish colonies or Brazil likely learned about the ways a slave might use the legal system to become free or otherwise to better his condition. So it is not surprising that some of the first records we have of self-purchase in Virginia involve slaves who had spent time in a Spanish jurisdiction. Through these interactions, slaves and slaveholders both participated in the creation of legal understandings and expectations concerning slavery and freedom in the colony.

Other slaves purchased their freedom in exchange for tobacco, livestock, or their own or their children's labor. William Harman purchased his freedom from William Kendall for 5,000 pounds of tobacco in casks, "cleer of ground leaves or trash." In Accomack County in 1671, John West recorded his agreement with his "mulatto" servant Thomas Webb, promising that Webb would be free after three years of work. In return, Webb promised to pay West 1,500 pounds of tobacco per year, a cow, and a calf, and to bind his daughter to West's daughter until she came of age. West promised to give Webb's daughter a mare colt and its female increase, with Webb to care for it and receive the male increase. Webb was "free to deal with anyone" but had to provide his own clothing. Thus, Webb was able to become legally free by exercising a significant level of autonomy while still enslaved, operating as his own business agent. Andrew James gained his freedom only after his owner John Griggs's death, but he did so based on a "covenant" that James would "worke for himselfe paying his sd master ... 2000 lbs sweet sented tobo & caske" and Griggs would not "hinder sd Andrew from working at his trade of Carpenter."[37]

For at least a few decades, some slaves appear to have understood that baptism into Christianity afforded them an avenue to freedom. In 1644 a mulatto named Manuel sued for his freedom before the Virginia Assembly in Jamestown on the basis of his Christianity, and in 1661 the Indian boy Metappin was freed, "he speaking perfectly the English tongue and desiring baptism."[38] Elizabeth Key, the daughter of a white man, Thomas Key, who had returned to England, and an African mother, made Christianity a fundamental part of her claim to freedom in 1654. Colonel Humphrey Higginson testified to an agreement he had made with Thomas Key, to care for Elizabeth as her godfather. "That shee hath bin long since Christened Col. Higginson being her God father and that by report shee is able to give a very good account of her fayth." Elizabeth Key won her suit, and married her attorney, staying in Virginia rather than returning to England with Higginson.[39] Several other slaves won suits for freedom based on their Christian baptism, and in other cases in which Christian baptism was not the basis for winning a freedom suit, it nevertheless appeared to bolster a slave's case. When John Graweere purchased freedom for his child, he told the General Assembly that "he desired [the child] should be made a Christian and be taught and exercised in the church of England, by reason whereof he ... did for his said child purchase its freedom." The court decreed the child should be free and that its Christian upbringing be provided for by Graweere and the child's godfather. Faced with the possibility that Christianity could become a widespread justification for enslaved people to emancipate themselves, perhaps it is no surprise that in 1667 the General Assembly, following all other Atlantic slaveholding jurisdictions, decreed that baptism would no longer be the basis for freedom.[40]

Even after the passage of the law, however, it appears that "enslaved people in Virginia were still using baptism as one among many reasons for freedom." William Catilla, a mulatto, sued Mrs. Margrett Booth for his freedom in 1695 because he was "the son of a free woman" and also because he "was baptized in the Christian faith." Baptism also remained a reason for treating free people of color as legal persons. For example, John Johnson gave testimony in Somerset County court in 1674 after giving assurance that he was Christian and "did rightly understand the taking of an oath."[41]

Other manumissions took place without any reasons recorded in court. For example, Elisabeth Walthum recorded a manumission in

Accomack County court in 1671 simply by declaring, "I, Elisabeth Walthum ... do fully acquit and discharge Jeane, a Negro ... from any further service either to me or any relating to me, declaring her to be a free woman." A deed by William Kendall in 1659 set forth that "whereas Capt. Francis Pott, Decesased, declared in his life time that when he departed this natural life ... [he would] set his negro Bashaw Free but did not mention ye same in his will, know ye that I doe by these presents sett ye said Bashawe att Liberty, proclaim him to be free of my servitude." Sometimes the court noted that the master had acquiesced to a slave's petition for freedom. For example, Henry Jackson, who was listed in one court record as "maletto servant to William Sterling," was noted in September 30, 1690 only as a servant: "servant to Wm. Sterling, petitioning for his freedom, the suit concluded (with the concession of ye said partys) the said Jackson is to serv the said Sterling one whole year from this day and he to be discharged from his said master's service with reasonable clothing."[42] For most of the seventeenth century, such manumissions remained routine events in the ordinary business of county courts, with little perceived need even to comment on the reasons behind them.

Yet by the end of the seventeenth century a dramatic shift began to occur, not only on the Eastern Shore of Virginia but also in the colony as a whole. Beginning in 1691, and decisively in 1723, Virginia legislators moved to restrict the ability of enslaved people to become free. This happened at a time of political upheaval as well as demographic and economic transformation for the colony. By the 1690s, white indentured servitude had declined dramatically, and white farmers had decisively shifted to enslaved Africans as their source of agricultural labor.

What explains the concomitant rise of race as a legal marker of degradation (described in Chapter 1), restrictions on manumission, and the move to import ever greater numbers of Africans for a lifetime of bound labor? The most famous explanation, that of Edmund Morgan's *American Slavery, American Freedom*, centers on elite Virginians' fear of alliances among poor white indentured servants, free people of color, and black and Indian slaves, who had banded together in Bacon's Rebellion in 1676. The slaveholding planters who dominated Virginia politics responded to this fear by banning Indian slavery, cracking down on the rights of free people of color and the possibility of manumission, and favoring the importation of Africans over troublesome English servants. As Morgan wrote, slaveholders passed legal measures in order to "separate dangerous free whites from dangerous slave blacks by a screen of racial contempt."[43] This was accomplished both by expanding the rights of white servants, especially once their indentures came to an end, and degrading the rights of free people of color.

This explanation is undoubtedly part of the answer, but it is incomplete. It does not take into account important demographic and economic shifts that preceded Bacon's Rebellion. First, the flow of English servants to Virginia began to dry up in the 1660s, and it fell off dramatically in 1680 owing to an improved English labor market and the growing attractiveness of other North American colonies, such as Pennsylvania. As the price of white bound labor rose by 60 percent, African slave prices bottomed out in the 1680s. By the 1670s the gentry were already replacing white indentured servants with African slaves, and by 1690 all of the gentry's bound workers were slaves, compared with 25 to 40 percent of those belonging to smaller farmers. There was no sudden trigger that caused the shift from servitude to slavery; rather, slavery expanded gradually in Virginia as the British Empire and its involvement in the slave trade grew and slaves became more available.[44]

Although the expansion of slavery was less a dramatic shift than a gradual response to market price and supply, politics also played an important role – especially when we consider the concomitant decisions to limit legal opportunities for freedom, and even to change the meaning of freedom along racial lines. It is this interaction between demographics and economics, on the one hand, and politics and law, on the other, that appears important in the comparative context. In Virginia, as compared to Cuba, where white indentured servants did not exist, the need for elite slaveholders to appeal to poor white Englishmen, and the fear that poor white servants might band together with unruly people of color, including Indians, prompted slaveholders to limit manumission in order to more effectively equate blackness with enslavement. Despite efforts to control people of color and instantiate racial distinctions in law, slaveholders in Cuba during this period did not conceive of the possibility of eliminating the slaveholders' right to grant manumission, or of limiting opportunities for slaves to become free. Such rights and opportunities were well entrenched in legal precedents and royal edicts and were not tied to race-making efforts.

In 1691, in response to political upheavals and the expansion of slavery, the Virginia General Assembly passed its first comprehensive slave code. The 1691 code borrowed a great deal from Barbados's 1661 "act for the better ordering and governing of Negroes," which consisted mainly of police regulations and laws about the apprehension and punishment of runaways.[45] But Virginia innovated by responding to rebellion and political turmoil with restrictions on manumission, to better align blackness with slavery, and whiteness with freedom. Legislators described the very existence of free people of color as an "inconvenience" that would produce all manner of negative social consequences. The assembly therefore decreed "that no negro or mulatto be after the end of this present session of assembly set free by any person or persons whatsoever, unless such persons ... pay for the transportation of such negro or negroes out of the country within six months after such setting them free, upon penalty of paying ten pound sterling to the Church wardens of the parish." The fine was to be used to "cause the said negro or mulatto to be transported out of the country" and to sustain the poor of the parish. Although the act of 1691 did not outlaw manumissions, and freed slaves continued to receive permission to stay in Virginia, the new law signaled official disapproval of the practice and placed a considerable additional burden on slaveholders wishing to manumit their slaves. Further restrictions followed. When in 1712 a slaveholder from Norfolk County "by his last Will set free sixteen Negro Slaves and [gave] them a considerable Tract of Land," the local council submitted the case to the General Assembly, requesting "a law against such manumissions of slaves, which in time by their increase and correspondence with other slaves may endanger the peace of this colony." In 1723 the assembly passed a law banning manumissions "upon any pretense whatsoever, except for some meritorious services, to be adjudged and allowed by the governor and council." Slaves who were set free without proper authorization were to be seized by the church wardens of the parish and sold back into slavery.[46]

Unlike the earlier laws, the 1723 ban achieved results: between the 1720s and the American Revolution in the 1770s, perhaps as few as two dozen Virginia slaves were freed by their masters, although there continued to be some successful freedom suits in county courts. The council does appear to have endorsed a fairly lax definition of what constituted "meritorious service," which was at times equated with such vague statements as "faithful service" or "fidelity and diligent service," clauses that were very similar to those invoked in Havana's manumission letters at the time.[47]

In a few cases, the merits required by law were spelled out in great detail, as in the rather exceptional case of Papaw, a slave who had performed "many extraordinary cures" and who was promised freedom in 1729 "to obtain from him a discovery of the secret whereby he performs the said cures." Papaw represented an early example of how enslaved Africans in the Americas made use of their ethnobotanical knowledge to heal themselves and members of their community. After Papaw "made an ample discovery of the several medicines made use of by him for that purpose to the satisfaction of the Governor and the Gentlemen appointed by him to inspect the application and operation of the said medicines," he was granted his freedom. Papaw also secured an annual pension of twenty pounds, for "the medicines discovered" by him were "tried and found effectual."[48]

Most of the slaves who managed to obtain freedom in the Virginia General Court, however, did so for more mundane reasons related to "faithful service," just as in Louisiana. Almost all of these manumissions were contained in wills and most were ratified by the council after the death of the master. In a typical example, Philip Ludwell's executors, "praying the approbation of this Board for the manumitting of Johnathan Pearse ... in Consideration of his faithful Services," represented the manumission as the will of the testator, for which he would be willing to exchange any of his other slaves. In 1735, the widow of John Smith declared that her husband, "being possessed of a Negro man named Robin for whom he had a very great affection did on his death bed declare his mind & earnest desire to be that the said Negro Robin for his fidelity and diligent service should immediately after his decease be free & discharged from all farther Servitude." To fulfill Smith's wish, the widow "humbly prayed the approbation of this Board therein pursuant to the Act of Assembly in that case made & provided," and the governor and council approved the manumission. In 1741, the nineteen-year-old slave Lilly, who was granted freedom by her female owner in her will "on account of Several very acceptable services done by her," was likewise declared free by the council.[49]

Occasionally not even the meager justification of good services was offered, as in this case from 1749: "Upon the Recommendation of his Honor the Governor it is ordered, that a Negro man, born a Slave, belonging to his Honor, named Captain John, be manumitted and set free." Only rarely did the council refuse to ratify a manumission, claiming that the petitioner had failed to provide adequate proof of meritorious service.[50]

Despite the explicit opposition of Virginia legislators and planters to manumission, therefore, a few slaves managed to litigate for their freedom, at the very least forcing authorities to consider their claims. In some cases, even informal claims succeeded. In 1745, for instance, a mulatto man name Abram Newton petitioned the council for his freedom, claiming that he had been married to Elizabeth Young, a free mulatto woman who had purchased him, that the two had lived together until her death, and that, "writing under her hand," she had given him "his discharge after her death." After inquiring if any party claimed to own Newton as a slave, the council "ordered that the said Abram be manumitted and set free according to the will" of his deceased wife and mistress. This was of course an exceptional case, as Abram petitioned for freedom after his owner's death, and the owner also happened to have been his wife.[51]

In those few cases in which slaves argued for their freedom against their masters, however, they faced not only formidable legal obstacles in proving that they had been wrongly enslaved but also the reprisals of their putative owners. In 1711 a black man named John Demerea petitioned the council "to prove his freedom" and obtained an order stating that "his master should not punish him for his coming without leave to present his petition." A few years later, in 1717, John Coomee argued that he had been wrongfully enslaved by a resident of Elizabeth City County and claimed to be a "freeman." Although in both cases the petitioners managed to lodge their claims, they both faced the ire of their alleged owners. Demerea complained that, as a result of his petition, the person who claimed to be his owner "had beat him in the most inhumane and severe manner." Coomee suffered a similar fate, as he was whipped, placed in irons, and threatened with transportation out of the colony.[52]

As other avenues were closed off in 1723, freedom suits centered on the existence of a free female ancestor. Some claimed an Indian or white mother, others that their mother, although a "negro," was free. For example, in 1723 in Northampton County, Thomas Ferrell, "mulattoo," petitioned for freedom on the ground that he had reached the age of thirty-one years (the statutory indenture for a bastard born of interracial fornication), but he then added to his petition "being born of a white woman." In 1732, Nanny Bandy ("alias Judea") petitioned that "she is illegally held as a slave, and born on the body of a white woman." In 1747, Will, "mulatto," petitioned for his freedom, and "Indian Will" sued in the same year, claiming that "his mother [was] very well known to be a free Indian." Although Indian Will lost his case, the others were successful.[53]

One case from Northampton County demonstrates the changing status of free people of color on the Eastern Shore in the early eighteenth century. Jane Webb, born in the early 1680s as the daughter of a white woman and a man of color, was a servant in the household of Henry Warren, a white planter. According to her lawsuit some years later, in 1703 she reached an agreement with Thomas Savage that she could marry his slave Left, and in return she would bind herself to him as a servant for a seven-year term, and the children she had with Left would serve Savage until age eighteen; at the end of her seven years of service, Left would be free, and any children they had after that would be free as well.[54]

At the end of Jane's term of service, in 1711, Savage had the court bind her three children to him "according to the law." This effectively extended Jane's children's service an additional three years, because the law of 1703 had set indentures for the children of a freedwoman at twenty-one years. Thus, when Jane began petitioning for the freedom of eighteen-year-old Dinah in 1722, the petition was dismissed. Dinah did not win her freedom until she turned twenty-one and brought her own suit in 1725. Jane also sued Savage in chancery in 1725 over the status of her other children, charging that he had violated the terms of their original contract. Angry at the court's decision in Savage's favor, Jane declared that "if all Virginia Negros had as good a heart as she had they would all be free." For these "dangerous words tending to the breach of the peace," she was sentenced to ten lashes the next day. Savage countered that he had never promised to free Left, and that he could not remember how long her children were to serve. Jane sought to introduce the testimony of other free people of color, and the court took several months to decide whether "Negro evidence" should be allowed. After four months, they decided that "none such ought to be allowed," and Jane gave up her suit. Jane's inability to protect her family, the corporal punishment she suffered for making a statement in favor of freedom, and the refusal to admit testimony by free people of color were all new developments in the Northampton County court. It is noteworthy, however, that the county court still thought it had to deliberate the question of whether free people of color should be allowed to testify, in 1725, even though the statute banning such testimony was passed in 1703.[55]

Jane Webb's son, Abimeleck Webb, also challenged boundaries, telling a white woman with whom he was working that "the Negroes ... would be free." When she asked him "how they would go about it," he answered, "with their one indeavour and godalmightys assistance or blessing, for what would it be fore the Negroes to go through this County in one nights time." This declaration set off a hue and cry about a "negro conspiracy" in the county and led to other slaves being rounded up for questioning, although there is no record of any convictions or punishments. Jane Webb herself finally gained some relief from the court in 1740 by playing on their sympathies to gain an exemption from the tax that women of color and all men of working age (but not white women) had to pay, writing, "Whereas your petitioner is very old and likewise decriped and am not able to git tobbco to pay my leavy."[56]

Although some slaves continued their efforts to win freedom, the 1723 ban on manumission severely limited their ability to do so, just as in Louisiana. Yet the people who had become free in the years before 1723 continued to appear in county court records, revealing how the courts tried – apparently unsuccessfully – to crack down on "fornication" and "bastard bearing" among whites, mulattoes, and negroes, free and enslaved. These records bear the evidence of extensive mixing among the "lower orders" of all races, blurring the lines between black and white, as well as those between slave and free.

INTERMARRIAGE, RACE MIXING, AND RACIAL IDENTITY

Wherever significant numbers of slaves became free, they mixed not only with other free and enslaved people of color but also with whites and sometimes Indians, given the relatively small overall populations of the three colonies. In Virginia, where this practice went on more or less unfettered in the seventeenth century, a spate of new regulations at the turn of the eighteenth century greatly limited manumissions and inter-marriages. It is not a coincidence that these limitations went hand in hand, as they shared the same purpose: to build a racial order in which blackness was synonymous with enslavement.

Stricter penalties for interracial sex outside marriage notwithstand-ing, a steady stream of interracial fornication and bastardy cases in eight-eenth-century county courts in Virginia testified to a growing "mulatto" population. Louisiana looked quite similar to Virginia during the same years: restrictive rules regarding manumission and intermarriage imposed from 1724 to 1769 meant relatively few people became free or married across racial lines, but illicit interracial relationships continued. In matters of intimate relations, legal restrictions seemed to be honored in the breach, in the sense that people continued to form interracial families without the benefit of legal recognition, and even when they paid penalties for doing so. Yet closing off legal marriage, and penalizing sex across the color line did have long-term consequences. Because of the rule of *partus sequitur ventrem*, much of the "mulatto" population of Virginia and Louisiana remained enslaved and illegitimate.

By contrast, interracial sex and marriage remained unregulated in Cuba, allowing the growth of a substantial population of free people of color, most of whom were mulatto, even if relatively few entered into the sacrament of marriage across racial lines. Spain did not attempt to regulate marriage on the basis of race before 1776. As with manumis-sions, the rules concerning slave marriage were anchored in traditional canon law and Roman principles not tied to a racial project. Although most marriages took place among people of similar stations, the canoni-cal principle of freedom of consent among Catholics was not formally challenged prior to 1776. In Havana, of the 3,098 marriages recorded in the years 1584–1622, 17.5 percent (539) were slave marriages, 2.6

percent (79) were marriages between two free people of color, and 4 percent (127) were marriages between a free person of color and an enslaved person. A small but significant number of interracial marriages were recorded as well: there were 91 marriages between a free person of color and a white person, making up 3 percent of the total, and 42 marriages between a slave and a white person, for another 1.4 percent. In Havana, almost as many people married across race lines as married across the line of slave and free. Furthermore, marriage godparents and witnesses also crossed racial lines. Although no black person performed these roles in marriages where both partners were white, the majority of godparents and witnesses in marriages among free people of color, or in interracial marriages, were white (81 and 98 percent, respectively). These marriages took place in the church, where both slaves and free people of color could receive the sacraments, and they were recognized as one of the rights of all Christians. Priests promised many benefits to baptism and receiving the sacraments, although freedom was not one of them.[57]

On the eve of the first law against unequal marriages, in 1776, free people of color made up about 14.5 percent of the total population of Cuba and 34 percent of the nonwhite population; people of mixed race made up 58 percent of the free population of color, and only 5 percent of the slave population. In Havana as well as in the colony at large, there was a substantial overlap between the populations of free people of color and "mulattoes," so that race and slave status came to be relatively closely linked: free people of color were likely to have a somewhat different racial status from those who remained enslaved, but the association between whiteness and freedom was nonetheless undermined.

Legal regulation of marriage did not take place until Spain's 1776 Royal Pragmatic on Marriage, aimed at preventing unequal marriages, made parental consent a formal requirement for those under twenty-five years old; in 1778 the law was extended to the colonies, with the penalty of disinheritance (see Chapter 5). Before that time, although interracial marriage was not a common practice in Havana, it occurred with regularity and received the same recognition as other marriages.

Louisiana authorities' first encounters with intermarriage and cross-racial sexual relationships occurred when French men sought to marry or enter into "concubinage" with Indian women, including slaves. Despite periodic efforts after 1716 to discourage marriages between French men and Native women, missionaries continued to sanctify their relationships, and secular officials conducted a decades-long debate about the advisability of marriages with Indians as a way of building alliances. This debate receded only as Louisiana "transform[ed] from an extractive colony to a proto-plantation society [w]ith the arrival of African slaves in large numbers beginning in the late 1710s." Familiarity with interracial marriage, combined with the shortage of white women, helped set the stage for French Louisianan men to seek partners across the color line.[58]

However, by the time the French settled Louisiana, the process of black debasement in their Caribbean colonies was already fairly advanced, so racial mixing was perceived – at least officially – as an unacceptable breach of the color line. Louisiana's Code Noir contained several significant revisions of the earlier code with regard to interracial sex and marriage. The 1685 Code Noir had included a fine of 2,000 livres in sugar for free men who had children in "concubinages" with enslaved women. If the father was the slave's owner, he was to be "deprived of the slave and children," who were to be sold for the benefit of the hospital and could never be freed. However, if the free man was not married to someone else "during his concubinage with his slave," he could legitimate the marriage and the child by marrying her in the church, thereby setting mother and child free. This possibility created a significant incentive for enslaved African women to enter into relationships with free men, white or black. The Louisiana code of 1724, however, forbade "white subjects, of either sex" to marry "les Noirs," free or slave, and also prohibited whites or free blacks from practicing "concubinage with slaves." In the 1724 code, an enslaved woman could gain her freedom only by marrying a previously unmarried free black man with whom she had lived in concubinage, not a white man. Thus, the 1724 code drew sharper lines both between free and enslaved and between white and black. Both lines sought to sustain a strict racial order.[59]

In spite of the ban on interracial marriage, a few racially exogamous marriages may have taken place in contravention of the Code Noir, including that of one white woman born in Bruges, Marie Gaspart, who married a free black man from Martinique, Jean-Baptiste Raphael, in 1725, with the permission of the colony's commandant general, a

Canadian officer who had administered the Illinois Country for the previous six years and seen many marriages between Frenchmen and Native women. Interestingly, a notation was added to their marriage record at a later point, designating both Raphael and Gaspart as "nègres libres," although in most records no race is attached to Marie Gaspart's name and she was almost certainly white. Furthermore, a handful of apparently interracial marriages that appear in the Spanish-era sacramental registers probably date to the French period. In one of those cases, a child baptized during the Spanish period was listed as the legitimate child of a white father and a woman of color for whom there is no surviving marriage record.[60]

In spite of the rarity of legitimate marriage, interracial unions may have been relatively common. The baptism registers of New Orleans began to include the racial designation "*mulatre*" (*mulâtre*) as early as 1730. This label appears more and more often in the late 1750s and the 1760s. During the years 1729–1733 and 1744–1755, the designation was used for enslaved children 81 times; from 1756 to 1769, it was noted 320 times. Additionally, from 1744 to 1755 only three "*quarterons*" or "*quarteronnes*" were baptized (among the enslaved), but in the years 1756–1769, 25 *quarteron(ne)s* and 10 "*griffes*" were baptized. By comparison, the notation "*negrillon*" or "*negritte*" (negro boy or girl), appears in the baptism registers 389 times from 1729 to 1733, on 948 occasions from 1744 to 1755, and 1,151 times from 1756 to 1769. There is also a much smaller number of children born to free women of color in the baptism certificates of New Orleans: for the entire time span, 19 *nègres*, 43 *mulatres*, 2 *quarterons*, 2 *métis*, and 35 children with no term of color. By the end of the 1750s, nearly one-third of the enslaved children for whom a term of color was noted in the New Orleans registers were of mixed ancestry.[61] Although there were many fewer Indian slaves than those of African origin, the rate of *métissage* (interracial sex) was higher among enslaved children of Indian descent (70 percent) than those of African descent (18 percent), as most Native slaves were women who had little opportunity for sex with an Indian male partner. The mixed-race children in these registers appear to have been almost entirely the children of enslaved women with white fathers. There also appear to have been significant numbers of long-term relationships or "quasi-marriages" between white men "of modest means" and free women of color, contradicting long-standing stereotypes of alliances between women of color and elite white men through "*plaçage*." The evidence from the sacramental registers suggests continuing relationships across racial lines, thus belying the image of a separate caste of free people of color in Louisiana, or a tidy "three-caste" society.[62]

In Virginia, sex ratios among the English immigrants were highly skewed in the early years (there were six men to one woman in the 1630s), so it would not have been surprising to find white men looking for black or Indian women as partners; what may be more surprising is the large number of white women servants who crossed racial lines.[63] Unlike in Louisiana, most of the so-called mulattoes on the Eastern Shore of Virginia were free, and they appear to have traced their roots to unions between white women and black men, further evidence of the fluidity of racial lines in Virginia during the seventeenth century. This led to a society of free people of color on the Eastern Shore in the seventeenth century that briefly looked more like Cuba than Louisiana or other mainland British American colonies. But whereas in Cuba the large proportion of "mulattoes" among free people of color can be explained only through selective manumission practices that targeted the offspring of interracial unions with enslaved women, in Virginia free people of color owed their freedom to the racial background of their mothers. The existence of white female indentured servants in Virginia, combined with the low proportion of women among European settlers in Cuba, help explain these parallels.

Before marriage across racial lines was banned in Virginia in 1691, a number of interracial marriages were recorded. One of the first, in 1656, involved Elizabeth Key, the young woman of color who had made her case for freedom based on her Christian faith, and William Grinsted (or Greensted), the white man listed as her "legal representative" in her successful suit the previous year. More common were marriages between men of color and white women. Philip Mongom, in 1651, married a white widow, Martha Merris, agreeing to reserve to her for her use the property she brought to the marriage, including both personal items and live-stock. Mongom signed the document with a picture of a bow and arrow rather than a signature or an *X*. He appears to have remarried within a decade, to a black woman, and then shortly thereafter he was charged with fathering the "mulatto bastard" of a white woman, Margery Tyer.

Francis Payne married a white woman, Aymey, in 1656, and they lived together without incident until his death in 1673. Emanuel Driggus, Richard Johnson, and Anthony Longo also married white women in the mid-seventeenth century in Northampton County.[64]

More common than marriage across the color line was interracial sex. John Johnson, the son of Anthony Johnson, was brought into the Accomack County court to admit paternity of white servant Hannah Leach's bastard child in 1664. He was released when his wife, Susanna, a free woman of color, petitioned for his return home, and a white man, Morris Mathews, gave security. Elizabeth Lang was sentenced to an additional three-year term of service in 1671 for bastard bearing, but begged the court that the child's "Indian [father] not have my child." Dorothy Bestick, a white woman, paid a double fine and received thirty lashes for bearing a bastard with "a Negro slave" in 1691. Numerous white women, as well as free women of color, were called into court between 1695 and 1710 in Accomack County for bearing "mulatto" children.[65]

As early as 1662, fines for fornication across the color line were set at double the amount for in-group nonmarital sex, typically 1,000 rather than 500 pounds of tobacco. However, the Northampton County court, at least, was slow to change. Several prosecutions for fornication between blacks and whites during the 1660s resulted in fines of 500 pounds of tobacco. Only much later is there any evidence that higher fines were enforced, around the time when the legislature passed a series of laws with harsher penalties for interracial sex and marriage. In 1691, the legislature decreed that any white person who married a person of color had to leave Virginia within three months. The law also addressed the status of the mixed-race children of white women. The white unmarried mother of a mixed-race child paid a fine of fifteen pounds, or was sold as a servant for a five-year term if she could not pay the fine; the child was bound out as a servant to the age of thirty. In 1705, the term of indenture for a "mulatto bastard" was raised to thirty-one, and a white person who married a "negro or mulatto" was sentenced to imprisonment for six months and a ten-pound fine, rather than banishment. The punishment was extended to the next generation in 1723, when children of mulatto or Indian women serving their thirty- or thirty-one-year indentures were also sentenced to serve thirty to thirty-one years (this was later reduced to eighteen for female children and twenty-one for males in 1765). Tamar Smith, a white woman in Northampton County, served the prison term and paid the fine in order to marry mulatto Edward Hitchens, but few other interracial marriages were recorded after 1705.[66]

By contrast, a significant number of women continued to be charged with interracial bastardy. In Northampton County there were numerous cases of interracial fornication before 1705, but after 1705, we see increasing charges against both white and mulatto women for bastard bearing as well, including Tabitha Cope, Hannah Carter, Margret Edsall, Esther Weeks, Anne Toyer, and Elisha Pitts. These women paid their fines or named the father to have him brought into court to "make the county harmless" and pay the church wardens. In Accomack County, Elizabeth Lang, a white indentured servant, gave birth to the child of an Indian, Oni Kitt, in 1671/72, and agreed to add three years to her indenture. In 1704, Mary Newman was accused of having a "bastard child by a Negro"; Mary admitted to fornication but named William Edgg, a white man, as the father. In 1707, white servant Rachell Wood, was sentenced to an extra year of service and sale for bearing a "bastard mulata female child." Wood resisted serving the extra year and was not sold.[67]

Thus, in Virginia, a significant number of white servant women continued to form relationships with men of color, often bearing mixed-race children, but they paid an increasingly heavy price for doing so. Women and men at the lower end of the socioeconomic spectrum defied increasing pressure from slaveholding elites to separate white from "negro," especially when it resulted in more free children of color born to white women. As in Louisiana, this was a small but important population in Virginia, one that maintained links with enslaved people of color as well as free white people. Legal proscriptions could not keep people apart; however, they did, in both Virginia and Louisiana, keep them from creating the kind of community that was already blossoming in Cuba.

COMMUNITIES OF FREE PEOPLE OF COLOR BEFORE 1770

The different legal regimes for manumission in Cuba, Louisiana, and Virginia produced, over time, dramatically different social structures, customs, and "rights." In some fundamental ways, the three societies were

TABLE 1. *Populations by Race and Status, ca. 1770*

Place, Year	Total Population	Whites (%)	Slaves (%)	Free People of Color (%)		
				Of Total Population	Of Free Population	Of Nonwhite Population
Havana, 1774	75,618	57.4	28.1	14.5	20.1	34.0
Virginia, ca. 1770	447,016	58.0	41.3	0.6	1.1	1.5
New Orleans, 1769	3,190	56.5	38.4	3.1	5.3	7.2

Note: These figures are presented only to suggest broad trends. The available data are not detailed enough to offer a better comparison.

Sources: Havana: Cuba, Comité Estatal de Estadísticas, *Los censos de población y vivienda en Cuba* (Havana: Instituto de Investigaciones Estadísticas, 1988). Virginia: figures are based on estimates provided by Herbert S. Klein, *Slavery in the Americas: A Comparative Study of Virginia and Cuba* (1967; Chicago: Elephant Paperbacks, 1989), 235, and the U.S. Census Bureau, *Historical Statistics of the United States, Colonial Times to 1970*, bicentennial ed., Part 2 (Washington, DC: U.S. Department of Commerce, Bureau of the Census, 1975), 1168. New Orleans: Charles Gayarré, *History of Louisiana: The French Domination*, 4 vols. (New Orleans: Armand Hawkins, 1867), 2:355. The New Orleans figures include 60 "domicilated Indians."

roughly similar. By the 1770s, whites constituted the majority of the population in each place, between 55 and 58 percent of the population. Slaves constituted a sizable minority, from 30 to 40 percent of the population, and were the economic engine of these colonial economies (table 1). By the size and economic role of their respective slave populations, these were all slave societies.

The most significant difference among these jurisdictions concerned the size and importance of their communities of free people of color. A socially identifiable and distinct community required a "critical mass" of free people of color.[68] This is where the divergent legal regimes of manumission in Cuba, Virginia, and Louisiana produced their deepest social effects: by the 1770s only Havana had that critical mass of free people of color. Identified as *negros* and *mulatos*, free people of color represented about 14 percent of the total population, 20 percent of the free population, and 34 percent of the nonwhite population of the city and its district. On the island as a whole, the free population of color represented an even higher proportion of the total, 18 percent. In New Orleans, still a small urban center in a frontier colony, the free people of color represented only 3 percent of the total population, 5 percent of the free population, and 7 percent of the nonwhite population. The proportion of free blacks was even lower in Virginia, where they represented less than 1 percent of the total population, and less than 2 percent of either the free or the black population. In the 1770s, then, the association between blackness and enslavement was tighter in Virginia and Louisiana than in Havana or in Cuba as a whole, where black freedom had made greater inroads.

Compared with Havana's sizable community, there is no doubt that the numbers in Louisiana and Virginia were very small. Yet a few caveats are in order. In certain Virginia counties, the proportion of free people of color was far greater. In Northampton County, up to 29 percent of the black population in 1668 was free and 19 percent of black males were tithable householders between 1664 and 1677.[69] When the first U.S. Census was taken in 1790, there were ten Virginia counties in which people of color made up more than 8 percent of the total free population, including Charles City County and York County, where they represented 15 percent of the free population. And in Louisiana, it is possible that the 1769 census of New Orleans did not reflect the entire population of free people of color. Gwendolyn Midlo Hall's database of surviving records shows a greater number of manumissions during the French period (119) than the number of free people of color recorded in the 1769 census. Also, a specialized census of free people of color commissioned by Governor O'Reilly in 1770, and administered by a free man of color, Nicolas Bacus, known as Capitaine Moraine, counted 195 free men of color eligible for the militia. As this number omitted women and children, it is possible that the total numbers were as high as 400 to 800 by 1770. Yet, even with these revisions, there is no doubt that free people of color in Virginia and Louisiana on the eve of the revolutionary era faced a radically different situation from that of their fellow freed people in Havana.[70]

By 1770, Virginia lawmakers and planters had achieved the greatest success in reducing free people of color to the status of "slaves without masters," as Ira Berlin called them. Yet they did not follow a straight line to reach that point. For two generations in the seventeenth century, some free men and women of English and African descent, in parts of Virginia, had interacted with great intimacy and, especially in the courts, at the same social level. During the seventeenth century, free people of color on the Eastern Shore lived dispersed among whites, raising livestock and growing tobacco. Some of the planters owned significant acreage, live-stock, guns, and other personal effects. They participated in networks of patronage and trade with whites as well as other free blacks. These free "negros" and "mulattoes" used the county courts frequently, to sue whites and other free people of color for unpaid debts, to record deeds trans-ferring cattle and other property, to bind out their children as servants, and to petition for the freedom of their children or to secure their own free status. They gave testimony against white people in court and often won their cases against whites.[71] Then, in eighteenth-century Virginia, the status of "negros" and "mulattoes" plummeted.

What accounts for this loss of status? One view is that the possibility of owning "property made the difference," that what had allowed free blacks on the Eastern Shore to live with their white neighbors on rela-tively equal terms was that they owned land, livestock, and even servants of their own.[72] Yet our research suggests that property was less important to blacks' shifting status than deliberate legal reforms that sought to debase blackness to the point of making it indistinguishable from en-slavement. That is, while free people of color were still able to own property in the eighteenth century, what made the difference to their status was that whites, fearing slave conspiracies and racial mixing, began to deny basic legal rights to free people of color, making black "freedom" a degraded status. In 1723, for example, the legislature passed a law against voting or officeholding by any "free negro, mulatto or indian." As the Virginia governor explained to royal officials, this exclusion was necessary in order to impose a "perpetual Brand" on blacks as different and inferior to whites.[73]

The dramatic shift in the fortunes of people of color on the Eastern Shore in the eighteenth century suggests the power of legal regulation. Of course, after Bacon's Rebellion, in addition to the legal changes instituted in Richmond there was an enormous demographic shift, as large numbers of slaves began to be imported directly from Africa, dwarfing the small population of free people of color. Virginia had become a slave society. Even demographic shifts, however, were affected by the legal changes. In response to their worsening status, some free people of color left the state or changed their status by joining Indian communities.

In Louisiana, as in Virginia, restrictions on manumission and inter-marriage meant that relatively few people became free or married across racial lines. However, people continued to form illicit interracial relationships. In New Orleans, there had been a free population of African descent since early colonial times, but as in Virginia, their numbers were extremely low. The restrictions the Code Noir placed on manumission effectively impaired the emergence of a community of free people of color, and no such separate, identifiable community existed by the time the Spaniards seized control of the colony in the 1760s.[74] Moreover, in addition to the legal obstacles built by the Code Noir concerning manu-missions, French colonial law allowed the reenslavement of manumitted slaves under various circumstances. According to article 34 of the code, free blacks who harbored fugitive slaves were subject to steep fines, and they were to be sold as slaves themselves if they could not afford to pay them. The law did not distinguish in this aspect between "freed" and "free-born" blacks. The ordinances of 1751 were even stricter, in that they eliminated fines and ordered the automatic reenslavement of "all free Negroes and Negresses" guilty of harboring fugitives. Free blacks found guilty of other crimes, such as theft, were also condemned to reenslave-ment. In 1743, for instance, the Superior Council condemned "free negro" Jean Baptiste "in reparation of his theft to be again reduced to slavery."[75]

The situation was different in Havana, where a well-established com-munity of free blacks had existed since the sixteenth century. As early as 1574, an important body of local law, the Cáceres Ordinances, made reference to the existence of "many" freedmen who lived in town and who were described as "vecinos." The community was large enough that by 1600 it sustained two religious confraternities, one devoted to Our Lady of the Remedies and the other to the Holy Spirit. Free blacks customarily gave alms to these confraternities in their wills and contrib-uted to the acquisition of real estate and ornaments for them. The confraternity of the Holy Spirit purchased its own building in 1604 and eventually became a new parish, created around the mid-seventeenth century. In 1635 the bishop reported that, owing to the growth of the city, "we will have a new parish because the blacks [*los morenos*] want to build a temple to the Holy Spirit . . . to have in it their burials; they are building it, they are many and it will be easy." In 1640 the members purchased a new house, which was probably used to build their church. By the 1640s the church was finished, and its square served as a social space that "all blacks" used in festivities "to dance and entertain themselves, with the approval of the Bishop and license from the Governor . . . [and] with this they collect charity for masses, for the dead, and for the service of the Holy Sacrament." When the first synod of the Cuban diocese reviewed the existence of religious confraternities in 1681, the one devoted to the Holy Spirit "of free blacks, in their parish" was confirmed.[76]

Free blacks had also performed military duties and participated in the colonial militia since the late sixteenth century. It is noteworthy that when local authorities produced the first military census in 1582, it included freedmen, who represented about 11 percent of all individuals deemed fit to serve. Among those listed was Hernandez de Salazar, "moreno," who was described as "captain of the blacks." In 1630 the "captain of the company of the freed blacks" (*negros horros*) was the free black officer Luis Rodriguez de la Soledad; in 1694 it was "captain Francisco Ponce." By 1760 the militia companies of free blacks (*morenos*) and mulattoes (*pardos*) had 2,493 soldiers, 60 percent of all the militiamen in the city. Participation in the militia conferred free blacks with status and privileges. Many of these soldiers were successful artisans and shop owners who were themselves slave owners. In 1757 the captains of the battalions of *pardos* and *morenos* provided uniforms for their own troops. A mid-eighteenth-century description of Havana made reference to this group of prosperous free people of color, arguing that locally born "negros" and "pardos" were very competent in the exercising of crafts, including those that required "greater ability, refinement and genius, such as silversmith, sculpture, painting, and carving, as can be seen in their marvelous works."[77]

The consolidation of a free colored community in early colonial Cuba did not happen as a result of the favorable attitude of local residents. In fact, there is evidence to sustain the opposite argument: that this community developed in spite of the efforts of the local elites, who sought to circumscribe and debase free blacks as much as possible. Nothing illustrates this better than the attempt, spearheaded by the town council of Havana between 1557 and 1577, to expel all freed people, on the argument that their presence was "damaging" to the city and the source of "many ills and inconveniencies." This attempt did not succeed, as the Audiencia de Santo Domingo declared it illegal, but the development of a free colored community in Cuba owed little to the generous attitudes of local powerbrokers. Not even military service protected *pardo* militiamen from humiliation and degradation. As the captain of one of the companies complained in a letter to the king in 1714, some people insulted them, calling them "dogs and mulattoes." His request was powerfully simple, an excellent illustration of how free people of color struggled to achieve social standing and respect. He simply wanted to be addressed by his name.[78]

**

Across the Americas, enslaved people sought freedom for themselves and their family members by any means possible. Most often, they achieved free status through hard work, financial accumulation, negotiation, and sometimes legal confrontation. Frequently, manumissions were not a private matter but involved the mediation and consent of public authorities. Yet opportunities for self-purchase and other forms of manumissions varied according to time and to place. Manumission never faced serious legal challenge in Cuba. Although there is evidence that slaveholders and local authorities resented the existence and social assertiveness of free blacks, they were constrained by a deep-rooted legal and institutional order in which the possibility of manumission was firmly entrenched and not tied to racial concerns. Furthermore, slaves in Cuba made use of customary practices of gradual self-purchase such as *coartación*, which led to the creation of ambiguous intermediate categories that did not fully fit with either slavery or freedom. In Louisiana, a restrictive legal code shaped by local slaveholding practices in the French Caribbean colonies guaranteed that manumission would remain a rare phenomenon during the years 1724–1763. By the time the

Louisiana Code Noir was promulgated, the manumission regime of the French Caribbean colonies had become increasingly restrictive, aligned with the requirements of a strict racial order. These restrictions were codified in the slave law of Louisiana. By contrast, in Virginia, where settlers had no comparable legal precedents to draw on, a period of relative racial fluidity and easy manumission and self-purchase in the seventeenth century was followed by severe restrictions in the eighteenth century, as legal efforts to debase blackness intensified. Compared with Cuba, where manumission was seen as primarily a slave owner's prerogative and a private matter, manumissions in the restrictive legal regimes of eighteenth-century Virginia and Louisiana required the approval of local authorities.

These varying trajectories led to the formation of significantly different communities of free people of color in the three colonies. Although free communities of color developed in French New Orleans and on Virginia's Eastern Shore, they paled in size and in power compared with that of Havana. The strength and size of the free community of color made an important difference to the efforts in all three societies to draw a sharp line between black and white, slave and free. The very existence of free people of color challenged the association between race and status, an ideal pursued by legislators in all three regions. Moreover, a larger community of free people of color could provide resources and networks of support for slaves seeking their own freedom.

Legal precedents did not necessarily determine the course of these histories, but they did play an important role in creating different demographic and social realities that had lasting effects. The key distinction between the manumission regimes of these jurisdictions concerns their connection to the project of black debasement. Whereas manumission remained independent of racial anxieties in Havana, where it was grounded in long-standing customs and legal precedents, it became a pillar of the racial regimes of Virginia and Louisiana. In the law of Virginia and Louisiana, freedom was linked to whiteness. In Cuba, black freedom became a contested but integral part of colonial society.

CHAPTER 3

"The Natural Right of All Mankind"

Claiming Freedom in the Age of Revolution, 1760–1830

B ETWEEN 1763, AT THE CLOSE OF THE SEVEN YEARS' WAR
(also called the French and Indian War), and 1831, when Nat
Turner's rebellion shook the U.S. South, the Atlantic world was roiled by
war, revolution, and slave rebellions. Slaves in both North and South
America took advantage of revolutionary ideologies and social unrest to
make their claims for freedom. During the American Revolution, thousands of slaves freed themselves by fleeing to British lines, and some
Virginia slaves sent as substitute troops for the rebel army also gained
freedom. In the northern United States, every state enacted some form of
general emancipation, although decades passed before all slaves in the
North became free. And in the jockeying among colonial powers at the
end of the French and Indian War, France transferred Louisiana to
Spain, to keep it from becoming a British colony. Thereafter, enslaved
people in Louisiana took advantage of Spanish law to buy or sue for their
freedom as legal obstacles to manumission were removed.[1]

Most cataclysmic of all, from the perspective of enslaved people, free
people of color, and slaveholding planters, were the events that transpired
in Saint-Domingue. On the eve of the slave rebellions that began there in
1791 and culminated in Haitian independence in 1804, French-owned
Saint-Domingue was the world's major exporter of sugar and coffee. The
tiny island colony had almost the same enslaved population as the entire
U.S. South. On January 1, 1804, revolutionaries led by Jean-Jacques
Dessalines declared the independence of the nation of Haiti. Haiti represented both the horrors and promises of the revolutionary Atlantic: it was a
beacon of freedom and equality for some; the prime example of black
barbarism and degeneracy for others. To white ideologues in Cuba, Haiti

was a "stupid, insignificant, impotent government of orangutans." To the groups of free black artisans and slaves participating in the Cuban anti-slavery movement led by José Antonio Aponte in 1812, Haiti was a source of inspiration, and they socialized with veterans of the rebel army of Saint-Domingue. Planters and colonial officials in Cuba, Louisiana, and Virginia feared that local communities of free people of color, inspired by all the revolutionary upheaval, might take up arms alongside slaves. In 1798 in Cuba, the Junta de Fomento, a planters' council, worried that the "seed of rebellion" had been "planted among our slaves." In Louisiana, after help-ing to take possession of the new Louisiana Territory on behalf of the U.S. government in 1803, General James Wilkinson warned that "the People of Colour are all armed, and it is my Opinion a single envious artful bold incendiary, by rousing their fears & exciting their Hopes, might produce those Horrible Scenes of Bloodshed & rapine, which have been so fre-quently noticed in St. Domingo."[2]

These fears notwithstanding, visionary defenders of slavery in Cuba saw a silver lining in Saint-Domingue's fall. Francisco de Arango y Parreño, a leading voice of the emerging planter class, characterized it as Cuba's "hour of our happiness." Arango and other architects of the new and growing sugar economy in Cuba saw promise in the collapse of the Caribbean's leading plantation economy, a development that helped to spur the rise in other parts of the Americas of what historians have called the "second slavery." As Ada Ferrer put it, "Cuban planters and merchants rushed to fill the void left by Saint-Domingue's collapse. They imported an ever-growing number of slaves and amassed greater and greater wealth in sugar." The second slavery also transformed the new territory and then state of Louisiana into a plantation society devoted to the production of sugar. Thus, in the wake of the Haitian Revolution, the specter of slave rebellion and possible alliances between enslaved and free people of color loomed over these societies just as they were becom-ing more and more dependent on and committed to slavery.[3]

Among people of color across the Atlantic world, news of Haiti did indeed inspire rebellion. The authorities of Virginia averted a wide-ranging conspiracy involving slaves, whites, and some free people of color in 1800. The leader of the rebellion, Gabriel Prosser, was not free, but he was a literate blacksmith hired out by his owner in

6. Battle of Santo Domingo. This painting done by a Polish artist depicts the Battle of Palm Tree Hill during the Haitian Revolution. January Suchodolski, *Bitwa na San Domingo*, or *The Battle of Palm Tree Hill*, 1845. Collection of Polish Army Museum, Warsaw, public domain.

Richmond, and he had heard about the uprisings in Saint-Domingue. In New Orleans, Charles Deslondes, a mixed-race slave most likely from Saint-Domingue, led a revolt in 1811 in which several hundred followers marched on the city in military formation and under uniformed officers. A local white resident referred to the rebellion as "a miniature representation of the horrors of St. Domingo." One year later, authorities in Havana uncovered the Aponte rebellion, a wide-ranging antislavery movement that reached into the plantation areas with the cooperation of slaves and free people of color. The rebellion led by José Antonio Aponte was one of at least a dozen conspiracies or rebellions uncovered in Cuba during the fifteen years following the initial slave uprising in Saint-Domingue in 1791. Its leaders not only knew a great deal about their Haitian counterparts but also testified at trial about the aid they hoped to receive from Haitian allies.[4]

A flood of refugees from Saint-Domingue found their way to Cuba, New Orleans, and to other parts of the mainland United States. Between June and December 1803, more than 1,800 refugees from Saint-Domingue arrived in Santiago de Cuba, doubling its 1791 population. White immigrants were allowed to stay and were given naturalization papers, but immigrants of color were to be deported, according to a law enacted to deal with the crisis. However, an 1808 census of Santiago counted 2,341 French free people of color living there, and 2,457 enslaved people of French origin. They were finally expelled from Cuba in 1809, and many traveled on to New Orleans. In 1809, 3,102 free people of color and 3,226 slaves, along with 2,731 white passengers, arrived in New Orleans, nearly tripling the free population of color, and bringing the city's total black population to 63 percent in 1810. Furthermore, despite the cavalier designations by ships' captains of "free people of color" and "slaves," Haitian law had freed all those who left the island after independence. Many of these immigrants would fight their reenslavement in freedom suits in Louisiana's courts.[5]

Slaveholding regimes, fearing a cascading chain reaction of slave rebellion and revolution after Haiti, responded with both retrenchment and reform. Ironically, the legal reforms that would make possible widespread claims-making by enslaved people resulted not from revolutionary fervor but its opposite: efforts by the Spanish Empire, as well as the new Virginia legislature, to protect the slave system in the face of new challenges. Slaveholders who freed their human property began to do so not out of any belief in freedom and equality, but because they saw an advantage in the new possibilities for self-purchase and conditional manumission. Now their slaves might work harder for a period of years in the hope of gaining freedom. The efforts at retrenchment also had other unintended consequences – some temporary and some lasting. Enslaved people took advantage of some of the legislation passed by Virginians to expand opportunities for freedom. And in both Cuba and Spanish Louisiana, Bourbon reforms meant to secure the slave system made it possible for enslaved people to expand practices of self-purchase that consolidated the power of communities of free people of color.

As a result, across the Americas, free communities of color grew, sometimes exponentially. For a time, it appeared as though Virginia and Louisiana might, like Cuba, build such substantial populations of free people of color that they could undermine the association between enslavement and blackness. Historians of Atlantic slavery and freedom have emphasized this revolutionary moment of convergence in favor of freedom across the Atlantic, or the dramatic increase in legal claims by subordinate groups in Spanish colonies.[6] In Havana, New Orleans, and Richmond, enslaved people used newly available tools to seek freedom, and pressed to transform customary practices into acknowledged legal rights.

The reaction was swift and severe. Beginning in 1806–1807, fearing black revolt, white elites in Cuba, Louisiana, and Virginia took systematic steps to increase control over slaves and to diminish the presence and rights of free populations of color. In all three jurisdictions, the first decades of the nineteenth century witnessed efforts to chip away at manumission and the interaction of free and enslaved people of color. In 1806, after debating a total ban on manumission, the Virginia legislature passed a law requiring freed slaves to leave the state within six months unless they procured special permission from the legislature to remain. In Louisiana, the new legislature of the territorial period (1804–1812) passed a Black Code in 1806 that repealed Spanish laws and added a number of regulations that applied to free people of color. A year later, a new law limited manumission by requiring permission of the legislature to free an enslaved person under the age of thirty. The territorial period was characterized by "the racialization and regulation of black people," paving the way to the Americanization of the state's legal system.[7]

In spite of these limitations, people of color persisted in seeking freedom and exercising rights in court in significant numbers through the first decades of the nineteenth century. They used the means available to them to secure lawyers, purchase family members' freedom, petition the legislature to stay in their homes, and to keep their families together. Free men of color continued to muster in militias in New Orleans and Havana. For free people of color in Cuba, Louisiana, and Virginia, the Age of Revolution did not end in 1806 or 1807 but lasted for several more decades. Cuba was particularly close to revolution, as the wars of independence in Spanish America raged through the 1820s.

The legal environments in which enslaved people maneuvered influenced the avenues they pursued and the channels they followed. In Virginia, for example, one avenue for freedom suits lay in claiming a nonblack, Indian identity. As freedom suits became easier to bring, people held in slavery pushed on that door as hard as they could, using one woman's freedom judgment, for example, as a wedge for dozens of family members to make claims based on their Indian foremother. This avenue would grow in importance in early nineteenth-century Virginia, as other grounds for freedom claims were reduced. In Louisiana and Cuba, enslaved people took advantage of Spanish law and practice to expand opportunities for self-purchase and to purchase family members.

In all three cases, the growth of free populations of color complicated considerably the association between blackness and enslavement that legislators had sought to enshrine in law, prompting new anxieties over race and status. But there was a crucial distinction: in Virginia, new regulations about manumission and anxieties about the growing free population of color became entangled with debates about general emancipation. Questions of manumission became inseparable from revolutionary ideas of equality, political participation, and the specter of black citizenship. In Cuba and in Spanish Louisiana, by contrast, manumission and the very existence of free communities of color were grounded on traditional understandings of slave-owning practices, black subjecthood, and vassalage. The menacing example of Haiti hovered over slave owners everywhere, but the political connotations of black freedom were very different in Virginia than in Cuba or Louisiana.

VIRGINIA

Virginia was the home of key leaders of the Revolutionary War and drafters of the Declaration of Independence and the Constitution, including George Washington, Thomas Jefferson, and James Madison. Perhaps prophetically, Thomas Jefferson's first draft of the Declaration of Independence, which attacked the slave trade as a "cruel war against human nature itself," was replaced by a new, milder admonition, that King George had incited "domestic insurrections among us." As Vermont, Pennsylvania, New Hampshire, Massachusetts, Connecticut, and Rhode

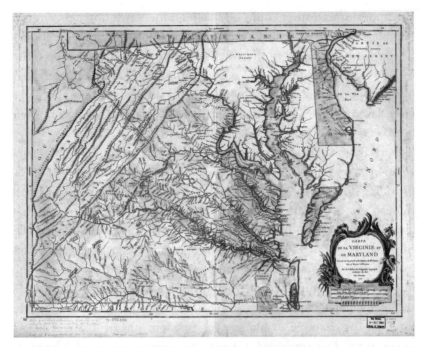

7. *Carte de la Virginie.* This detail showing the Eastern Shore of Virginia (Accomack and Northampton Counties) is from a French map of the Virginia, Maryland and "De la War" colonies. Gilles Robert De Vaugondy, Joshua Fry, Peter Jefferson, and E. Haussard, *Carte de la Virginie et du Maryland* (Paris?, 1757). Map, Library of Congress, Geography and Map Division, http://www.loc.gov/item/74692500/.

Island adopted policies between 1777 and 1787 to abolish slavery, some thought there was a chance that Virginia might follow suit. However, despite pressure from Virginian Quakers to emancipate all slaves, Virginia did not take the route of "general emancipation." Instead, legislators made small legal changes that made it easier to free individual slaves. These changes had unexpected consequences, both in terms of the claims enslaved people brought, and in the political shifts they set in motion.[8]

What set the stage for the expansion of freedom was a new, booming legal landscape in Virginia after the Revolutionary War. In 1789, new courts expanded the number of venues where enslaved people could bring freedom claims. A network of eighteen district chancery courts that heard cases from multiple counties was established in 1802. Now a slave seeking freedom could bring her case in chancery or in a county court of law, appeal it to district court, or take it all the way to the new Virginia Supreme Court of Appeals. She might also petition the legislature for her freedom, or to remain in the commonwealth after emancipation. The expanding legal system led to a boom in lawyers, who, although they likely supported the institution of slavery, stood ready to take advantage of enslaved people's new opportunities to become free as part of their bread-and-butter court business.

Early national legislation greatly expanded the possibilities for emancipation. The most important law was the Manumission Act of 1782, providing for private manumissions as well as the enslaved person's right to sue for freedom. The Freedom Suit Act of 1795 declared that lawyers would be appointed to represent indigent slave petitioners. The Importation Act of 1778 banned the importation into Virginia of slaves from Africa or from other states and provided slaves with a major opening for freedom suits. Because the penalty for illegally importing slaves included emancipation, a slave who had been brought from Maryland to Virginia, for example, could sue for freedom on the basis of illegal importation. This remained a significant source of successful freedom suits for several decades, especially in border counties, until the loophole was closed in 1806 – and courts continued to hear such cases for more than a decade after 1806, based on earlier importations.[9]

White Virginians eventually came to find the new laws threatening. Yet at the time they were adopted, there was little recognition of how enslaved people might take advantage of them. The Importation Act was an effort to shore up the local economy of eastern Virginia; as the freeholders of Prince George County argued, "The African Trade is injurious to this Colony, obstructs the Population of it by Freemen, prevents Manufacturers and other useful Emigrants from Europe from settling among us, and occasions an annual increase of the Balance of Trade against this Colony."[10] The torrent of freedom suits that resulted from the act seems to have been an unanticipated consequence.

The Manumission Act of 1782 was the result of four years of debate in the Virginia House of Delegates that began with a rather routine petition for freedom from an enslaved man named George. He had petitioned the legislature in 1778, as had all other slaves in the previous half-century who wished to enforce a deceased master's promise for freedom. Instead of passing an individual bill to free George, the House of Delegates instructed a committee to broaden its consideration to a general manumission law. Although the bill did not pass in 1778, Quaker activists continued to push Virginia politicians to address the issue, through lobbying and petitioning and by carrying out their own acts of emancipation without legal sanction, which led to an increasing number of disputes over manumissions in wills. A 1780 petition to the legislature from James Ladd on behalf of "sundry Members of the Society of People called Quakers . . . being fully persuaded that Freedom was the natural Right of all Mankind," and having "prohibited their Members several years ago from purchasing any slaves," warned the delegates that the efforts of Quakers to emancipate their slaves was being thwarted by probate courts and individual executors, and called for legislation to allow them to manumit freely. The "act to authorize the manumission of slaves" that finally passed in 1782 did two important things to ease manumission: it dispensed with the requirement of legislative approval, and it allowed freed slaves to remain in Virginia. Although the act did protect the interests of white creditors, it also significantly loosened the eighteenth-century restraints on manumission, and it produced a community of free people of color larger than had ever existed in Virginia. Authorizing slave owners to manumit their slaves was certainly not revolutionary, as the examples of Cuba and Spanish Louisiana illustrate. But in Virginia it overturned sixty years of strict limits.[11]

Some slaveholders advocated the repeal of the Manumission Act almost as soon as it was passed. In their early petitions to the legislature, they focused on the immediate problems resulting from individual manumissions, especially the problem of freed and escaped slaves running to the British Army. The first such petition, by sixty-two residents of Accomack County, came to the House of Delegates on the eve of the act's passage in 1782, urging the delegates to vote it down. The petitioners were "much alarmed" at several Quakers' applications to manumit all of their slaves. They argued that "however desirable an object that of universal Liberty in this country may be" and "however religious or upright the intentions of their owners," large-scale emancipation would be undesirable because free people of color would harbor runaway slaves sympathetic to the British, or they could become charges of the state.

Emancipation, they said, should be for "Meritorious Services" only; furthermore, they claimed, tax revenue would go down if the slave population diminished.[12] Two petitions signed by hundreds of Virginians from Hanover and Henrico Counties in the aftermath of passage called for greater regulation of newly freed slaves. The language of the petitions was identical, bewailing the "evils of partial emancipation." The chief complaint was that free people of color acted as "agents for slaves," selling property stolen from their masters, and that slaves would now be able to pass as free to join the British Army. They called for a requirement that free people of color carry papers signed by the county clerk, and for a restriction on trading with slaves, but they stopped short of demanding an end to – or even restrictions on – manumission.[13]

A flurry of petitions responded to proposals for the gradual emancipation of all slaves that made a brief appearance in Virginia in 1785, first in the proselytizing of Methodist preacher Thomas Coke, and then in Jefferson's *Notes on the State of Virginia.* Coke and Francis Asbury journeyed to the United States in 1784, and founded the Methodist church at the Baltimore Christmas Conference held that year. They agreed to try "extirpate this abomination [slavery] from among us." Not only were they unsuccessful in swaying many Virginians, but Coke brought a mob upon himself in Halifax County. In 1875 the Virginia Baptist General Committee also declared "heredit[ar]y slavery to be contrary to the word of God," but had no power to impose the rule on its congregations.[14] And Thomas Jefferson proposed gradual emancipation in his *Notes on the State of Virginia,* published in the same year. In response, hundreds of legislative petitioners from the Piedmont counties of Amelia, Halifax, Pittsylvania, Brunswick, and Mecklenburg warned that "the Enemies of Our Country" were attempting to "dispossess us of a very important Part of our Property . . . to wrest from us our Slaves by an Act of the Legislature for a General Emancipation of them." They urged the legislature to "Discountenance and utterly reject every Motion and Proposal for emancipating our Slaves."[15]

In Virginia, then, manumission became entangled with broader debates concerning emancipation. After the uprising known as Gabriel's Rebellion in 1800, a petition from the Tidewater county of King and Queen to the legislature drew the connection between "a

General Emancipation," which, "in their present condition is impossible with our safety," and individual manumission, urging that the 1782 law be repealed, and freedom once again be limited to manumission for "Meritorious Services."[16] The legislature did not act on that petition, and in 1803 it voted down another proposal for restrictions on manumission. In November 1804, in the wake of Haitian independence, a Petersburg, Virginia, grand jury presented a list of grievances to the county common council that included "the law relative to Free Negroes & Mulattoes going from place to place . . . for we daily see strangers of that description setting among us who to appearance do not apply themselves to any honest way of obtaining a livelihood."[17] In December, the council forwarded a petition to the House of Delegates, warning that "Large numbers of free blacks flock from the country to the towns," bringing "fraud, idleness, treachery, and every Species of vice ... [and] corrupt[ing] the slaves." They reminded the legislature that unruly free people of color had set off the chain of events "in St. Domingo that totally annihilated the whites." Therefore, the petitioners argued, manumission should be banned and free blacks' mobility restricted.

A proposed ban on manumission by will or deed failed to pass the House of Delegates in January 1805. Some argued in favor of the property rights of slaveholders – which included the right to emancipate a slave – as well as the principle of liberty. One delegate, John Minor, argued that free people of color were not natural allies of slaves, and that the wisest strategy in a slave society was "divide and conquer." The law that Virginia delegates finally passed was a limited provision requiring slaves freed after May 1, 1806, to leave Virginia within the year or risk reenslavement. In addition, they changed the penalty for illegal importation of slaves from out of state, so that emancipation was no longer the result. After five years of debate, this legislation was very much a compromise, protecting a right to manumit and adding only the requirement to leave the state.[18]

Although 1806 did not mark a major shift in the status of free people of color in Virginia, the legislative debate in 1806 signaled a concern with manumission as a matter of public policy that presaged some important differences between Virginia, on the one hand, and Cuba and Louisiana, on the other. In Cuba, as well as in Spanish Louisiana, manumission was a tradition steeped in paternalistic and religious values, a customary trans-action between social unequals. Manumitted slaves became free subjects, but within societies stratified according to multiple stations and *calidades*, or qualities. There was nothing subversive or revolutionary about a practice woven into the fabric of the ancien régime, certainly nothing that would presume a connection with the abolitionist ideas crisscrossing the Atlantic during the Age of Revolution and beyond.

In Virginia, however, after the fall of Saint-Domingue, individual manumission became connected to larger questions of slave emancipa-tion in legislative debates. In public discourse, the idea that manumission was an individual slaveholder's choice, a humanitarian or pious act, began to give way to a notion that individual manumission was a public-policy matter, tied to the prospect of general emancipation.[19] This can be seen in the petitions that referred to "partial emancipation" when urging repeal of the 1782 law, suggesting that each slave freed led down a slippery slope to the end of slavery. Although this remained a minority viewpoint in 1806, the seeds were planted for later contests.

For ten years, the 1806 law suppressed manumissions, as the reward of freedom was less desirable if it meant having to leave home or remain in the state illegally. Still, slaveholders continued to free some slaves in their wills, and enslaved people, to purchase themselves or family members. The best evidence about manumissions suggests a great burst of them in the spring of 1806, followed by a big dip, but only in the first few years after 1806. Ten years later, in 1816, the legislature revised the law to allow slaves to remain in the state after successfully petitioning local courts, rather than the legislature. Manumissions picked up again until 1831, when there was a precipitous drop during the final decades before the Civil War (see Chapter 4).[20]

Although the Virginia legislature did not seriously entertain proposals for general emancipation, many Quakers, and some Methodists and Baptists, especially on the Eastern Shore, took advantage of the greater ease of freeing individual slaves in the first decade after the Manumission Act was passed. In Accomack County in the 1780s, manumissions by deed and by will increased tenfold. Slaveholders were often quite explicit in their deeds and wills about their religious antislavery motivations. For example, in 1787 Charles Stockly emancipated thirty-one enslaved people by deed, explaining that he was "impressed with the fullest Sensibility of the Equal rights of Human Nature to Personal Liberty and being desirous of contributing thereto as far as the Emancipation of my Slaves."[21] The following year, Levin Teackle freed twenty-six slaves, declaring, "Know ye that I Levin Teackle of Accomack County in Virginia having weighed in the Scale of Justice the Condition of Slavery am sensibly convinced that it is unwarrantable as well by the laws of religion as morality, and that as God originally distributed equally to the Human Race the unalienable right to the Enjoyment of Personal Liberty so it behoves [sic] each man to restore to his fellow Creations the invaluable blessing of which he by unjust and impolitic Laws is possessed." Only one will in the county attempted to manumit slaves before 1782; after that date, 295 wills included manumissions.[22] In many of the manumission deeds from Charles City County between 1780 and 1806, the phrase "being fully persuaded that freedom is the natural right of all mankind and being desirous of doing to others as I would be done by" is repeated verbatim.[23] In Chesterfield County, the phrase repeated in several deeds is "all men are by nature equally free and from a clear conviction of the injustice and criminality of depriving my fellow creatures of their natural right, I do emancipate." One historian estimates that, across eight Virginia counties, half of the manumissions of the first decade after 1782 were based on antislavery sentiment, and nearly 70 percent of the manumissions by deed set free all of the people held by a slaveholder, rather than a select few.[24]

Not all enslaved people whose masters attempted to set them free were fortunate enough to escape their bonds, sometimes because family members sought to thwart the efforts of religiously inspired manumitters. Ann Roberts, whose husband, Humphreys, had disappeared during the Revolutionary War, wrote in a deed of emancipation that she identified with the experience of forcible separation from loved ones,

> being possessed of a number of negroes as slaves and through the adverse occurrences permited by divine Providence, under the present calamitous Dispensation to overtake us, whereby I am separated from my Husband and one child, thereby in my own experience have to witness the grievous hardship of being forcibly separated from these near connexions,

whereunto the African slave has for a long series of Time been subjected by the oppressive practice of making them slaves.

She went on to declare that slavery, "I am fully persuaded[,] is inconsistent with Christianity and totally derogatory to the Injunction of Jesus Christ our holy Saviour, where he injoins his followers that whatsoever they would that others should do unto them, they should suffer it to be the governing rule of their conduct to do so by them, which I do fully believe to be indispensibly obligatory on me." Because of the Golden Rule, she saw it as her duty to "set absolutely free all the negroes I am possessed of." Unfortunately for the people she tried to emancipate, her son Edward took possession of them and refused to set them free. When the slaves Thomas and Mary brought freedom suits based on Ann's deed, they both lost. Although Ann had possession of the slaves, she was not their owner.[25]

These early religiously inspired manumissions notwithstanding, far more important to the expansion of freedom in Virginia were the efforts of enslaved people themselves. By the early 1790s, the number of self-purchase agreements surpassed recorded manumissions by deed and by will.[26] For example, J. Peterfield of Chesterfield County charged the executor of his will with hiring out Cesar and Harry "until such time as they shall have earned the sum of one hundred pounds each," after which they would be "emancipated and exonerated forever from slavery." Likewise, Eady Cary had made an agreement to pay Rebecca Brown, a "free negress" herself, for her freedom. The judge in her freedom suit recognized that Cary had paid her full purchase money to "Becky" Brown or her husband John, and that she had been "going at large probably" for some years. But Brown had sold Cary to Stith Burton, and he had a right to her. Witnesses testified that Brown had paid thirty dollars for Eady Cary and had the bill of sale transferred to her, and that it was agreed that "when Edy repaid it to her, it would be given up to her. Edy says she has paid the money long ago – the woman Brown says she has not." The judge thought that "under these circumstances, clearly, at law, she could not recover her freedom."[27]

When enslaved people purchased their own freedom or freedom for a family member, they sometimes enlisted the help of a sympathetic white person or free person of color, and they often used a lawyer. Some enslaved people used the legal fiction of assault and battery and false imprisonment to bring their claims under the writ of trespass. In this legal form, the slave complained of being "with force and arms, to wit, with swords, staves, knives, and fists" assaulted and "imprisoned & restrained ... of their liberty & held in bondage." This would lead the slaveholder to answer that he was not liable for trespass because he owned the slave, and then the enslaved plaintiff would reply that she had not been legally enslaved.[28]

The 1795 Freedom Suit Act allowed claimants to dispense with this legal fiction. Instead, they could submit a petition stating simply that they had a right to freedom, and asking to sue *in forma pauperis*, as a pauper. They could sue on their own behalf, without a "next friend" or guardian, although it is likely that most enlisted a lawyer ahead of time, as had been the practice before the Revolutionary War. The petition could be submitted without a lawyer, however, and the judge would then appoint one to investigate the claim and determine whether the slave should be allowed to sue. If he found merit in the case, the judge would appoint the lawyer to represent the slave, and the lawyer's fees would be paid by the court. Almost every extant record of such cases contains a statement from the appointed lawyer that "in [his] opinion, the plaintiff is entitled to her freedom" or "has a claim to freedom." At times, the appointed attorney gave a more detailed report on the basis for his opinion, as in the Accomack County case of *Maria v. Robert Saunders*. The lawyer wrote: "I have not in coming to a conclusion as to her right to freedom rested exclusively on her affidavit but have called in aid of my opinion all the circumstances connected with the case," including a number of depositions by witnesses from Delaware who had known Maria as a slave in Delaware, which supported her claim for illegal importation.[29] Similarly, Thomas R. Joynes, assigned as counsel for petitioner Harry in his claim for freedom from Samuel Trader's estate, gave his opinion on the interpretation of Trader's will giving Harry his freedom on the condition of self-purchase. The will stated: "I desire that my negroe man Harry may be liberated after he earns at twenty five dollars a year, seventy Pounds, which was what he cost me." The clause was ambiguous as to whether the computation should be made from the time of the purchase or from the time of Trader's death. Joynes concluded that, "on attentively considering the manner in which the expressions are used, and the low annual reduction which the Testator has put on the Petitioner's services, I am of the opinion that the Testator meant the computation should commence from the time he purchased the Petitioner, and that therefore Harry has a right to freedom." Attorneys, thus, appear to have played an intermediate role, between advocate and decision maker, although we found only one petition that did not go forward because the attorney determined it was not worth pursuing.[30]

Whereas, before the act was passed, lawyers took on freedom suits pro bono, now they could collect fees for these cases. This new opportunity coincided with a "dramatic increase in the number of practicing lawyers," owing in large part to the expansion of legal education in Virginia with a new law faculty at the College of William and Mary.[31] Several of the students of law professor George Wythe took on slaves' freedom suits; in particular, George Keith Taylor represented a number of slave plaintiffs. Taylor, himself a slaveholder, became a resource for the enslaved Coleman family, who tenaciously pursued freedom claims across several generations. The Coleman plaintiffs drove this litigation as much as their attorney did, and several played important roles in taking depositions, sharing knowledge, and making connections between cases. Taylor's close working relationship with his enslaved clients facilitated their claims.[32]

If a freedom suit was allowed to proceed, the case would be decided by a jury. Juries were quite sympathetic to plaintiffs, most often finding in their favor. Judges were less sympathetic, as they sometimes overturned jury verdicts. Most of the records contain only a notation of the verdict, although on occasion, the jury made a report or gave a conditional verdict. These conditional verdicts shifted the power to the judge to make the final decision. For example, one jury found: "If the law be for the plaintiff then we agree judgment shall be entered for him and one cent damage and the costs & if the law be for defendant than judgment shall be entered for him."[33] No record remains of what the judge decided in that case.

Slaves who could trace their roots to both Indian and African ancestors used that fact to their advantage in their claims to freedom. Although

Indians had been enslaved throughout early America, including in large numbers in late seventeenth- and early eighteenth-century Virginia, Indian ancestry had become a basis for freedom claims by the later part of the eighteenth century. Late-eighteenth-century Virginia newspapers were filled with advertisements for runaway slaves who insisted they had Indian ancestry. In October 1772, for example, Paul Michaux advertised for "a Mulatto Man named Jim, who is a Slave, but pretends to have a Right to his Freedom." Jim was the son of an Indian man and had "long black hair resembling an Indian's"; Michaux suspected that "he was gone to the General Court to seek his freedom." Likewise, William Cuszens complained that his "Mulatto Slave" David, who "sa[id] he [wa]s of the Indian breed" had gone "down to the General Court, as I imagined, to sue for his freedom."[34]

The first freedom suits based on Indian ancestry began to appear in the Virginia General Court in the 1770s. The General Court wrestled with the question of when in fact the legislature had ended Indian slavery, which had been legalized in 1682, immediately following Bacon's Rebellion. There was no clear-cut repeal of the 1682 act, but rather successive legislation on servants and slaves in 1691 and 1705 that referred obliquely to servants who had been "shipped." A series of eighteenth-century cases affirmed that Indians could only legally have been held as slaves between 1682 and 1705; an 1807 case narrowed this window to 1682–1691. These cases involved the same extended family, who claimed to descend from one Indian woman, Judith, purchased by Francis Coleman Sr. in South Carolina sometime after 1705. The family first brought suit in the General Court in *Robin v. Hardaway* in 1772, although plaintiffs' attorney Thomson Mason referred in that case to "hundreds of the descendents of Indians" who had "obtained their freedom on actions brought in this court," of which no records remain. The family's claims reached the Virginia Supreme Court in *Coleman v. Dick and Pat, Jenkins v. Tom,* and *Pegram v. Isbell.* Historian Honor Sachs has traced the legal history of this Afro-Indian family through the courts of Dinwiddie County, Brunswick County, and the General Court.[35]

Many enslaved people brought their claims in county court, without making the trek to the capital. In Accomack County, Indian ancestry was the most common basis for freedom suits, and the court heard many such claims after 1795. For example, George brought suit against John Walker Jr. in May 1796, claiming that his mother, Mary Cook, "had been taken in some war & brought into Accomack County & sold a slave to Edmund Scarbrough." Furthermore, according to a deposition by Priscilla Johnson, "Peter Major, Mary's Indian husband, served said Edmund Scarbrough a certain number of years for the freedom of said Mary, by which means she obtained it." According to Johnson, however, Mary's eldest daughter, Lucy, lived and died a slave of the Scarbrough family, and "she never heard that the said slaves had the most distant thought of claiming their freedom" until another family member won a freedom suit based on Indian descent. Another witness testified that "Mary alias Major, who by her long black hair, yellow or copper complexion, & her manners appeared to this Deponent to be indisputably one of the Native Indians of North America," had lived as a free person for many years. He explained that the "common report" was that she had been held in bondage by Edmund Scarbrough until she "threatened to sue for her freedom." Scarbrough freed her in order to "pacify" her, and to "prevent her procuring the liberty of her child or children" born during her enslavement. Although the outcome of George's suit is unclear, another apparent family member, also known as Major, won a similar suit several years later against another slaveholder. Several slaves belonging to the Andrews, Roberts, and Scarbrough families brought additional freedom suits, with varying results, all basing their claims on descent from the same Indian foremother.[36]

In cases involving an Indian foremother, witnesses for the defendant typically argued that the ancestor was in fact a "mulatto," not an Indian, especially by testifying to the texture of her hair. On behalf of William Roberts in Ibby's freedom suit, Priscilla Johnson remembered a "negroe woman who had frizzle looking hair" who "had a Daughter by name of Pathena [Ibby's great grandmother] who also had a brushy Head of hair." Johnson "never heard or had any reason to believe that the said Pathena had any claim to any free blood and that she verily beleaves that she was a mulatto." In *Wells v. Lewis*, the plaintiff claimed to be the descendant of a free white Englishwoman named Ann Wells who had come to Maryland as an indentured servant. According to P. R. Kendall, the counsel appointed for Wells, affidavits regarding the "short woolly

hair" of Rachael (Daniel's grandmother and Ann's granddaughter) actually "operate[d] in favor of the petitioner's claim, it being, I understand,
the opinion of some eminent physiologists that the child's hair resembles
the father."[37]

In bringing lawsuits for freedom based on a claim of Indian maternal
ancestry, slaves took advantage of a growing contrast in the legal treatment of "negros" and "Indians." In Revolutionary Virginia, the category
of "race" crystallized in contrast to the new sense of "nation" as the unit of
political organization, a people with a state. In the American context, the
"negro" came to stand for "race" – a race fit for servitude – in contrast to
the "Indian" as a member of a nation inferior in civilization but capable
of improvement. Drawing the distinction between blacks and Indians
served to divide and conquer two groups that threatened the new slave
societies being built in the American republic. At least to some degree,
the legal construction of slaves' racial status grew out of the contrast
between "Indian" and "negro" in Virginia and Louisiana, in a way that it
did not in Cuba.[38]

The most important rules about racial and slave status were laid out in
the 1806 case of *Hudgins v. Wright*, in which Hannah sued for her freedom based on the Indian ancestry of her mother, Butterwood Nan.
Hannah's witnesses agreed that Hannah appeared white, that her father
had been an Indian, and that Butterwood Nan, though enslaved, was
"called an Indian." Hannah's owners argued that Nan was legally
enslaved, whether black or Indian. In the end, no one could prove that
Nan was an Indian or just reputed to be one, or that Hannah's mother
had been legally or illegally enslaved. But the Supreme Court ruled that
Hannah enjoyed a legal presumption of freedom because of her "red
complexion." People with a "red" or "white" appearance would begin
with a presumption of freedom, and those with a "negro" appearance
would be presumed slaves unless proved otherwise. Indians were by
default citizens of a free nation; Africans were by default members of
an enslaved race.[39]

This contrast between race and nation extended to different modes of
fact-finding. One of the rare freedom suits to be appealed all the way to
the U.S. Supreme Court, *Negro John Davis v. Wood*, in 1816, established the
rule that hearsay and reputation evidence would be allowed only to

establish "pedigree" (that is, race) and not, for example, one's status as enslaved or free. Community members could testify as to their understanding of a person's race, and the jury could rule on it accordingly. To determine "slave" or "free" status, however, documentation would be required. The same was true for "negro" versus "Indian" identity. James Baugh sued his Chesterfield County owner for his freedom in 1826, claiming that his mother's mother was an Indian woman entitled to her freedom. Twice Baugh won at trial, and twice his owner appealed to the state supreme court. At the second trial, Baugh submitted the deposition of an eighty-three-year-old witness discussing his grandmother's Indian identity. The Virginia Supreme Court ruled that hearsay testimony about Indian tribal status was inadmissible – in striking contrast (as the dissent pointed out) to the general rule about the admissibility of reputation evidence to prove pedigree, or race. The community could decide who was black or red or white, but not who was a citizen of an Indian nation, or who was legally owned as a slave. The court sharply distinguished "the country, nation or tribe, of [James Baugh's] ancestor" from her "pedigree." Thus, Indian ancestry cases helped the Virginia Supreme Court articulate the meaning of "negro" in contrast to "Indian."[40] In other words, the comparison with Indians brought home the uniqueness of blackness; only black people could be enslaved, and their racial identity could fix them as enslaveable.

In northern Virginia counties that bordered Maryland, enslaved people took advantage of another opening in the law, the rule against illegal importation of slaves. Before 1806, numerous slaves petitioned the Arlington County courts or the District of Columbia courts in Alexandria, claiming that they had been illegally imported from Maryland or elsewhere. In typical form, the petitioner would state that she had been brought from Maryland on a particular date, "contrary to the Act of Assembly prohibiting further importation of slaves into Virginia[,] and in consequence became entitled to her freedom."[41] A petitioner also had to show that the slaveholder did not take the oath within sixty days of coming to Virginia stating that he did not bring in slaves to be sold. Although most petitioners were successful with illegal importation claims, there were a few cases in which the judge overturned a favorable jury verdict. Silvia, for example, claimed that she had been illegally imported from New Jersey, because she had spent two years there. Although there was ample precedent to the effect that residence on free soil would set a slave free, the judge found that "during the time out of the commonwealth [the owner] never gave up his property or estate in her" and "never received any profit or hire for the plaintiff during her absence from this commonwealth," and thus that "the importation aforesaid was not such an importation as intitles the pl[ainti]ff to her freedom."[42]

Even without going to trial, enslaved people could use the threat or initiation of a freedom suit based on illegal importation as a way to bring an owner to the bargaining table, either for outright manumission of an enslaved person or to enable her to buy herself. For example, Terry petitioned for freedom from William Mitchell on August 7, 1797, claiming illegal importation, and Mitchell freed her the next day. After David threatened to institute a suit against Andrew Trouin in 1804, Trouin agreed to allow David to purchase himself for $100 and his wife, Mary, for $50.[43]

Freedom suits based on importation were surprisingly successful. It is doubtful that legislators ever imagined that the penalty for importation would be enforced, let alone that so many enslaved people would use it successfully to wrest their freedom from unwilling owners. The legislature began considering ways to narrow this loophole in the illegal importation law during its 1796 session, but it was not until 1806 that legislators changed the penalty for illegal importation from emancipation of the illegally imported slaves to their sale and export from the state. Even after that date, however, enslaved people continued to sue for several decades, based on earlier importations.[44]

By 1790 the population of free people of color in Virginia had reached 12,000, or about 1.7 percent of the total population. Thirty years later, it had tripled in size and represented about 3.5 percent of the whole population. The proportion was higher in some parts of the state. In Norfolk, for instance, free people of color represented more than 6 percent of the total population in 1810, and in Petersburg, one-third of the black population was free. More than half of Richmond's population was of African descent, and 20 percent of those residents were free. In 1810, of 1,256 households in Richmond, 256 were headed by a free person of color, and another 313 free people of color lived in a household headed by a white person. The Eastern Shore also had substantial populations of free people of color. In Accomack County they made up 29 percent of all nonwhites in 1810, and 12 percent of the total population; free people of color also made up 12 percent of the total population in slave-majority Northampton County and more than 20 percent of the county's nonwhite population.[45]

These populations continued to grow over the next two decades. By 1830, free people of color represented 4 percent of the total population in the state and 15 percent in Accomack and Northampton Counties. By then, however, new and more effective limits had been placed on manumission and freedom suits (see Chapter 4). The phenomenon of claiming freedom on the basis of Indian ancestry had eclipsed self-purchase and other bases for emancipation after 1806 and helped to solidify new legal and cultural understandings of race and nation. Hence, the paradox of the Revolutionary era: the simultaneous expansion of freedom and slavery.

CUBA

This paradox applied to Cuba as well, where the Age of Revolution was an age of entrenchment and expansion of plantation slavery. The slave revolution in Saint-Domingue preoccupied slave owners and colonial authorities in Cuba, but they also saw an opportunity to expand sugar production after the collapse of the French colony. The number of Cuban sugar mills doubled between 1790 and 1830, while the number of slaves on the island multiplied fivefold. On the ruins of the sugar economy in Saint-Domingue, Cuban slave owners built one of the most successful plantation slave economies in the Western Hemisphere. The lust for profits outweighed the fears of black rebellion. As a representative of the city council of Havana stated in 1802, "Let the blacks come, which is the only way to cultivate the lands."[46]

Cuban planters and colonial authorities coped with the fear of revolt by increasing military forces and repression, as illustrated by the execution of rebel leader José Antonio Aponte in 1812. But they also argued repeatedly that slavery had never been as harsh in Cuba as it was in Saint-

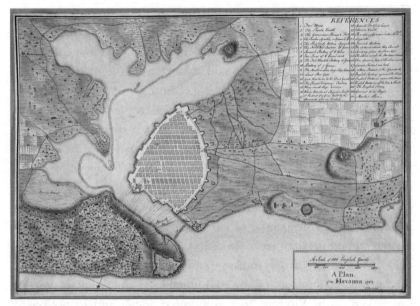

8. Map of the city and harbor of Havana. Manuscript colored map of the city and harbor of Havana, created while the city was under English occupation in 1762, with detailed military information. John Carter Brown Library Map Collection, Brown University.

Domingue and that slaves were better treated in Cuba than elsewhere. At least in part, this argument revolved around manumission and the alleged ease with which industrious and well-behaved slaves could obtain freedom in Cuba.

Although opportunities for manumission were never as great as the planters and colonial officials made them out to be, they increased during the last few decades of the eighteenth century, just as the sugar economy and plantation slavery began to expand. In this sense, like Virginia, Cuba experienced the simultaneous expansion of slavery and freedom. By 1792, free blacks and mulattoes represented 38 percent of the nonwhite island population and 20 percent of the population as a whole. About 19 percent of the inhabitants of Havana and its suburbs were counted as "negros" or "mulatos" "libres." They played a prominent role in local militias, an important route to social standing. African-descended soldiers made up 20 percent of the total military forces and 42 percent of the militias in the colony in 1770.[47]

Size was, precisely, the problem. In 1792, Francisco de Arango y Parreño, the leading spokesman for the emerging planter class, warned that militias staffed by free blacks and mulattoes could join forces with slaves. "They are all blacks," he said; "they have more or less the same grievances and the same reason to live resenting us."[48] Concerns about alliances between free people of color and slaves led to an ordinance approved by the colonial governor in 1779 that stipulated draconian punishments against "any black or mulatto who took arms against a white person, even without hurting with them." The aggressor was to suffer 100 lashes, plus hand nailing. If it happened a second time, the punishment increased to mutilation of the hand.[49]

Suspicion of free people of color did not translate into efforts to restrict manumission or freedom claims, however. Not only was the free colored community simply too large and consequential to be eliminated, but in Cuba manumission was a traditional legal and religious practice, not linked, as in Virginia, to revolutionary ideals and to notions of political freedom and republican equality. In fact, some of the leading voices of the planter class argued that the existence of a "large" population of free people of color in possession of "all the civil rights enjoyed by any other free man" contributed to "the subordination of the slaves."[50] This was in marked contrast to Virginians' fear that manumitting slaves was the first step toward general emancipation.

Nevertheless, the Cuban expansion of freedom was almost entirely the product of enslaved people's tenacious pursuit of emancipation, not of new policies or legislation designed to increase manumissions. Some cases were connected directly to the conflicts and displacements produced by revolutionary processes and imperial rivalries in the Caribbean. In one such case, initiated in 1819, four slaves demanded their freedom as well as back pay, alleging that by the time their mother had arrived in Havana from Haiti, she was free. They argued that Francisca Lorignac had wrongfully kept them as slaves, even though their mother, Maria Coleta, now deceased, had obtained her manumission from her previous owner, who had committed suicide. Lorignac, in turn, argued that they were not beneficiaries of the freedom decreed by the French nation because the girls' mother had left the island in a Spanish vessel. She was also able to show that in the baptism records of each child, Maria

Coleta was always described as Lorignac's slave. Yet apparently there were enough witnesses who could testify that Coleta was in fact free by the time of her arrival, because by 1823 Lorignac agreed to grant the petitioners' freedom if they dropped their demands for back pay.[51]

Most of the increase in freedom cases in Cuba was linked not to the revolutionary conflicts in the Caribbean, however, but to the legal and administrative reforms introduced by the crown during the eighteenth century, the so-called Bourbon reforms. These reforms sought to "curb smuggling, curtail the power of the Church, modernize state finances, establish firmer political control within the empire, end the sale of bureaucratic appointments, and fill the depleted royal coffers."[52] In Cuba, the Bourbon reforms levied new taxes to finance the growing military needs of the colony, which were made painfully obvious after the English occupation of Havana in 1762 as part of the Seven Years' War. To this end, between 1764 and 1765 the crown increased the *alcabala*, a tax on all sales that had been tentatively introduced in 1758, from 2 to 6 percent. In exchange, the crown extended new commercial concessions to the island, inaugurating the era of "free trade."[53]

As in Virginia, legal reforms had unintended consequences. None of the Bourbon reforms sought to modify manumission practices, yet they ended up producing new opportunities for slaves to gain their freedom in Cuba. Colonial officials were forced to contend with manumission, rarely a topic of policy disputes, because it was not altogether clear whether the new *alcabala* taxes applied to self-purchase contracts or to other forms of manumission, and who should pay them. Did slaves have to pay the tax in cases of self-purchase? Did owners have to contribute in cases of gracious manumissions? Who was to pay the *alcabala* in regular sales, the seller or the buyer?

As colonial officials raised these questions with their superiors in Madrid, they conveyed information about customary and frequently contentious manumission practices that received, for the first time, detailed attention from imperial bureaucrats and regulators. In 1766, for instance, Governor José María Bucareli requested instructions for how to handle the disputes concerning taxation over the "voluntary and involuntary" sales of slaves who were *coartados*, people who had paid a portion of their self-purchase price. Two years later he sought further clarification, asking whether *coartados* should be treated like other slaves, whom he referred to as *enteros* (entire, or completely enslaved persons), suggesting in the process that *coartados* were not, in fact, fully or totally enslaved.[54] Requests like these forced the Consejo de Indias (King's Council) to look into the matter. Under the imperial gaze, some of the traditional customary arrangements and practices acquired increased levels of certitude and clarity. Slaves, in turn, tried to use the new regulations to their advantage, seeking to consolidate and to enlarge precarious customary "rights" and understandings that had been produced after decades, if not centuries, of interactions among slaves, masters, legal mediators of various sorts, and government officials.

Administrative changes helped to shift the balance of power in favor of the enslaved. Slaves' initiatives received considerable and unexpected support from another of the Bourbon reforms, one geared toward the more efficient management of royal justice and governance in the colony: the creation of the office of *síndico procurador* in the 1760s. A municipal institution transplanted to the colonies in 1766, the *síndico* was to provide legal representation for slaves and mediate in their conflicts with masters. The royal cedula of 1789, "on the education, treatment, and occupation of the slaves," referred to the *síndico* as the "slaves' protector" and established that no slave could be criminally prosecuted without his intervention. He was also responsible for entering charges against slave owners and overseers in cases of excessive punishment. Since the *síndico* was elected by the town council and the position was considered an honorable public duty, we can assume that many who held the position were themselves slave owners and not particularly concerned with the well-being of the slaves. Over time, however, the *síndicos* appear to have developed procedures that many owners perceived as intolerable intrusions against their own rights of ownership.[55]

Even if *síndicos* supported slavery, their very presence expanded the colonial state's involvement in the master-slave relationship and created institutional channels through which enterprising slaves could claim rights. The *real cédula* of 1789 added legitimacy and visibility to those channels, which is why slaveholders adamantly opposed its dissemination and enforcement, in Cuba as well as other colonies. In their view, the mere existence of a new legal text that sought to regulate slave-master relations would result in endless litigation and insubordination. As a group of Cuban planters explained to the king, "this law ... in an of itself, is extremely just. But, once the slaves come to understand it, they will rise up against their masters. Owners will suffer unwarranted insults from their slaves on a daily basis ... [and] no one will be able to restrain their arrogance."[56]

New institutions also created new avenues for slaves' claims. The creation in 1800 of an appeals court in the island, the Audiencia de Puerto Príncipe, made it easier to litigate cases beyond the *alcaldes ordinarios* (city councillors) and the governor. The new court was also a product of the Age of Revolution: conflicts taking place on the neighboring island of La Española, where the Audiencia de Santo Domingo had resided since the sixteenth century, prompted its transfer to Puerto Príncipe. All these factors help explain why slaves "demanded outright freedom more frequently" and why legal suits "began to have a new meaning in the late eighteenth century, one that implied the recognition of individual rights."[57]

Among those rights were the poorly defined and highly contentious privileges supposedly associated with *coartación*. By the 1760s and 1770s, some of the elements associated with the institution were well known and widely shared. As mentioned before (see Chapter 2), these included a fixed manumission price that, once agreed to, could not be altered, as well as a slave's right to make partial payments toward that end. Owners were obligated to accept such payments, and these conditions could not be altered by subsequent sales. In other words, when a *coartado* slave was sold, the price was reduced in proportion to the payments the *coartado* had already made to the original owner, and on the condition that the new owner accepted the terms of the *coartación*. What had begun as a slave owners' prerogative had been transformed into a slave's right. It is interesting to note the semantic evolution of this term during the eighteenth century. In 1729, the dictionary of the Spanish Royal Academy defined *cortarse* as the action by which slaves "adjusted" with their masters the terms of their freedom, "cutting" their total purchase price into pieces – payments over time. By the late eighteenth century, however, the practice was known as *coartación*, which literally means "hindrance" or "restriction." The old usage still showed up in some documents as late as the 1760s, as in the legal case of Francisco Josef, a slave who in 1763 was requesting "el corte de su libertad," that is, "to cut" his freedom price. Whereas *cortar* refers to the slave's action, *coartar* refers to limitations on the master's power. Over time, slaves' actions had become a constraint on the master's dominion.[58]

Initial inquiries about *alcabalas* in cases of manumission and *coartación* were quickly solved by the Consejo de Indias in 1768. Building on the long-standing principle of *favor libertatis* (favoring freedom), the crown ordered that gracious manumissions or self-purchases were exempt from the tax. As the council noted, "Everything is sacrificed for the benefit of freedom, which is always or most of the time of public interest, which prevails over the private interests of individuals." In cases of sales involving *coartado* slaves, the *alcabala* would apply only to the unpaid portion of the manumission price. The same doctrine was invoked by the crown to hold that owners could not refuse freedom when slaves managed to come up with the funds needed to purchase it. As a royal order stated in 1778, masters were "obligated, according to custom, to give [slaves] their freedom whenever they showed the corresponding price." It was not as clear whether owners were equally obligated to accept a down payment on manumission and to allow any slave to become *coartado*, although this seems to have been the implication of another royal order of 1768, which stated that any payment made by the slave "as part of the price paid for him" by the owner, was to be noted in the corresponding title to facilitate manumission. The *síndicos* appear to have imposed manumission and *coartación* even on reluctant masters. As a *síndico* representing the slave Santiago argued in 1826, none of the reasons alleged by Santiago's reluctant master nor "any other of greater importance can have the effect of delaying or creating obstacles" for freedom. In this way, the *síndicos* contributed to the transformation of a slaveholder's prerogative (manumission) into a slave's right (self-purchase).[59]

One of the key issues in litigation was the manumission price. Initially, some royal documents equated the original purchase price of a slave with the manumission price, and some contracts used purchase price as a reference for manumission and *coartación* valuation purposes. In 1778, the governor and his legal advisers clarified "many questions concerning the slaves' freedom pretentions" when they encountered the case of

9. *Santiago v. Antonio Moreira* freedom suit, 1826. "The Sindico Procurador [legal representative of slaves] ... in the name of the *moreno* [black] Santiago against Antonio Moreira claiming his freedom," 1826. Archivo Nacional de Cuba, Escribanías (Salinas), leg. 676, no. 7858.

Maria de los Dolores Abileyra. Maria requested her freedom letter for a payment of only 80 pesos, a valuation made during the execution of a will when she was only eight years old. She had been subsequently sold, in 1763, for 300 pesos, and the judge used that figure as her manumission price. The legal advisers of the governor agreed, noting that the previous valuation was not binding for *coartación* purposes because it had taken place before the royal order of 1768. The 1768 regulation, they noted, "obligated" masters to observe slave valuations for manumission only following its promulgation, and not before.[60]

The same principle was applied to the manumission of Jose Maria, a slave of the city council of Havana who worked as a cook in the city jail. In 1800, Jose sent a formal petition to the council, requesting "the amount that he must exhibit for his freedom." The petitioner argued that he had been employed at the jail for about nine years, since his arrival in a slave ship, that he had always fulfilled his obligations, and that he was ill and needed medical attention. After hearing reports about the allegations of the slave, the council gave "freedom to the black Jose Maria for the price of his acquisition, in attention to his good services and the illness that he suffers." Such funds were to be used, in turn, to acquire a new enslaved cook.[61]

Slaveholders, however, managed to disassociate the manumission or *coartación* price from the purchase price. They argued that they had incurred expenses in the training and the sustenance of their slaves, many of whom had acquired valuable skills that commanded higher market prices. On this point the Cuban governor José María Bucareli sided with the owners, arguing in 1768 that equating the manumission or *coartación* price with the purchase price was detrimental to slaveholders and to colonial agriculture. The crown responded that any slave who was able to pay the purchase price should be entitled to buy her freedom.

Most slaves were in fact unable to pay the full amount, choosing instead the route of *coartación* or gradual payments. Thus, the price of freedom became something to be negotiated through competing appraisals.[62] Typically, slaves who were unable to reach an agreement with their masters would approach a *síndico* to be appraised. The *síndico* would then appoint an assessor, and the owner would do the same. Their estimates were frequently far apart, prompting the appointment of a third assessor by a local judge, whose verdict became the manumission price for the slave.

In a typical case, Martin Arostegui in 1818 approached one of the alcaldes of Havana to request his freedom. To start, Martin, who worked in a rural farm on the outskirts of the city, had had to "run away to present himself" before the judge to claim his freedom. According to the petition, which was written by a *síndico*, Martin had worked at the farm for more than twenty years, was about sixty years old, and had made various payments across time to his owner that he wanted to apply toward his manumission. In this case there had been no agreement on the manumission price, so Martin was not a *coartado*, and he requested a valuation. As was typical in these cases, the slave and his representative made a case for a low market price, equivalent to $250, claiming old age, several diseases, and "the circumstance that the owner had never taught him any trade." The slaveholder assessed his worth at $500. As was customary, the judge then appointed a court assessor, who set the price at $300, the price that José María Alfonso, the owner of Martin, had originally paid for him. Unlike most slaves, Martin was able to produce written receipts from his owner for the payments he had made, which on inspection amounted to the price set for his manumission. He was promptly declared free.[63]

Only rarely could the *coartación* price be altered. Royal regulations ratified the invariability of the price. The principle seems to have been widely accepted by all involved, as this does not appear to have been a point of contention in what was otherwise a fairly contested and poorly defined institution. In cases in which the slave requested to be sold without just cause – that is, without proving extreme abuse – the *alcabala* could be added to the price to be paid by the slave. Likewise, if a *coartado* slave initiated a criminal proceeding against a master but did not succeed, some of the procedural costs could be added to the manumission price. This is what happened to the slave Juana Josefa de la Torre, who in 1802 accused her owner of "enjoying her virginity" under false promises of freedom. The claim was rejected, and the owner was allowed to charge half of the proceeding costs to Juana Josefa's price, "even if she is *coartada*."[64]

When slaves began to make payments toward their freedom, how did that affect their living and labor arrangements? Were they entitled to control a portion of their time and labor? In one of his consultations with the Consejo de Indias, Governor Bucareli had requested clarification on precisely this point, but the council replied categorically that *coartado* slaves were for all practical and legal purposes to be considered *enteros* until they obtained their manumission. Still, as Martin Arostegui and the *síndico* representing him argued in their previously mentioned 1818 case, it "was not in any way just that having received most of his price or almost everything, the owner enjoys him [the slave] *por entero* (in all) the way he has done it."[65]

Coartado slaves, with the aid of the *síndicos*, also made the radical claim that one who had paid a portion of her price had in effect purchased a portion of herself, and thus was owed wages for a portion of her labor. Some early sale contracts of *coartado* slaves suggest that a customary understanding developed on this point over time. As mentioned in the Introduction, the 1690 sale of Juana, who had already paid half of her manumission price, included an explicit acknowledgment that this entitled her to half her time and half the products of her labor: "Concerning this sale it is only on half of the said mulatto woman. The buyer must use her in the same form and if he uses her whole service or rent, collecting it entirely, he must grant her half of the time that belongs to her and discount it from her price."[66] In such cases, the customary understanding of what *coartación* implied was built into the sale contract, limiting considerably the options of the new owner.

In other cases, however, masters refused to surrender partial control over their slaves. In 1826, for instance, Don Francisco Prado went to court over the earnings generated by his slave José Genaro. The *síndico* demanded that a portion of the profits Genaro had produced during the two and a half years he had been *coartado* be credited toward his *coartación*. The owner refused. The record does not include the result of this case, but we do know that some lawyers shared the owners' view and decried the custom of reducing slaves' obligations according to the portion of the full price they had paid toward their freedom. As one stated in 1830, "Some *síndicos* have attempted to alleviate slavery, so as to pretend to concede a half of their time to slaves who are bound in service of their masters (when they have paid half of their value to their owners); but this opinion is not in conformity with the law. . . . *Coartación* . . . was not established to reduce slavery into halves, but only to prevent any alteration in the price of slaves." Although this question continued to be litigated well into the nineteenth century, there is evidence that at least some of the *coartados* reached agreements with their owners that allowed them to control a portion of their time and labor. As mentioned before, by the late eighteenth century, non-*coartado* slaves were referred to as *enteros*, which suggests that the status of the *coartados* arguably distinguished them from those fully enslaved. As one local official reported in 1826, *coartados*, "not being free, can barely be called slaves." Or, as a *síndico* noted several decades later, by paying a portion of his price, a slave "became associated with the ownership of himself."[67]

In finding that *coartados* were to be considered as *enteros*, the Consejo de Indias also clarified another contentious point: the alleged right, claimed by some *coartados*, to change masters at will. Governor Bucareli referred obliquely to this practice when he mentioned the existence of "involuntary sales" that proceeded against the will of the owners. It is possible that some *coartados* sought to change masters in order to inscribe in the contract of sale the sort of explicit acknowledgment of their situation that was included in the 1690 sale of Juana. A change in ownership could give slaves the opportunity to negotiate the terms of their enslavement with a new owner, something that was perhaps more difficult to do with those who had owned them for years. To change masters, a slave would request a written license from his or her owner – *papel* – which signaled the owner's willingness to sell. When masters refused to issue the license, which they appear to have done with some frequency, slaves and the *síndicos* representing them went to court, claiming abuse. Some *síndicos*, however, went further, invoking a vernacular understanding of *coartación* according to which *coartados* slaves had the "right" to change masters at will, on the theory that freedom was to be favored in all cases. This elaboration of the right of *pedir papel*, or carrying paper, gave *coartados* another legal weapon in their contests with masters.

When enslaved people brought claims of abuse to a *síndico*, they referred not only to physical mistreatment but also, more broadly, to neglect of the duties associated with slave ownership. Clearly and repeatedly elaborated in Castilian and colonial law, these duties included the provision of proper nourishment and medical care, clothing, and the avoidance of "extreme punishment." Slaves used the breach of any of these duties to request a change in ownership. In 1795, for example, the slave Manuel de la Trinidad escaped from the sugar mill where he worked. He wanted his master to "give him paper to find another whom he would serve, for they do not attend to him as is required and they give him too much work." To substantiate the charge of abuse,

Trinidad also referred, using language that closely mirrored that of established legal doctrine, to the lack of "necessary food" and "the cruelest treatment that can be imagined." Another slave, Cristobal del Castillo, placed the standard of abuse much lower. In 1836, he complained that he was being mistreated on the cattle farm where he worked because his owner did not allow him to "earn a few *reales* with which to buy his freedom nor would he give him paper to search for a new master."[68]

By making partial payments toward their freedom, *coartado* slaves were in a stronger position to claim that any limitation on their ability to complete such payments represented a form of abuse and thus entitled them to seek a new owner. Some slaves and *síndicos* claimed, in fact, that obtaining *papel* and changing owners were rights ancillary to *coartación*, the legal pronouncement of the Consejo de Indias notwithstanding. This was the argument of slave Micaela O'Farrill to the court of the colonial governor in 1835. O'Farrill reported "unbearable" although unspecified "ill treatments" at the hands of her owner, but requested her *papel* on the ground that "the laws allow the slave to change owners, particularly when . . . she is *coartada*." In this case the owner decided not to litigate, so O'Farrill obtained her paper without further process. The *síndico* representing *coartado* slave Pedro López claimed that he should receive his paper because this was, "in his unfortunate situation [slavery], the only relief that the law gives him." Other *síndicos* put it more forcefully, as in this 1837 case: "Her master must give her paper to search for a new master because this is a prerogative of *coartado* slaves."[69] In these cases, abuse was not even invoked. The argument was, rather, that *coartación* represented a specific legal status that served as the foundation of new rights, such as the alleged right to change owners at will.

Planters and slave owners fought back. Many slaveholders opposed what they perceived as gross interference with their ownership rights. In 1820, for instance, Leandro García agreed to the petition of his slave Bernardo Lucumí to become *coartado*, but rejected his request for *papel* so that he could change owners. The judge found the slave's petition without merit: "As the causes put forth by Bernardo Lucumí are not sufficient to compel his master Leandro García y Sanabria to this alienation," he was not entitled to *papel*. The owner, however, had to accept "the amounts that his slave may give him for his freedom." Equally successful in rejecting his slave's petition for *papel* was the Marquis of Campo Florido. He alleged, in 1833, that "he could not be forced by the *síndico*" to sell, and that the petition did not conform to reason, the law, or the "delicate political order" in a country where slaves outnumbered masters. The judge concurred, stating further that the *síndico* did not have jurisdiction in this case to begin with.[70] Not all *síndicos* sided with the slaves on this question, although those who did left a more visible trail, as those are the cases that ended up in court. As one *síndico* noted in 1836, *coartación* did not "give a slave the right to change owners, just for his pleasure," and the institution's only legal effect was to limit the sale price.[71]

According to José Mojarrieta, who in the 1820s worked as a lawyer at the Audiencia of Puerto Príncipe, that court of appeals always rejected the *coartados'* demands to change masters. Mojarrieta reasoned that this was not a difficult legal question, as *coartado* slaves were to be treated under the law as *enteros* and did not enjoy any specific rights: "And what difference can there be between one and the other, when we see that the yoke of slavery on all is the same? If slaves [*coartados*] do not enjoy the rights of freemen, on what principle can they claim the right of changing masters at their pleasure?" Still, the fact that these cases reached the court of appeals indicates that some judges favored slaves' claims during the ordinary process and continued to see *papel* as an ancillary right to *coartación*. In the second half of 1800, for instance, the Audiencia de Puerto Príncipe reviewed nine cases concerning freedom, four of which were brought by aggrieved slaveholders – meaning the enslaved claimants had won at the lower court level. Thus, lower court judges were not unanimous in their view of masters' prerogatives, which left openings that enslaved people could exploit to keep making claims.[72]

As with so many of the complexities of heritable slavery, children were especially vulnerable. A final issue clarified by the Consejo de Indias concerned the status of the unborn children of slaves who became pregnant while they were *coartadas*. In 1835, slave Pedro Pascasio claimed the right to freedom based on the argument that his mother had been *coartada* by the time of his conception and that his 1796 baptism record did not describe him as a slave. The fact that the baptism notation made no reference to the status of Pedro may have reflected lingering doubts about the status of children of *coartado* slave mothers.[73] The judge, however, found the allegation to be without merit. By 1835 the prevalent legal doctrine characterized *coartación* as a personal benefit, not transferable to the children. Initially, colonial authorities had reasoned that, as children followed the condition of the mother, they should benefit from the *coartada* status of the mother. After consulting with some of his legal advisers, in 1786 Governor José de Ezpeleta issued a preliminary finding that provided legal guidance on this matter. It stated that the price of the children of slaves should be reduced in a proportion similar to that of the mothers who had begun making payments toward their own freedom, a position that was informed by the widely accepted principle of *partus sequitur ventrem* but in some tension with the idea that *coartadas* were *enteras*. The Consejo de Indias, however, reversed this decision, stating that it was "contrary to law, for *coartación* in mothers is something that only pertains to them, so personal that it cannot be transmitted to their children," a principle that was ratified by a royal cedula of 1789.[74] Although this decision seemed to violate two important principles of Castilian slave law – *favor libertatis* and *partus sequitur ventrem* – the council justified it by the political and economic needs linked to colonial agriculture. When it came to progeny, *coartado* female slaves were in fact treated, following the council's own doctrine, as *enteros*.

The notion that *coartado* slaves should be deemed *enteros* for all legal purposes was repeatedly contested by slaves and their representatives in court. But at the same time, their cases eventually put long-standing and contentious customary manumission practices on more solid legal footing. The existence of these practices was now acknowledged by imperial authorities and colonial officials, raising complex questions concerning slavery and freedom, many of which had been prompted by the actions and demands of slaves themselves. These questions continued to be the subject of intense debate and litigation well into the nineteenth century. Then, at the height of plantation slavery, slaves and their allies managed to obtain some of their most important legal victories. Slaves' actions and initiatives would have long-term and consequential legal effects.

LOUISIANA

As in Cuba and Virginia, in Louisiana the Age of Revolution, which coincided with the passing of the colony into Spanish hands in 1763, was an age of expansion for slavery. As Rashauna Johnson puts it, "The

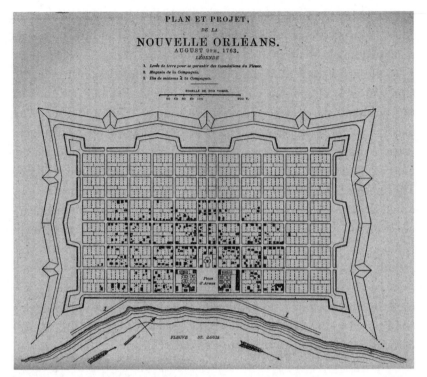

10. New Orleans fort map, 1763. New Orleans and its fortifications at the time Louisiana changed hands from France to Spain. "Plan et Projet de la Nouvelle Orléans, August 9, 1763, 1763," from *Report on the Social Statistics of Cities*, compiled by George E. Waring Jr. U.S. Census Office, Part 2, 1886.

Age of Revolution was the age of African slave importation." It was also, paradoxically, a period when slaves and free people of color carved out greater opportunities for freedom. Although the explosion in Louisiana's class of *gens de couleur* is often attributed to the substantial immigration of refugees from Saint-Domingue in the early nineteenth century, that is only partially correct. At least half of the rise in population happened earlier, during the Spanish period, when enslaved individuals took matters into their own hands to become free. During the four decades of Spanish rule, the practice of *coartación*, as well as more liberal rules regarding manumission, contributed to substantial growth in the population of free people of color. Slaves in New Orleans were nearly three times more likely to win their freedom than slaves in post-

Revolutionary Virginia. Even after Louisiana became a U.S. territory in 1803, and then a state in 1812, rates of manumission and freedom suits remained higher there than in other states.[75]

In the first decade after rules were loosened under Spanish rule, the largest number of "*gracioso*" emancipations took place, and in total almost two thousand slaves were manumitted between 1763 and 1803. The majority of those freed were children, and most of the adults were women; it appears, therefore, that in the first decade of Spanish rule, most of those freed were the enslaved family members of slaveholders. The increase in manumissions following the change in jurisdictions would suggest that, in the absence of onerous legal requirements, manumission rates in New Orleans would have been comparable to those in Havana. Even more frequent, however, were self-purchase agreements, including gradual payment arrangements such as *coartación*. Louisiana came under Spanish control just as authorities in Cuba and in Spain were clarifying the contours and implications of *coartación*, and this probably contributed to the dissemination of the practice there. By the last two decades of the eighteenth century, enslaved people in Louisiana had moved to take control of their own emancipation.[76] In total, perhaps 1,500 people bought their freedom through self-purchase and *coartación* over the course of the Spanish period, and others were purchased and freed by family members or white allies. Although estimates vary, they all agree that the population of free people of color grew significantly, from 3 percent of the total New Orleans population in 1771 to almost 14 percent in 1806. With the considerable influx of refugees from Saint-Domingue, their proportion would increase even further by 1810, when they made up 44 percent of the free population of New Orleans. Although the majority of free people of color in the Louisiana Territory lived in New Orleans, the population in the territory as a whole grew as well, to 7,585 free people of color in 1810, about 10 percent of the total population.[77]

It appears that enslaved people learned of the legal changes brought by Spanish rule very quickly, judging by the immediate appearance in the records of *coartación* agreements. Where did this knowledge come from? One source might have been the 160 free militiamen of color who arrived in New Orleans with Governor Alejandro O'Reilly from Cuba in 1769. He also brought several legal officials who would have been familiar with the Cuban practice.[78] What is clear is that legal knowledge passed quite quickly among the enslaved and free people of color, so that they not only began to institute self-purchases but also to demand rights in court.

As in Cuba, *coartación* was an important route to freedom for Louisiana slaves, and it provided them an opportunity to challenge their masters directly in courts of law and to claim other rights as well. Maria Juana, for example, appears to have been requesting *papel* when in 1776 she demanded "the recourse that for charity is conceded to all slaves, namely to go look for masters more to their liking." She invoked "Divine Law which is in her favor," to escape "captivity [in which] she, herself, is exposed continually to punishment where through suffocation or desperation she might die." She also invoked "Natural law," which "recommends freedom more than any other law"; "royal law . . . because there is not any Law unfavorable to my claim"; and the Siete Partidas, which "states that if a slave had two masters and one of them grants him freedom gratuitously while the other one does not want to, the Judge shall order the latter to do it." Her owner, Don Juan Suriray de la Rue, insisted that Maria Juana had no right to "pass into the ownership of an Englishman with whom she is in collusion I do not know to which end." As many judges were doing in Havana, the Louisiana court agreed that *coartación* did not include the right to force an owner to sell to another buyer.[79] Her abuse claim thus failed.

The case of Maria Luisa Saly illustrates some of the dangers that slaves claiming to be *coartados* had to face when such agreements were not properly recorded and acknowledged. Saly claimed that she had already paid 250 pesos toward her 300-peso price, "from the commerce of fowl, pigs, &c.," but that her putative owner had beaten her and shackled her to prevent her from claiming her freedom. Witnesses for the owner testified that she had been earning money in the underground economy and that they had urged her to emancipate herself through her commercial enterprise, but that they had no specific knowledge of a self-purchase agreement. The owner, Mateo Parin, declared that "she has never given me any amount or treated with me about her freedom . . . regarding that I have beaten her with clubs and put her in shackles it is true for as a slave of mine that she is I can execute so, and I made sure that she deserved it for the disrespect and insolence with which she treats me and which is evident from her own pleadings." Saly lost her suit.[80]

A somewhat different strategy was followed by the slave Maria Theresa who demanded her freedom from Marie-Françoise Girardy in 1782. The slave owner refused to answer the suit, arguing that Maria Theresa was a runaway who should be instead compensating *her* for lost labor; Maria Theresa claimed that she had served her mistress for twenty-five years and that she had the right to purchase her freedom. The case followed the typical procedure in *coartación* cases, which was the same in Cuba and in Louisiana. The slave demanded the right to have an appraiser appointed to set her purchase price. One appraiser would be appointed on her behalf, one on behalf of the owner, and if they disagreed, a third would settle the matter. Such arguments over valuation are interesting; slaves argued infirmity and age, while masters emphasized slaves' skills and abilities – even a slave who was a fugitive. Maria Theresa's owner insisted that she was "one of the most perfect servants in this Province, a good washer and ironer, also a seamstress and embroiderer, as well as an excellent cook, in one word all the proper talents ... which have cost so much to teach them to her," and that the only significance of her being a runaway was that she owed her master wages for the time absent. Nevertheless, Maria Theresa succeeded in winning a low purchase price (600 pesos, where she had claimed 500 and her owner 900) based on her advanced age, which was between forty-three (according to her master) and fifty (according to her); she did, however, have to pay back wages for her time as a runaway. She herself claimed that she had left her master only to claim her rights, and that the claim of back wages "should be denied as Impertinent and as an absurdity [*fuera de propósito*] for its Spirit is none other than preventing me the Freedom that the Laws and subsequent Pragmatics of the Sovereign recommend." Nevertheless, she was ordered to pay seven pesos per month for her sixteen months as a fugitive.[81]

Like Maria Luisa Saly, the slave Antonio of Pointe Coupée also lost his claim for freedom because of the absence of proper documentation, in his case, in a will. Antonio tried to gain his freedom based on a document written by his mistress, witnessed by seven people.

However, the deceased mistress's will did not mention Antonio's freedom, and the minor children, who claimed him as their slave, scoffed at the writing as a "simple paper that he has produced." Several witnesses testified that Antonio's owner, Dame Stephan, had purchased Antonio in order to free him if he worked for her for four years. Unfortunately, Governor Unzaga declared "the much-mentioned Paper of no Value and unable in law to produce the effect for which it was generated." Indeed, although holding paper did not guarantee the victory of a freedom claim, those who did not have adequate documentation remained especially vulnerable.[82]

It is important to recognize that procedurally, these cases were quite different from freedom suits in Virginia or other U.S. states. In Louisiana, enslaved people could obtain letters of freedom, *cartas de libertad*, from a notary, a public official with no counterpart in the American system. The notarial records of New Orleans are full of proceedings for freedom that were not adversarial, although they could be if the one claiming ownership refused a slave's emancipation. As in Havana, those were the cases that ended up before the court of the governor or before an alcalde, a judge sitting on behalf of the governor. Nevertheless, the volume of testimony in the records is limited, and the chief dispute was typically over the sum of money required for self-purchase. In other words, these cases were usually "battles of the experts" between competing appraisers, with the court often accepting the average of the two, but sometimes appointing a third appraiser to cast the deciding vote.[83]

As in Cuba, those disputes that ended up before a magistrate involved such competing appraisals. Helena, a "free Negress" seeking to free her son Magloire, complained of the owner's "maneuvers" to have him appraised at a high value, some 800 pesos, in spite of her offer of proof that "my son, his slave, was a thief and a drunkard whose trades he had learned while under his services for more than five years." Helena gave examples of numerous skilled slaves, "such as Carlos, a shop carpenter and a former slave of Madame Bienvenue," and "Andres Nata, an ironsmith master and slave of D. Patricio Magnimara," who had been appraised at values between 750 and 800 pesos without a third appraiser. She concluded that

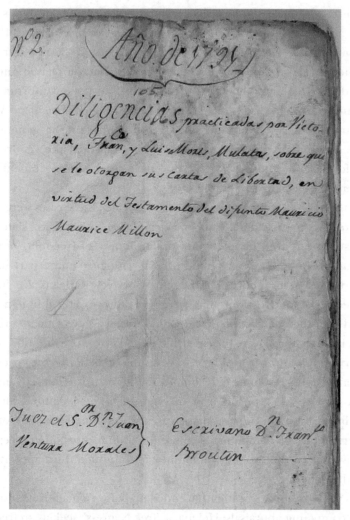

11. Victoria, Francisca, and Luisa request letters of freedom. This notarial act documents "proceedings conducted by Victoria, Francisca, and Luisa Moris, *Mulatas*, regarding the granting of their letters of Freedom, by virtue of the Will of the deceased Mauricio Maurice Millon" before the judge, Señor Don Juan Ventura Morales, and the notary Don Francisco Broutin. Victoria, Francísca, y Luisa Moris v. Estate of Millon, in Francisco Broutin, *Notary – Acts – Court Proceedings*, vol. 6 (1791), 105, New Orleans Notarial Archives.

the appraisers, out of respect for said Don Henrique Depres, have estimated my son in an exorbitant price so that he cannot have his freedom because a Negro without trade, drunkard and thief cannot be worth more than a twenty-five year old mulatto and master carpenter such as Madam Bienvenue's one above referred, or as much as a thirty year old master ironsmith as the cited slave of Don Patricio Magnimara, or as much as the Negro named Luis, a carpenter by profession and excellent master in his trade who belongs to the Capuchin friars and who was lately estimated in eight hundred pesos.

Nevertheless, her son was appraised by a third appraiser at 800 pesos, and she was unable to buy his freedom.[84]

As in Virginia, descent from an Indian woman became an important way for enslaved people to claim freedom. Governor O'Reilly issued a decree in December 1769 prohibiting Indian slavery. There is some disagreement about whether the decree required all those who held Indian slaves to free them or applied only prospectively; it certainly prohibited the transfer or sale of Indian slaves.[85] The governor also required *comandantes* of each post in the colony to take a census of Indian slaves, although there are only two records of such censuses. It was two decades before substantial numbers of slaves began to sue based on Indian ancestry, apparently after a later governor, Esteban Miro(acute) (1782–1792), asked the St. Louis *comandante* Francisco de Cruzat to republish O'Reilly's decree. Between 1790 and 1794, there were at least thirteen lawsuits filed for claims of Indian ancestry. In most cases, the slave owners did not challenge the enslaved person's claim to be descended from an Indian ancestor but instead argued that "negro" paternity should trump Indian maternity, or that it was wrong to allow descendants of Indians to go free when they had been enslaved legitimately, or because they were third-party purchasers who had bought their slaves in good faith. In 1795, a group of planters petitioned Governor Francisco Carondelet, Miro(acute)'s successor, arguing that the flood of lawsuits was causing an "irreparable wrong . . . to all in this colony" and that a "contagion" of emancipations might result. In response, Governor Carondelet repealed the law, asserting that it threatened "a complete reversal of the fortune of many inhabitants." Instead, he allowed enslaved people who could prove descent from the Natchez the right to purchase themselves at their estimated price, and those from other Indian tribes to redeem themselves for 250 piastres, folding these suits into the more common practice of *coartación*.[86]

Some of the enslaved traveled from outlying plantation areas to New Orleans to demand legal rights, demonstrating not only great initiative but also knowledge of the Spanish laws as well as customary practices that had the force of law. For example, in 1774 the *comandante* at Pointe Coupée seized some horses belonging to slaves in order to raise revenue, citing article 29 of the Code Noir, which restricted slaves' ownership of animals. Three of the slaves whose horses had been taken set off for New Orleans to demand the proceeds of the sale from Governor Luis de Unzaga (1770–1777). Although at first they were jailed for traveling without a pass, several weeks later they returned from New Orleans with the money, having successfully invoked the customary right to own property in the form of pigs, chicken, horses, and crops on provisions grounds. Similarly, the enslaved woman Françoise traveled from Pointe Coupée to New Orleans to see Governor Unzaga to insist that her children not be sold away from her. Comandante Villers wrote to the governor, "I was good enough not to take away the youngest from her, but she is not satisfied." We do not know the outcome of this case, but it is striking that Françoise appears to have known the provision in the Code Noir restricting sales separating mothers from children under age ten, and to have thought she had a right to invoke it. Such knowledge probably spread more quickly as the colony grew and the slave trade between New Orleans and outlying areas accelerated. Enslaved women and men used this knowledge to make claims that challenged military and colonial officials to see them as legal agents.[87]

As the population of free people of color in New Orleans grew, the community became more assertive. The Spaniards who took over New Orleans, many of whom, like Governor O'Reilly, came directly from Cuba, were accustomed to free militias of color. Although the French had relied on free men of color as soldiers to a limited extent during the Natchez revolt in 1729 and other wars against Indians in the 1730s, the Spanish government created a formal militia company for *morenos* and one for *pardos*, and awarded free militiamen of color medals, cash bonuses, officer commissions, and military pensions if they served well. By 1800, there were three militia companies, with more than two hundred men. Some historians have argued that Spanish authorities recognized the value of "divide and conquer" and consciously sought to create a separate class of free people of color, distinct from enslaved people and free whites. The creation of "colored" militias, however, followed well-established institutional patterns in the Spanish Empire.[88]

By 1786, the growing visibility of free people of color in the city of New Orleans had become a cause for alarm. Governor Miró issued a proclamation in 1786 restricting assemblies of free people of color and concubinage between women of color and white men; he denounced free women of color for "idleness," "incontinence," and "libertinism," and issued restrictions on their mode of dress, including the requirement that they wear a *tignon* (head kerchief) to mark them out from the rest of the population. He also placed restrictions on slaves' dancing and religious practices. These regulations do not appear to have been widely enforced, but they do suggest Spanish officials' rising anxiety. The news from Saint-Domingue in 1791 fueled growing fears of insurrection, and colonial officials, from Pointe Coupée to New Orleans, investigated allegations of a number of slave conspiracies and revolts during those years, many of them involving free colored militiamen. As Governor Carondelet wrote to the cabildo in 1793, "[We must] always fear that the free men of color and the slaves will allow themselves to be tempted by the corruption of the French government." In 1795, he again warned that, "by means of secret and undercover plots, the colony, is on the verge of being submerged in the horrors which have ruined the French colonies."[89]

After its transfer to the United States, the Louisiana Territory was home to an extraordinarily large free community of color, by American standards. The subsequent history of the territory and state continued to be shaped by the innovations of the Spanish period for several decades into the nineteenth century. To take one significant example, the free militia of color remained an important institution. In New Orleans in the summer of 1804, local officials urged Territorial Governor William C. C. Claiborne to crack down on politically assertive free men of color and to disband their militia. Claiborne, too, feared that "the Misfortunes of St. Domingo" would "visit ... on this quarter of the Union." But in his view, the threat did not originate among free people of color; rather, "the events which have Spread blood and desolation in St. Domingo originated in a dispute between the white and Mulatto inhabitants, and that

12. Mathew Carey's Louisiana. Mathew Carey, *Louisiana* (S.l., 1814). Map, Library of Congress, Geography and Map Division, http://www.loc.gov/item/2002624016/.

the too rigid treatment of the former, induced the Latter to seek the support and assistance of the Negroes." The militiamen themselves formally petitioned to continue their service, invoking their proud record of service and promising to do so "with fidelity and zeal." Claiborne concluded that "the recognition of the Militia Corps composed of the People of Colour, is certainly under existing circumstances the wisest Course to pursue." He appointed white officers to oversee the black militia, but he also met and negotiated with free black leaders and praised them for helping to put down the 1811 Deslondes slave uprising "with great exactitude and propriety." The first state legislative session in Louisiana, in 1812, passed the Organization of Creole Free Men of Color Militia Act. The two battalions of free men of color who fought in the Battle of New Orleans in 1815 were led by free men of color from Saint-Domingue, and in a joint resolution of the Louisiana legislature on

February 1, 1815, they were singled out for praise. Although free men of color themselves showed less interest in mustering during the years 1816 to 1828, the legislature continued to authorize their militia until 1834.[90]

American authorities were also forced to recognize that in Louisiana, legal understandings concerning slavery, manumission, and race were grounded on a set of French and Spanish colonial rules and customs. The residents of Louisiana lived under a legal regime that incorporated regulations and understandings from multiple sources, including the French Code Noir and Spanish traditions and codes such as the Siete Partidas. The Black Code of 1806 aimed to overturn many of the most liberal aspects of Spanish law, including *coartación*, and to add many provisions to quell rebellions and assemblies of slaves and free people of color. Swaths of regulations were imported directly from other American states' slave statutes, especially those of South Carolina, and a number targeted free people of color. All free men of color from the island of Hispaniola, for example, were to be denied entry; free people of color had to carry certificates of freedom and should not "presume to conceive themselves equal to the white . . . and never speak or answer to them but with respect."[91] The language of the laws was far more brutal than Louisiana practice, however. Over the course of the next several decades, between the adoption of the Digest of the Civil Laws in 1808 and the new Civil Code in 1825, slavery law in Louisiana exhibited "advancing Spanish-Roman influence." The 1817 case of *Cottin v. Cottin* held that the Digest had not abrogated Spanish law, so anything not covered specifically within the Digest remained governed by Spanish law. The Civil Code of 1825 recognized a new category of *statu liberi*: an enslaved person who had contracted for freedom, not unlike a *coartado*, but using the language of Roman law rather than Iberian. It also recognized the slave's *peculium*, or earnings, which could be inherited, and the slave's ability to act as agent for her master, all of which were part of the Roman law of inheritance.[92]

Although Anglo-American residents complained about "all the rancor manifested . . . against the common law," courts invoked French and Spanish regulations and legal principles well into the nineteenth century.[93] When in 1810 the slave Adèle sued for her freedom, her representative responded to the defense's claim that she had to "prove that she was born free or has been emancipated" by invoking the Siete Partidas. He argued that "even if the defendant could prove his possession of the plaintiff as his slave, still the Spanish law would require him to produce some written title, or at least that he acquired possession of her without fraud. Partida 3, tit. 14, 1. 5." The court found that "the law cited by the plaintiff" was "certainly applicable to the case" and held in favor of Adèle's freedom. This case also established a legal distinction between "negroes" and "persons of color." A person of color was presumed free, given the likelihood that someone with Indian, white, or mulatto heritage was free, whereas a "negro" was presumed enslaved. Like the Virginia court in *Hudgins v. Wright*, the Louisiana state court determined that presumptions of slavery or freedom could be reached based on color and appearance, and blackness bore the presumption of enslavement. The clear difference was that in Louisiana people who appeared to be mixed-race – "mulattoes" – would start with a presumption of freedom, whereas in Virginia, the racially ambiguous person could not be presumed free or slave but had to have her racial identity determined in court.[94]

Although slaves continued to make claims based on Indian ancestry after Louisiana became a U.S. state, they were less successful than claimants in Virginia, because defendants could point to the legal basis for Indian slavery in Louisiana law. In *Seville v. Chrétien*, in 1817, a number of enslaved plaintiffs claimed descent from an Indian woman. After numerous witnesses testified about the common practice in "not only law, but custom and usage of buying and selling Indians, women and men alike, as slaves ... just like negros" in Spanish Louisiana, the Louisiana Supreme Court upheld the jury verdict for the slaveholder.[95]

Slaves and free people of color continued to use Spanish legal and social foundations after Louisiana became a state in 1812, and systematic steps were taken to legally restrict manumissions and to diminish the rights of free people of color. In 1806, the territory adopted a Black Code for the regulation and punishment of slaves that reenacted many of the provisions of the Code Noir, including restrictions on free people of color. In 1807, one year after Virginia issued its own restrictive act concerning manumission, an act regarding emancipation decreed that "no person shall be compelled either directly or indirectly, to emancipate his or her slave or slaves," thereby implicitly abolishing *coartación*. Building on French Code Noir precedents, the 1807 act required judicial permission for manumission, including proof that a slave was thirty years old and had not been convicted of bad behavior for four years, and limited the slave's right of recourse against a cruel master; only with a criminal conviction of the master could a slave be sold away as of right.[96] After 1807, some form of official permission was required for manumissions to take place, either from the Superior Council (1807–1812), the state legislature (1812–1827), the police jury of the parish (after 1827), or an emancipation court (after 1846).

Nevertheless, in the face of an increasingly restrictive legal regime concerning manumissions, slaves continued to seek out whatever legal opportunities remained to sue for freedom and to enforce self-purchase agreements. The 1825 Civil Code's recognition of slaves' legal capacity in cases concerning manumission – "when he has to claim or prove his freedom" – and the legal possibility of self-purchase – "the slave is incapable of making any kind of contract, except those which relate to his own emancipation" – provided platforms for freedom suits.[97]

Trials of self-purchase disputes were common, and the courts invoked Spanish as well as Roman law. In 1818, Maria Cuffy, the daughter of a free man and an enslaved woman, sued for her freedom based on her father's contract with her mother's owner to purchase her and her three siblings for 2,400 pesos. The trial record contained a copy of the contract: "I am agreeing with Cofy my black freedman to give liberty to Pedro, Honoré, Maria, and J. Baptiste, my black slaves and his children, for the price of 2,400 pesos after he has paid me the said quantity then I will free them and for this I give the present receipt. In New Orleans on July 4, 1789, Signed Andrew Almonaster y Roxas." Furthermore, the Louisiana court cited the ruling of the earlier Spanish tribunal, that her mother had already paid 316 pesos, and therefore must be allowed to work for the "residue" of her purchase price, according to the principles of *coartación*. However, Maria Cuffy lost her case. The jury found for her owner, the trial court refused a motion to overturn the verdict, and the Louisiana Supreme Court upheld the judgment. In their opinion, the court at once affirmed the applicability of Roman-law principles, including the principle that the slave's work could provide part of the purchase price. But the justices resisted *coartación*, insisting that the principle applied only "to such persons who are made free instanter, on condition of paying a certain sum in futuro."[98]

Another New Orleans slave who had raised most of his purchase price "by voluntary contributions among the free people of color," Louis Doubrère, won the appeal of his freedom suit to the Louisiana Supreme Court, citing not only the Louisiana Civil Code but also the Siete Partidas. Doubrère, a trading-ship pilot, was captured by his former owner's creditors, and the issue in the case was whether a contract for freedom was like any other private contract for "immoveable property" that could be reversed as a fraudulent conveyance in anticipation of bankruptcy. The Supreme Court heard a number of appeals in which slaves tried to enforce self-purchase contracts, and found for the slaves in some cases. As late as 1842, a Louisiana jury found in favor of the freedom of an enslaved man who had purchased himself. Indeed, Louisiana was the only Southern state where slaves' self-purchase enjoyed some legal support. Enslaved plaintiffs were less successful, however, in winning the ancillary rights that Cuban slaves had won, such as the right to force a sale to a new owner through *papel*, or to own a percentage of themselves. For example, in 1819 a New Orleans slave, Marie, whose owner had directed the executor of his will to purchase her and her child in order to emancipate them, had the right to sue for freedom – but not to force a sale to a new owner. The court cited Spanish law but dismissed her claim. Self-purchase agreements also had to be in writing, although in one case, again citing Spanish law, the Louisiana Supreme Court allowed a self-purchase agreement to be proven with five witnesses to an oral contract.[99]

Finally, enslaved plaintiffs pushed a novel claim in the Louisiana courts, that of freedom by prescription, in which an enslaved person claimed to be free by virtue of having lived as free for a prescribed number of years. Although emancipation by prescription had existed in Roman law, there was no precedent for it in Louisiana. In a pair of cases in 1818 and 1819, Adelaide Metayer, who had lived as a free woman in Haiti as well as in Havana for more than twenty years and then in Louisiana for another year, won her legal freedom by convincing the court to recognize the years she had lived as free in Haiti and Havana as well as in the United States.[100]

For the first several decades of the nineteenth century, freedom suits and manumissions continued in a variety of forums. Before 1827, thousands of slaveholding Louisianans petitioned the legislature for permission to manumit their slaves. In their work, Kotlikoff and Rupert registered petitions to the police jury in New Orleans to manumit 1,770 slaves between 1827 and 1846, all but a handful of which were granted. Furthermore, despite an 1830 amendment requiring manumitters to post a $1,000 bond to ensure the freed person left the state within thirty days, "unless the police jury said otherwise," those who appealed the rule were all allowed to remain, without exception. Enslaved Louisianans continued to bring freedom suits to parish courts in great numbers, many of which found their way to the Louisiana Supreme Court. In addition to those involving self-purchase contracts, there were more than one hundred suits seeking to enforce wills that contained manumission provisions, as well as several dozen involving "free soil" claims, in which an enslaved person claimed freedom based on a sojourn or residency in a free jurisdiction. The enslaved plaintiff was victorious in nearly all of these cases, as the Louisiana Court followed the rule that "as she was a free woman there [e.g., in Ohio], she must be held so every where."[101]

***

The period from 1763 through the 1820s could be said to be the era of greatest commonality across our three jurisdictions. During this period, both Louisiana and Virginia developed significant communities of free people of color, especially in urban areas. By the early nineteenth century, New Orleans had a free population of color similar to that of Havana, although in the state as whole it was nowhere near the percentage of the total free population of color in Cuba. In all three jurisdictions, manumission had become a regular aspect of the regime of slavery during a period of rapid growth in the staple plantation economy and the scope of the slave trade. In all three, slaveholders used manumission to reward service, and to provide incentives for hard work during the term of slavery. And in all three, slaves and free people of color took advantage of the new opportunities created by political and institutional change to press claims for freedom. In Cuba and in Spanish Louisiana, slaves used *coartación* and other customary practices to try to transform what had always been a slave owner's prerogative into a slave's right.

Although the numbers of freedom suits surged during the Age of Revolution, this period also laid the groundwork for the divergent trajectories of the nineteenth century. Manumissions increased in all three jurisdictions, but the increases had radically different political connotations. In Virginia, manumissions became linked to wider debates about slave emancipation and were opposed by numerous state residents as representing a dangerous step toward freedom and citizenship for black people. In Cuba – and by extension in Louisiana under Spanish control – manumission was linked to the regulation of customary practices that had nothing to do with abolition or with republican notions of equality. By the 1760s, Cuba already boasted a sizable community of free people of color. Unlike in Virginia, the existence and standing of this community were linked to traditional understandings of vassalage, status, and royal justice. In Cuba, the free community of color was a product of the ancien régime, not of the revolutions in the Atlantic world, as in Virginia. This community was too large and too powerful to be obliterated, regardless of the fears voiced by some slave owners, such as Francisco de Arango y Parreño.

This may begin to explain why, as news of slave uprisings spread, abolitionist ideas gained traction, and the populations of free people of color continued to grow, white elites in Virginia, and in Louisiana after the U.S. takeover, were considerably more successful than their Cuban counterparts in turning back the tide of freedom. The ironic aftermath of the Age of Revolution and the adoption of the U.S. Constitution was the full-fledged commitment of the U.S. law and polity to the enslavement of Africans, and an increased emphasis on race in adjudicating freedom. Without legal support for self-purchase arrangements and other routine manumissions, racial claims became the most common basis for freedom suits in Virginia, and increasingly so in Louisiana after the end of the Spanish period.

Communities of free people of color peaked in population and power in the first decades of the nineteenth century. We turn now to the antebellum era, when legal, political, and demographic trends overtook the free communities in Virginia and Louisiana; in Cuba, slaveholders and colonial authorities took significant and consequential steps to curb the privileges and standing of the free community of color, but their efforts were not as successful as in the other jurisdictions. In the U.S. South, anxiety increased over people who belied the white-free/black-slave duality, leading to hotly contested trials over racial identity, especially in suits for freedom. Similar anxieties played out in Cuba; trials contesting unequal marriages, in which typically the parents of one of the parties opposed the union, frequently focused on the racial backgrounds of the participants. Over the course of the antebellum era in the United States, as sectional conflict increased the saliency of white supremacy as the justification for slavery, legal regimes of race and freedom in Louisiana and Virginia converged, outlawing or greatly curtailing opportunities for manumission. In Cuba, on the other hand, slaves continued to invoke traditional practices and rights, not only maintaining but in some ways even expanding the avenues to emancipation. In the process, the association between blackness and enslavement, whiteness and freedom, remained less strict and precise in Cuba than in Virginia and Louisiana.

CHAPTER 4

"Rules ... for Their Expulsion"

Foreclosing Freedom, 1830–1860

BY 1831 THE CITIZENS OF NORTHAMPTON COUNTY, ON Virginia's Eastern Shore, noted with "well-founded uneasiness" the disturbing information revealed by the latest census: "The proportion of free persons of colour to ... white inhabitants is annually increasing." At about 15 percent, this proportion was indeed much higher than in the state as a whole, and higher even than in some of the urban areas, such as Norfolk. "From the number of our free negroes, and from the idle and vicious habits of most of them, we have stronger reason ... to suspect dangerous intrigues with our slaves," county residents argued. They added that in Virginia, free persons of color represented "an anomalous population" indelibly marked by "the stain which attaches to their colour" and by the multiple legal barriers that limited their civil and political rights. Anxious white petitioners asked that to secure their "peace and security ... all free persons of color should be promptly removed" from the county.[1]

Such fears were common among whites living in slave societies, regardless of legal and cultural differences. In the 1850s, Louisianans complained about the rising number of free blacks coming into the state. One East Feliciana native wrote to the *New Orleans Semi-Weekly Creole* in 1854, calling for laws that would make these migrants "unhappy and discontented with their present condition," so they would leave. In his 1857 message to the legislature, Governor Robert C. Wickliffe bemoaned the migration of free blacks into Louisiana, and declared that "the interests of the people require, that immediate steps should be taken at this time to remove all free negroes who are now in the State," as "their example and association have a most pernicious effect upon our slave population."[2] Even in Havana, where the large free population of color had deep colonial roots, it was perceived as a potential danger. As a Spanish official stated in 1825: "Free blacks in the island are already to be feared in towns because of their excessive number in relation to whites." Several years later, the town council of Havana informed the crown that the existence of free blacks was one of its concerns, as they represented "no small portion of the population that without being enslaved, wishes the extermination of the white race."[3] Indeed, as noted in Chapter 3, the population of free people of color in all three places had grown significantly by 1830. In Virginia, the number of free people of color increased by 21 percent in the 1810s and 28 percent in the 1820s. In Louisiana, the rate of growth was 38 percent in the 1810s and 59 percent in the 1820s, while population in Havana doubled between 1792 and 1817.

Slaveholders feared that free people of color might join forces with slaves to overthrow the racial order and obtain social equality. "It is not wise to place black slaves in contact with those who are free," the town council of Havana admonished in 1826.[4] Asked about whether free blacks saw themselves as closer to whites or to slaves, and whose side they would take in case of an insurrection, James Madison was unequivocal in 1823: "More closely with the slaves and more likely to side with them in case of an insurrection." The citizens of Northampton County agreed: "Standing thus in a middle position between the two extremes of our society, and despairing of ever attaining an equality with the higher grade, it is natural that they connect themselves in feeling and interest, with the slaves, among whom many of their domestic ties are formed, and to whom they are bound by the sympathies scarcely less strong, which springs from their common complexion."[5]

These anxieties notwithstanding, in the final decades before slavery ended in the United States and Cuba, the institution appeared to be stronger than ever. Sugar plantations in Cuba and Louisiana churned out their staple commodity with a speed never imagined – Cuba's sugar production was the greatest in the world, growing from 147,000 long tons in the 1830s to 345,000 in the 1850s; in Louisiana, the figures were 38,000 and 138,000, respectively. Between the 1830s and the 1850s, as many as one million enslaved people left the slave markets of the Upper

South, of which Richmond and Alexandria, Virginia, were the largest, for plantations in the Lower South, many of them passing through New Orleans. The wealth concentrated in the hands of planters continued to grow.[6]

Yet slaveholders felt pressure from all sides: rebellious slaves threatened their sleep and security; newly emboldened abolitionists threatened to block slave ships to Cuba and undermine Southern power in the U.S. government; and populations of free people of color seemed to be the harbingers of both rebellion and abolitionism. Beginning in the 1830s, and with increasing fervor in the 1840s and 1850s, white slaveholding elites across the Americas sought to crack down on free people of color and manumission. They also looked for ways to remove free people of color from their midst, to realize the old dream of a perfect, and perfectly dichotomous, social order of blacks and whites, enslaved and free.

Cuban slaveholders were manifestly less successful than those in Virginia and Louisiana in the implementation of this project. Whereas legislators in Virginia and Louisiana imposed increasingly onerous conditions on manumission, in Cuba it was not feasible to alter long-standing slaving practices. Manumission was a well-established practice with important religious implications. It was also frequently claimed as a "right" by slaves and their family members. As mediators of increasingly tense social and race relations that at some points threatened the very stability of the colony, Cuban officials were forced to reconcile contradictory demands and expectations, including those of the free people of color and the enslaved. That is why the Reglamento de Esclavos (Slave Ordinance) of 1842 expanded legal avenues for freedom just as plantation slavery was growing in western and central Cuba. Proposals to remove free people of color from the island were considered but quickly dismissed by Cuban authorities as being "filled with thousands of difficulties."[7]

In Virginia and Louisiana, free blacks' claims to citizenship and belonging were grounded in the right to a homeland, to stay close to friends and families in their communities of birth. Such rights were not under assault in Cuba. As the captain general of Cuba candidly acknowledged in 1832, "Having made the mistake of not placing obstacles to freedom, to make it difficult and slow, and making matters worse by the indifference with which their [free blacks'] propagation has been met," it was now "imprudent" to try to correct old "omissions and defects." However undesirable, free people of color were a social reality that slaveholders and colonial authorities would have to live with. In the final decades of slavery, legal understandings and performances of black freedom in Cuba came to differ significantly from those in Virginia and Louisiana.[8]

ABOLITIONISTS AND REBELS

In 1829, David Walker, a free man of color, sent shock waves throughout the southern United States with his incendiary pamphlet, *Appeal to the Coloured Citizens of the World*, warning white slaveholding Americans that their days were numbered: "Unless you speedily alter your course, you and your Country are gone!!!!!!! For God Almighty will tear up the very face of the earth!!!"[9] Walker's *Appeal* inaugurated the abolitionist movement of immediatism, the demand that slavery be ended right away, not in some distant future. The *Appeal* went through several editions in 1830 that were smuggled into all the Southern states and circulated by free people of color. Walker himself was born free, to a free woman of color and an enslaved father in North Carolina, and moved to Boston in 1825, where he wrote for the first black newspaper in the United States, *Freedom's Journal*. Walker's *Appeal* shocked and terrified white readers by directly urging people of color around the world to rise up, claim citizenship, and if necessary, take up arms against slavery: "Look upon your mother, wife and children, and answer God Almighty; and believe this, that it is no more harm for you to kill a man, who is trying to kill you, than it is for you to take a drink of water when thirsty."[10]

Walker drew the connections between manumission and black citizenship, noting that "as soon as a slave among the Romans obtained his freedom, he could rise to the greatest eminence in the State, and there was no law instituted to hinder a slave from buying his freedom."[11] He fanned white fears concerning free people of color by unequivocally claiming black birthright citizenship – "This country is as much ours as it is the whites, whether they will admit it now or not" – and by

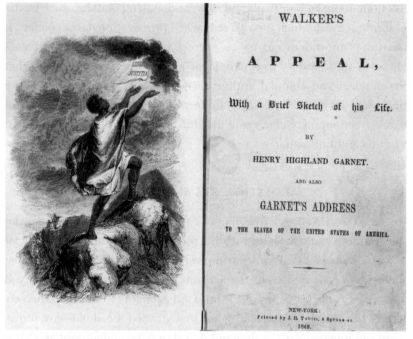

13. David Walker's *Appeal.* First published in 1829, the *Appeal to the Coloured Citizens of the World,* by David Walker, struck fear into the hearts of slaveholders. The frontispiece to this edition, *Walker's Appeal, with a Brief Sketch of His Life by Henry Highland Garnet,* shows a slave atop a mountain with his hands raised up, reaching for a paper, labeled "libertas justitia," that appears in sky. Childs, frontispiece to David Walker, *Walker's Appeal* (New York: J.H. Tobitt, 1848). Photograph, Library of Congress, Rare Book and Special Collections Division, www.loc.gov/item/92513183/.

highlighting the links between slaves and free blacks: "For if the free are allowed to stay among the slaves, they will have intercourse together, and, of course, the free will learn the slaves *bad habits,* by teaching them that they are MEN, as well as other people, and certainly *ought* and *must* be FREE." The specter of this social and political "intercourse" terrified slaveholders.[12]

William Lloyd Garrison amplified the call for immediate abolition shortly thereafter in his new newspaper *The Liberator.* Garrison's paper gave a platform to many black abolitionists, advocated immediate and unconditional abolition of slavery in all the states of the union, and envisioned a future of equality and black citizenship. "Assenting to the 'self-evident truth' maintained in the American Declaration of

Independence, 'that all men are created equal, and endowed by their Creator with certain inalienable rights – among which are life, liberty and the pursuit of happiness,' I shall strenuously contend for the immediate enfranchisement of our slave population," Garrison stated in his first editorial.[13] Echoing Walker's *Appeal*, Garrison vowed to fight for emancipation "till every chain be broken, and every bondman set free! Let southern oppressors tremble – let their secret abettor tremble – let their northern apologists tremble – let all the enemies of the persecuted blacks tremble." Garrison's leadership among white abolitionists, along with growing British abolitionism across the Atlantic, brought the message of immediatism to a broad audience. Although abolitionists remained a small minority of white Northerners, they did influence the political landscape of national politics in the United States, which was increasingly divided along sectional lines. The Missouri Compromise line, drawn at the parallel latitude of 36°30′ north, symbolically split the country into a free North and a slave South, and white slaveholders feared their section would be swallowed by the more populous North, just as they feared white abolitionists would join with black rebels to turn on them, even murdering them in their sleep.

Perhaps most terrifying to white slaveholders in Walker's *Appeal* was "the image of a messianic black leader, a black Moses, who Walker predicted would soon emerge to lead slaves to freedom and revenge."[14] Only months later, Nat Turner fulfilled that prophecy. On August 21, 1831, Turner, a fiery preacher and visionary, led a small group of free men of color and enslaved rebels in an insurrection in Southampton County, Virginia, seizing arms and horses and killing at least fifty-five white men, women, and children. The revolt was quickly crushed, however. Not only were Turner and most of the rebels executed, but several hundred other black men, women, and children were tortured and killed in an orgy of vengeance that dismayed even staunch supporters of slavery.

Echoes of Nat Turner's rebellion reverberated across the South but especially in New Orleans. The largest slave market in the United States at the time was in New Orleans, and it received many of the tens of thousands enslaved Virginians sent to the Deep South each year. Usually reluctant to report on matters concerning slave resistance – beyond the typical advertisements for runaway slaves – the local press took note of

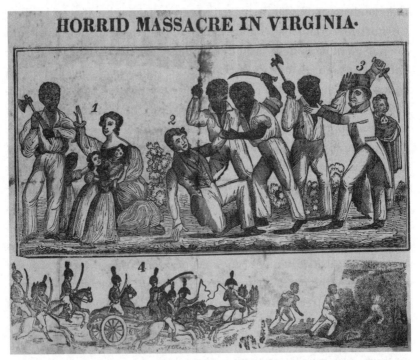

14. "Horrid Massacre in Virginia." This image illustrated the *Authentic and impartial narrative of the tragical scene which was witnessed in Southampton County,* published in New York in 1831. News of Turner's rebellion spread far and wide in 1831, leading to a crackdown on free people of color across the U.S. South. "Horrid Massacre in Virginia," Southampton County, Virginia, 1831. Photograph, Library of Congress, Rare Book and Special Collections Division, www.loc.gov/item/98510363/.

what it called "the banditti of Southampton" and reported on "the depraved character of that monstrous impostor, Nat Turner" and his "nefarious plans." The newspaper *The Bee* called on local authorities to take preventive action: "However persuaded we may be that the authorities of Virginia will put the captured insurgents in the impossibility of doing any more mischief on this earth ... it were highly politic nay imperiously required that the proper officers of the state should take measures to prevent the introduction of slaves from the infected section of the country."[15]

The news from Southampton arrived on the heels of David Walker's incendiary pamphlet. An Englishman named James E. Alexander, who sailed to New Orleans from Havana in September 1831 – at roughly the same time that news of the rebellion was reaching the city – reported that, on his arrival, "there was an alarm of a slave insurrection" when authorities discovered copies of Walker's *Appeal*. Alexander also reported that weapons had been found at the house of a "colored man" and that armed citizens and regular troops were patrolling the city. Rumors of revolt also came from the sugar-producing areas north of the city, where slaves were allegedly arming themselves to claim their freedom.[16]

Fears of slave revolt resulted in a flurry of legislative activity. A special session of the legislature debated *The Bee*'s request to exercise caution with slave imports from the "infected sections" of Virginia and decreed a temporary halt to all slave imports. An 1829 law already prohibited bringing into Louisiana any slave "accused of any conspiracy or insurrection, or who had resided in any county of any State or Territory of the United States, during the time of any conspiracy or insurrection in such county." The law passed in 1831 also sought to curb smuggling – which might bring in enslaved people who had insurrectionary ideas – by prohibiting the importation of slaves from neighboring Mississippi, Alabama, and Arkansas.[17]

According to Alexander, however, smuggling also came from another direction: from Havana. Commerce between the two port cities was frequent and active. These contacts facilitated not only trade, legal or not, but also the circulation of rumors and information concerning slave insurrections and abolitionist efforts across jurisdictions. Citing a Louisiana planter as his source, Alexander denounced the existence of "a set of miscreants in the city of New Orleans who are connected with slave-traders of Cuba, and who at certain periods proceed up the Mississippi as far as the Fourche mouth" to sell slaves. In 1835 New Orleans authorities requested an armed ship to patrol the waters between Cuba and Texas and "to capture and bring here any American vessels found engaged in transporting African negroes from Cuba to our coast or to Texas."[18]

Cuban slaveholders did not need to have heard about Nat Turner to be apprehensive, however. Cuban colonial authorities recorded more than twenty slave rebellions in the three decades between Aponte's movement in 1812 and 1844, the year of "La Escalera," a vast conspiracy involving plantation and urban slaves, as well as free people of color, reaching from the sugar districts of Matanzas to Havana.[19] Several of the revolts were organized by recently arrived African slaves, many of whom had fought in wars in their societies of origin. On numerous coffee and sugar estates, large concentrations of Africans had come from the same region, some were surely also related through links of community and kinship. This meant that planning revolts could be done in broad daylight because they shared African languages unintelligible to overseers. Many slaves participated in these revolts not by seizing arms or actively engaging in violence against whites, but by refusing to protect the estates where they labored, or the lives of the white residents. At the Alcancía sugar mill in the sugar-producing region of Bemba, Matanzas, a major slave revolt broke out in March 1843. The manager complained that many of the mill's slaves did not help to put out the fires set by the rebels. Some simply walked away during the confusion, searching for loved ones and crafting their own routes of escape and experiences of freedom. In the process, they contributed to the momentary collapse of socioracial hierarchies in Cuba, "the kind of massive undermining (and in some cases complete dissolution) of plantation control" that had terrified slaveholders since the days of Saint-Domingue. And although repression was swift – one report indicated that 300 slaves were killed or committed suicide after the rebellion at the Alcancía mill – it "presented a horrible spectacle, while the deserted estates, the burnt fields and dwellings, added still more to the air of desolation spread around."[20]

Other factors contributed to the climate of fear and dread, among them, the spectacular rise in the number of *cimarrones* (runaways) and the formation of *palenques*, or maroon communities, in various parts of the island. Although most runaways were recaptured within the month, their escape still undermined the strict control that slaveholders deemed central to a stable slave society. Some managed to live as free for years. That was the case for an African named Gil who escaped in 1847 but was not detained until 1861.[21]

Particularly worrisome to slaveholders was the possibility of a coordinated alliance between the mostly African slaves in the rural areas and urban slaves and free people of color. They were terrified to learn, for instance, that according to the testimony of one of the rebels, slave revolts on the coffee-growing plantations of Guacamaro, Matanzas, in 1825, were planned with free people of color from Matanzas and Havana. When, in November 1843, the slaves at the Triunvirato sugar mill promised to "wage war and kill the whites" in what was probably the largest slave revolt in colonial Cuba, they articulated a message that inspired not only other slaves, but also free blacks.[22]

The prospect of this alliance made La Escalera particularly frightening. The 1844 conspiracy included overlapping plots and networks connecting rural estates and urban areas. To contemporary observers, La Escalera was the outcome of the great slave rebellions of March and November 1843 (in Bemba and Triunvirato). Many elite free blacks and mulattoes were involved, including some militia officers.[23]

To make matters worse, authorities discovered in 1844 that La Escalera conspirators had coordinated their actions with British abolitionists and their agents. Several free blacks detained for the conspiracy testified that they had received offers of material and moral support, including military supplies, from various British agents. The revolt allegedly was "the Englishmen's idea" and the British would "arrange everything with the people from Santo Domingo in order to send weapons and a general to command the rebels once the planned uprising had begun."[24] British consul David Turnbull, whom Cuban slaveholders labeled "a violent apostle of abolitionist propagandists," was identified as one of the masterminds of the revolt.[25]

CRACKDOWN ON FREE PEOPLE OF COLOR

White fears and anxieties concerning free people of color, slave resistance, and open rebellion, as well as abolitionist threats, led to new regulations and to stricter enforcement of existing laws. After Nat Turner's rebellion, the Virginia governor called for "the revision of all the laws, intended to preserve in due subordination the slave population of our state." In Cuba, an American observer reported that La Escalera "had the effect of obliging the government to become stricter in the execution of the existing laws." In New Orleans, the *Daily Picayune* warned in 1857 that "times are at least urgent for the exercise of the most watchful vigilance over the conduct of the slaves and free colored persons" and called for the strict enforcement of all regulations.[26]

In Virginia and Louisiana, the crackdown began with Walker's *Appeal*. The Louisiana legislature reacted to the arrest in New Orleans of a free black merchant who circulated the *Appeal* in early March 1830 by immediately prohibiting the immigration of free people of color into the state, and it made all recent immigrants of color subject to deportation. Enforcement of the new law was weak, and the legislature walked back elements of it soon afterward, but it signaled heightened levels of concern that free people of color might foment slave rebellion. The Louisiana legislature also passed an act in 1830 that punished anyone writing, printing, publishing, or distributing "anything having a tendency to produce discontent among the free colored population of the state, or insubordination among the slaves." The same act criminalized "the use of language in any public discourse" or even in "private discourses of conversations" that sowed discontent among slaves and free people of color. In Virginia, when the mayor of Richmond learned that Walker had mailed thirty copies of his *Appeal* to Thomas Lewis, a free black resident of that city, he dispatched patrollers to confiscate them, recovering only twenty copies, and wrote to the governor urging statewide action. In April 1831, the first edition of *The Liberator* prompted a closed-door session of the Virginia legislature, which passed a ban on teaching reading and writing to free people of color.[27]

In 1831–1832, the threats of Walker's *Appeal*, the Nat Turner rebellion, and the ensuing white terror prompted the Virginia House of Delegates to debate the future of slavery and the fate of free blacks in the commonwealth. The very survival of the institution was at stake, it seemed, and there was no consensus about what to do. Benjamin Watkins Leigh, a conservative, argued for perpetual slavery and stricter discipline for slaves. Others claimed, spuriously, that the slaves of Virginia were "as happy a laboring lot as exists upon the habitable globe." Thomas Roderick Dew articulated what would be one of the strongest defenses of slavery in a white men's democracy: slavery brought white Virginians "to one common level" as "nearly as can be expected or even desired in this world." This "spirit of equality" among whites, he said, "is both the generator and preserver of the genuine spirit of liberty." White equality was conceived as a function of black enslavement.[28]

Black freedom had no place in such a vision. Even those who hoped for emancipation frequently linked it with the removal of free blacks. John Marshall hoped that the legislature would take advantage of "the excitement produced by the late insurrection" to pass sweeping legislation on the removal of free blacks to a colony in Africa. The members of the Society of Friends of Charles City County attributed their "present difficulties and dangers" to the evils of slavery, an institution that violated "the laws of justice and humanity." In their view, the only way to restore divine law and to serve "the best interests of the Commonwealth at large" was to implement "some efficient system for the abolition of slavery." Such a system was proposed by Thomas Jefferson's nephew Thomas Jefferson Randolph, who offered a plan for gradual emancipation that failed by only fifteen votes, along regional lines, with Virginia's high-slave-population Southside carrying the day. Although Virginia's legislature came close to passing general emancipation at that tumultuous moment, the only thing that did unite the legislators was their agreement on free black removal: both those who favored gradual emancipation and those who wanted to strengthen slavery believed that free people of color should not remain in Virginia.[29]

Only rarely did slave revolts prompt the sort of debate that took place in Virginia. Most frequently, slaveholders reaffirmed their support for the institution by exercising tight control over any information that could throw the legitimacy of slavery into question. Cuban slaveholders, under constant attack from British abolitionists and slave rebels, refused even to discuss the future of slavery on the island. Such debates, they claimed, inevitably led to revolution, as slaves interpreted them as proclamations of freedom and emancipation. Such had been the case since "a delirious deputy" raised the possibility of abolition at the Cortes de Cadiz in 1812, and that is why colonial authorities refrained from disseminating information about the treaties abolishing the slave trade in 1817 and 1845. "I will be careful," the governor stated apropos the 1845 treaty, "that this resolution does not create fear or doubts concerning ownership of

existing slaves, as these rights cannot be doubted or examined without threatening the security of the country."[30]

Colonial authorities in Cuba tried to control the dissemination of any
information related to slave emancipation, but their ability to do so was
limited. On the one hand, the issue was a topic of political debate in
Spain and any news that emancipation would be included in the agenda
of the Spanish parliament provoked a strong reaction from Cuban slaveholders, who constantly warned that such discussions would lead to the
destruction of the island. When a newspaper announced in late 1840 that
the parliament might consider several laws "leading to emancipation,"
a general sense of "alarm" took over Havana and the rest of the island. On
the other hand, it was impossible to prevent the dissemination of news
concerning emancipation elsewhere in the Caribbean. Alarm increased
with each report of abolition in the neighboring islands. In 1831 the
governor banned the introduction of any slaves from Jamaica, arguing
that, "seduced by the spirit of freedom propagated by revolutionary
societies and the sectarians of Methodism," black and mulatto slaves
and freedmen on that island were planning to revolt against the whites.
News of the British Slavery Abolition Act of 1833 caused great apprehension in Cuba. The town council of Havana argued that the "negrophiles"
had begun to create abolitionist societies to "upend order in Cuba" and
predicted that final emancipation in Jamaica would lead to a general
black revolt. They also anxiously monitored any discussions or efforts,
organized on the neighboring island, concerning possible slave emancipation in Cuba. When news about emancipation in the Danish colonies
reached Havana in 1847, authorities feared that they would provoke
a rebellion. In 1848, the governor acknowledged that information
about emancipation in the French Antilles had "inevitably circulated"
and that "some agitation" was to be expected.[31]

Abolitionist literature was confiscated in Cuba, and those charged with
its dissemination treated as inciting sedition. When an American Methodist
preacher from Providence, Rhode Island, described as "a mulatto," was
apprehended in Havana in 1837 with abolitionist materials, the colonial
government rejected the petition of deportation issued by the British
Consul and prosecuted him to the full extent of the law. The preacher
was found to be in possession of "several subversive papers, notebooks, and

illustrations that sought to propagate principles contrary to slavery and to energetically speak to the imagination of the Africans." Cuban authorities saw all distribution of antislavery writings as a direct threat to the institution of slavery on the island and moved quickly to curtail it.[32]

In the United States, the imperatives of sectional politics, and especially the increasingly assertive Northern abolitionists, led Southern slaveholders to articulate an explicit defense of slavery in the 1830s. Instead of describing it as an unfortunate but unavoidable evil inherited from the colonial past, slaveholders argued that slavery was a "positive good" – economically, morally, and socially favorable to the Southern states, and to the slaves themselves. This positive-good argument not only answered Northern critics but also enlisted nonslaveholding white men in the South in the defense of a Southern way of life, and it had the potential to align all white Americans behind white supremacy. A note published in *The Liberator* in 1847 claimed that at the time of the newspaper's creation, "not a human being defended slavery in the abstract." But by the late 1840s, "powerful" arguments were being articulated "in all parts of the South" in defense of the institution. Writing in 1856, a New Orleans observer concurred:

> In the earlier discussions, it was admitted by southern men that slavery was an evil which it was desirable to get rid of, but for which the existing generation was in nowise responsible . . . . It is probable that the South would have continued merely to apologize but for the denunciations of the abolitionists, which led to the . . . consequent conviction that slavery, as it exists in the United States, in all its aspects, moral, social, and political, is not inconsistent with justice, reason, or religion.[33]

This apology for slavery was grounded on black inferiority. Theorists writing from the perspective of religion, science, and law argued that slavery reflected the unbridgeable barrier between blacks and whites. Thomas Reade Cobb, author of a treatise on the law of slavery, explained that "a state of bondage, so far from doing violence to the law of [the African's] nature, develops and perfects it; and that, in that state, he enjoys the greatest amount of happiness, and arrives at the greatest degree of perfection of which his nature is capable."[34]

This ideology implied that Africans belonged only in slavery and not in freedom. "It must be admitted," physician and scientist Josiah Nott remarked in one of his New Orleans lectures, "that the slaves of the South, as a mass, are more intelligent, more moral, and more happy than any free negroes on the face of the globe .... The negroes of the South ... are now the most contented population of the earth." A citizen of Virginia agreed, noting that slaves there were "as happy" as workers anywhere in the world. Allegedly happy slaves were also to be found in Cuba, where slaveholders and authorities constantly argued that they were better treated "than anywhere else in the world."[35]

Happy slaves did not translate into black citizens, however. The restrictive regulatory regime that came to characterize all three of these slave societies in the mid-nineteenth century targeted free blacks, seeking to erode their tenuous freedom and, if possible, to get rid of them altogether. In Cuba, Virginia, and Louisiana, the decades of the mid-nineteenth century featured openly racist attacks on the decency, intelligence and humanity of people of African descent. All three jurisdictions reinvigorated old bans against the immigration of free people of color and approved new prohibitions. Virginia banned the immigration of free blacks as early as 1793 and reiterated this prohibition in 1834, in 1841, and in the criminal code of 1848. In the port city of New Orleans, several laws passed in the 1840s required the incarceration of out-of-state black sailors arriving in the city and banned them from working on the wharves.[36] The prohibitions applied to any "free negro, mulatto, or person of color" arriving aboard "any vessel or steamboat, as a cook, steward, or mariner, or in any employment ... or as a passenger." In Cuba, old prohibitions targeting blacks from the French islands were recycled and expanded in the mid-nineteenth century. A royal order of 1837 prohibited any free black person from landing on the island "under the shadow of any pretext whatever," and free black sailors were imprisoned in the port until their departure, very much as in New Orleans. In 1844, the colonial governor expelled all free men of color who had come to the island from "any other country." New measures also limited the mobility of free blacks, particularly in regions thought to be linked to revolution and abolition. The Louisiana legislature placed several conditions on free blacks traveling out of the state and banned all travel to "the West India

Islands" in 1830 and 1831. In Cuba, a rule issued by the colonial governor in 1842 banned issuing passports to any "individual of color, natural of the Spanish domains," who sought to visit "foreign possessions."[37] The circulation of free people of color came under assault in all three jurisdictions.

Legislators went further, trying to devise ways to get rid of free people of color altogether. In all three jurisdictions, the outright removal of free blacks was seriously considered, through proposals for onerous residency requirements and colonization schemes. Such policies were explored even in Havana, home to a large community of free people of color that had been part of local society since the sixteenth century. In 1832 the Spanish minister of war asked the governor whether free people of color were "convenient" to the island and, if not, "which rules were the most appropriate for their expulsion." The governor replied that mass deportations should be "entirely proscribed" because such a move would provoke widespread resistance among blacks and disapproval among whites. The most that could be done, he said, was to exile, going forward, all free blacks and mulattoes convicted of crimes.[38] Thirty years later, racist ideologue José Antonio Saco advocated an absolute ban on black immigrants, including slaves; the deportation of individuals of the "free African race" convicted of any crime and "vagrants" without a known trade or occupation; and the imposition of residency requirements on future manumissions, so that any slave younger than fifty who obtained freedom did so on condition that she "leave the island."[39]

Saco's residency requirements mirrored those implemented in Virginia and Louisiana. The delegates involved in the great debate concerning slavery in Virginia in 1831–1832 could not agree on the future of the institution, but they did agree on one thing: the undesirability of free blacks. As Representative James Gholson stated in 1832, "The public mind is definitely settled [on] the propriety of removing the free colored population beyond our limits." Free blacks, said another, carried "a mark" that could never be erased, so free people of color were "the very drones and pests of our society." The *Martinsburg Gazette*, the *Norfolk and Portsmouth Herald*, and the *Richmond Enquirer* editorialized that the removal of free people of color was "vital" to the "peace and welfare" of Virginia. Josiah Nott echoed this vision, noting that "several millions of such idle, vicious vagabonds" could never be allowed to "live and propagate" among whites.[40]

COLONIZATION

To implement their perfect world of free whites and enslaved blacks, slaveholders concocted several colonization plans. The idea of "removing" free people of color to a colony far away, whether on the American continent or back in Africa, tantalized Americans and Cubans who stroved to rid their societies of these troublesome "in between" individuals. As a group of Havana planters argued in 1841, emancipation would alter "social relations" and place blacks and whites "on an equal legal footing, creating social ties between two races who display in their faces the irrefutable mark of physical separation."[41] Fueled by racism, slaveholders and policy makers first crafted plans to deport free blacks to Africa. The authorities of Havana had tried to implement this drastic solution, without success, as early as the sixteenth century.

In the early nineteenth century, colonization captured the imagination of national leaders across the United States. Thomas Jefferson, among others, argued that slavery should come to an end gradually, but that whites and freed slaves could not live side by side. The American Colonization Society (ACS) was founded in 1816 by clergy, who hoped to garner large-scale government support for purchasing slaves, freeing them, and sending them to a colony in Africa where they, in turn, would Christianize Africans. Liberia was established the following year, with help of the U.S. government, and it became the destination of about 12,000 black Americans between the 1820s and the 1860s.

Virginians were heavily involved in colonization from the start, led by John Randolph of Roanoke and President James Monroe, as well as other leaders from the Upper South, such as Senator Henry Clay. Often in response to popular petitions, the Virginia legislature approved funding to subsidize various colonization activities, particularly after Nat Turner's rebellion, when petitions to remove the free population of color from the state intensified. At the urging of ACS leader Charles Fenton Mercer, the legislature also pressed the federal government to sponsor colonization.

In the 1850s, Virginia imposed an annual tax on free black men ages twenty-one to fifty-five to subsidize "the removal of free Negroes." The ACS eventually had more than thirty chapters across the state; nearly one-third of the people of color who left for Liberia came from Virginia.[42]

Petitioners to the Virginia legislature elaborated the argument for removal. In 1825, the Richmond colonization society explained that free people of color, "placed midway between freedom and slavery, ... know neither the incentives of the one, nor the restraints of the other; but are alike injurious by their conduct, & example, to all other classes of Society." They suggested that colonization would benefit free people of color, who would find in Liberia "political liberty ... social happiness ... [and] moral and religious improvement."[43] Two years later, their petition was more urgent: free people of color in Virginia, they warned, were a "positive evil" whose increased numbers were "alarming in prospect."[44] For the most part, however, early colonization petitions were optimistic, emphasizing the "crowning success" of Liberia and the "individual and general good" resulting from the "noble enterprise" of colonization.[45]

After the 1830s, however, colonization came to be seen primarily as a way to support and defend slavery. As abolitionists' demands for immediate emancipation intensified and the possibility of slave rebellion became real, the connections between colonization and eventual emancipation withered. Advocates increasingly emphasized the "removal" of free people of color as a way to ensure that blackness was coterminous with slavery. Virginians' petitions for colonization, for example, changed in tone after Nat Turner's rebellion. Now, they stressed that free people of color might foment rebellion, and blamed "the awful scenes" of the Nat Turner rebellion on their negative "influence." Free people of color, they declared, were "degraded, profligate, vicious, turbulent and discontented"; their "wretchedness" and "idleness" were a "great and annually increasing evil." Petitioners drew the connection between racial inferiority and removal explicitly, as they had not before. Ninety-six citizens of Northampton County signed a petition stating that free people of color were "inferior to the whites in intelligence & information; degraded by the stain which attaches to their colour; excluded from many civil privileges which the humblest white man enjoys, and denied all participation in the government," and that therefore "it would be wholly absurd to expect from them any attachment to our laws & institutions or any sympathy with our people." The petitioners recommended numerous restrictions on free people of color. Forced removal to Liberia was the final measure on the list. Throughout the 1830s, petitions for forcible removal used the same language, describing free people of color as "highly injurious" and an "intolerable burthen." As a report of the ACS put it in 1833, "Causes, beyond the control of the human will, must prevent their [free blacks] ever rising to equality with the whites."[46]

Free people of color vociferously opposed colonization, forcefully contesting the actions and rhetoric of the ACS. At a large meeting in Philadelphia in January 1817, just after the founding of the ACS, participants opposed banishment from the United States: "We will never separate ourselves voluntarily from the slave population of this country; they are our brethren by the ties, of consanguinity, of suffering and of wrong." As these views gained ascendance with the rise of immediatism, moderate white abolitionists gradually abandoned the colonization movement. Baptist minister Thomas Price elaborated on his change of sentiments in 1833. He declared that he had first heard of Liberia "with joy and gratitude to God," but that his views about the ACS had been "totally altered . . . changed into aversion and abhorrence," and he had come to see colonization as an effort "unworthy of the patronage of the religious and anti-slavery public." Although in their fund-raising efforts ACS claimed to be advancing the cause of abolition in the United States, Price explained that their true purpose was "to perpetuate the enormous evil. It is the enemy of immediate abolition." Although Price acknowledged that colonization schemes had brought "freedom to a few slaves," its main effect had been "to confirm the slave system." Colonization, he said, was an expression of the fears of whites who, "not having enough either of religion or honesty to restore to the negro his rights, devised this scheme of transporting the free, in order to perpetuate the bondage of the enslaved black." The ACS's own Southern auxiliaries contributed to the proslavery profile of the institution. As a member from Virginia explained, "The Society has reiterated the declaration, that it has no ulterior views diverse from the object avowed in the constitution; and, having declared that it is in nowise allied to any Abolition Society in

America, or elsewhere, is ready, whenever there is need, to pass a censure upon such Societies in America."[47]

African American activists also contested the notion that blacks could not be educated enough to become enlightened citizens of the United States. Baltimore minister and educator William Watkins, a free man of color, "mocked those who suggested that black men could never 'enjoy the unalienable rights of man' and the 'privileges of freemen.'" To Watkins, colonization was a covert mechanism to eliminate "the general mass of the free blacks ... a greater nuisance than even slaves themselves." Free black opponents of colonization claimed the right to their homeland: "Resolved, That we consider the land in which we were born, and in which we have been bred, our only 'true and appropriate home.'" Garrison supported these views, arguing that colonization schemes denied black people any opportunity to be "elevated, enlightened, or happy, in their native land," propagated "prejudice against their color," and slandered them "in the most cruel manner, representing them as nuisances, vagabonds, more degraded and miserable than the slaves, the wild stirrers up of sedition."[48]

Colonization efforts became popular in New Orleans only after the idea was firmly associated with the "removal" of free blacks, and not at all with emancipation. In 1842 the ACS reported that it had sent four expeditions to Liberia, two of which departed from Norfolk, Virginia, and one from New Orleans. That same year, the Louisiana State Colonization Society acquired a tract of land in Liberia to establish its own colony, although it never did so.[49] In 1852, those who opposed emancipation in Louisiana won an important victory when the legislature required all freed slaves to be sent to Liberia within one year of manumission. The owner had to pay passage of $150, and slaves who refused to leave would lose their freedom.[50] In 1858 the state of Louisiana was one of the largest contributors to the national ACS, second only to Mississippi. Virginia was the third.[51]

The largest single group to go to Liberia from New Orleans were the slaves belonging to John McDonogh. In the 1820s McDonogh crafted a self-purchase plan in which his slaves worked for several decades to raise the funds to buy their freedom and move to Liberia. McDonogh was clear that the freedom he promised could be enjoyed only elsewhere: "That is, your freedom in Liberia, the land of your fathers, a great and glorious land. For let it be understood between us, it is your freedom in Liberia that I contract for. I would never consent to give freedom to a single individual among you, to remain on the same soil as the white man . . .. My object is your freedom and happiness in Liberia." The ship sponsored by the ACS that left New Orleans in 1842 carried about eighty of McDonogh's emancipated slaves, and another forty-two sailed in 1859, having worked for seventeen additional years to pay for their freedom.[52]

Colonization schemes to remove newly freed Africans also developed in Cuba. Unlike Virginia and New Orleans, however, in Cuba colonization debates centered mainly on the so-called *emancipados*, slaves captured by the British navy in its efforts to stop the illegal slave trade. When a ship with a cargo of 159 slaves was captured off the coast of Havana in December 1824, the question of what to do with them immediately came up. The captain general said that it would be "extremely harmful to this island and a terrible example for these blacks . . . to remain in the island," as slaves would surely question their own situation, "having these freedmen around." The Cuban members of the international tribunal established to adjudicate cases against vessels charged with illegal slave trading agreed. They argued that the presence in Cuba of the *emancipados* among those of "their color and origin as members of the free class gratuitously," that is, without the usual manumission process, would be "a fatal seed." They therefore proposed to ship them to Africa or the British colonies.[53] Concerned with "the excessive number" of *emancipados*, the town council of Havana issued a similar proposal a year later. Havana authorities feared that the *emancipados* would contribute to British abolitionism by explaining to slaves, many of whom had surely been imported illegally, that they had been freed under international law. They successfully requested royal support to "reinstate them to their homelands and households" so that they "would not remain in the island." The king eventually ordered that *emancipados* be transported to Spain, Sierra Leone, or the British colonies in the Caribbean. Out of about 11,000 slaves liberated by the mixed commission of Havana between 1824 and 1841, about 3,000 were relocated to the British colonies of Trinidad, Bahamas, British Honduras, Grenada, and Jamaica. Some found their way back to Africa, but their numbers were limited. The bulk of the liberated slaves, which by the 1860s exceeded 25,000, stayed in Cuba.[54]

Faced with the very limited success of efforts to remove free people of color, slaveholders concentrated their efforts on attracting white settlers. Thus, in Cuba colonization came to be associated mostly with plans for white settlement rather than the removal of the free black population.[55] Although Cuban slaveholders and white intellectuals had the same racial fears as their social equals in Virginia and Louisiana, their approach to colonization, particularly as it applied to free blacks, points to some of the fundamental differences that characterized these slave societies by the mid-nineteenth century. Concerns over *emancipados* illustrated the Cubans' belief that Africans should come to the colony only as slaves, a belief they shared with slaveholders in Virginia and Louisiana. Furthermore, in the debates over *emancipados* and their problematic insertion into Cuban society, the size of the community of free people of color was sometimes mentioned. Yet even colonial officials who complained about the "excessive" number of free blacks in Cuba had to acknowledge "the fact that most of them [free blacks] owe their freedom to the honesty that they have displayed and to their savings," that is, to practices (saving) and perceptions (honesty) that were deeply ingrained in local law and custom.[56] Racial fears notwithstanding, slaveholders in Cuba operated in a legal culture in which the possibility of black freedom was widely accepted. Indeed, nowhere were differences among these mature slave societies clearer than in the legal and political treatment of manumission.[57]

MANUMISSION AND FREEDOM

By the 1830s, communities of free people of color were large enough in Cuba, Virginia, and Louisiana to complicate each jurisdiction's rigid associations between race and legal status. It was simply no longer possible to assume that every black man or woman was a slave, as it had been in a place like Virginia before the revolutionary era. Even though the courts repeatedly asserted the presumption that, as a Virginia judge stated in 1806, "a person visibly appearing to be a negro ... is, in this country ... a slave," the existence of free people of color complicated such

15. *View of the Main Promenade of Havana.* This detail of a color aquatint by Hippolyte Garnery, ca. 1830, shows both enslaved, chained workers and street vendors who may have been free. The Miriam and Ira D. Wallach Division of Art, Prints and Photographs, Print Collection, New York Public Library.

presumptions.[58] They blurred the line between freedom and slavery and destabilized the association between freedom and whiteness. Many fugitive slaves found refuge in the cities, where they could hide among free people of color and even among slaves, who lived under regimes of labor and mobility very different from those on the plantations. In Virginia, many fugitives found sanctuary in Norfolk and Richmond, where slaves often hired themselves out, thus enjoying what a Virginia judge grudgingly described as "a modified quasi state of freedom." New Orleans also attracted large numbers of fugitive slaves: 8,500 of them were recaptured there by the police just in the 1850s. Runaway slaves were common in Havana as well. Between 1829 and 1833 the Deposit of Runaway Slaves, a detention center where they were held until claimed by their owners, registered more than 11,000 *cimarrones*, most of whom had been recaptured in the city or its vicinity.[59]

Free black communities were key to the expansion of black freedom. They provided not only sanctuary to runaway slaves but also resources to help free their relatives and loved ones from bondage. Self-purchases were rarely an individual affair. Between 10 and 20 percent of all manumissions in Virginia and New Orleans were paid for by relatives. Likewise, a study of manumissions in the rural hinterland of Havana during the period from 1800 to 1881 found that 20 percent of all manumissions were paid for by relatives. Moreover, free black slave owners were responsible for manumissions at much higher rates than their percentage in the total population. In the city of Petersburg, Virginia, free blacks were responsible for one-third of all manumissions between 1806 and 1860. In New Orleans, the likelihood that a slave owned by a free black person would obtain manumission was more than three times greater than it was for slaves who were owned by whites.[60] Something similar was true in Havana, where, in addition to individual black slaveholders who manumitted their slaves, the Afro-Cuban cabildos raised funds to facilitate the manumission of some of their members and affiliates.[61] In this very concrete sense, at least, the size of the free community was crucial, because it provided key cultural and financial resources for those seeking to escape from slavery.

These communities were large enough to sustain themselves through natural growth, even without further manumissions and in the face of growing white hostility. Contributing to this growth was the fact that manumission rates were higher for women, which of course meant that their progeny would be free as well.[62] Virginia had the smallest community in relative terms; the proportion of free people of color never reached 5 percent of the total population during the nineteenth century (see table 2). New Orleans and Havana were home to much larger communities. At various points during the century, one out of four or five residents of those cities was a free person of color. However, although people of color remained a small percentage of its total population, Virginia was the only jurisdiction where the *absolute* number of free people of color grew steadily between 1810 and 1860. This suggests

TABLE 2. *Free Population of Color as Percent of Total Population, 1770–1860*

	Virginia / Northampton County (%)	Louisiana / New Orleans (%)	Cuba / Havana (%)
1770	0.6/	/ 3.1	/14
1780			17.1/20.3
1790	1.8/12.5		19.9/19.1
1800	2.5/ 9.7	/13.6	
1810	3.4/12	9.9/23.3	
1820	3.9/13.2	6.8/17.4	16.6/25.4
1830	4.5/15	8.0/23.9	
1840	4.8/ 9.8	7.2/18.8	15.2/26.0
1850	4.8/ 9.9	3.4/ 8.3	16.6/17.3
1860	4.7/12.3	5.4/ 6.3	16.2/17.4

Sources: Historical Statistics of the United States: Millennial Edition Online, https://hsus .cambridge.org/HSUSWeb/index.do. Virginia figures based on estimates in Herbert S. Klein, *Slavery in the Americas: A Comparative Study of Virginia and Cuba* (1967; Chicago: Elephant Paperbacks, 1989), 235, and the U.S. Census Bureau, *Historical Statistics of the United States, Colonial Times to 1970*, bicentennial ed., Part 2 (Washington, DC: U.S. Department of Commerce, Bureau of the Census, 1975), 1168. For Louisiana and New Orleans 1780–1810, see Charles Gayarré, *History of Louisiana: The French Domination*, 4 vols. (New Orleans: Armand Hawkins, 1867), 3:170–171, 215 (for 1785 [reported under 1780] and 1788 [reported under 1790] in Louisiana); Kimberly Hanger, *Bounded Lives, Bounded Places: Free Black Society in Colonial New Orleans, 1769–1803* (Durham, NC: Duke University Press, 1997), 18 (for New Orleans, 1788); Paul F. Lachance, "The 1809 Immigration of Saint-Domingue Refugees," *Louisiana History: Journal of the Louisiana Historical Association* 29, no. 2 (1988): 112 (for New Orleans, 1806 [reported under 1800] and 1810). For Cuba and Havana: see Cuba, Comité Estatal de Estadísticas, *Los censos de población y vivienda en Cuba* (Havana: Instituto de Investigaciones Estadísticas, 1988).

that, despite attempts to ban free blacks through colonization or residency requirements, enslaved people continued to achieve freedom through manumission or self-purchase, and continued to remain in the state as free people, through a variety of legal, personal, and family strategies. They were most successful in the first two decades of the nineteenth century, during which the free population of color grew by 78 percent. The community grew only 35 percent larger between 1820 and 1840, and it increased by 16 percent from 1840 to 1860.

Communities of color in New Orleans and Havana showed similar growth patterns to that in Virginia. The free population of color in New Orleans and Havana grew fastest in the 1800–1820 period (it tripled in New Orleans and doubled in Havana), followed by significant but smaller growth in 1820–1840 (a 166 percent increase in New Orleans; 68 percent in Havana). The 1840s were an inflection point. The free population of color of Havana remained basically stationary between 1840 and 1860, at about 35,000 people. That of New Orleans contracted dramatically, as the number of free people of color living in the city declined by almost half during the same period. Their proportion of the total population was only 6 percent by 1860, compared with 17 percent in Havana. But even in Havana, where the population held steady, the lack of growth in the free population of color after the 1840s reflected growing hostility. The repression unleashed in the wake of La Escalera resulted in the imprisonment and exile of hundreds of free blacks and mulattoes, as well as in the deportations of free black foreigners.[63] These events obviously took a toll on the Havana community, even though manumission was not restricted there as it was in Virginia and Louisiana.

The free communities of Havana and New Orleans existed in very different social and racial contexts, however. New Orleans was an oasis of black freedom in a sea of rural plantation slavery in which almost every person of African descent was enslaved. Excluding New Orleans, free blacks and mulattoes represented only 2.5 percent of the total population of the state in 1840, 1.4 percent by 1860. Outside New Orleans, to be black in Louisiana was to be enslaved. To put it differently, most free individuals of color in the state lived in New Orleans: 75 percent of the total, in 1840. In the same period, the free people of color living in Havana represented a much lower percentage (23 percent) of the total free population of color in Cuba. By 1861, the proportions of free people of color in the Havana population (17 percent) and across Cuba (16 percent) were almost identical. Furthermore, whereas the slave population of Cuba as a whole declined by 15 percent between 1840 and the 1860s, that of Louisiana experienced an astonishing 97 percent growth.

By 1860, on the eve of the U.S. Civil War, Virginia and Louisiana were part of a region, the U.S. South, that had committed itself, economically and politically, to slavery and to an ideological defense of slavery that linked slavery to white supremacy and to the elimination of free people of color as a class. Cuba, although equally committed to slavery and racism, had not been able to advance as far toward making the connection between them. In 1860, Louisiana was a flourishing, fast-growing slave society in which being black was almost coterminous with being a slave. Ninety-five percent of all blacks in the state were enslaved, although the proportion was much lower in New Orleans (57 percent). The association was less extreme in Virginia, but there, too, free blacks remained a small minority – by 1860, 89 percent of all blacks living in the state were enslaved. The link between slavery and blackness was further solidified in both places in the 1850s, when even the possibility of manumission came under attack in Virginia and Louisiana. In Cuba, by contrast, slaves represented a minority (45 percent) of all blacks in Havana and a small majority (62 percent) on the island as a whole by 1860. There, blackness was not a proxy for enslavement the way it was in Virginia and most of Louisiana. The contrasts between these communities grew stronger as Virginians and Louisianans of color faced increasingly restrictive and oppressive legal regimes.

VIRGINIA. In Virginia, it was still possible for enslaved people to become free through manumission by will or deed, and through freedom suits. However, the rule that freed people had to leave the state within one year introduced powerful uncertainty into the lives of Virginians of color. Although many stayed in the state, their situation became increasingly precarious, and they depended on white patronage for their security. They mustered white support to obtain legal documents that could secure their place in Virginia society and keep them safe when they were out on the roads. They did so by drawing on powerful invocations of the right to liberty and to homeland.

On February 15, 1848, Arthur, a freedman from Chesterfield County, petitioned the General Assembly of Virginia for permission to remain in the state. His arguments were simple and powerful. He mentioned his "love of country, home, wife, children and friends," adding that these feelings were shared by all black people, especially by those who, like him, had been "properly reared by a Kind owner." Blacks' affective bonds were similar to those of whites, he said, and black freedom ought to be comparable, as well, to the freedom experienced by whites. Arthur was actually talking about himself when he asked: "What is liberty to the white man if he, to enjoy it, is to be banished from his home, his wife, … his children, as dear as his own life's blood, his fellows, with whom he has labored day after day for half a century, his friends, who have stuck to him as close as a brother, to be driven into exile."[64]

We do not know whether Arthur was allowed to stay in the state, close to his friends and family. His petition was neither uncommon nor implausible, however, as many such requests were granted. In some cases, the legislature explained why it was allowing a free person of color to remain in Virginia, but in most cases it did not. George Butler, for instance, who was described as "an old man," was allowed to remain "because he is attached to his family, who are slaves, and cannot be taken from the state." Sterling, "who had been left money by his mistress to purchase his freedom before the passage of the act," also won the right to remain. Such explanations were rare, however. Freed blacks could not easily know if they would be allowed to remain in the state.[65]

The law stated that free people of color who remained more than a year in the state after their manumission would be reenslaved, but in fact most freedwomen and men were not resold into slavery. There were few prosecutions of such cases before 1830, and just a few afterward. In Richmond, "one of the most repressive localities," between 1830 and 1860 only 124 people were charged with remaining in the state illegally, and of those, only 12 were convicted. Eighty percent of illegal residency prosecutions were dropped before going to trial, perhaps because many of the defendants left the state or went into hiding rather than face trial. Equally important, 60 percent of Richmond residents' petitions to remain were successful. According to the most extensive study of reenslavement and self-enslavement in the state, "the thousands of illegal free black residents whose names surface in census rolls, tax lists, and court books managed to belong in their neighborhood by living lives according to the laws of the land, in direct violation of Virginia statutes."[66]

The new residency requirements did not halt manumissions or other legal avenues to obtain freedom. Slaveholders continued to free their slaves by will and by deed, and a significant number of slaves sued for freedom and won their suits.[67] Although the 1806 law had closed off illegal importation as a basis for manumission, scattered suits for freedom based on illegal importation were still filed as late as 1852, and plaintiffs continued to win those suits into the 1840s.[68] There were also occasional suits based on Indian ancestry, both in the lower courts and in the Virginia Supreme Court. The great majority of the litigation for freedom in the last decades of the antebellum period involved wills. Of fifty-two freedom suits that reached the state supreme court, thirty-six involved wills (and three, deeds). Plaintiffs were often victorious. Out of a sample of thirty-four cases from six Virginia counties in 1831 to 1861, the plaintiff won in thirteen, lost in five, and the outcome could not be determined from the records in sixteen cases. Likewise, enslaved people who brought suits in chancery courts were frequently successful.[69] Contested wills that reached the state supreme court were handled routinely until the 1850s, when "the Court abandoned its relatively neutral position on the issue of manumission and instead interpreted the legal right to manumit as a threat to the established order of Virginia's slave society."[70]

Slaveholders did not always acknowledge the new residency requirements in their wills. Some made no mention of the enslaved people thereafter leaving the state. In 1831, for instance, John Peyton freed all of his slaves over age forty. One of those was Samuel, who received a certificate of freedom and lived "for several years in the enjoyment of those rights and privileges of free negroes" before one of Peyton's creditors tried to reenslave him. In 1835 in Accomack County, Sally Savage's will freed all her slaves and left them much of her property. Other wills mentioned vaguely the limits of the law, without making specific allowance for it. William Walters's will, in 1839, gave Harriet her freedom "when she arrives at age 28, provided the law will permit her to be FREE." Elizabeth Garrison, in 1835, stated in her will that she wanted "All my Negroes . . . free in the manner the law directs & I give each of them $5 in order for them to obtain their free papers & follow the direction of the law." In 1838, the will of William Henley emancipated all his slaves and left his slave Peggy and her children $300 annually during their lifetime, with no mention of their leaving the state; they litigated for the will's enforcement in 1844.[71]

Many wills, however, attempted to comply with the changed manumission law and the requirement that all freed people had to leave the state. Probably the most common solution was to condition the slaves' freedom on their willingness to leave the state, as required by law, or else they would remain enslaved to the testator's heirs. Revell Twiford Sr., in a will dated March 11, 1828, and probated on January 29, 1838, instructed, "My man Frank, after my death, provided he will leave the state of Virginia, to be emancipated & if he does not prefer to leave I give him to my heirs." Walter D. Bayne freed six of the people he had enslaved, as well as their "future increase," provided "they all leave the state of Virginia at the same time within 12 months of their freedom .... If my Executors think best they shall hire them all out until they raise a sum sufficient all together to send them to Philadelphia, Liberia or any better place, it being understood that they are not to be hired out for this purpose if the Colonization Society of the State of Virginia will furnish the means of sending them away." Mary P. Stran gave all of her slaves to her sister, to be freed at her sister's death, unless "at any time they should be willing to go to a free state, I do hereby set them free."[72]

Other slaveholders tried to keep their former slaves in Virginia. Judge Thomas H. Bayly, who sat as justice of the peace in many of the freedom suits in Accomack County, in his own will of July 7, 1853, freed his two "house servants," but "enjoin[ed] upon them to live with my wife & children & to be as faithful to them when I am dead as they were to them & to me while I was living." He prevailed on the court to allow them to remain in the state, declaring that he had "served the people of Accomac & of the state of Virginia in one public capacity or another for 17 years without pecuniary compensation," and now "ask[ed] for the first time & for the last as a favor to me, as an act of justice & as a matter of public policy ... that those two servants may be permitted to remain in the Commonwealth of Virginia." Others attempted to evade the law by setting up their slaves in a kind of quasi-freedom. For example, in 1863 Sallie Parsons stated in her will that "I desire my negro woman old Fanny to live to herself forthwith. And my negro man James after 3 yrs or payment of $120 and then live to himself." William Bragg of Amelia County, in 1846, provided that "my man Jarret should be free and have the liberty of selecting some of my connections to stand as master or mistress for him and require good care shall be taken of him." These arrangements may have worked in practice for some period of time, but they usually failed if challenged by heirs or creditors.[73]

A number of slaveholders conditioned manumission on slaves' leaving for Liberia. For example, in 1832, in Petersburg City, Mary Parish provided that her slaves "shall have their free choice of liberty on the condition that they agree, within one year from the day of my decease to go to the colony of Liberia in Africa." If any refused to accept those terms, her statement continued, "then it is my will that they be valued by three judicious men and that they have the privilege of choosing their own purchasers at the prices fixed in the said valuation." One enslaved woman who was "willing to accept her freedom on the terms (hard as they may be) prescribed by the will" complained that the will's executors had refused to free her because of unpaid debts. Other slaveholders enlisted the American Colonization Society directly, not always with the desired results. Noah Meund left his slaves to "the agent of the new Colonization Society in Africa to do as he pleases with them," but none of them obtained freedom because of the will's vagueness, whereas the slaves of John Stockdell, who had placed them "in the hands of the American Colonization Society," were freed because they had an affidavit from the ACS saying it was ready to transport them and had the means to pay for it.[74]

Finally, some slaveholders tried to provide for their slaves to go to the North. In *Billy v. Blankenship*, in 1847, the slaveholder left $250 for his freed slaves to go to "one of the non slave holding states and to pay their expenses in going to the same." Craddock Vaughn of Halifax County created a trust to ensure freedom for Eleanor, her six children, and another woman named Dicy. Vaughn stipulated that "if the Laws of the Commonwealth of Virginia will allow them to remain in the state, and receive and enjoy their freedom, that the aforementioned trustees shall see that all legal and proper steps are taken for that purpose." If the trustees failed "to procure an act of the general assembly for that purpose," however, the emancipated slaves should be removed to "a free state and locale." In fact, they relocated to Ohio, and the trustees purchased land for them there.[75]

Remaining legally in the state became harder after Nat Turner's rebellion, when white fears skyrocketed. In 1831, a new act stipulated that those who remained in the Commonwealth "contrary to law" were to be "sold publicly," while the state constitution of 1851 reiterated that slaves emancipated after that date would "forfeit their freedom by remaining in the Commonwealth more than twelve months." These laws were never enforced systematically, but they could be invoked punitively. For example, immediately after the Nat Turner rebellion the Accomack Superior Court charged forty-two free people of color with remaining in state illegally. Two received formal permission to stay – the rest apparently stayed on illegally, despite the prosecution. Eleven were eventually acquitted in jury trials, but twelve others were convicted and sold at auction.[76]

The legislature rarely gave a reason for rejecting a petition to stay in Virginia but simply stated that freed individuals were to leave the state, as required by law. In 1819, the will of Izar Bacon, a slaveholder from Henrico County, freed all of his slaves. The assembly acknowledged that "the dictates of justice and humanity require the right of freedom of the said slaves should be confirmed," but asked the chancellor of the Superior Court of Chancery of Richmond to ensure "that none remain within the Commonwealth more than twelve months." Philip Vass manumitted six slaves in his 1831 will. After years of litigation concerning the estate, the slaves secured their freedom in 1841. With the endorsement and support of white patrons, they petitioned the assembly to remain in the state, as each of them had close relatives there. One of the petitioners, thirty-three-year-old Jacob, had a wife and three children who were very "endeared to him by the most tender ties of affection," while the others had "many near relations" or a "tender and kind" husband. Their petition was nevertheless rejected. One of these slaves, Patsey Daniel, submitted a new petition for residence a year later, arguing that she was married to a free black shoemaker, Terry Daniel, a legal resident of Halifax County, and had several adult children living in the area. Even though Daniel secured a letter of endorsement signed by fourteen white residents, her request was denied again. A similar fate awaited the slaves of Reuben Howard, of Hanover. Howard manumitted all of his slaves by will and also left them land and other properties for their sustenance. The assembly agreed that the slaves should be manumitted, but ordered that the land be sold "for the use of the emancipated persons and to pay their removal expenses out of the Commonwealth."[77]

It is difficult to know how many of these freedmen and women remained in the state, although as the example of Patsey Daniel shows, many of them did, even after their petitions were denied. Leaving the state was more easily said than done. In addition to the pain of breaking family and social relations, relocating to another state was expensive, and many neighboring states had laws against the immigration of free blacks. Vass, for example, had made provisions to buy tracts of land for his emancipated slaves in North Carolina, but that state also rejected their petition for residence.[78]

In desperation, some freedmen and women chose "voluntary" reen-slavement under an act passed in 1857. Sarah Bell, a seventy-year-old slave, arranged to be purchased for one dollar in an attempt to avoid deportation. In 1856, Simon, his wife, Martha, and their daughters Judy and Margaret, of Southampton County, requested to be reenslaved, obviously so the family could remain together in the state. Free blacks purchased their own relatives and loved ones, to make sure that they could remain within the state. However, even this possibility became increasingly restricted, as acts of 1832 and 1858 regulated free blacks' ownership of slaves. The 1832 act allowed ownership only of close family members such as a husband, wife, or children. However small, this loop-hole was closed in 1858, when the acquisition of new slaves by free blacks was eliminated: "No free Negro shall be capable of acquiring, except by descent, any slave." The increasingly rigid and draconian racial order of the mid-nineteenth century rested on the notion that all blacks were supposed to be enslaved. Black ownership of slaves, previously common, had come to represent a blatant violation of such order and was conse-quently banned. It was another turn in the relentless process of legal black debasement, a logical step toward a tighter racial regime. The number of black slaveholders consequently declined dramatically between 1830 and 1860.[79]

For many emancipated slaves, then, the only option was to stay illegally in the state, a decision that frequently depended on the complicity of local whites. It has been estimated that between 20 and 30 percent of free blacks in Virginia resided in the state illegally by 1860. Theirs was an uncertain freedom, as they risked reenslavement and were at the mercy of local authorities and white patrons. Even those who obtained permis-sion to stay did so under precarious conditions, as they were warned that the courts could revoke permits "when they shall think fit," were forced to post bonds for good conduct, or knew they could lose residence rights in case of any offense. Ongoing residence thus entrenched subordination and social control, as many nominally free blacks were in relations of abject dependency on whites. As acknowledged by Governor William "Extra Billy" Smith, who in 1846 "made free black removal a legislative priority," although the law was unlikely to be enforced, it would send a message that would "'materially aid us in the management of this unhappy race' by making them fearful and obedient."[80]

Free people of color carried papers – certificates of freedom and certificates of good character – to avoid kidnapping, harassment, and prosecution. Although large numbers of free people of color never registered with local authorities and stayed on in Virginia illegally, someone without papers took grave risks. Local court records are filled with requests for duplicate papers from free people of color who had lost theirs, as well as writs of habeas corpus from people who claimed wrongful enslavement based on lost papers.[81]

These draconian limitations on black freedom cast a shadow of uncertainty. They also had a chilling effect on manumissions over time. Brunswick County registered 222 slave manumissions between 1782 and 1809, compared with only 34 between 1810 and 1860. After 1840, manumissions virtually ceased. In Sussex County, only 5 manumissions took place after 1830, compared with 60 earlier, between 1782 and 1800. Comparable figures in Powhatan County were 8 and 30, respectively. "The odds that a slave might attain his freedom through manumission dropped from about one in ten in the 1790s to about two in one hundred in the 1850s," according to economist Howard Bodenhorn. It also appears that manumission became increasingly regionalized, persisting in the cities and nose-diving in rural areas. By 1860 Virginia's cities, all of which were rather small compared with New Orleans and Havana, boasted large free populations of color in relative terms. Petersburg had the largest proportion of free blacks (18 percent), followed by Alexandria (11 percent), and Norfolk (7 percent). In the largest city, Richmond, free blacks represented 6.8 percent of the total population, which was still higher than in the state as a whole (4.7 percent).[82]

By the 1850s, Virginians had concluded that free people of color were, as College of William and Mary president Thomas Dew put it, the "pests of society." The Virginia constitution of 1851 was unambiguously opposed to black freedom, ratifying the 1806 and 1831 regulations requiring free people of color to leave the commonwealth. But the constitution went further. On the one hand, it gave authority to the members of the General Assembly to "impose such restrictions and conditions as they shall deem proper on the power of slave owners to emancipate their slaves." On the other, it placed strict limits on the assembly's power to approve manumissions: "The General Assembly shall not emancipate any slave, or the descendant of any slave, either before or after the birth of such descendant." By 1860, Virginia leaders had acted to ensure that free people of color represented, as a white resident stated in 1854, "an absurdity."[83]

LOUISIANA. One could not argue that free people of color represented an absurdity in New Orleans. Some of the wealthiest free blacks in the entire South, including black slave owners, lived in New Orleans. At least until the 1840s, free black people had access to numerous skilled occupations in the city and dominated some of them. Most of them lived in the "virtually autonomous creole municipal districts," where "free and slave black creoles continued to gather for festivities, frequent bars and dance halls, and cohabit despite the state laws." Most white Americans, who "abhorred many of the colonial racial practices" identified with the local free population of color, lived in the American sector of the city. Unlike the other municipalities, which registered official documents in French, those in the American sector were kept in English, offering a graphic example of how different legal and administrative traditions coexisted in New Orleans. The city continued to attract large numbers of free blacks from other jurisdictions. They settled there to take advantage of better economic and social opportunities. The creole municipalities were safe havens because they did not enforce laws against unregistered or out-of-state blacks.[84]

As in Virginia, however, the legal standing of free people of color in Louisiana deteriorated dramatically during the 1850s. An 1852 act required all persons emancipating slaves to pay for their passage to Liberia, and all manumissions were banned in 1857. Like Virginia, Louisiana passed a reenslavement law in 1859, and the *Daily Picayune* "delighted in printing reports of slaves preferring bondage to freedom."

The relative numbers of free people of color in New Orleans collapsed during the 1850s. By then, toleration for manumission, for newly emancipated blacks, and for black visitors to the city was quickly dwindling. Sectional tensions, the threat of Northern abolitionism, and the influx of poor white immigrants from Ireland and Germany all helped to erode the standing of the free black community. The new immigrants fought to displace black workers from their traditional occupations and economic activities. An increasingly restrictive legal regime, parallel in many ways to that of Virginia, crippled the standing and growth of the largest community of free people of color in the United States, which was reduced to a shadow of its former self by 1860. Free people of color, many of them with means, migrated from the city in the 1850s. Some went to France; others went to Haiti. The last years of slavery in Louisiana also saw night-riding vigilantes in the countryside beating and terrorizing free people of color, causing them to flee the state.[85]

The Louisiana legislature began to take steps to limit the numbers of free people of color in 1830, but enforcement remained lax well into the 1850s. An 1830 act required slaveholders who manumitted a slave to post a $1,000 bond to guarantee that the freed person would "permanently depart from the state within one month." This requirement was lifted if the slaveholder secured permission from the police jury or the council of the municipality. The state thereafter experimented with different ways to regulate and control the stream of petitions from both slaveholders and enslaved people for manumission, or for freed people to remain in the state. Between 1831 and 1846, parish police juries granted or denied such petitions. The Orleans Parish Police Jury did not require a single freed slave to leave in those years. A sample of manumission cases in the New Orleans "emancipation courts" between 1846 and 1851 also found that no one was required to leave the state.[86] Slaveholders and enslaved people continued to petition the legislature for individual acts of manumission and for the right to remain in the state, especially after the 1852 law requiring the removal of freed slaves to Liberia. Fed up with the constant petitions, the legislature passed a law in 1855 turning over all questions of manumission to the district courts. This resulted in a torrent of 159 suits to free 289 slaves, all registered in a sixteen-month period. Juries deciding these cases often freed enslaved people so rapidly and routinely that they did not get up from their seats to go to the jury room. They simply found for the plaintiff and went on to the next case. It was in reaction to the resulting flood of newly free people of color that the legislature finally prohibited all manumissions in 1857: "That from and after the passage of this act no slave shall be emancipated in this state."[87]

The courts of Louisiana clamped down on traditional manumission practices during the 1850s. In the mid-1850s, for example, contracts for slaves' self-purchase were declared no longer enforceable in the New Orleans district court unless slaves could provide written evidence.[88] In free-soil cases heard before 1850, the Louisiana Supreme Court routinely freed enslaved people who had traveled to France or a free state, but after the U.S. Supreme Court's opinion in *Strader v. Graham* (1851), the Louisiana courts finally "f[e]ll in line with national precedents" and began to find for the slaveholder in such cases.[89] The Louisiana Supreme Court treated enslaved plaintiffs more skeptically, increasingly finding against the plaintiff on the ground that her value as a slave amounted to more than 10 percent of the estate, too large a percentage to be "donated" in manumission.[90]

Although slaves and freed people faced an increasingly hostile environment, they continued to press claims for freedom. Enslaved plaintiffs took several cases all the way to the Louisiana Supreme Court, where they raised arguments expanding on the alleged right to purchase one's freedom. For example, Azela Gaudet argued in 1848 that she should be free because her mother, Clarisse, had purchased her freedom when she was pregnant with her. The jury at trial had found for her owner, but the Louisiana Supreme Court reversed in Azela's favor. Similarly, during years of litigation, Eulalie argued for her freedom on the basis of her many years living as a free woman. The Louisiana Supreme Court ratified a jury verdict in favor of her and her family, based on the novel principle of prescription, by which any claim to ownership over her had expired owing to the passage of time. One effort to expand the right of self-purchase, however, did not succeed. François, a skilled hatter, sued his master for freedom based on a self-purchase contract for $300. On appeal to the Supreme Court, his lawyer raised the argument that François had purchased five-eighths of himself through his partial payments, and therefore should have been entitled to five-eighths of his monthly wages. This argument, controversial but sometimes successful in Cuba, was soundly rejected by the Louisiana Supreme Court: "A slave cannot become partially free, nor can he, until legally and absolutely emancipated, own any property, without the consent of his master."[91]

Freed persons faced growing pressure to abandon the city and the state, especially after the 1852 law requiring the removal of manumitted slaves to Liberia. Ben, his wife, Clarissa, and their three children, Edward, Susan, and Mary, were emancipated by will for "meritorious services" to their deceased master, Samuel Estelle, in 1852. The state legislature approved, but only on condition that they abandon the state in compliance with the 1852 law, "never again to return"; otherwise the emancipation would be "null, and the slave or slaves not strictly complying with this act, shall become a slave again." The same condition applied to Nanny, a slave also emancipated by will, "for faithful and meritorious services rendered by her during the long and painful illness of her deceased master." Some freed people of color obviously had no choice but to leave, as "six liberated slaves" of Eliza Barker of New Orleans did in 1848. The group went to New Bedford, Massachusetts, "to be settled upon a farm." Following in the steps of the Virginia legislature, in 1859 the General Assembly of Louisiana passed a law that made it "lawful for any free person of African descent, over the age of twenty-one years ... to select his or her master, or owner, and to become a slave for life."[92]

As in Virginia, many free people of color nevertheless remained in the city illegally and "refused to take out their papers," or did not register with authorities. But there is little doubt that the legal and social spaces available to them were rapidly shrinking. Racial repression became overwhelming after 1852, when the traditionally autonomous municipalities of New Orleans were consolidated and many of their enforcement functions transferred to state authorities. The number of free people of color who sought to register to remain in the city multiplied during the 1850s, particularly during the second half of the decade. No registrations were recorded in 1852 and 1853, followed by 11 in 1854, 43 in 1855, and 238 in 1856. By 1859 the number had jumped to 420. The number of police arrests for free-black residency violations jumped from fewer than 10 per month in the early 1850s, to almost 100 per month by 1859.[93]

Residency requirements rendered black freedom as vulnerable and precarious in Louisiana as in Virginia. That is why some black slaveholders who purchased their own family members sought to obtain legal permission for their relatives to stay in case something happened to them. This was the case for Marie Louise Bitaud, who in 1832 petitioned the police jury of the city of New Orleans to confirm the manumission of her daughter Françoise and her grandson Gustave, both of whom she had purchased. By then the act of 1830, as mentioned, required slaveholders manumitting a slave to post a bond. Bitaud had been "very much alarmed" to learn from a lawyer that "in case of death without a last will, her daughter and her children should belong to the State of Louisiana and should continue to be slaves for life." She presented a certificate, signed by several freeholders, that her daughter was "of good morals and character and may easily maintain herself." The jury confirmed the liberation of Françoise and Gustave, but imposed a $500 bond to allow them to remain in the state.[94]

As Bitaud's case illustrates, slaves and free people of color tenaciously insisted on sorting out the growing legal obstacles placed on the paths to their own freedom, that of their loved ones, and to their right to a homeland. In 1853, a correspondent of the *New York Times* reported from New Orleans that there were "a number of cases, now in our courts, where negroes are suing for their freedom, they having been once emancipated," likely because they had not fulfilled the draconian conditions imposed by the 1852 act. As late as 1858, after manumissions had been outlawed in the state, an unnamed "colored woman" claimed to have been freed under an "arrangement made previous to the recent law prohibiting emancipation." A year later, three recently freed slaves from New Orleans, Anthony Gustave, Lucy, and her infant child, sought to have their "manumission papers recorded in the Probate Court" of Cincinnati, Ohio. By doing this, they hoped to be recognized as "citizens of Ohio" and to "henceforth endeavor to do here what the Republican State of Louisiana prohibits their class from doing." On the eve of the Civil War, after several decades of Americanization of the state's legal system and mores, and in the midst of the state's fast-growing slave population, Louisiana had reached a position concerning manumissions that was identical to that of Virginia – and indeed, the rest of the slave South. The local *De Bow's Review* summarized the underlying assumption neatly: "Free negroism and slavery are incompatible with each other."[95]

CUBA. Cuban slaveholders followed events in the United States closely. Like slaveholders in Louisiana and Virginia, they despised abolitionists. They witnessed with apprehension how emancipation expanded in the rest of the Caribbean, first in the British colonies, then in the Danish and French islands. In the 1840s and 1850s, as slavery appeared to be under siege everywhere, Cuban slaveholders looked to the U.S. South as their last hope for survival. Annexation became a popular political option.[96]

Cuban slaveholders took note of the growing limitations placed on manumission in the U.S. South. In an 1826 report to Madrid, the Havana town council noted approvingly how difficult it was for slaves to obtain freedom in the British colonies and the United States: "In the English colonies they give freedom to a slave only for very specific reasons and under exquisite precautions. In the United States, it is absolutely prohibited for any master to give freedom to his slaves, because they believe that freedmen awaken fatal ideas and desires among those who are not. In light of this, is it just, reasonable and political for Spain to work on its own perdition?"[97]

Although Cuban authorities clearly sympathized with the restrictive manumission regimes of the U.S. South, they stopped short of insinuating that manumission policies should change. Slaveholders on the island grumbled about slaves' legal initiatives and demands for freedom and sought to circumvent those initiatives to the extent possible. But a systematic legal assault on manumission, similar to those orchestrated in Virginia and Louisiana, did not take place.[98] As the Consejo de Administración, the highest consulting body in the colonial government, candidly acknowledged in 1862, it was not "prudent" to attack "rights or concessions sanctioned by law" that affected a large segment of society, especially as the island was living through "difficult circumstances," part of "an evidently transitional period."[99]

What the Consejo de Administración described as "rights or concessions" referred not only to standard manumission practices, by which slaveholders agreed to grant freedom to their slaves, but also to the set of practices and

16. A legal demand presented on behalf of the enslaved driver Agustin, who requested *coartación* for 400 pesos. "The black Agustin versus the Sub-Lieutenant D. Federico Cordova about *coartación*," 1841. Archivo Nacional de Cuba, Escribanías (Guerra), leg. 246, no. 4035.

"rights" associated with *coartación*, discussed in Chapter 3. Through these practices slaves could obtain their freedom, even against the will of their masters, and for prices and under conditions that were not set or fully agreed to by them. In other words, these were true rights that, at least under some circumstances, slaves managed to enforce, limiting in the process the dominium of the owners in fairly concrete terms. Cuba's slaveholders abhorred such rights, which they perceived as an assault on their own power, and petitioned constantly to eliminate them. That is, precisely, what prompted the Consejo's recommendation.[100]

By 1862 it was too late, however. Until the 1840s, *coartación* and its effects were linked to a set of practices, vernacular understandings, and contested legal interpretations that various actors – slaves, *síndicos*, masters, jurists, judges, and government officials – invoked as they litigated these cases. This changed, however, when Captain General Gerónimo Valdés approved a new slave ordinance, the Reglamento de Esclavos, in 1842. Produced in large measure in response to British abolitionism and the slave rebellions of the 1820s to 1840s, this code had several purposes. It sought to harmonize previous regulations concerning the management of slaves and to prevent new revolts by placing limits on the abusive practices of the owners. The Reglamento also reaffirmed the centrality of the colonial government as the main guarantor of colonial slavery and the arbiter and mediator of growing social tensions. Valdés claimed to represent the colony's "true interests," which of course did not perfectly align with the slaveholders' demands for total autonomy when it came to managing their farms and their slaves. Slaveholders condemned the new code as a dangerous attack on their power.[101]

Contributing to that perception was the Reglamento's approach to *coartación* and *papel*. Article 34 defined *coartación* as a true slave right, stating that owners "may not refuse" the *coartación* of any slave who offered at least fifty pesos toward his or her price. The *coartación* price, the next article asserted, could not be altered, although "if the slave wished to be sold against the will of his master and without just cause," the master could add the sales tax to the price. Article 34 built on precedents such as the regulation issued by the Consejo de Indias in 1778, according to which slaveholders could not refuse manumission payments. Article 35 broke new legal ground. It appeared to acknowledge that a *coartado* slave could in fact be sold "against the will of his master," a right for which there was no precedent in the codes of Castile or in colonial legislation. This new right owed its existence to slaves' own legal initiatives over time.

Although slaveholders sought to repeal the Reglamento and also litigated against the rights associated with articles 34 and 35, they had to contend with a new regulation that placed slaves' demands for freedom and *papel* on a more solid footing. It was now possible to argue, as several jurists and

17. Luisa Vasquez requests a new master. "The *morena* [black] Luisa Vasquez, slave of Don Leon Vasquez, declares that about a month ago she was sold to her master ... for the amount of 650 pesos, and because it is not convenient for her to continue in that house, she requested *papel* from her master, who appraised her at 900 pesos." Vasquez requested a lower price in order to seek a new master. "Case in which the black Luisa Vasquez pretends to change master," 1854. Archivo Nacional de Cuba, Gobierno Superior Civil, leg. 949, no. 33545.

síndicos did in the 1850s, that changing masters was "a right of the *coartado* slave, established by the law and sanctioned by an old custom." One *síndico* offered a typical argument on behalf of the slave José Casanova in 1846, stating that "according to article 35 ... *coartados* can change masters at will."[102]

Slaves made use of these new legal rights to challenge the power of their masters, to escape abusive owners, to avoid being sent to the countryside, and to oppose masters' decisions that were not favorable to them. For instance, in 1852 Filomeno Lula, a *coartado* cigar maker, requested *papel* to prevent his master from sending him to the countryside. Paulino, a slave described as *criollo*, complained that his master was sending him to work at a sugar mill "as if he was a complete [*entero*] slave," even though he had been *coartado* at 250 pesos. The free black man Felipe Herrera deposited 150 pesos with the *síndico* of Havana in 1864 to initiate his *coartación* and secure the transfer of his children and their mother, Clara Diago, back to Havana from *el campo* – the countryside. And when in 1859 sugar mill owner Máximo Arozarena tried to transfer nineteen slaves from a cattle farm to the Mercedes sugar mill, the slaves walked to town and presented themselves to a *síndico* in Havana to request their *coartación*. Through this action, they could proceed to find a new owner and a more congenial labor regime. That is why Arozarena described *coartación* as "the most terrible and destructive weapon against territorial property."[103] The practice appears to have been fairly common in Havana even before the approval of the Reglamento. Visitors to Cuba reported that slaves approached them with the question, "Would you like to buy me?" The enslaved poet Juan Francisco Manzano mentions the practice in his 1840 autobiography, and so does Cirilo Villaverde, in *Cecilia Valdés* (1839).[104]

It is difficult to know how many slaves took advantage of *coartación* to gain a modicum of control over their lives or to escape slavery altogether. Laird Bergad and his colleagues found that in a random sample of notarized Cuban slave sales between 1790 and 1880, 13 percent of those sold were *coartados*; generally, however, only a fraction of *coartados* ever completed the payments toward manumission.[105] For slaveholders, the question was not how many slaves managed to obtain freedom through these legal procedures – although they complained about those numbers. Their main concern was that whatever slaves obtained through *coartación*, it was without, or even against, the will of their masters. "I heard frequent complaints from slave-holders and those who sympathized with them, as to the operation of these provisions," abolitionist Richard Henry Dana reported during his visit to Havana in

1859.[106] It is possible that slaveholders managed to at least slow down manumissions, which would explain why the free population of color of Havana did not grow between 1840 and 1860. It is certain, in turn, that *coartación* did not become a path to general slave emancipation in Cuba.[107] In the hands of assertive and restive slaves, however, the institution challenged the "stern and unrelaxing discipline" on which slavery was supposed to rest. Cuban lawyer José Ignacio Rodríguez concluded as much in 1856: "The *coartado* slave is not as enslaved as the *entero*."[108] As lawyer and *síndico* Antonio Bachiller y Morales asserted in 1859, slavery "was not compatible with the rights of the *coartado* slaves."[109]

***

In contrast to Louisiana and Virginia, Cuba's legal regime for manumission did not grow increasingly restrictive, and there is evidence that manumissions continued to be relatively common in the mid-nineteenth century, even in rural areas.[110] But free people of color came under attack in Cuba as well as in Virginia and Louisiana, even though no systematic efforts were undertaken in Havana to expel the free black population. In Cuba, colonization was about removing *emancipados* – freed slaves captured by English patrols – and attracting white settlers to the island; it was not about the removal of all free blacks. As Governor Vives candidly acknowledged, by the nineteenth century it was impossible to correct the centuries-old "mistake of not placing obstacles to freedom." Nor did Cubans defend slavery as a "positive good," as apologists did in the U.S. South.[111]

Large-scale slave revolts, the rise of abolitionism as a major political force, and the central role of free people of color led to crackdowns against free people of color everywhere. Slaveholders sought to remove free black people from their midst, to limit their ability to come into contact with enslaved people, to prevent the distribution of abolitionist literature, and, as we shall see in Chapter 5, even to prohibit slaves from learning to read, in case they got ahold of such dangerous materials.

But by 1860 these jurisdictions were on truly divergent paths concerning slavery, race, and freedom. Although embattled, the community of free people of color in Havana was three times as large as that in New Orleans, four times as large as in Virginia. Black freedom, described as an anomaly or a legal absurdity in Virginia and Louisiana, remained normal in Cuba. On the eve of the Civil War, being black was nearly synonymous with being enslaved in most areas of Louisiana and Virginia. The same could not be said about Cuba generally or Havana. Yet the opposite – that blackness was coterminous with freedom – was certainly not true either. These tense associations remained works in progress and were constantly contested and policed.

CHAPTER 5

"Not of the Same Blood"

Policing Racial Boundaries, 1830–1860

A S SLAVEHOLDING ELITES IN CUBA, LOUISIANA, AND Virginia drew ever sharper lines between slave and free, they also reinforced the line between black and white. The more anomalous, troublesome, and threatening free people of color seemed to be, the more urgent the policing the color line became. Ideologues proclaimed the inferiority and civic incapacity of black people. By the mid-nineteenth century, racist scientists even suggested that people of African origin might belong to a different species, or that they had degenerated to such a degree that they were biologically different and hopelessly handicapped.

The research of such eminent biologists and phrenologists as Samuel Morton in Philadelphia and Louis Agassiz of Harvard University sought to ground black inferiority in physiology and biology. Southern doctors dissected black bodies, searching for signs of inferiority, which they claimed to find in every possible organ, from limbs to lungs. Cranial measurements added weight to the widespread belief that, as Agassiz noted, "they are not of the same blood of us." These measurements, Josiah Nott emphasized in his New Orleans lectures in 1848, established "the fact" that blacks and other "dark skinned races" had smaller heads, a "deficiency . . . especially well marked in those parts of the brain which have been assigned to the moral and intellectual faculties." Combined with other shortcomings, such as the "physiological fact that negroes consume less oxygen," these attributes were said to lead to dullness and a "hebetude of mind and body" that could be managed only under direct white supervision. Slavery, said a New Orleans doctor, was "a system of ethics" and "a rule of action in the Southern states." Under it, enslaved black people could enjoy "the comforts and pleasures of life." As an article in *De Bow's Review* argued in 1859, "the negro race" would reach civilization not "through a process of freedom" but rather "through long periods of servitude." This argument resembled that of the Catholic priest Juan Bernardo O'Gavan in Cuba: "In the end, those men, who in Africa would have been indomitable savages, learn and practice among us the religious maxims of peace, love and kindness." Or, as University of Virginia professor Albert Taylor Bledsoe stated in his *Essay on Liberty and Slavery*, "No fact is plainer than that the blacks have been elevated and improved by their servitude in this country."[1]

Such theories circulated freely across the Atlantic but were particularly popular in the American South. In response to Northern abolitionists and sectional conflicts, Southern slaveholders articulated the coherent, race-based defense of slavery as a positive good. Improvement for black individuals was possible, but only under white supervision and within the limits of their adverse physiology. Racial inferiority explained slavery, not the other way around. Science had merely confirmed black inferiority and placed it on different, nearly unassailable ground. As an English traveler remarked in 1855, the belief that "the colored is by nature a subordinate race" that under no circumstances could be "considered equal to the white" was virtually universal "throughout the whole of the states, whether slave or free." "This opinion lies at the root of American slavery," he added, "and the question would need be argued less on political and philanthropic than on physiological grounds."[2]

The racial justification for slavery "quickly became the dominant mode of proslavery apologetics in the United States." As George Fredrickson explains, "The South turned to a more militant defense of servitude at precisely the time when it was succumbing to Jacksonian pressures to extend the franchise and otherwise increase the democratic rights of the white population." This "ideological marriage between egalitarian democracy and biological racism" shored up "inter-class solidarity between planters and nonslaveholders within the South." The most famous exposition of slavery as a positive good, John C. Calhoun's speech to Congress in February 1837, attacked abolitionists' petitions and defended slavery as the best arrangement when "two races of

different origin, and distinguished by color, and other physical differences, as well as intellectual, are brought together," as in the South.
Calhoun claimed that racial slavery "exempted" the South "from the
disorders and dangers resulting from ... conflict between labor and
capital." In his view, racial slavery produced a stable "political condition"
among white men in the South, who were united by race and therefore
not riven by class.[3]

In Virginia, however, it was only in the 1850s that white man's democracy and free blacks' removal finally gained traction. And they went hand
in hand. At the Constitutional Convention of 1830, reformers lost their
bid to expand suffrage and shift the basis for representation from property holding to white male identity alone. The Southside conservatives
who narrowly defeated the proposal for gradual emancipation and the
colonization of freed slaves likewise defeated efforts at political reform.

Twenty years later, white delegates at Virginia's "Reform Convention"
of 1850 "revolutioniz[ed] the structure of state and county government."
They instituted popular elections for statewide offices, including the new
position of lieutenant governor; removed property qualifications for
voting; and reapportioned representation away from property (i.e., slaveholding) toward a "white basis," shifting power to the nonslaveholding
western section of the state.[4] Several delegates stressed the connection
between this expanded political power for whites and control over free
people of color. Western Virginia delegate Stephen B. Wheeler called for
more stringent laws aimed at expelling free blacks, by taxing them heavily
and offering rewards for informants who turned in those who remained
in Virginia illegally. Delegates proposed stronger removal laws, which
were eventually adopted in 1852.

The *Richmond Enquirer* explained the relationship between constitutional reform and free black removal: "We are now about to enlarge the
right of suffrage and give a more popular tone to all our institutions, and
it becomes more important that the State should not be divided upon
castes, nor, indeed, should there be a population among us, upon which
such dispute could, by possibility, be raised."[5] In a white man's democracy, where whiteness was the sole basis for political power, free people of
color could never be citizens. Although the reforms were motivated by
nonslaveholding whites in Virginia's western counties, the logic of

a white man's democracy knit all white Virginians together. And all agreed that free people of color had no place in it.

This association between white man's democracy and slavery did not have a parallel in Cuba. The specter of republican equality and black citizenship fed racist ideology and practices in the United States in ways that were not politically required in societies such as Cuba's, which did not operate under a presumption of equality.[6] It is not that notions of racial differentiation were absent in Cuba. They became more entrenched there too, as illustrated by the fact that in 1861, for the first time, instead of counting people as *blancos, pardos* or *mulatos*, and *morenos* or *negros*, slave or free, the colonial census now grouped individuals into just two categories: *raza blanca* and *raza de color*.[7]

Racial justifications for slavery were more ubiquitous in Virginia and Louisiana than in Cuba, however, leading to several key distinctions among these three jurisdictions. The legislatures of Virginia and Louisiana sought to isolate and degrade people of color in every realm of the public sphere, closing down the arenas in which whites and blacks might mix, and also where free people of color might seek an education or a religious awakening. Legislators took aim at free blacks' churches, schools, and militias; they eliminated rights to bear arms, to mingle with whites and to gather in groups, to testify in court, to travel without papers, and even to own or transfer property, including slaves. Regulations based on race rather than status predictably led to litigation over racial identity. Of course, trials of racial determination had taken place across the United States since the beginning of the republic. But the higher stakes attendant on drawing racial boundaries produced an upswing in litigation after 1850.[8]

White Southerners feared their inability to know and determine racial identities. A growing "mulatto" population, the increasing domestic slave trade from the Upper to the Lower South, and rising geographic mobility in Southern society made it harder to discern who was white or black, and who was a slave. The mandate to align slavery with racial status made it considerably more difficult after 1850 for an enslaved litigant to convince a jury or a judge that she was white or free. But most striking in the cases of racial determination was the new fervor with which the trials were conducted. The 1850s trials garnered local and national attention. They fed into abolitionist claims about white slavery and "tragic octoroons," as well as Southern fantasies about the rule of law. Litigants became more invested in the search for the essence of race, deploying two types of arguments, based on racial science and on the performance of whiteness.[9] By arguing in court that white people were those who performed citizenship, and people of color were those who could not, trials of racial determination drew an ever tighter connection between whiteness and citizenship, blackness and incapacity for citizenship.

Analogous trials regarding racial identity took place in Cuba when individuals of social backgrounds legally defined as unequal sought to enter into matrimony, prompting conflicts over race, lineage, honor, and status in colonial society. The 1776 Royal Pragmatic on Marriage allowed parents to object if their son or daughter wanted to marry someone who was not of the same noble lineage, wealth, reputation, or race. As racial boundaries and categories were defined and contested, cases contesting unequal marriages became privileged sites for race making. Participants were, in fact, "creating race."[10] But the possibility of legal interracial marriages in Cuba, in contrast to their prohibition in Virginia and Louisiana, represents a telling distinction between the racial legal regimes of these jurisdictions. Although interracial marriages came under legal assault in nineteenth-century Cuba, they were never banned. Those seeking dispensation to enter into racially mixed marriages also created race, but they did so by negating, or downplaying, the centrality of racial boundaries, or by highlighting the importance of other indicators of difference, such as honor, income, and legitimacy. Thus, although they did not necessarily contest the degradation of people of color relative to whites, they did not foreclose the possibility that people of color could be rights-bearing subjects.

REGULATING FREE PEOPLE OF COLOR AND THEIR INSTITUTIONS

Louisiana and Virginia cracked down on free people of color with unprecedented ferocity in the mid-nineteenth century. Across the South, two waves of regulations targeted free people of color: the first in the year following Nat Turner's rebellion, and a second in the 1850s. Furthermore, many laws passed earlier, in Louisiana as well as Virginia, were not enforced until the 1850s. For example, in Virginia a broad set of laws passed in March 1832 classed free people of color with slaves in many new respects, providing that they be tried for criminal offenses in the same special courts established for slaves, and face the same punishments. Also like slaves, "free negroes and mulattoes" were restricted from preaching, assembling at night, and bearing arms. The 1832 laws even targeted the one area in which free people of color had exercised unfettered freedom: the ownership of property. From that time forward, free people of color were prohibited from "purchasing or otherwise acquiring permanent ownership, except by descent, to any slave, other than his or her husband, wife or children."[11] This law was expanded and strengthened in March 1858, when the acquisition of new slaves by free blacks was prohibited, without exceptions (see Chapter 4). During the 1850s, new statutes further encroaching on the rights of free people of color included: an annual head tax; an act to prevent free blacks from owning dogs; new harsher penalties, including the death penalty, for violent crimes committed by free people of color; and, finally, the 1860 act authorizing sale into slavery rather than imprisonment as the punishment for a number of crimes.

In Louisiana, where free people of color could testify in court, freely hold and transfer property, and were not required to register or carry papers, the first limitation on free people of color was an 1830 registration law, which itself exempted those who had lived in the state before 1812. Only in the 1850s did Louisiana's legislature crack down on free people of color, banning assemblies of free people of color with slaves; outlawing "religious, charitable, scientific or literary societ[ies] composed of free people of color"; restricting immigration of free blacks; banning liquor licenses for people of color; and, in 1859, requiring free people of color who arrived in Louisiana ports to be "lodged in the parish jail" while their ship was moored in New Orleans.[12]

Historians who have mined the records of local county courts in the U.S. South, including in Louisiana's river parishes, have demonstrated the ways in which free people of color claimed citizenship in the antebellum era through litigation. Especially in routine cases involving property transactions – suing for debt, or for trespass, sometimes against other people of color, but often against whites, and often victoriously – free people of color used property law to claim basic rights. Yet even these property rights came under attack during the 1850s. Louisiana's Constitutional Convention of 1852 considered, but did not pass, a proposition to prohibit free people of color from purchasing or inheriting property, and in 1859, Saint Landry Parish planters petitioned the legislature to ban free persons of color from owning "beings of their own color, flesh, and blood." In New Orleans, free people of color lost ground economically in the 1850s, both in terms of real estate and slaveholding, although this was offset by gains in other parishes.[13]

During the 1850s, the claim to citizenship was fundamentally a claim to the right to stay in the land of one's birth, the right to remain in one's homeland with family and community. From a comparative perspective, this form of claims-making suggests how tenuous the possibilities of citizenship had become for people of color in the United States. In Cuba, the right to remain never came into question, and the exercise of citizenship was tied more robustly to participation in public life through long-standing schools, churches, militias, cabildos, and confraternities. Such institutions came under attack after the 1840s, but they remained much stronger than their counterparts in Virginia and Louisiana.[14]

MILITIAS, SCHOOLS, AND CHURCHES

Free people of color built secular, religious, and, when possible, military institutions to sustain their communities, to socialize, and to promote various forms of belonging and respectability. Three of the most important institutions in the daily lives of free people of color, across jurisdictions, were militias, schools, and churches. By 1850, free people of color had been mustering in their own militia companies in Cuba and Louisiana for two centuries. They had also established their own churches and schools in the late eighteenth and early nineteenth centuries. Although urban churches for free people of color continued to function almost unabated in all three jurisdictions, schools came under increasing attack, and the Louisiana militias for free people of color were disbanded. And in all three places, the specter of armed black men terrified white slaveholders.

Across the Americas, slaveholders' fears of black rebellion led them to try to keep weapons out of the hands of people of color, both enslaved and free. In Cuba, the Bando de Gobernación issued by Gerónimo Valdés in 1842 reiterated old prohibitions concerning slaves' right to carry arms but also prohibited free blacks from carrying weapons. Fears of rebellion also led to the elimination of the free black and mulatto militia battalions in 1844, a significant blow against Cuba's free community of color. By then, the free colored militias were already diminished, at least compared with in the late eighteenth century. In 1830, free colored militias represented about 10 to 15 percent of all military forces on the island, compared with 20 percent in 1770. The militias were reinstated in 1854, but they lost much of their traditional function as a platform for social mobility and respect for the free community of color. The colonial government even found it difficult to enlist new soldiers.[15] The fear and repression unleashed by La Escalera resulted in additional restrictive regulations concerning free people of color. In 1844, Governor Leopoldo O'Donnell ordered local authorities to increase their vigilance over free black sharecroppers and to register all free blacks without known properties, trades, or occupations as "vagrants ... harmful to society." Blacks could not be employed in pharmacies, and they were also excluded from occupations, such as muleteer and carter, that required independent mobility and contact with rural slaves. Finally, the circular stipulated that at least 5 percent of all laborers on any farm had to be *empleados blancos*, that is, "white employees."[16]

Virginia and Louisiana legislators acted on similar concerns. As early as 1806, following Gabriel's Rebellion, the Virginia General Assembly required free blacks to obtain a license to carry firearms. All guns were banned for people of color in 1832: "Free Negroes are not to carry firelocks of any kind, under penalty of thirty-nine lashes." The legislature sometimes authorized county courts to issue individual licenses for free blacks to "carry a fire lock and also powder and lead," but such licenses appear to have been rare. Free black ownership of dogs also became an offense. In Louisiana, some members of the free colored militias had obtained pensions after their participation in the Battle of New Orleans in 1815, but under American rule the militias were slowly disbanded, and military duties in the state became an exclusively white prerogative. The last two battalions of free men of color disbanded in 1834. An act of 1830 defined militia service as the duty of "every white inhabitant," and the state constitution of 1845 ordered "the free white men" of the state to be "armed and disciplined for its defense." Slaves were prohibited from carrying arms of any sort; those authorized by their masters to hunt could do so only on their plantations. Free blacks were allowed to carry weapons only with a license.[17] These prohibitions deprived free men of color of a key marker of masculine civic standing, one that had in earlier times set them apart as a group with significantly higher status than enslaved people.

The assault on the free communities of color in Louisiana and Virginia targeted their most important institutions. Several new regulations limited black literacy and education, always tied in slaveholders' minds to the potential for rebellion. A Virginia act of 1838 stipulated that any free person of color who went out of the state to receive an education could not return, although this provision would have been difficult to enforce. There were few opportunities for people of color to get an education within the state. An act of 1831 qualified any gathering of "free Negroes or mulattos" anywhere and at any time for "teaching them reading or writing" as an unlawful assembly, subject to corporal punishment. A white teacher would be fined and sentenced to up to two months in prison, although slaveholders could legally teach their own slaves.[18] Some slaveholders, such as William Henry Ruffner of Lexington, Virginia, taught Sunday schools in which hundreds of slaves and free people of color learned to read in the 1840s and 1850s. Free people of color also operated small schools, in contravention of the law, usually through churches. Mary Peake, for example, the daughter of free parents in Norfolk, lived with an aunt in the District of Columbia while she attended school there. In 1847 she moved to Hampton, Virginia, where she taught black children and adults until the Civil War.[19]

By the 1850s, these small schools alarmed whites who feared abolitionism and slave rebellion. One white teacher, Mary Douglass of Norfolk, was prosecuted for "unlawfully assembl[ing] with divers negroes for the purpose of instructing them to read and to write" in 1853. Douglass had operated a school for free children of color with about twenty-five pupils, for almost a year; it was apparently the first such institution in the city.

Free black children attended a Sunday school at Christ's Church in Norfolk, where they received religious teaching that apparently included some Bible reading, but no formal instruction. The judge who presided over the case noted that Douglass was to be punished for "assembling with negroes to instruct them to read or write, and for associating with them in an unlawful assembly." He sentenced her to a month in prison. He based the sentence on the 1848 code, noting that the law was a justified "self-defense" against abolitionist propaganda that incited "our Southern negroes ... to cut our throats."[20]

The larger and more powerful community of free people of color in New Orleans created educational opportunities for children that were unusual in the context of the South. By as late as 1850, about 1,000 free children of color attended schools in the city. An 1854 list of the occupations of free people of color in New Orleans listed fifteen active teachers. The wealthiest members of the community even sent their children abroad to study, especially to France, or to local schools with white teachers, such as the school operated by Ursuline nuns in the 1830s. Even in New Orleans, however, educational opportunities declined under an increasingly repressive legal regime. In 1850, the Louisiana assembly ruled that the state's act for the organization of corporations did not apply to any religious or other associations of free persons of color, an exclusion that would include black schools. Although Louisiana did not ban the teaching of free children of color like Virginia did, their school enrollment in New Orleans declined by about 75 percent between 1850 and 1860.[21]

Among the few institutions still providing educational services to free children of color in 1860 was L'Institution Catholique des Orphelins Indigents, a school created in 1848 through a bequest from Marie Justine Sirnir Couvent. An African-born free black woman who had been enslaved in Saint-Domingue, Couvent bequeathed property to the Catholic church for the explicit purpose of creating a school to offer free education to orphaned children of color. The school was incorporated by a benevolent association of free people of color in 1847, before the restrictive law of 1850. At a moment when opportunities for free people of color in the city were rapidly dwindling, L'Institution Catholique represented a rare space for black intellectual freedom. It was staffed and administered by prominent intellectuals of color in New Orleans – a new generation of activists and professionals, among whom was Alphonse Desdunes.[22]

The school epitomized the determination of free people of color to educate their children, even in the face of growing racist hostility. New Orleans created a system of public education in the 1840s, but as the public school law of 1847 stated, it was "for the education of the white youth of this state." L'Institution Catholique managed to obtain some support from the state and the city in the early 1850s, but such funding was eliminated in 1858.[23] White public opinion against education for black students had hardened, as illustrated by a dispatch from a New Orleans correspondent in 1853, who referred to the "education of free negroes" as an "evil . . . which should be eradicated, root and branch." In 1859, John Francis Cook Jr., the son of a noted black Presbyterian and educator in Washington, DC, was forced to close his school for children of color and leave New Orleans. Cook faced arrest for violating residency requirements against free persons of color and for operating the school illegally.[24]

Notably, such legal restrictions were not enacted in Havana. Access to formal schooling for free children of color was limited, however, and may have in fact declined during the nineteenth century. The first school census conducted in the city, in 1793, listed seven schools for boys with a total enrollment of 552 students, one-fourth of whom (144) were free blacks and *pardos*, a proportion roughly similar to their representation in the general population. With one exception, these schools were racially mixed, and the largest school, led by a *pardo* teacher named Lorenzo Melendez, who was also a militia officer, had 120 pupils, including 40 white students, 60 *pardos*, and 20 *negros*. This was also the school with the most comprehensive curriculum, in which, in addition to writing, reading, Christian doctrine, and elementary arithmetic, there were classes on grammar and orthography. There were also thirty-two schools for girls of both races, many of which were led by women of color. That is, many white students were taught by teachers who were free people of color. A report issued in 1801 complained that most schoolteachers were "women of color, who lack instruction, order, or method." However, it said, such "bad schools" should not be "destroyed," because they "at least" taught children reading, writing, and the "rudiments of the faith." By 1816, the largest elementary school in the city was the free school at the Belen Convent, attended by 310 white male students and 69 students "of color." In the city as a whole, one-fifth of all pupils were children of color; among girls, the proportion was even higher: approximately one-third were students of color.[25]

Most of these schools were established by individual teachers or religious orders. The fact that some militia officers worked as teachers, or petitioned colonial authorities to establish schools for the children of their "class," illustrates that individuals of standing and respect in the free community of color valued education, which they saw as a platform for mobility and belonging.[26] That prospect, however, is what worried slaveholders and authorities the most. When the planter-controlled Sociedad Económica de Amigos del País began to create a regulatory system for education in 1816, it systematically built new racialized barriers to schooling. The society's Education Section prohibited coeducational schooling, which was common at the time, and banned white and free pupils of color from attending classes together. The society's 1831 annual prize for the best paper in education, written by a school principal, addressed the need to separate pupils by race: "Free people of color know perfectly well that is not up to us to abolish a distinction that is impressed on the face." According to the writer, the "manifest inferiority" of free children of color would always be on display in integrated schools. Other commentators, however, were even more candid, claiming that the "confusion of all colors and castes in the same room" sowed "moral corruption."[27]

These regulations had the intended effect: they transformed the educational landscape of Havana. By the 1830s, schools were segregated racially and the racial gap in school enrollment had grown dramatically. In 1836, Havana had 208 schools for white boys and girls, but only 14 for children of color. The pupils of color represented only 5 percent of all children attending school in the city. Their proportion in the total student population had declined by two-thirds compared with 1816, a trend particularly pronounced among girls, who represented less than 2 percent of all female students. This devastating decline was permanent, with free students of color representing between 4 and 5 percent of all pupils in 1851 and 1861.[28]

By segregating schools, the Education Section of the Sociedad Económica erected formidable barriers to educational opportunity for free people of color, but it stopped short of its outright elimination. In contrast to New Orleans, in Cuba the 1841 plan for public education ordered the creation of "separate schools for the children free of color," at least in those towns "where circumstances demand it." The revised public education plan of 1863 mandated the creation in every town of "one or more public schools for children of color."[29] However, available statistics strongly suggest that these mandates were not implemented and that in fact children of color had very limited access to public education.

Black teachers, numerous in the early nineteenth century, performed a key social role in the reproduction of the community of free people of color and in people's aspirations for mobility. They also subverted the racial order, as many of their students were white. That is why the Sociedad Económica prohibited free people of color from working as teachers. As the head of the Education Section explained in 1827, it was necessary to prevent "the disorder that [is created when] a person of color commands a white by being his teacher, as under no circumstance should that right be granted." Section reports constantly disparaged the quality and preparation of teachers, particularly of poor female black teachers who operated neighborhood "little schools," or *escuelitas*, of *amigas* (friends), where poor children were watched during the day and where they learned basic reading and writing. They described those "poor *negras* who do not have any other means to sustain themselves with any decency" as "ignorant, without principle, and education."[30]

Growing regulation and professionalization of teaching displaced free people of color, but it is highly unlikely that popular educational practices and institutions such as the *escuelitas* simply disappeared. In 1837, for instance, Antonio Bachiller y Morales, secretary of the Education Section, opposed the actions of an "overzealous inspector" who, on a single day, closed "many *escuelitas*" in the poor neighborhood of Horcón because they were not licensed. Bachiller proposed instead to "officially tolerate" the activities of the *escuelitas*, while distinguishing between proper teachers and those running the *escuelitas de amigas*. Teachers were to be licensed through rigorous exams and proper training. Furthermore, all schoolteachers, including those staffing the schools for children of color, were required after 1841 to certify their *limpieza de sangre* ("blood purity") – that is, they had to be white. Colonial statistics reflect these trends. According to the census of 1846, all elementary school teachers were white. The census of 1861 listed only two male professors "of color" among the sixty-eight listed in the city. Yet we know that in 1841, free *morena* Maria Faustina Peñalver, a resident of the popular Jesús Maria neighborhood, obtained a recommendation from the neighborhood's inspector to open a school for girls "of her class." Matías Velazco, a *pardo* who served as a sergeant in the militias in the early 1800s, operated a school in the same neighborhood from the 1820s to the late 1850s. In fact, between 1830 and 1840 the Education Section of the Sociedad Económica issued 332 teaching licenses, 21 of which were given to *pardos* and *morenos*.[31] These teachers may not show up in censuses and other official statistics, but they were clearly active. This parallel assortment of educational practices, institutions, and arrangements suggests, in turn, that education for free people of color was more widespread than official statistics reflect. Otherwise, it would be difficult to understand how, in 1861, an official report listed more than 10 percent of free women of color in Havana as literate.[32]

Despite regulatory efforts to undermine their standing and mobility, the free people of color in Havana had institutional resources strong enough to withstand such efforts with some degree of success. They also continued to enjoy a comparatively advantageous position in another key area: religious practice. Regulations limiting the assembly of free people of color and slaves existed in Cuba, Louisiana, and Virginia, but legislators in the American South specifically targeted religious gatherings, which they saw as breeding grounds for rebellion. In 1832, following Nat Turner's rebellion, the Virginia legislature banned free blacks from preaching, and criminalized any assembly of free and enslaved blacks for the purpose of religious worship.[33] Free people of color nevertheless established churches in several denominations, some of which grew to a great size. They used creative measures to avoid shutting down in the face of discriminatory legislation.

Black churches in Virginia were some of the largest institutions in the Baptist Association, including the Gillfield Baptist Church of Petersburg, which had 441 members in 1821 and 1,361 in 1851. Williamsburg Church, which had been founded by black preachers in the 1780s, disbanded after the Turner rebellion but was reorganized in 1843 and grew to 505 members by 1860. Other black churches survived and

18. First African Baptist Church, Richmond, Virginia. This photograph of Richmond's First African Baptist Church, established in 1841, was taken shortly after the end of the Civil War. First African Baptist was one of the largest black churches in the South and probably had the largest congregation of any church in Virginia. [Richmond, Va. First African Church (Broad Street), 1865], Library of Congress, Prints and Photographs Division, www .loc.gov/pictures/item/2018666798/.

flourished by calling in a white minister, who was at least nominally in charge: the First African Church of Richmond, formed in 1841, had 2,056 members within two years and 3,260 members in 1860. The First African Church of Petersburg had 1,635 members in 1851.

In Louisiana, free black Catholics worshipped alongside whites throughout the state. At Saint Augustine's Cathedral in New Orleans, free people of color rented about half the pews and helped raise funds for the building. Only slaves were segregated in church activities. There were also four independent African Methodist Episcopal (AME) churches in New Orleans, with membership totaling 1,700 and property worth $10,600, established in 1842 by former slaves from Virginia.[34]

In 1858, however, a New Orleans ordinance declared all black religious bodies illegal. The African Baptist churches immediately reached an arrangement with the white churches to "enable the Colored people to occupy their House of Worship again," by declaring that each "Colored Church is constituted a Branch of the [white] Coliseum Place Baptist Church." Although this did create a structure of white supervision, they kept their institutions open, and the mayor of New Orleans approved the plan. By contrast, Saint James AME, the largest of the New Orleans AME churches, described by a New Orleans correspondent as "a large brick church ... which is under the control of a negro bishop, and where the services are performed by a negro minister, in direct violation of the laws of the State," was shut down by the police on the grounds that "such assemblages are dangerous to the institution of slavery. They create discontent among the slaves."[35] The AME Church sued the City of New Orleans and won an injunction in the district court. The following year, however, church members lost on appeal to the Louisiana Supreme Court. The "African race are strangers to our Constitution, and are subject of special and exceptional legislation," the court declared.[36] The church shut its doors in 1859 until after the Civil War, and black congregants had to meet secretly in homes around the city.

The free population of color in Havana, on the other hand, continued to enjoy the social and religious community they found in their cabildos and *cofradías*, mutual-aid associations that provided material and spiritual sustenance, as well as cover for African and Afro-diasporic religious practices. Colonial authorities regulated these associations, overseeing, for example, the election of cabildo officers. Local officials were charged with surveillance of dances, religious gatherings, and funerals, but the events themselves were not prohibited. Cabildos and confraternities gathered on Sundays and religious holidays. They paraded publicly on specific dates, such as the feast of the Epiphany, or Reyes Magos (Three Kings' Day). Well into the nineteenth century, these institutions sustained and reproduced crucial economic, social, and family networks, as well as the celebration of black cultural traditions. Many of the elected officials of the cabildos and religious fraternities were also militia officers

19. "The Holy King's Day." This engraving by Pierre Toussaint Frederic Mialhe depicts the popular celebration of the Epiphany in mid-nineteenth-century Havana, when enslaved Africans and their descendants were allowed to parade in the city and to request alms for their cabildos and religious associations. From *Album Pintoresco de la Isla de Cuba* (Berlin: Oilprinting Storch & Kramer [for] B. May y Ca., 1855).

and successful artisans, people of standing in their communities. Freedman Antonio Maria del Castillo, for instance, was one of the leaders of the important cabildo of the Carabali Isuama "nation" in 1827. He was also a captain in the Battalion of Free Morenos. At the time of his death, Castillo bequeathed 3,000 pesos to the cabildo to support "the house of my nation." Another leader of the cabildo was Antonio Potestad, who was also a soldier in the militia. He and his wife, Catalina Blanco, lent money to the cabildo, which probably used it to extend credit to other members. Their daughter Rosa Maria, in another militia connection, married Rafael Hernandez, a sergeant of artillery in the Battalion of Pardos.[37]

REGULATION OF INTERRACIAL MARRIAGE

Through these unions and institutions, free people of color accumulated property, passed it on to their progeny, and built family alliances. Some of the daughters of the most successful families also married across racial lines. The final area of social life in which legal regulation intruded much farther in Virginia and Louisiana than in Cuba was in the area of marriage and family – in particular, the rights of free people of color to form legal, legitimate families and to inherit property across racial lines. Interracial unions were common in all slave societies in the Americas, including Virginia and Louisiana. In Cuba, however, interracial marriages were legally recognized. Spanish law did not build what Chief Justice Roger Taney described in the United States as a "perpetual and impassable barrier" between whites and people of color, or perceive their union as necessarily "unnatural and immoral." Indeed, one Cuban colonial official even predicted that "by authorizing marriages between one and the other the links of subordination of the colored people to the white will tend to be subverted and weakened" and people of color "will aspire impetuously to achieve a rank which society denies them."[38] Informal marriages across the color line, performed by priests or within churches, took place in Louisiana and Virginia, but they remained outside the law.

Yet even in Cuba interracial marriages became subject to regulation during the nineteenth century. The intervention of civil authorities into what had traditionally been a religious sacrament was part of a wider effort by the crown to assert control over its subjects. It also reflected growing anxieties about racial hierarchies and the mobility of the so-called lower castes. The "absolute and disorderly freedom" under which vastly unequal marriages were taking place in the colonies prompted the crown to extend its 1776 Royal Pragmatic on unequal marriages to the colonial territories in 1778.[39]

Just as manumission crossed the barrier between black enslavement and white freedom, interracial marriages bridged the gap that separated whites from blacks. Starting in 1805, a family member, local official, or priest could challenge such unions by invoking the "royal cedula on marriages that persons of known nobility seek to enter with members of the castes of negroes and mulattoes." The decree prevented the marriage of individuals of known "nobility and purity of blood" with people of color without official permission.[40] Over the course of the first half of the nineteenth century, this decree was increasingly applied to interracial marriages involving ordinary white people, not just those from the upper classes. Thus, "unequal marriages" between people of color and whites could be challenged, but they were not automatically illegal. For example, in 1820, the priest of the parochial church Nuestra Señora de Regla in Havana refused to marry one couple because they were "not of the same class" and did not have a license from the civil authorities. The case did not involve a member of the nobility, however. Joaquín Vázquez was a seaman described as "a white man of the common estate [*estado llano*] and of irreproachable behavior," who was seeking to marry the "parda" Catalina Guerrero. In principle, the royal cedula should not have applied to Vázquez, given his humble status.[41] But the interpretation that came to dominate in the colonial territories, including Cuba, was that no member of the nobility *or* individual of known *pureza de sangre* could marry a member of the lower *castas* without official approval. Any white person seeking to marry across racial lines was presumed to be of known blood purity, regardless of his or her personal circumstances. After the 1805 royal decree, interracial marriages became "the direct province of the civil authorities."[42]

Clearly there were white people of the *estado llano*, or common estate, who wanted to form legally recognized families that crossed racial lines. The Cuban authorities complained about "the constant trend by persons of different color to achieve marriage," while arguing, paradoxically, that such unions "conflicted with the genuine sentiments of the inhabitants of these Antilles."[43] Particularly before the 1830s, few Cuban couples requested licenses for such marriages. Verena Martínez-Alier, who analyzed 199 license applications in the Cuban National Archives, from 1810 to 1882, found that couples initiated proceedings in 124 cases. Most of those proceedings (90 out 124) took place after 1830, however. In the early decades of the nineteenth century, those entering interracial marriages rarely initiated the request for a dispensation on their own; typically they were forced to do so by the dissent of parents or other family members. Indeed, 80 percent of the 54 cases of parental dissent studied by Martínez-Alier were filed prior to 1830.

Supporting the notion that some interracial marriages took place without any kind of intervention by civil authorities is the fact that at least some priests interpreted the existing regulations as applicable only to members of the nobility.[44] The royal cedula of 1805 was apparently issued precisely because some parish priests continued to perform mixed marriages on their own. Otherwise, it is difficult to explain why Governor Gerónimo de Valdés stressed, in his 1842 instructions to *pedáneos* (district captains and neighborhood commissioners), the "obligation to exhort parish priests and vicars, in person or in writing" to "suspend" marriages involving "inequality of caste" or "status" until civil authorities had a say in the matter. As late as the 1850s, one archbishop performed thousands of mixed marriages during several pastoral visits to central and eastern Cuba, on the understanding that "the diversity of races was not an impediment in canon law for marriages, neither is it on civil law, when the white belongs to the common estate." As another priest put it, "Before God everybody is equal." According to a report published in *Gaceta de la Habana*, just over 200 "unequal marriages" were celebrated in Havana in 1853 and the first semester of 1854.[45] This report suggests that the actual number of interracial marriages was considerably larger than those documented in the existing legal records, which originated in disputes. In the absence of a challenge by relatives, priests, or civil authorities, interracial marriages were valid to the full extent of the law.[46]

In colonial Louisiana, as in Cuba, Spanish law allowed interracial marriages. Yet evidence from notarial archives suggests the resilience of earlier French legal and social practices regarding interracial relationships. During the Spanish colonial period, there were few legal interracial marriages, although inheritance by illegitimate children of color from white fathers was common.[47] When Louisiana became part of the United States, the new civil code of 1825 declared the "incapacity and ... nullity" of "marriage contracted by free white persons with free people of color." Nevertheless, a number of unlicensed Catholic sacramental marriages crossed racial lines.[48] Some antebellum writers referred to these marriages in New Orleans as *mariages de conscience* (marriages of conscience). When the women and children in these interracial families claimed the right to inherit, however, they were often unsuccessful. Free women of color were much more likely to be labeled "concubines" than white women, who were treated as common-law wives in the same circumstances. The strong preference in Louisiana law for "legitimate" children hurt such interracial families. In the late 1850s they were also

20. Free woman of color with her daughter. This painting by an unknown artist depicts the woman of color and her "quadroon" daughter posing in front of their home. *Free Woman of Color with Quadroon Daughter*, late eighteenth century, New Orleans, public domain.

targeted by extralegal vigilantes, a precursor to the Ku Klux Klan mobs that murdered interracial couples during Reconstruction.[49]

Interracial marriages had been illegal in Virginia since the early colonial period. The laws proscribing interracial marriage went back to the seventeenth century, but they underwent modifications in the antebellum era. In 1792, the General Assembly criminalized a white man or woman "intermarrying with a negro or mulatto, bond or free" subjecting them to six months' imprisonment or a $30 fine, plus a $250 fine for a minister who performed such a ceremony. An 1848 revision doubled the prison sentence and raised the maximum fine to $100, but reduced the fine for a minister to $200. Despite these laws, some interracial families in Virginia lived together "trouble-free" for years, although "only with the assent of a white community that constantly watched them." David Isaacs and Nancy West established an interracial family and lived for several decades in antebellum Albemarle County, in spite of their 1822 prosecution for "umbraging the decency of society and violating the laws of the land by cohabiting together in a state of illicit commerce as man and wife." After five years of litigation, the case was finally dismissed in 1827. Other communities recognized and acquiesced to interracial marriages, but they never considered them legal. Robert Wright, a free man of color, petitioned the legislature in 1816 for a divorce from his white wife, Mary Godsey, on grounds of desertion and adultery. The legislature rejected his petition because they were not legally married, and so could not divorce. The court noted that "although Wright could be married to a white woman in his community, he could not be married to her in law." In Nansemond County, a census taker in 1830 noted nine households in which a "free negro" man lived with "his white wife."[50]

Thus, in Virginia and in Louisiana interracial unions might be tolerated socially and escape criminal prosecution, but they did not enjoy the protections of the law. The law, moreover, did not allow families of free people of color to inherit freely from white fathers and to build up the property and benefits of legitimacy. Furthermore, the legal constraints placed on interracial marriage implied that race was an impassable barrier, and reserved the most important rights of citizenship for whites.

TRIALS OF RACIAL IDENTITY AND THE MAKING OF RACE

Building a solid racial barrier is what legislators tried to accomplish in all three jurisdictions, with various degrees of success. As states sought to make race the most powerful dividing line in society, those who straddled racial lines found themselves increasingly in the cross hairs of the law. In Havana and New Orleans, most free people of color were of mixed ancestry – identified as *pardo* or, in the U.S. Census, "mulatto." In Virginia and the rest of Louisiana, by contrast, a larger number of free people identified as "negro." Nevertheless, those who could pass as white, or who inhabited a middle ground between black and white, found their racial identity on trial in a variety of contexts. In Cuba, racial identity was central in cases challenging "unequal marriages" across racial lines. In Virginia and Louisiana, legal arguments and claims concerning race were central in freedom suits, as well as in cases concerning access to benefits typically reserved for white citizens. In some ways, the Cuban cases resembled those of Virginia and Louisiana, yet they also differed in crucial ways.

Across the U.S. South, trials of racial identity arose when an enslaved person sued for freedom based on a claim of whiteness, or when a third party brought someone's racial identity into question. For example, a criminal defendant might try to disqualify a witness's testimony on the ground that the person was not white; or a defendant might challenge his own prosecution for a crime particular to free people of color, such as carrying a handgun, traveling without a pass, or intermarrying with a white person. There were lawsuits for slander when a person holding himself out as white was called a negro. Steamboat owners might counter a lawsuit for transporting a slave across state borders with the defense that the passenger was white. In Virginia, an 1833 law required people who were "Indians or other people of color" who were "not free negroes or mulattoes" to obtain certificates from the county court exempting them from the restrictions on free people of color. Those seeking such exemptions brought a series of petitions in county courts to declare their racial identity. These cases took on greater urgency in the 1850s, as free people of color were hemmed in on all sides and questions of racial identity became increasingly fraught. Many who had lived in a state of racial ambiguity were now forced to one side of the line or the other.

At trial, witnesses translated legal rules based on ancestry and "blood" into wide-ranging testimony about appearance, reputation, and, in particular, a variety of forms of racial performance: dancing, attending parties, associating with white people or black people on a social level, sitting on a jury, voting, mustering in a militia, and testifying in court. By deferring to juries, judges allowed evidence of racial performance to become as important to the definition of race as fractions of ancestry were in the statutory law. Judges especially privileged particular kinds of racial performance. At the appellate level, when a man's identity was at issue, courts found civic performances determinative. For example, in *Dean v. Commonwealth*, the Virginia Supreme Court found it significant that the "grandfather [of the Ross brothers, whose racial identity was at issue], who was spoken of as a respectable man though probably a mulatto, was a soldier in the revolution and died in the service."[51] Courts singled out evidence of the exercising of rights and privileges as markers of white manhood. When women's whiteness was at stake, sexual purity and moral character were the key attributes.

In Virginia, people of ambiguous racial identity petitioned the government to be exempted from the legal disabilities of a "free negro or mulatto," claiming whiteness or in some cases Indian ancestry. In early 1833, fifty-one white men signed a petition to the General Assembly regarding five newly freed people seeking permission to stay in Stafford County. The petitioners explained that the Whartons were "all white persons in complexion and in fact; and although they are remotely descended on one side from a coloured person, more than three fourths of their blood is derived from white ancestors." The petitioners conceded that the Whartons had been "nominally" the slaves of John Cooke, now deceased, but argued that they had been "for several years past ... entirely free from the control of the said John Cooke and of all other persons, having paid a full consideration for their freedom, and have continued to live as free persons and to exercise all the rights of free persons in the acquisition of property and otherwise without interruption – until the last term of the County Court of Stafford when they were presented for remaining in the state as free persons contrary to law." The petitioners stressed the Whartons' "excellent character," industry, and lack of "associations with coloured persons." In fact, they added, "some of them have intermarried with white persons and their partialities are decidedly for the whites," having helped catch runaway slaves. "These acts together with their general deportment and associations" were the main argument for their being allowed to remain.[52]

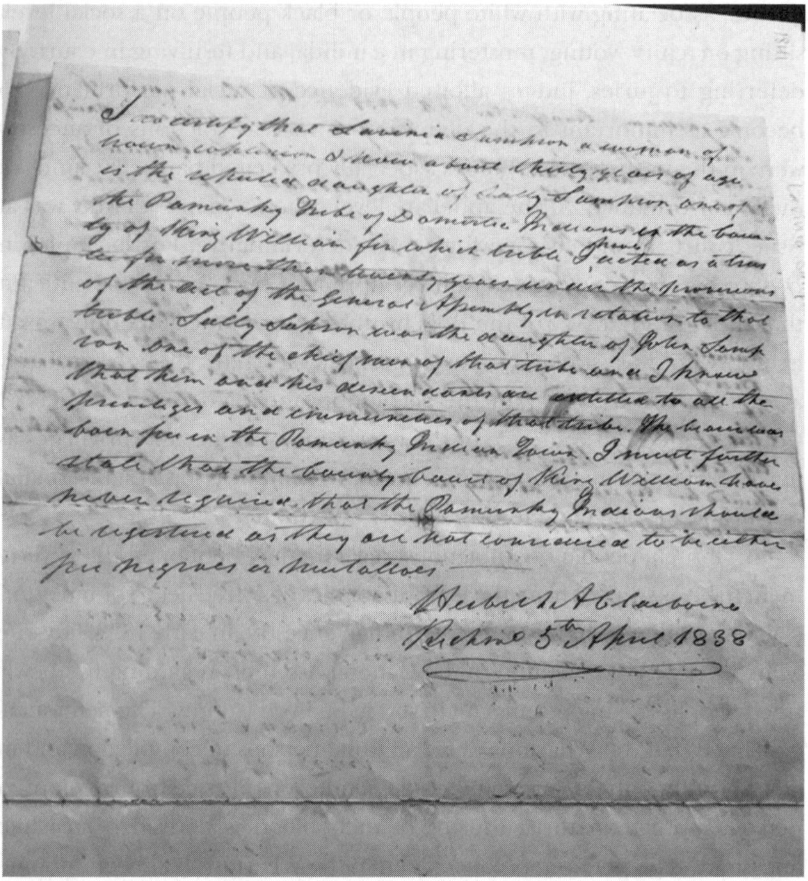

I do certify that Lavinia Sampson a woman of
brown complexion & now about thirty years of age
is the reputed daughter of Sally Sampson one of
the Pamunky Tribe of Domestic Indians in the Coun-
ty of King William for which tribe I acted as a trus-
tee for more than twenty years under the provisions
of the Act of the General Assembly in relation to that
tribe. Sally Sampson was the daughter of John Samp
son one of the chief men of that tribe and I know
that him and his descendants are entitled to all the
privileges and immunities of that tribe. She was
born free in the Pamunky Indian Town. I must further
state that the County Court of King William have
never required that the Pamunky Indians should
be registered as they are not considered to be either
free negroes or mulattoes

Herbert A Claiborne
Richmd 5th April 1838

21. "Not a negro" certificate of Lavinia Sampson. When Virginia passed a series of restrictive laws regarding free people of color in 1832, legislators left a loophole allowing some free people of color to petition for certificates stating that they were "not a negro." In this document, dated April 5, 1838, Herbert A. Claiborne certifies that "Lavinia Sampson a woman of brown complexion and now about thirty years of age is the reputed daughter of Sally Sampson one of the tribe of Pamunky Tribe of Domestic Indians in the County of King William," that her family "enjoyed all the privileges & immunities of that tribe," and further that "the County Court of King William have never required that the Pamunky Indians should be registered as they are not considered to be either free negroes or mulattoes." "Lavinia Sampson certified as Indian not free negro nor mulatto, 1841." City of Petersburg Circuit Court Free Negro and Slave Records, 1809–1865, Box 1, Barcode 1152180, LVA.

By admitting that the Whartons had been enslaved, but were white, the petitioners pointed out the irony of the removal law: "These persons are neither free negroes nor mulattoes. They are white persons. . . . If they

should leave the state, in obedience to the literal requirement of the act of 1806, and become citizens of another state as white persons (which they can unquestionably do) will they not have the right to return immediately to this state and become citizens thereof? There is now no law which would prohibit them." Based on this unassailable argument, the assembly approved the petition on March 9, 1833, declaring that they were "not negroes or mulattoes, but white persons, although remotely descended from a coloured woman."[53]

Just a week or so later, out of concern for other "free people of color" who found themselves in the predicament of the Whartons, Assemblyman John Murdaugh of Norfolk introduced a resolution to the General Assembly to exempt "Indians and other persons of mixed blood who are not free negroes or mulattoes" from the new regulations passed in 1831–1832 and the stiffer criminal penalties aimed at free people of color, and to issue these in-between people (not white but "not a negro") certificates of exemption. In March 1833, the assembly adopted the resolution, whereby county courts could issue such a certificate "upon satisfactory evidence of white persons being adduced." In that year, eighteen members of the Perkins, Bass, and Newton families petitioned the Norfolk City Court for certificates, claiming that they were "not free negroes or mulattoes, but [were] of Indian descent," and each received a certificate to that effect, "embracing their ages, height, complexion & marks or scars." Another petitioner, Lavinia Sampson, was certified as an Indian by the Petersburg Hustings Court in 1841, after she proved that she was the daughter of Sally Sampson, "one of the Pamunky Tribe of Domestic Indians."[54]

As restrictions on "free negroes and mulattoes" increased, efforts to evade these limitations with certificates apparently also increased. The *Richmond Dispatch* claimed that free people of color "continually annoy" the Richmond Hustings Court with applications. Furthermore, the *Dispatch* editors worried, "mixed bloods" could never have been intended to exercise the privileges of citizenship – of whiteness – "to become governors, judges, jurors, soldiers or lawyers . . . to exercise the right of suffrage, or marry with white persons."[55] The city courts of Norfolk, Petersburg, and Richmond all heard repeated petitions in the 1850s from people of "mixed blood" who claimed not to be "free negro or mulatto." Most of the records of these petitions contain only the certification that these individuals were "not a negro," but some include more detailed depositions or summaries of testimony. In 1852, John Scott Bailey brought Sarah Burton and Francis Burton, both white, to testify about the racial identity of his ancestors going back several generations. These included one female ancestor who was "nearly white and had less than one fourth negro or Indian blood in her veins" and one male ancestor who was a "thorough Indian." Of twelve applications for certificates that have survived in the archives, only one was denied, regardless of the testimony of three white neighbors that Braxton Smith, "a man of most excellent habits," was descended from a white woman.[56]

Some newly free people of color also continued to petition the legislature for the right to remain in the state, using a whiteness claim. For example, Eleanor Vaughan and her family petitioned the assembly in 1851, arguing that Craddock Vaughan had emancipated her and her children (who were also his children), and "that though they were by laws of the land necessarily regarded as Slaves, (their mother being a slave), and are now taken by the laws to be noted as Free negroes – they are in fact, and in truth much more than three fourths white so far as blood is Concerned, and in Colour almost entirely so." Although they recognized the "popular prejudice" against free people of color, they hoped "that such feelings have not become so radically fixed in the minds of enlightened Statesmen as to preclude a fair, and impartial discrimination where Circumstances will justify it." In this case, "they are themselves in their own estimation beyond the sphere of the Free negro Class generally so degraded ... they have been respectably raised, know how to conduct themselves – and have always conducted themselves well."[57]

The perception that more free people of color were trying to pass as white led some white Virginians, like the editors of the *Dispatch*, to call for repeal of the "not a negro" law, and to demand greater rigidity in racial definitions. The process of racial determination in the courtroom involved neighbors' testimony about reputation and performance, which the editors found imprecise, manipulable, and dangerous. In December 1853, Assemblyman Travis Epes proposed repealing the "not a negro" law and replacing the definition of a negro or mulatto by one-fourth ancestry with a rule that any African ancestry would signify a mulatto classification. The *Richmond Enquirer* approved of Epes's resolution: "The blood of the Caucasian cannot continue pure and undefiled, while the law compels a fellowship with negroes." But "A Lawyer" wrote in a letter to the editor that these worries were overblown, as no law could compel "amalgamation."[58] The following month, the Committee of Courts of Justice decided that it would be "inexpedient" to change the law. After some legislative maneuvering, the bill eventually died in March 1854, although the attempt to equate any black ancestry with blackness was a telling illustration of hardening racial lines.

As late as 1858, white neighbors petitioned the assembly on behalf of the children of James Corsey, arguing that they should be able to inherit his land because Corsey was "at least three fourths white" and therefore the children were white. Twenty white citizens claimed that Corsey was

> much esteemed and respected by the citizens generally of the county to whom he was known, that he conducted himself in most respects well, and associated mostly with the white people of his neighborhood and was free from the vices and bad habits ... of the free negro population. That he formed a connection with a white woman, with whom he lived as his wife for many years and by whom he had children ... though never married to her because their marriage was prohibited by law, they lived together it is believed in entire conjugal fidelity to each other, and always recognized the above named children as his.

Of the children, they said that they "conducted themselves ... virtuously and respectably, that they all now pass as white people and are recognized as such with and among those with whom they associate and ... a daughter ... has actually intermarried with a white man and is now residing in this county with him." This petition, however, was not successful – it died in committee. [59]

Thus, in Virginia, the crackdown on free people of color that began in the 1830s led some people to petition the state for exemption from the new, harsher system that equated all free people of color with debased and enslaved "negros." For a time, the legislature even issued certificates to those people of "mixed blood" or "Indian" ancestry who could muster their white neighbors to vouch for the fact they were "not a negro." This suggests the extent to which, by the 1850s, free people of color in the commonwealth felt themselves caught in a tightening vise.

Louisiana, too, saw a series of heated disputes over racial identity in the 1840s and 1850s, many litigated all the way to the Louisiana Supreme Court. For example, there were several cases of racial slander in which an individual claimed that he was white, and that being called a "negro" had caused him to lose several of the benefits of whiteness. In each of these cases, witnesses testified as to the respectability, reputation, and honor of the man claiming whiteness, constituting whiteness as a category of privilege and distinction. A typical example is the case of Stephen Boullemet, who had served in the Fourth Regiment of the Louisiana Greys militia and was being considered for a commission as first lieutenant, which would have been put to a two-thirds vote of the militia. Another member, however, refused to support the commission, arguing that the aspirant was "a colored man." Boullemet's friends traced the rumor to Alexander Phillips.[60] Boullemet, who was concerned that the rumor would imperil his impending marriage to a white woman, brought suit against Phillips. At two trials in quick succession in 1840, witnesses appearing on behalf of Boullemet insisted that he had lived his life as a white man, that he had been accepted into white society, and that his mother was reputed to be, if not white, then Indian, but certainly not "colored." One of them asserted that Boullemet was "received in good circles of society . . . as a white man"; another, that Boullemet "was always considered a white boy at school." A third testified that Boullemet's children played with his children, although he had heard the rumor that Boullemet's mother was colored. Boullemet, in addition to serving in the militia, had worked as a clerk and saddle maker for employers who insisted he was white. Furthermore, according to Boullemet's witnesses, he behaved and performed like a white gentleman: a "modest and retiring young man" whose "conduct has always been that of a gentleman in every respect"; "retiring and sober," or "sober and industrious."

Some of the testimony regarded the associations and reputation of the Boullemets in Santo Domingo, which was captured by France in 1802 and then reclaimed by the Spanish in 1809. Several witnesses from Santo Domingo confirmed that the Boullemets had been a respectable white family there before they emigrated in 1809, and that "if a white person was to unite to a coloured woman he was immediately considered as degraded." These witnesses reported that blacks and whites might share a table on the ship leaving Santo Domingo, but that whites would not "admit [people of color] in families." Another emigrée, Mrs. Lavigne, had seen Boullemet's father at various white people's balls, and gave the names of those who had socialized with them.

Boullemet's witnesses claimed that Boullemet and his mother were descendants of Indians ("descendants de Sauvages"), and several witnesses reported that his grandmother hunted in the woods like an Indian woman. These witnesses also said that she looked like many whites: Jean Fauchet "knew many white persons who had the same complexion and had no African or Indian blood in their veins;" Jean Chaillot "did not think that the complexion of the plaintiff's mother was darker than that of a white person of her age."[61] By contrast, witnesses for the defendant described Boullemet's mother as his father's mulatto "menagère." Norbert Vaudry explained that Boullemet's father was "a very respectable man" but his mother "never associated with white ladies," and Vaudry "always took her for a coloured woman." Another witness from Santo Domingo claimed that "the mother of the woman who calls herself Mrs. Boullemet she had no more the appearance of an Indian than witness himself has that of a broom stick [l'air d'un Indien comme mien d'un manisse à balet]." Furthermore, "her complexion was more that of a grenadier than that of a woman. . . . [T]he children might have been considered as interesting children but not as white children." The first jury in *Boullemet v. Phillips* could not reach a verdict. The second decided in favor of Boullemet. The trial judge suggested that he disagreed with their conclusion but let the verdict stand. The Louisiana Supreme Court overturned the verdict as "contrary to the evidence" and remanded for a new trial, but there is no record of a new trial. This was a case in which dozens of white witnesses could not agree about the racial identity of the plaintiff, although all agreed that white identity was vitally important.[62]

In *Cauchoix v. Dupuy*, the plaintiff sued for slander because the rumor that his aunt in New York was a woman of color prevented him from accessing an important social benefit: marrying a white woman in New Orleans. Witnesses on both sides reported that they had known the plaintiff and his family in Havana and had known his aunt, Madame Allien, in New York, but gave conflicting views of their racial status. Some witnesses claimed that they had never even heard a rumor in Havana that the Cauchoix family had "coloured blood"; others claimed to have known them as colored people. One witness said that Madame Allien "was invited by a great many ladies of the City of New York," and another that "there was a current report there in Circulation that she was a coloured woman." In the end, the jury awarded Cauchoix $250 of the $6,000 in damages he had claimed; the Louisiana Supreme Court affirmed, because Cauchoix had "traced his descent, through unmixed blood, for upwards of a century."[63]

Attributions of whiteness frequently depended on the civic activities of the plaintiff and of family members, including voting. In the 1851 slander case of *Dobard v. Nunez*, witnesses' depositions were entered into the record with the following responses: "Third Interrogatory – They are generally known and treated as white persons. To the Fourth Interrogatory – I have known them to vote, and serve on juries. ... Fifth interrogatory – married white persons." In another deposition: "Fourth interrogatory – I have known them to vote at elections, serve on juries and occupying the position in society belonging exclusively to white persons I have known them about 10 years"; "I have seen them vote, also seen them serve as jurors, hold public offices, and occupying a position in society exclusively the privilege of white persons, these facts are known to me for the last eleven years."[64] As in many racial identity trials across the U.S. South, the most important evidence was that a man had voted, sat on juries, held office, mustered in the militia, or married a white woman – all acts of citizenship that could not be performed by black men.

The most dramatic and widely followed trials of racial identity in New Orleans were two cases in which enslaved women sued for freedom, claiming they were whites. These women could not claim that they had exercised the rights of white men. Rather, they dazzled their neighbors and jurors with feminine evidence of whiteness: beauty, sexual purity, and moral character. The written evidence, by contrast, pointed toward black ancestry, or at least slave status. Yet the two women won their cases by behaving like white women in the courtroom and for the popular press. In the 1845 case *Miller v. Belmonti*, the plaintiff Sally Miller claimed to be a German Redemptioner, separated from her family when they got off the boat from Holland and then sold or bound to service in Attakapas Parish to John F. Miller, who sold her to Louis Belmonti at public auction. The chief argument that Sally's attorney made in favor of her whiteness was a moral one: "the perseverance, the uniform good conduct, the quiet and constant industry, which ... have always been found in her ... *these traits prove her white nature.*" Her lawyer hastened to clarify that her whiteness did not rest only on her reputation or association with other whites. He mentioned public opinion only "to shew her moral power, and weight, and influence. An influence, which I contend no one but a white woman could possibly raise up and control – an influence as inconsistent with the nature of an African, as it would be with the nature of a Yahoo."[65]

Similarly, in *Morrison v. White*, Alexina Morrison convinced the majority of jurors in two trials that she was white, despite evidence of her slave status. Witnesses for her putative owner James White used the language of racial science and physiology to declare her colored, talking about her mouth, eyes, teeth, and backbone. They cast aspersions on her sexual purity and moral character, suggesting that she had borne her jailer's child. Morrison's witnesses, by contrast, emphasized that she attended balls and socialized with other white women.[66]

Race was performative in trials involving both men and women. Sally Miller and Alexina Morrison displayed sexual purity and moral goodness, while men voted, sat on juries, held office, and married white women. The practical effect of this kind of evidence was to make white identity in Virginia and Louisiana equal to a set of moral and civic virtues that characterized only white people. In both places, one had to claim whiteness to qualify for basic rights, including the right to marry a person perceived as white.

In Cuba, litigants also drew on a distinct set of beliefs about honor, morality, and racial difference. Yet in trials of unequal marriage, honor and civic virtue were not tied inextricably to whiteness. The "unequal" spouse could argue that she was honorable and industrious *in spite of* her blackness. Thus, in Cuba such rights and attributes were not – or at least not completely – beyond the reach of free people of color. Cases involving interracial marriage became a privileged space in which to articulate, contest, and assemble notions of difference, including lineage,

22. A portrait, in the *costumbrista* tradition, of free women of color. Works in this style depict local Cuban customs and scenes: here, three women of color like those described in the "unequal marriage" cases as virtuous and honorable *pardas*. Victor Patricio Landaluze, *Damas en la ventana* (*Ladies by the Window*), ca. 1860, oil on canvas. Courtesy of Cernuda Arte, Coral Gables, FL.

honor, income, and occupation. These cases were centrally about race, as the very definition of *unequal* marriage was based on the marriage of racially "pure" individuals with members of the lower *castas*. As Patricia

Seed notes, "Substantial social inequality was given a very strict definition ... racial disparity, and racial disparity only." But the fact that inequality could be overlooked, condoned, or compensated for through other attributes of social worth and standing gave litigants considerably more space to negotiate the meanings and the impact of race as a category of difference in Havana. This happened precisely as discourses developed on *raza* (race) in the modern sense, illustrating the contradictory and contested nature of racial law in Cuban colonial society. In the 1840s, the traditional notion of "blood purity" ceased to be an issue in legal procedures, and the question was framed instead in terms of "marriages between people of *different race and color* [*distinta raza y color*]."[67] Whereas "blood purity" was linked to issues of religious orthodoxy, in addition to lineage, *raza* referred to phenotypical and other biological markers that distinguished blacks from whites. Still, such marriages were not banned. To evaluate differences of "race and color," civil authorities looked at the social reputations of the couple and their families, including legitimacy, occupation, honor, wealth, and other markers of social status. In the majority of cases, when dispensation was requested by the couple, the process resulted in the scrutiny of the free person of color – most frequently, of a woman described as *parda* and her family – as it was assumed that the white male partner was the one who would sacrifice the most by marrying someone of the lower *castas.* Most white men who requested licenses to marry were, like Joaquín Vázquez, mentioned earlier, of the *estado llano.* They were poor, working immigrants whose social and residential worlds were very close to those of the free population of color. These immigrants typically did not have relatives in the city, "people to whom the union may be prejudicial" and who might have challenged the marriage. That was the case for Florencio José Curbelo, who applied for permission to marry the *parda* Nicolasa Josefa Camacho in 1827: "This union that may seem unequal at first sight is not, given the obscure birth of the suitor, who is a common white [man]." In another case, the low social status of the white man was key to a successful application: "The quality of the suitor is not much above that of the bride ... although he is held to be white, his purity of blood has not been certified and on the other hand the occupations he has held have been low ... if not of the servile kind."[68]

Like Curbelo, some would-be spouses chose to cast aspersions on their own white identity to reduce the social distance between themselves and their bride of color. When Manuel de Jesus applied to marry the *parda* Maria de la O in 1813, Jesus placed his own whiteness in doubt. His baptismal record indicated that he was the child of "unknown parents, although seemingly white," an argument that he deployed effectively: "This expression does not prove that I could be legitimately white, as I do not really know my origin." Authorities agreed, noting that in this case the harm, if any, was "too small" and affected only "his own person," because he did not have any known relatives. Authorities also allowed the marriage of Agustin Telles to the *parda* Luisa Martinez, despite the opposition of Telles's brother, who argued that Martinez's ancestors, including her own father, had "all" been enslaved. Officials did not dispute this fact but authorized the marriage nonetheless, arguing that although Telles "passes as white, he is not."[69]

In Cuban society, certain occupations were identified with enslavement and with free people of color to such a degree that they made individuals "socially black." These included workers in numerous skilled occupations characterized as "mechanical or liberal arts," such as tailors, masons, painters, sculptors, and others, that were dominated by workers of African descent, enslaved and free. Cuban abolitionist priest Felix Varela wrote in 1823 that most free people of color "devote themselves to the trades and the arts, be they mechanical and liberal, so one could say that for each white tradesman there are twenty of color." Varela lamented this racialized occupational structure: "In fact, since the arts found themselves in the hands of blacks and mulattos, they became degraded for whites," who became socially "debased" when they performed such occupations, usually in the company of free workers of color.[70]

This debasement was frequently invoked to justify mixed marriages. As authorities argued in 1855, the fact that a white suitor was "an artisan, establishes equality between him and the '*parda*' whom he wishes to marry." Mason Mathias Maruny described himself as a "natural of Europe" who worked alongside many people of color who were "as poor" as he. That is how he met his bride, referred to as the *mestiza* Josepha Estrada, whom he sought to marry in 1826. Among the occupations understood to be socially black was that of tailor. In 1823, Simón de Jesús Barcañela, a painter by trade, obtained a license to marry the "parda criolla" Feliciana Pascuala Tolet y Cargnes. Barcañela came from a family of tailors, a trade that "in this country is not exercised generally speaking but by people of *pardo* quality, or very suspicious of being it [*pardo*] or having it [*pardo* quality]." Another white suitor argued that he belonged to "the class of workmen, being a tailor, which in this country markedly diminishes those whites who engage in these occupations." He also noted that his bride, although of "clase parda," was of such light complexion that she was frequently seen as white.[71]

The social standing and respectability of women were key factors in the determination of these cases, and in the reproduction of patriarchal control. The gaze of state authorities was thus frequently concentrated on free women of color and their families. They noted the caste of the female partner, whether she was *parda* or, more rarely, *morena*, and inquired about her family and reputation. This included whether the woman and her parents were freeborn, whether she was the offspring of a legitimate marriage, and whether her conduct and demeanor were "respectable." In the case of seaman Joaquín Vázquez, his bride was identified as the "parda" Catalina Guerrero, a woman of "proper conduct and well-known manners, born from legitimate marriage, both she and her parents in both lines." The "parda" Nicolasa Josefa Camacho, in turn, was described as "a young woman raised in the best education, full of virtues."[72] In another case, a neighborhood authority reported of a family that "their good qualities of honesty and Christianity have gained them the highest distinction on the part of the first families of this municipality, so that this family only lacks the color as it is commonly said, for anybody I asked [was] full of praise of them, as much with regard to the good upbringing and education M. [the bride] has received as to the probity of master carpenter her father."[73]

Wealth, and especially the possibility of a dowry, were also compensatory factors in unequal marriages. In one such case, the authorities reasoned that the white suitor would "improve his situation, because the bride ... had goods that will be of use to the happiness of this marriage." As a Spanish immigrant noted in a petition to marry the *parda* María de la Luz García in 1824, the marriage would be "his happiness, given the virtues that adorn his bride, because the accident of color does not detract from her, and her parents, who in addition to their honesty and good behavior, have real estate that root the petitioner, with the father's commitment to give him a shop to roll cigars." García was free-born, the legitimate daughter of two freeborn *pardos*, which elevated her status even further.[74] Such privileged *pardo* families deployed considerable economic resources to guarantee a suitable marriage for their daughters.[75]

These women did not claim to be white, and they complied with the conventions of a patriarchal social order. Their status, however, was linked to gendered markers of female virtue, education, and respectability that were identified with whiteness, markers that the women of color claimed for themselves. Some commentators described the *castas mestizas* as transgressive, "one thousand times more dangerous" than blacks, because of their "audacity and their pretentions of equality with whites." These pretensions frequently found expression in marriages that free people of color used to construct lineages of respectability that distanced them from the stigma of slavery. Since many poor people lived in extramarital unions, a legitimate marriage indicated distinction. Couples used the church's requirement for information concerning *soltería* (singleness), religion (being Catholic), and the lack of impediments to construct their own histories and to build paper trails of respectability: "as we are free *morenos*, single, Christian, Roman Catholic apostolic, without family relationship or any other impediment." Documentation typically included baptismal registers, noting legitimacy of origin, plus proof of the identity of the parents and grandparents on both sides. If one of the future spouses was a minor, "paternal authorization" was included.[76] Many of the *pardas* marrying white men came from families like these.

Some unequal marriages bridged a greater social gap, when, for example, a white man sought to marry a woman described as *morena* or who, through family links, was barely removed from slavery. Rafael Garzés, an immigrant and discharged soldier, wanted to marry María Josefa de Regla Travieso, a "free *morena*" who was the daughter of "freed blacks [*negros libertos*]," that is, of individuals who had experienced enslavement. In 1826, Jorge Graverán applied to marry the *parda* Margarita Dau, who was the daughter of a white man and an enslaved *parda*. Juan Tenreyro's bride was the *parda* daughter of a white father and an enslaved mother.[77]

Institutionalized white male control required the subordination of women in general, and policing the sexuality of white women, in particular. Unequal marriages involving white women and free men of color were particularly transgressive, and less frequent. They were justified by denigrating the morality and standing of the women, some of whom were described as destitute and in "utterly miserable circumstances." In one such case, the woman "appear[ed] to be white" but was of "a very humble condition; her conduct ... extremely reprehensible by virtue of the illicit affair she has been having ... with the *moreno* José Joaquín for the period of eight years causing public scandal and police intervention." In a comparable case, Anna Josefa Fernández, a white woman, wanted to marry Pedro Estrada, "of *pardo* or mulatto color." Fernández described herself as a "sacrilegious daughter," that is, the illegitimate daughter of a priest or member of a religious order. She was "absolutely helpless," had lived as Estrada's concubine for many years, and had a child with him. Although the authorities noted "the difference of colors," they granted the license for Fernández and Estrada on the ground that "the defects that they suffer are mutually compensated." The stain of Fernández's origin was of such magnitude that it rendered her a social equal to her mulatto partner.[78]

Proposed marriages between less destitute white women and men of color frequently encountered parental and family opposition, forcing the couple to obtain a dispensation. Following patriarchal conventions, authorities took a father's consent to such a marriage as sufficient. In most cases, however, relatives of the white woman challenged her plan to enter a mixed marriage, claiming that it would do irreparable damage to the honor and standing of the family. As the relative of one woman stated, the union between a girl of "the pure, white race" and someone from "an entirely opposite race" should not be allowed, because it resulted in "the introduction into the family of a subject in whose veins no white blood flows." Tomás Alvarez opposed the marriage of his widowed sister to "the *pardo* Pedro Vargas" in 1822 because such unions were "scandalous" and "opposed to our laws and customs," given the "absolute and essential inequality" of the parties.[79]

Unequal marriage cases implied certainty about the racial backgrounds of the parties. Only exceptionally was this element either ambiguous or unclear. Marcos Jose Garcia, a "free *pardo*," sought to marry Maria Josefa de las Mercedes Suarez in 1856. In marriages among free *pardos* or *morenos*, a suitor usually noted that his bride was of his "own class and condition." In this case, however, there was no notation of Maria Josefa's class. She was simply described as "born in the city of Seville, capital of the province of the same name, the legitimate daughter of Ciriaco de las Mercedes Hurtado de Suarez and of Maria Josefa Isariga." The baptismal record of Maria Josefa contained no racial notation, stating that she was of legitimate birth and that her parents had been born in the colonies, in Panama and Guayaquil. It is possible that Maria Josefa was perceived to be of indigenous or partially indigenous origin, which would explain why the father of the suitor, Marcos Jose, opposed the marriage. In a case like this, in which authorities did not have explicit information about the racial background of Maria Josefa, they had no choice but to make a determination. Without such information, it was impossible to establish if the marriage was unequal. In this case, despite her peninsular origin, Maria Josefa was obviously not considered white either by the groom, who mentions the absence of "impediments to our marriage," or by authorities, who described her as of "the same class" as him in their marriage license. The specific factors that allowed them to define her class, however, remain opaque.[80]

Arguments against mixed marriage became sharper in the 1850s and 1860s in Cuba, as explicit allusions to notions of racial difference gained prominence. The "dividing line between the white and the African race" ought to be "very clearly marked," argued relatives opposed to such marriages, because the "special conditions" of colonial society demanded a clear "line between the white class and that of color." Authorities reasoned that interracial marriages were dangerous, because they could lead to "presumptions on the part of the colored class," who may "derive from the said marriages the idea of equality between the classes." Marriage and informal interracial unions eroded the "indispensable subordination and respect with which the colored race must regard the white." Some colonial officials took these dangers seriously. An *alcalde mayor* (district judge) described his approach to these cases in 1853, saying that he issued licenses for "whites" to marry "*pardos* or *morenos*" only when there was "a powerful cause."[81]

Still, licenses for mixed marriages were routinely granted until the mid-1860s, when they were halted for a ten-year period when racial anxieties increased during the Civil War in the United States and Cuba's own war of independence in 1868. But the halt was temporary. Extra administrative requirements for mixed or "unequal" marriages were totally eliminated in 1881; after that date, interracial marriages were no longer subject to any special regulation. In the case of minors, however, parents could still register their opposition to a mixed marriage. But as a nineteen-year-old white groom argued in a petition for a marriage license against his father's wishes in 1882, by then the law gave "people of different races complete freedom to enter marriage."[82]

***

That "freedom" was a fundamental difference in the legal treatment of race in Cuba, Virginia, and Louisiana. The hardened legal barriers that by the 1850s separated whites and blacks in the Southern states had no parallel in Cuba. Race was a shared idiom of difference and social subordination, but it had come to have different meanings and social implications. In Virginia and Louisiana, blackness was coterminous with enslavement and exclusion from the political order. Free blacks were a social and political anomaly, "strangers" to the Constitution, as the Louisiana Supreme Court stated. The association between citizenship and whiteness was so strong, in fact, that the performance of civic duties was taken as proof of an individual's white racial background, regardless of other circumstances. Public services such as education were available only to whites, and even the basic right to reside in a state as a free person came to be racially defined. By the eve of the Civil War, the legal regimes of Louisiana and Virginia had relentlessly and systematically constituted blackness as a category of abjection.

Individuals could challenge their racial identity in court. A few managed to escape from the handicaps reserved for what a Virginia litigant described as the "free negro class, generally so degraded." These cases, however, helped to constitute whiteness as a category of social super-iority, inseparable from the privileges of citizenship and from gendered notions of purity, beauty, and propriety. In the unequal marriage cases in Cuba, by contrast, whiteness was sometimes degraded to account for other markers of status, such as income, origin, and occupation. In the eyes of the law, poor working whites were socially close enough to free people of color that their marriages were not that unequal after all. And some "stains" of origin were of such a magnitude as to eliminate the privileges that individuals normally derived from whiteness. The same applied to certain manual occupations. Free people of color entering unequal marriages could indeed have entertained, as authorities feared, "the idea of equality" between whites and blacks. In Cuba, this idea had some foundation in law.

Furthermore, in Cuba, where the colonial state could not afford to alienate the free black population, and where black freedom did not threaten fragile white political coalitions, free people of color managed to withstand the slaveholders' assault on their traditional rights and institutions. Some of those rights – membership in the militia, access to publicly funded schools, the ability to legally sustain their cabildos and religious confraternities, marriage across racial lines – while greatly restricted and at times denied, were not construed as incompatible with blackness. The law defined blacks as socially inferior, legally handi-capped subjects in all three jurisdictions, but the process of constituting blacks as subjects without rights, without even the right to have rights, went considerably further in Virginia and Louisiana than in Cuba.

Conclusion

"Home-Born Citizens": The Significance of Free People of Color

B Y THE MID-NINETEENTH CENTURY, CUBA, VIRGINIA, AND Louisiana were all mature slave societies. In all three, slavery was a part of life, a key element in systems of production and social organization that had been in place for centuries. The enslavement of Africans and their descendants was seen as regrettable to some and commendable to others, but it was acceptable to most white people, grounded in the belief, widely shared across Atlantic societies, that blacks were hopelessly inferior in political, moral, intellectual, and civilizational terms. In all three societies, the racial order placed blacks at the bottom of society. Yet by 1860, the racial orders of Cuba, Virginia, and Louisiana differed in important ways. In many parts of Virginia and Louisiana, an enslaved person could live his entire life without ever meeting a free person of color. Blackness was equivalent to enslavement. This was virtually impossible in Cuba, where free people of color represented a significant proportion of the total population. In Virginia and Louisiana, when people of color challenged their enslavement or their racial designations in court, legal institutions tied their claims of citizenship to whiteness. The link between whiteness and citizenship, so important to the ideology of white supremacy and white man's democracy in the United States, did not crystallize in the same way in Cuba. A free person of color in Cuba could be a rights-bearing subject, participate in public life, and marry across racial lines; on the eve of the Civil War, a person of color in Virginia or Louisiana could do none of those things. Legal traditions, enslaved people's actions, imperial institutions, politics, and the twists and turns of history all shaped these differing trajectories.

Ironically, the strong Iberian legacy of slavery law and practice had contradictory and unexpected effects in the New World. In Cuba, colonists arrived with a set of Iberian legal and institutional precedents that already constituted blacks as socially debased subjects. Yet at the same time, manumission was a well-established practice in Mediterranean Spain that applied to individuals of different religious and ethnic backgrounds. Iberian legal traditions helped build racial distinctions into law more quickly in Cuba than in the other jurisdictions, but they also helped entrench the practices of manumission and self-purchase, independent of race. By contrast, the manumission regimes of Virginia and Louisiana became pillars of their respective racial orders. French colonists in Louisiana drew on precedents developed in France's Caribbean colonies during the seventeenth century to include not only racial distinctions in the law but also limitations on manumission and racial intermarriage. Virginians, after a period of relative openness in the seventeenth century, began to impose similar limitations in the late seventeenth and early eighteenth centuries. By that time, all three jurisdictions had built racial orders that rested on legal regimes associating blackness with enslavement, but Virginia and Louisiana had limited the master's right to free a slave.

Slaveholding elites never managed to create the perfectly dichotomous world that they envisioned. Free and enslaved people of color subverted the racial orders by exploiting and sometimes creating ways to escape from enslavement, by contesting the negative features associated with blackness, and by entering into sexual relations and even marriages across racial lines. In all three places, these strategies resulted in the creation of intermediate groups that did not fit the discrete categories of free white people and enslaved people of African descent.

Legal traditions were very important in the early establishment of the colonies, but the initiatives of enslaved people themselves proved just as important over the course of their histories. In all three jurisdictions enslaved people took advantage of legal reforms, not intended for their benefit, to carve out greater freedoms for themselves. They sued for freedom using statutes passed for other purposes, shared information with other people of color across great distances, labored and amassed property to purchase freedom for themselves and others, and demanded ancillary rights once they had paid a part of their purchase price. In Cuba, enslaved, free, and *coartado* people transformed the customary practice of *coartación* into a right eventually enshrined in statutory rules. Similar efforts on the part of people of color in Virginia and Louisiana were less successful.

In this process, the size of the community of free people of color was key. Many enslaved individuals who purchased their freedom did so with the financial backing and the legal support of free black neighbors and kin. The larger the community, the greater the opportunities for freedom. Free black residential communities also represented safe havens for fugitive slaves and places for the dissemination of important information about freedom – from the identity of lawyers who could aid freedom suits to news of abolitionist activity. Larger and wealthier communities of free people of color represented a formidable deterrent against slave owners' visions of a perfectly dichotomous social order in which blackness meant enslavement. In a place like Havana, for example, it was difficult to sustain that association. Furthermore, the free black communities created institutional spaces and performed rituals of respectability and belonging, disrupting elite white narratives associating blackness with debasement. As Catholic subjects, they constituted honorable families and played important roles in institutions, such as the militias, that conferred status and prestige.

The community of free people of color in Havana, and the New Orleans community, which expanded significantly under Spanish control after the 1760s, owed their existence to legal understandings and customary practices anchored in the ancien régime. Slaves who managed to purchase their freedom or, more rarely, obtained manumission through other means became members of highly stratified societies in which social stations were defined along multiple axes of lineage, income, religion, respectability, and so on. Black freedom did not imply social equality and it was grounded in traditional legal and religious principles. By contrast, in Virginia the rise of manumission, and of freedom suits, became inextricably linked to the military conflicts, tensions, and expectations associated with the Age of Revolution. In Virginia, the expansion of manumission was tied to questions of citizenship, of black participation in the new political order under conditions of equality. Slaves and free people of color infused these questions with a sense of urgency, as they made use of every available legal loophole to purchase or make claims for their own freedom. Their actions produced dramatic results: by the early nineteenth century, the proportion of free people of color in the commonwealth had increased significantly.

White citizens witnessed these trends with horror and petitioned to outlaw manumissions. It was, literally, a reactionary request: to restore the colonial law of freedom. The 1806 law requiring freed slaves to leave the state fell short of that goal, but it marked the first step toward a social order in which blacks could participate only as slaves. After Nat Turner's rebellion in 1831, white Virginians' political will to exclude free blacks intensified. Slaveholding states in the U.S. South responded to threats of rebellion, and to Northern abolitionists' demands for immediate emancipation, with a defense of slavery as a "positive good": claiming it was the best possible condition for debased "negroes." To galvanize the support of nonslaveholding whites and cement white solidarity, they defined citizenship and voting rights along racial lines – thus, the paradox that egalitarian democracy went hand in hand with the expansion of racist practices and ideologies.

By 1860, free people of color in Virginia and Louisiana were under attack, increasingly forced to leave the state upon emancipation or to live under threat of prosecution. A few even chose "voluntary" reenslavement in order to remain with their family members. Free people of color continued to claim freedom in court, and to fight tenaciously for the basic right to a homeland, to remain close to friends and kin, to simply live in their communities of origin, as "home-born citizens."[1] Yet they saw their militias and schools shut down, their churches survive only under white leadership. Increasingly contested battles in court over racial identity attested to both the growing anxiety over the line between free and enslaved, black and white, and the need to prove whiteness to claim basic rights. What Chief Justice Roger B. Taney described as the "perpetual and impassable barrier" between the races was never as impassable as he wanted it to be – but the process of building that barrier was much further advanced in Virginia and Louisiana than in Cuba. The community of free people of color in Cuba, far larger as a percentage of the population,

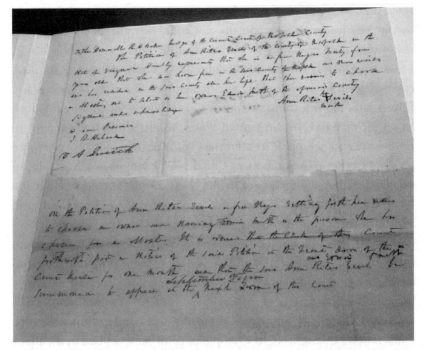

23. Petition of Ann Riter for reenslavement. After Virginia courts began to crack down on free people of color who did not leave the state after their emancipation, a small number of freed people petitioned to be reenslaved in order to stay with their families. In this document, Ann Riter "humbly represents that she is a free negro twenty four years old that she was born in the said county of Norfolk and now resides and has resided in the said county all her life. That she desires to choose a Master, and to select as her owner Edwin Smith of the aforesaid county." Petition for reenslavement of Ann Riter, 1861, Norfolk County Free Negro and Slave Records, Box 2, Barcode 1188995, LVA.

retained greater institutional resources and mounted a more successful legal resistance.

All three were successful, brutal slave societies. Their main and most consequential difference lay not in their regimes of slavery, however, but in their regimes of race. And what mattered most in the development of those regimes of race was not the law of slavery but the law of freedom. Although free people of color were few in number compared with enslaved people, and they lived on the margins of the three plantation societies in many ways, the contests over their identities, status, and rights formed the terrain on which race was made. If their condition was reduced to something closer to slavery, as in Virginia and Louisiana by

1860, then race rather than enslavement would be the true "impassable barrier." If, instead, free people of color could be rights-bearing subjects, as in Cuba, then enslavement was the dividing line.

Laws regulating free people of color also served as templates for post-emancipation societies seeking ways to keep black people in their place. Slavery laws did not translate forward in the same way that regulations based on race did. In the United States, when Southerners sought to restore the antebellum order after the Civil War, they could not reimpose slavery, but they passed the Black Codes, whose language echoed almost exactly the antebellum laws regarding free people of color. Under the Black Codes, freedmen could enter into contracts, own property, and appear in court on their own behalf. But in myriad other ways their lives were constricted, just as they would have been before 1861. Slavery-era laws limiting the immigration of free people of color from one state into another were the first immigration restrictions, and they have echoed – through the twentieth century and to the present – in numerous limitations on the right to immigrate based on racial and national identity. Laws limiting the rights of free people of color have echoed in the Black Codes, in a host of facially neutral but racially discriminatory laws from 1865 to the present, and in the racial logics that still inform much of our legal system. In Cuba, on the other hand, legal racial barriers came under additional attack even before the final end of slavery in 1886. In the 1880s, limitations on interracial marriages were eliminated and racial segregation in public services and education were outlawed. As the colonial state sought to retain control over its restive colony, it had to cultivate the political support of the black population. By 1898, the island's short-lived political regime granting "autonomy" to the colony recognized black men as voting subjects with equal rights.

The transition from black slavery to black citizenship in all three jurisdictions was neither linear nor preordained. The process was as contentious and ferociously contested in Cuba as it was in Virginia and Louisiana. But the new struggles, after slavery, for standing and citizenship took place against a backdrop of significantly different legal regimes of race. From black slave to black citizen, the connecting tissue before and after emancipation was not "from slave to citizen," but from black to black.

Notes

INTRODUCTION

1. ANC, PNH, ER, 1690, fol. 44 and 45. Our emphasis.
2. Hudgins v. Wright, 11 Va. 134 (1806); Hudgins v. Wright Trial Record, Box 71, Tucker-Coleman Papers, Special Collections Research Center, Swem Library, College of William and Mary, accessed March 19, 2019, http://hdl.handle.net/10288/16635. See also Gregory Ablavsky, "Making Indians 'White': The Judicial Abolition of Native Slavery in Revolutionary Virginia and Its Racial Legacy," *University of Pennsylvania Law Review* 159 (April 2011): 1457–1531; Pegee v. Hook, Franklin County Judgments (Freedom Suits), 1808, LVA. Pegee v. Hook, Augusta County Chancery Causes, 1746–1912 (Augusta County Chancery Court, 1809), LVA, accessed March 19, 2019, http://ead .lib.virginia.edu/vivaxtf/view?docId=lva/vi03107.xml; see also Hannah Fender v. John Marr (August 1788), Henry County Freedom Suits, LVA; Harry v. Sterling Ruffin (1801), Brunswick County Freedom Suits, 1790–1808, LVA; Rachel Findley v. John Draper Sr. (1820), Powhatan County Freedom Suits, LVA; Petition of Sally, etc. (1811), Louisa County Freedom Suits, LVA; Maria, etc. v. Mary Moore (April 1814), Prince Edward County Freedom Suits, LVA; Edwin L. Harris v. Sinah, etc. (1817), Arlington County Freedom Suits, 1795–1822, Box 1, LVA.

   Tellingly, one witness revealed the way in which whiteness could work against a slave: he testified that Nan's owner wanted him to buy Nan, but "he would not buy a white negro, saying that if he . . . bought said woman and she should afterwards breed, the Neighbours would probably say that the children were his or some of his sons." Franklin County Judgments.
3. Eulalie v. Long and Mabry, Docket No. 3237, Louisiana Supreme Court Records, Historical Archives of Louisiana, University of New Orleans, 11 La. Ann. 463 (1856) and 9 La. Ann. 9 (1854). See also Rebecca J. Scott, "Social Facts, Legal Fictions, and the Attribution of Slave Status: The Puzzle of Prescription," *Law and History Review* 35, no. 1 (2017): 1–22.
4. *See* Frank Tannenbaum, *Slave and Citizen: The Negro in the Americas* (New York: Vintage Books, 1946); Stanley M. Elkins, *Slavery: A Problem in American Institutional and Intellectual Life* (Chicago: University of Chicago Press, 1959); Herbert Klein, *Slavery in The Americas:*

A Comparative Study of Virginia and Cuba (Chicago: University of Chicago Press, 1967); Carl Degler, *Neither Black nor White: Slavery and Race Relations in Brazil and the United States* (Madison: University of Wisconsin Press, 1971). The most recent and important contribution to this tradition is that of Robert J. Cottrol, *The Long Lingering Shadow: Slavery, Race, and Law in the American Hemisphere* (Athens: The University of Georgia Press, 2013).

5. For an in-depth summary of the literature, see Alejandro de la Fuente, "From Slaves to Citizens? Tannenbaum and the Debates on Slavery, Emancipation, and Race Relations in Latin America," *International Labor and Working Class History* 77 (2010): 154–173; Alejandro de la Fuente, "Slave Law and Claims-Making in Cuba: The Tannenbaum Debate Revisited," *Law and History Review* 22, no. 2 (Summer 2004): 339–369.

6. We review the scholarship up to 2010 in Alejandro de la Fuente and Ariela Gross, "Comparative Studies of Law, Slavery and Race in the Americas," *Annual Review of Law and Social Science* 6, no. 1 (2010): 469–485, and in Ariela J. Gross, "Beyond Black and White: Cultural-Legal Histories of Race and Slavery," *Columbia Law Review* 101, no. 3 (2001): 640–690. Key recent works that have influenced us include Bianca Premo, *Enlightenment on Trial: Ordinary Litigants and Colonialism in the Spanish Empire* (New York: Oxford University Press, 2017); Rebecca J. Scott and Jean M. Hébrard, *Freedom Papers: An Atlantic Odyssey in the Age of Emancipation* (Cambridge, MA: Harvard University Press, 2014); Sue Peabody and Keila Grinberg, *Free Soil in the Atlantic World* (New York: Routledge, 2014); Martha S. Jones, *Birthright Citizens: A History of Race and Rights in Antebellum America* (New York: Cambridge University Press, 2018). Newer works on manumission and freedom suits include Adriana Chira, "Affective Debts: Manumission by Grace and the Making of Gradual Emancipation Laws in Cuba, 1817–68," *Law and History Review* 36, no. 1 (February 2018): 1–33; Kelly M. Kennington, *In The Shadow of Dred Scott: St. Louis Freedom Suits and the Legal Culture of Slavery in Antebellum America* (Athens: University of Georgia Press, 2017); Kimberly Welch, *Black Litigants in the Antebellum American South* (Chapel Hill: University of North Carolina Press, 2018); Loren Schweninger, *Appealing for Liberty: Freedom Suits in the South* (New York: Oxford University Press, 2018).

7. Keila Grinberg, "Freedom Suits and Civil Law in Brazil and the United States," *Slavery & Abolition* 22, no. 3: 66–82 (December 2001).

CHAPTER 1 "A NEGRO AND BY CONSEQUENCE AN ALIEN"

1. *Actas Capitulares del Ayuntamiento de la Habana* (Havana: Municipio de la Habana, 1937), 1(2):229; Alejandro de la Fuente, *Havana and the Atlantic in the Sixteenth Century* (Chapel Hill: University of North Carolina Press, 2008); Irene A. Wright, *Historia documentada de San Cristobal de la Habana en el siglo XVI*, 2 vols. (Havana: Imprenta El Siglo XX, 1927) and *Historia documentada de San Cristóbal de la Habana en la primera mitad del siglo XVII* (Havana: Imprenta El Siglo XX, 1930).

2. *Actas Capitulares del Ayuntamiento de la Habana*, 1(2):177, 189, 201 (sessions January 9, 1559; March 13, 1559; and August 17, 1559). The earliest town council minutes available date to July 1550. For an early example of how manumission letters described the status

of freedmen and women, see ANC, PNH, ER, 1579 in María Teresa de Rojas, *Índice y extractos del archivo de protocolos de la Habana*. 3 vols. (Havana: Imprenta Ucar, García y Cía, 1947), 1:410.

3. ANC, PNH, ER, 1600, fol. 396v.; 1628, unnumbered fol. (will of July 20); 1637, fol. 543v.; de la Fuente, *Havana and the Atlantic*, 176.

4. *Actas Capitulares del Ayuntamiento de la Habana* 1(2):201; ACAHT, vol. 1599–1604, fol. 498; Testamento de Sebastian Vazquez, ANC, PNH, ER, 1637, fol. 543v.

5. See *Northampton County, Virginia, Record Book: Orders, Deeds, Wills &c*, ed. Howard Mackey and Marlene E. Groves, 17 vols. (Rockport, ME: Picton Press, 1999–2006): *Northampton County Deeds and Wills 1645–1651*, folder 75, 237; *Northampton County Orders, Deeds, Wills 1651–1654*, 123 (January 10, 1647); ibid., 226 (February 28, 1652); *Northampton County Deeds and Wills 1654–1655*, folder 10, 35 (March 8, 1655); *Northampton County Orders, 1655–1658*, 10. John Johnson v. John Johnson, *Northampton County Deeds and Wills 1657–1666*, 57–58, 103; *Northampton County Deeds, Wills 1651–1654*, folder 200; Somerset County, Maryland Court Records, July 2, 1667, January 13, 1674/5, Maryland State Archives, Annapolis. For more detail, see Paul Heinegg, *Free African Americans of North Carolina, Virginia, and South Carolina*, vol. 2 (Baltimore: Clearfield, 2005), 705–707; J. Douglas Deal, *Race and Class in Colonial Virginia* (New York: Garland, 1993), 219–221.

6. Heinegg, *Free African Americans*, 706.

7. We fully sympathize with the argument of scholars such as Michael Gomez, *Exchanging Our Country Marks: The Transformation of African Identities in the Colonial and Antebellum South* (Chapel Hill: University of North Carolina Press, 1998), who emphasize the agency of the enslaved and their descendants in the creation of new identities based on race (208–209). The evidence presented in this chapter, however, disputes the notion that "race as a unifying ideal was not imposed upon the community" (220).

8. Residencia de don Antonio Maria Bucarelli, Havana, 1774, AHN, Consejos (CI), leg. 20889, pieza 1, fol. 183v.; "Bando del Gobernador Diego José Navarro," May 4, 1779, in Leví Marrero, *Cuba: Economía y sociedad*, 15 vols. (Madrid: Editorial Playor, 1971–1992), 13:207.

9. On the importance of blacks among slaves in Seville, Lisbon, and the Canary Islands in the sixteenth century, see José L. Cortés López, *La esclavitud negra en la España peninsular del siglo XVI* (Salamanca: Universidad de Salamanca, 1989), 204–205; Alfonso Franco Silva, *La esclavitud en Sevilla y su tierra a fines de la Edad Media* (Seville: Diputación Provincial de Sevilla, 1979), 150–151; Manuel Lobo Cabrera, *La esclavitud en las Canarias Orientales en el siglo XVI (negros, moros y moriscos)* (Las Palmas: Cabildo Insular de Gran Canaria, 1982), 147–149; W. D. Phillips Jr., *Historia de la esclavitud en España* (Madrid: Editorial Playor, 1990), 163–166; A. C. de C. M. Saunders, *A Social History of Black Slaves and Freedmen in Portugal, 1441–1555* (Cambridge: Cambridge University Press, 1982), 54, 166, 174; Frank Tannenbaum, *Slave and Citizen* (Boston: Beacon Press, 1992), 48, 103.

10. Debra Blumenthal, *Enemies and Familiars: Slavery and Mastery in Fifteenth-Century Valencia* (Ithaca, NY: Cornell University Press, 2009); de la Fuente, *Havana and the Atlantic*,

147–148; Cortés López, *La esclavitud negra*, 91–94; James H. Sweet, "The Iberian Roots of American Racist Thought," *William and Mary Quarterly* 54 (1997): 143, 154; Cortés López, *La esclavitud negra*, 45; María Elena Martínez, *Genealogical Fictions: Limpieza de Sangre, Religion, and Gender in Colonial Mexico* (Stanford, CA: Stanford University Press, 2008), 11–13; George Fredrickson, *Racism: A Short History* (Princeton, NJ: Princeton University Press, 2002), 31–33.

11. Saunders, *A Social History of Black Slaves*, 54, 76–77, 106, 166, 178.

12. This argument contradicts Alan Watson's claim concerning the allegedly nonracist character of slave law in Latin America compared to the British colonies. See Alan Watson, *Slave Law in the Americas* (Athens: University of Georgia Press, 1989), 64, 76.

13. By contrast, Klein argues that slaveholders in Virginia enjoyed such a degree of judicial, legislative, and administrative independence that they were free to create "their own slave regime," whereas in Cuba slaveholders "were totally excluded from political and social power" and did not have the institutional means to legislate slavery according to their own interests. Klein acknowledges the existence of "New World institutions generating law" but does not place this legal production at the center of his analysis. See Herbert S. Klein, *Slavery in the Americas: A Comparative Study of Virginia and Cuba* (1967; Chicago: Elephant Paperbacks, 1989), 68.

14. Cortés López, *La esclavitud negra*, 45–46; Silva, *La esclavitud en Sevilla*, 59; Phillips, *Historia de la esclavitud*, 164–167, 194–195; Saunders, *A Social History of Black Slaves*, 54; Alessandro Stella, *Histoires d'esclaves dans la péninsule Ibérique* (Paris: Editions de l'Ecole des Hautes Etudes en Sciences Sociales, 2000), 78; Jennifer C. Geouge, "Anglo-Portuguese Trade during the Reign of João I of Portugal, 1385–1433," in *England and Iberia in the Middle Ages, 12th–15th Century: Cultural, Literary, and Political Exchanges*, ed. María Bullón-Fernández (New York: Palgrave Macmillan, 2007), 119–133; Marc Bloch, *Slavery and Serfdom in the Middle Ages* (Los Angeles: University of California Press, 1975), 24–25; William D. Phillips Jr., *Slavery from Roman Times to the Early Transatlantic Trade* (Minneapolis: University of Minnesota Press, 1985), 61–63, 68–69.

15. "Fernando Appeals His Suit to the General Court, 1667," Lower Norfolk County Order Book, 1666–1675, folder 17, reprinted in Warren M. Billings, ed., *The Old Dominion in the Seventeenth Century: A Documentary History of Virginia, 1606–1700*, rev. ed. (Chapel Hill: University of North Carolina Press, 2007), 200. Borrowing is central to Alan Watson's understanding of legal development, as exemplified in his *Slave Law in the Americas*, which argues for the heavy borrowing of Roman precedents. See also Christopher L. Tomlins, *Freedom Unbound: Law, Labor, and Civic Identity in Colonizing English America, 1580–1865* (New York: Cambridge University Press, 2010); Bradley J. Nicholson, "Legal Borrowing and the Origins of Slave Law in the British Colonies," *American Journal of Legal History* 38 (1994): 38–54.

16. Philip P. Boucher, *France and the American Tropics to 1700: Tropics of Discontent?* (Baltimore: Johns Hopkins University Press, 2008), 156; Guillaume Aubert, "To Establish One Law and Definite Rules: Race, Religion, and the Transatlantic Origins of the Louisiana Code Noir," in *Louisiana: Crossroads of the Atlantic World*, ed.

Cécile Vidal (Philadelphia: University of Pennsylvania Press, 2014), 35; Jacques Petit Jean Roget, *La société d'habitation a la Martinique: Un demi siècle de formation, 1635–1685*, 2 vols. (Lille: Université de Lille III, 1980), 2:1135.

17. See generally Michael Guasco, *Slaves and Englishmen: Human Bondage in the Early Modern Atlantic World* (Philadelphia: University of Pennsylvania Press, 2014); Kathleen M. Brown, *Good Wives, Nasty Wenches, and Anxious Patriarchs: Gender, Race, and Power in Colonial Virginia* (Chapel Hill: University of North Carolina Press, 1996), 109; Sally E. Hadden, "The Fragmented Laws of Slavery in the Colonial and Revolutionary Eras," in *The Cambridge History of Law in America*, ed. Michael Grossberg and Christopher Tomlins (New York: Cambridge University Press, 2008), 253, 257–258; Anthony S. Parent Jr., *Foul Means: The Formation of a Slave Society in Virginia, 1660–1740* (Chapel Hill: University of North Carolina Press, 2003), 107; Hadden, "The Fragmented Laws of Slavery," 258–264. Other North American colonies established after Virginia adopted slavery codes by borrowing and transplanting from slave systems that were already up and running. Christopher Tomlins has argued that the "first explicit definition of those who might be appropriately enslaved that was advanced by the English on the American mainland" appeared in Nathaniel Ward's 1641 *Body of Liberties*. Ward's definition borrowed from biblical principles and was codified in the Massachusetts *Lawes and Libertyes* in 1648. South Carolina adopted the slave code of Barbados almost verbatim when it passed the Act for the Better Ordering of Slaves in 1690–1691. The mid-Atlantic states adopted similar regimes as well, between the 1690s and the 1710s, including Barbados's system of slave courts. Christopher Tomlins, "Transplants and Timing: Passages in the Creation of an Anglo-American Law of Slavery," *Theoretical Inquiries in Law* 10 (2009): 389–421.

18. Vernon Valentine Palmer, "The Origins and Authors of the Code Noir," *Louisiana Law Review* 56, no. 2 (1996): 389–390; Aubert, "To Establish One Law." Palmer, in "The Origins and Authors," concludes that "where slave law was concerned, Louisiana was more the heir of Martinique and St. Domingue than of Rome" (390). Other scholars, however, argue that the code was a product of French legislators and "European legal scholars who knew far more about ancient Roman jurisprudence than about New World plantations." See Laurent Dubois and John Garrigus, *Slave Revolution in the Caribbean, 1789–1804: A Brief History with Documents* (Boston: Bedford, 2006), 49. See also Alan Watson, "The Origins of the Code Noir Revisited," *Tulane Law Review* 71, no. 4 (March 1997): 1041–1172; "The 'Code Noir' (1685)," trans. John Garrigus, accessed August 10, 2018, https://s3.wp.wsu.edu/uploads/sites/1205/2016/02/code-noir.pdf.

19. Roget, *La société d'habitation a la Martinique*, 2:1002.

20. De la Fuente, *Havana and the Atlantic*, 179–185.

21. Traslado de las Ordenanzas de los Negros, Santo Domingo, 1522, AGI, Patronato, leg. 295, no. 104. This document is reproduced, with a transcription by Anthony R. Stevens-Acevedo, on the website of the Dominican Studies Institute, City University of New York. We are grateful to Richard Turits for bringing this document to our attention. Subsequent local ordinances are reproduced in Malagón Barceló, *Código negro Carolino (1784)* (Santo Domingo: Ediciones Taller, 1974), 128–146.

22. De la Fuente, *Havana and the Atlantic*, 179; *Actas Capitulares del Ayuntamiento de la Habana* 1(2):89; ACAHT, 1616–1624, fol. 126.

23. *Actas Capitulares del Ayuntamiento de la Habana*, 1(2):75.

24. These ordinances are quoted and discussed in de la Fuente, *Havana and the Atlantic*, 179–180.

25. Pieza que contiene los cargos y descargos de la sentencia dada al Exmo. Sr. don Francisco Cagigal de la Vega en la residencia que se le ha tomado, Havana, 1762, AHN, Consejos (CI), leg. 21467, pieza 5, fol. 64; Primer cuaderno de autos de la residencia del señor Marques de Casa Cagigal, 1770, AHN, Consejos (CI), leg. 28898, pieza 1, fol. 324; Cargos y Exculpación del Sr. Marques de la Torre, 1777, AHN, Consejos (CI), leg. 20892; Bando 1 September 1786, in Juicio de residencia de Josef de Ezpeleta, 1789, AHN, Consejos (CI), leg. 20920, pieza 1, fol. 58; *Bando de buen gobierno del Excmo. Sr. conde de Santa Clara, gobernador y capitán General* (Havana: Imprenta de la Capitanía General, 1799), article 88.

26. De la Fuente, *Havana and the Atlantic*, 179–180; Residencia de don Antonio Maria Bucarelli, Havana, 1774, AHN, Consejos (CI), leg. 20889, pieza 1, fol. 183v.; Bando sobre prohibición del uso de armas, July 16, 1792, ANC, Asuntos Políticos, leg. 4, no. 37.

27. Tannenbaum, *Slave and Citizen*, 91–93; Tamar Herzog, *Defining Nations: Immigrants and Citizens in Early Modern Spain and Spanish America* (New Haven, CT: Yale University Press, 2003), 7; Governor Francisco de Venegas to the King, Havana, August 12, 1622, AGI, SD, leg. 101, ramo 1. See also Isabelo Macías, *Cuba en la primera mitad del siglo XVII* (Seville: Escuela de Estudios Hispanoamericanos de Sevilla, 1978), 36–37.

28. RC of July 21, 1623, in Richard Konetzke, *Colección de documentos para la historia de la formación social de Hispanoamérica, 1493–1810*, 3 vols. (Madrid: CSIC, 1953), 2:278; Marrero, *Cuba*, 5:26–28; Gabriel de Villalobos, "Grandezas de Indias," ca. 1670, Biblioteca Nacional de España, Mss. 2933; de la Fuente, *Havana and the Atlantic*, 180; ACAHT, vol. 1630–1639, fol. 139; Teniente Gobernador, Conde de Ripalda, Bando, June 5, 1777, in Residencia del Marques de la Torre, 1777, AHN, Consejos (CI), leg. 20893, pieza 22, fol. 177; ACAHT, 1599–1604, fol. 606–606v.

29. The language used in this regulation resembles closely a royal cedula of 1577 that ordered free blacks and mulattoes to live with "known masters" for tax purposes. See RC of April 29, 1577, in Diego de Encinas, *Cedulario Indiano*, 4 vols. (Madrid: Ediciones Cultura Hispánica, 1945–1946), 4:390. This RC became Ley 3, Título 5, Libro 7 in *Recopilación de Leyes de los Reynos de las Indias*, 4 vols. (Madrid: Julian de Paredes, 1681), 2:285v.

30. ACAHT, vol. 1609–1615, fol. 126–126v. For a similar regulation of 1624, see ACAHT, vol. 1616–1624, fol. 346; ACAHO, vol. 1616–1624, fol. 348v.–349. For similar sumptuary laws, see Ley 28, Título 5, Libro 7 of the *Recopilación* of 1680; "Ordenanzas de la Real Audiencia de Nueva España sobre juntas y trajes de negros y mulatos," April 14, 1612, in Konetzke, *Colección*, 1:2, 183; and Tamara J. Walker, *Exquisite Slaves: Race, Clothing, and Status in Colonial Lima* (New York: Cambridge University Press, 2017). Klein, *Slavery in the Americas*, 205–211, notes how in practice some of these prohibitions were ignored; George Reid Andrews, *Afro-Latin America, 1800–2000* (New York, NY: Oxford University

Press, 2004), 44–45; El Licenciado Manuel de Murguia y Mena a S.M., Havana, May 18, 1685, ANC, AH, leg. 90, no. 606. The Diocesan Synod of 1680 prohibited the admission into the sacred orders "the children of those condemned by the holly office, or blacks, mulattoes, or mestizos." See Juan García de Palacios, *Sínodo Diocesano* (Havana: Oficina de Arazoza y Soler, 1814), 18.

31. *Actas Capitulares del Ayuntamiento de la Habana*, 1(2):294 and 2:204.
32. For an example, see "Relación del Obispo Alonso Enríquez de Almendariz a S.M. 12 August 1620," *Memorias de la Sociedad Económica de Amigos del País* (Havana, 1847), 3:188, in which the population is divided into two categories: Spaniards and *negros*.
33. Antonio Vázquez de Espinosa, *Compendio y descripción de las Indias Occidentales* (Washington, DC: Smithsonian Institution, 1948), 293.
34. Early colonial understandings of race in the law are discussed extensively in A. Leon Higginbotham Jr., *In the Matter of Color: Race and the American Legal Process: The Colonial Period* (New York: Oxford University Press, 1978); Parent, *Foul Means*; Rebecca A. Goetz, *The Baptism of Early Virginia: How Christianity Created Race* (Baltimore: Johns Hopkins University Press, 2012); Edmund S. Morgan, *American Slavery, American Freedom: The Ordeal of Colonial Virginia* (New York: Norton, 1975); Brown, *Good Wives*; T. H. Breen and Stephen Innes, *"Myne Owne Ground": Race and Freedom on Virginia's Eastern Shore, 1640–1676* (New York: Oxford University Press, 2005); and Winthrop Jordan, *White over Black: American Attitudes to the Negro, 1550–1812*, 2nd ed. (Chapel Hill: University of North Carolina Press, 2012).
35. Act of January 6, 1639, in William Waller Hening, ed., *The Statutes at Large: Being a Collection of All the Laws of Virginia*, 13 vols. (New York: R. & W. & G. Bartow, 1819–1823), 1:226; Jordan, *White over Black*, 78; Parent, *Foul Means*, 109; Higginbotham, *In the Matter of Color*, 32. Breen and Innes summarize this debate well in *"Myne Owne Ground,"* 25–26.
36. Higginbotham, *In the Matter of Color*, 27.
37. William Waller Hening, ed., *The Statutes at Large; Being a Collection of All the Laws of Virginia from the First Session of the Legislature, in the Year 1619*, 13 vols. (New York: R. & W. & G. Bartow, 1819–1823), 2:26. ("ACT XXII: English running away with negroes. BEE itt enacted That in case any English servant shall run away in company with any negroes who are incapable of makeing satisfaction by addition of time, Bee itt enacted that the English so running away in company with them shall serve for the time of the said negroes absence as they are to do for their owne by a former act.")
38. Philip D. Morgan, *Slave Counterpoint: Black Culture in the Eighteenth-Century Chesapeake and Lowcountry* (Chapel Hill: University of North Carolina Press, 1998), 11–12, 308, 477; Morgan, *American Slavery, American Freedom*, 155, 328.
39. See "An Act for the Dutch and All Other Strangers for Trading to this Place" (1659), in Hening, *The Statutes at Large*, 1:540; "Negro Womens [*sic*] Children to Serve According to the Condition of the Mother" (1662), ibid., 2:170; Brown, *Good Wives*, 132; "Negro Women Not Exempted from Tax" (1668), in Hening, *The Statutes at Large*, 2:540; Brown, *Good Wives*, 108, 133.
40. "An Act Declaring that Baptisme of Slaves Doth Not Exempt Them from Bondage" (1667), in Hening, *The Statutes at Large*, 2:260; "Noe Negroes nor Indians to Buy

Christian Servants" (1670), ibid., 2:281; "What Tyme Indians to Serve," (1670), ibid., 2:283.

41. Conway Robinson, "Notes from the Council and General Court Records, 1641–1672," April 23, 1669, reprinted in *Virginia Magazine of History and Biography* 8, no. 3 (January 1901): 243.

42. "An Act for the Apprehension and Suppression of Runawayes, Negroes and Slaves" (1672), in Hening, *The Statutes at Large*, 2:299; "An Act for Preventing Negroes Insurrections" (1680), ibid., 2:481; "An Act to suppress outlying slaves" (1671), ibid., 3:86–88; "An Act for the more speedy prosecution of slaves committing Capitall Crimes" (1692), ibid., 3:102–103.

43. "An Act Concerning Servants and Slaves" (1705), in Hening, *The Statutes at Large*, 3:447–448.

44. Ibid., 3:448–449. Distinctions between (white) servants and (black) slaves were reiterated in the 1753 "Act for the better government of servants and slaves," which restated, with minimal revisions, the code of 1705. It reiterated, for instance, that "all petitions of servants to the court of the county wherein they reside for diet, clothing, lodging, correction, whipping, freedom or freedom dues, shall be received at any time." By 1753 it was unnecessary to state explicitly, however, that the servants' right to seek judicial redress did not apply to slaves and the notation was eliminated. See "An Act for the better government of servants and slaves" (1753), ibid., 6:358.

45. Higginbotham, *In the Matter of Color*, 44; Cortés López, *La esclavitud negra*, 142; Saunders, *A Social History of Black Slaves*, 40–42; de la Fuente, *Havana and the Atlantic*, 161–165; Steven Epstein, *Speaking of Slavery: Color, Ethnicity, and Human Bondage in Italy* (Ithaca, NY: Cornell University Press, 2001), 147, 175–179; "Act directing the trial of Slaves, committing capital crimes," (1726) and "An Act for the better government of servants and slaves," (1753), in Hening, *The Statutes at Large*, 4:131–33 and 6:361, respectively.

46. Philip J. Schwartz, *Twice Condemned: Slaves and the Criminal Laws of Virginia, 1705–1865* (Union, NJ: Lawbook Exchange, 1988), 62.

47. On this debate, see Aubert, "To Establish One Law," and Watson, "The Origins of the Code Noir," 1054–1055.

48. An English translation of the code is included in B. F. French, *Historical Collections of Louisiana* (New York: D. Appleton, 1851), 3:89–95. For an analysis, see Thomas N. Ingersoll, "Slave Codes and Judicial Practice in New Orleans, 1718–1807," *Law and History Review* 13, no. 1 (Spring 1995): 23–62.

49. Aubert, "To Establish One Law," 23.

50. Charles Gayarré, *History of Louisiana*, 2 vols. (New Orleans: Armand Hawkins, 1885), 2:53–55.

51. Gayarré, *History of Louisiana*, 2:364–366. See also articles 20 and 25: "Negroes or Negresses" not to assemble "under the pretext of dancing, or for any other cause" unless "the Negroes" belonged to a single owner – "excepting the Negroes whom they may own themselves"; those "Negroes" who used horses "immoderately" or who stole horses "to be shot at when they are thus met."

52. "Ordinance of Governor Kerlerec and Intendant-Commisary D'Auberville for suppression of cattle stealing by slaves," June 1, 1753, *Louisiana Historical Quarterly* 3 (January–October 1920): 89–91. On the racial order built by these regulations, see Thomas N. Ingersoll, "Free Blacks in a Slave Society: New Orleans 1718–1812," *William and Mary Quarterly* 48, no. 2 (April 1991): 173–200.

53. Carta de Manuel de Rojas a S.M., November 10, 1534, in *Colección de documentos inéditos relativos al descubrimiento, conquista y organización de las antiguas posesiones españolas de ultramar*, second series, 25 vols. (Madrid: Establecimiento Tipográfico "Sucesores de Rivadeneyra," 1885–1932), 4:333; ACAHT, vol. 1599–1604, fol. 468.

54. There are several copies of these "Ordenanzas redactadas por el cabildo habanero para la reducción de negros cimarrones" dated July 14, 1600. The original is in the original series of the town council records, ACAHO, vol. 1603–1609, fol. 3v., which is reproduced in the copied ("trasuntadas") series, ACAHT, vol. 1599–1604, fol. 4. There are additional copies in AGI, SD, leg. 116, and in ANC, AH, leg. 31, no. 289.

55. ACAHT, vol. 1599–1604, fol. 502v.–503; ACAHT, vol. 1609–1615, fol. 126; ACAHT, vol. 1683–1691, fol. 260v.; Condiciones formadas por los Sres. Comisarios y Procurador General para la captura de negros cimarrones, May 31, 1690, ACAHO, 1688–1691, fol. 530–531v.; the "Reglamento de Cimarrones" of 1796 is reproduced in Fernando Ortiz, *Los negros esclavos* (Havana: Editorial de Ciencias Sociales, 1975), 416–422.

56. "An act for preventing Negroes Insurrections" (1680), in Hening, *The Statutes at Large*, 2:481–482; "An act for the more speedy prosecution of slaves committing Capitall Crimes" (1692), ibid., 3:102–103.

For a summary of Virginia's criminal statutes targeting slaves and "negroes," see June Purcell Guild, *Black Laws of Virginia* (Richmond, VA: Whittet & Shepperson, 1936), 151–171.

57. Gilbert C. Din, *Spaniards, Planters and Slaves: The Spanish Regulation of Slavery in Louisiana* (College Station: Texas A&M University Press, 1999), 5; "Attorney General on Desertions," August 17, 1726, *Louisiana Historical Quarterly* 3 (January–October 1920): 414; See articles 26, 32–34 of the Code Noir.

58. Quoted in Parent, *Foul Means*, 238.

59. ACAHT, vol. 1654–1661, fol. 198v.–199.

CHAPTER 2   THE "INCONVENIENCE" OF BLACK FREEDOM

1. Petition to Redeem Slave wife, June 28, July 6, and Oct. 29, 1737, Documents 1737-07-06-01 and 1737-06-28-06, Box 46, LCJR, LHC; Emancipation of Marie Aram, a slave, by her husbands labor during seven years, March 6–10, 1744, no. 3785 (23780), Document 1744-03-06-03, LCJR, LHC. "Contract of Tiocou with Director of Hospital (July 15, 1737)" is reprinted in *Louisiana Historical Quarterly* (*LHQ*) 4 (1921): 366–368. On the origins of the hospital, see John Salvaggio, *New Orlean's Charity Hospital: A Story of Physicians, Politics and Poverty* (Baton Rouge: Louisiana State University Press, 1992), 11–13; "Olographic Will of Jean Luis, 1735," *LHQ* 3 (1920): 555–557; Gwendolyn Midlo Hall, *Databases for the Study of Afro-Louisiana History and Genealogy, 1699–1860: Information from Original Manuscript Sources* (Baton Rouge: Louisiana State University Press, 1999).

2. "Petition of the Directors of the Charity Hospital of New Orleans to Grant Freedom to Marie Aram, a Negress Slave (March 6, 1744)," Document 1744-03-06-03, pp. 2–3, LCJR, LHC, excerpted in *LHQ* 3 (1920): 551–553.

3. "An Act to Free Will, a Negro Belonging to Robert Ruffin" (1710), in William Waller Hening, ed., *The Statutes at Large: Being a Collection of All the Laws of Virginia*, 13 vols. (New York: R. & W. & G. Bartow, 1819–1823), 3:537–538.

4. "Petición y Sentencia en La Causa por La Libertad de Los Negros Esclavos Cristobal Mina y Jose Mina," November 17, 1691, ANC, PNH, Escribania Fornaris, 1691, fol. 343.

5. See Chapter 1. We also explore these efforts in Ariela Gross and Alejandro de la Fuente, "Slaves, Free Blacks, and Race in the Legal Regimes of Cuba, Louisiana and Virginia: A Comparison," *North Carolina Law Review* 91 (2013): 1699–1756.

6. Stuart B. Schwartz, *Sugar Plantations in the Formation of Brazilian Society: Bahia, 1550–1835* (New York: Cambridge University Press, 1985), 252; Alejandro de la Fuente, *Havana and the Atlantic in the Sixteenth Century* (Chapel Hill: University of North Carolina Press, 2008), 171–173; Carmen Bernard, *Negros esclavos y libres en las ciudades hispanoamericanas* (Madrid: Fundación Histórica Tavera, 2001), 118–119; Alfonso Franco Silva, *La esclavitud en Sevilla y su tierra a fines de la Edad Media* (Seville: Diputación Provincial de Sevilla, 1979), 246–248; see also George Reid Andrews, *Afro-Latin America, 1800–2000* (New York: Oxford University Press, 2004), 86–92; Marixa Lasso, *Myths of Harmony: Race and Republicanism during the Age of Revolution, Colombia 1795–1831* (Pittsburgh: University of Pittsburgh Press, 2007), 9–11.

7. The phrase comes from Richard Frucht, *Black Society in the New World* (New York: Random House, 1971), 196.

8. Marvin Harris, *Patterns of Race in the Americas* (New York: Walker and Co., 1964), 84–92; Carl Degler, *Neither Black nor White: Slavery and Race Relations in Brazil and the United States* (Madison: University of Wisconsin Press, 1971), 44 ("The free blacks and mulattoes were needed. . . . They filled the innumerable petty jobs, the interstitial work of the economy."); Degler, *Neither Black nor White*, 39–47; T. Ingersoll, *Mammon and Manon in Early New Orleans* (Knoxville: University of Tennessee Press, 1999), 221–234; D. G. Eder, "Time under the Southern Cross: The Tannenbaum Thesis Reappraised," *Agricultural History* 50, no. 4 (1976): 600–614; D. C. Rankin, "The Tannenbaum Thesis Reconsidered: Slavery and Race Relations in Antebellum Louisiana," *Southern Studies* 18, no. 1 (1979): 5–31.

9. Camillia Cowling, *Conceiving Freedom: Women of Color, Gender, and the Abolition of Slavery in Havana and Rio de Janeiro* (Chapel Hill: University of North Carolina Press, 2013), 9.

10. A. C. de C. M. Saunders, *A Social History of Black Slaves and Freedmen in Portugal, 1441–1555* (Cambridge: Cambridge University Press, 1982), 138.

11. J. L. C. López, *La esclavitud negra en la España peninsular del siglo XVI* (Salamanca: Universidad de Salamanca, 1989), 228–235; W. D. Phillips Jr., *Historia de la esclavitud en España* (Madrid: Editorial Playor, 1990), 175–176; Silva, *La esclavitud en Sevilla*, 247, 261–272; Saunders, *A Social History of Black Slaves*, 54–57; Phillips, *Historia de la esclavitud en España*, 177.

12. Steven Epstein, *Speaking of Slavery: Color, Ethnicity, and Human Bondage in Italy* (Ithaca, NY: Cornell University Press, 2001), 170–171; M. Bloch, *Slavery and Serfdom in the Middle*

Ages (Los Angeles: University of California Press, 1975), 14; Saunders, *A Social History of Black Slaves*, 138; Gonzalo Aguirre Beltrán, *La población negra de México, 1519–1810: Estudio etnohistórico* (Mexico City: Fondo de Cultura Económica, 1972), 281.

13. Debra Blumenthal, "Demandes de Libertat: Demandas de esclavos en el medioevo tardío valenciano," *Debate y Perspectivas* 4 (2014): 23–36; El Rey al Gobernador y los Oficiales Reales de Cuba, November 9, 1526, ANC, AH, leg. 80, no. 7; RC, April 15, 1540, later Ley 8, Titulo 5, Libro 7 in the *Recopilación de Leyes de los Reynos de las Indias*, 4 vols. (Madrid: Julian de Paredes, 1681), 2:286; RC, May 11, 1527, in Diego de Encinas, *Cedulario Indiano*, 4 vols. (Madrid: Ediciones Cultura Hispánica, 1945–1946), 4:385–386.

14. The discussion of manumission in early colonial Havana (1585–1610) is based on de la Fuente, *Havana and the Atlantic*, 170–179, and Alejandro de la Fuente, "Alforria de Escravos en Havana, 1601–1610: Primeiras conclusões," *Estudo Econômicos* 20 (1990): 139–159; Frederick P. Bowser, "The Free Person of Color in Mexico City and Lima: Manumission and Opportunity, 1580–1650," in *Race and Slavery in the Western Hemisphere: Quantitative Studies*, ed. Stanley L. Engerman and Eugene D. Genovese (Princeton, NJ: Princeton University Press, 1975), 331–368; the eighteenth-century Havana figures come from Manuel Moreno Fraginals, "Peculiaridades de la esclavitud en Cuba," *Del Caribe* 4, no. 8 (1987): 4–10.

15. Herbert S. Klein, *African Slavery in Latin America and the Caribbean* (New York: Oxford University Press, 1986), 227; for a discussion of gender and manumissions, see Kathleen J. Higgins, *"Licentious Liberty" in a Brazilian Gold-Mining Region: Slavery, Gender, and Social Control in Eighteenth-Century Sabará, Minas Gerais* (University Park: Pennsylvania State University Press, 1999), and Frank T. Proctor III, "Afro-Mexican Slave Labor in the Obrajes de Panos of New Spain, Seventeenth and Eighteenth Centuries," *The Americas* 60 (2003): 33–58.

16. The importance of children in manumissions is not a Cuban phenomenon but is noted in other colonial territories. For examples, see Stuart B. Schwartz, "The Manumission of Slaves in Colonial Brazil: Bahia, 1684–1745," *Hispanic American Historical Review* 54 (1974): 615; Bowser, "The Free Person of Color in Mexico City and Lima," 350; Lyman L. Johnson, "Manumission in Colonial Buenos Aires, 1776–1810," *Hispanic American Historical Review* 59 (1979): 262; Kátia M. de Queirós Mattoso, *To Be a Slave in Brazil: 1550–1888* (New Brunswick, NJ: Rutgers University Press, 1986), 163–164; Klein, *African Slavery in Latin America*, 227.

17. ANC, PNH, ER, 1602, fol. 48; ANC, Protocolos Notariales de Santa Clara, Escribanos Salvador Gonzalez y Manuel Rodriguez, 1691–1696, fol. 4.

18. ANC, PNH, Escribania Fornaris, 1690, fol. 45.

19. ANC, PNH, Escribania Fornaris, 1694, fol. 257.

20. These cases are registered in the Actas Capitulares del Ayuntamiento de la Habana, 1650–1700. The records contain only a brief notation about each case, not the cases themselves. The actual judicial dossiers do not seem to exist.

21. Moreno Fraginals, "Peculiaridades de la esclavitud en Cuba," 7.

22. ACAHT, vol. 1672–1683, fol. 329v.; RC, September 24, 1750, ANC, Reales Cédulas y Ordenes, leg. 2, no. 120. Additional references to these regulations appear in

José M. Zamora y Coronado, *Biblioteca de legislación ultramarina*, 7 vols. (Madrid: Imprenta de Alegría y Charlain, 1844–1846), 3:128, and Fernando Ortiz, *Los negros esclavos* (Havana: Editorial de Ciencias Sociales, 1975), 320.

23. Ingersoll, *Mammon and Manon in Early New Orleans*, 77–78; Daniel H. Usner, "From African Captivity to American Slavery: The Introduction of Black Laborers to Colonial Louisiana," *Louisiana History: The Journal of the Louisiana Historical Association* 20 (1979): 192.

24. Gabriel Debien, *Les esclaves aux Antilles françaises, XVIIe–XVIIIe siècles* (Basse-Terre and Fort-de-France: Societés d'Histoire, 1974), 371–373; Gillaume Aubert, "To Establish One Law and Definite Rules: Race, Religion, and the Transatlantic Origins of the Louisiana Code Noir," in *Louisiana: Crossroads of the Atlantic World*, ed. Cécile Vidale (Philadelphia: University of Pennsylvania Press, 2014), 39.

25. Hall, *Databases for the Study of Afro-Louisiana History*; Thomas Ingersoll, "Free Blacks in a Slave Society: New Orleans, 1718–1812," *William and Mary Quarterly* 48 (1991): 177.

26. Manumission of Marie Charlotte and Louise (October 9, 1735), no. 23589–90, Document 1735-10-09-01, LCJR, LHC, excerpted in *LHQ* 8 (1925): 143–144. In this case, however, freedom was denied the mother and daughter because their master "owed three times as much as his goods were worth."

27. Manumission of Jeanneton, July 11, 1737, Document 1737-7-11-01, Box 046, LCJR, LHC, excerpted in *LHQ* 5 (1922): 403; Manumission of Mimi, April 8, 1762, Document 1762-02-28-02, LCJR, LHC, reprinted in *LHQ* 23 (1940): 924; "Emancipation Paper (Oct. 1, 1733)," *LHQ* 5 (1922): 250. See also Manumission of slave by Governor Bienville, Document 1743-07-16-01, LCJR, LHC.

28. Manumission of Louis Connard et al., Document 1739-03-06-02, LCJR, LHC, summarized in *LHQ* 6 (1923): 283, 303–304; "Excerpt from Register of Superior Council, petition for freedom by Pantalon, freed by Dartagnette in his will, May 10, 1747," *LHQ* 18 (1935): 430, 440; see Manumission of Marie Charlotte and Louise, October 9, 1735; Manumission of Françoise and Laplante, January 22, 1762, Document 1762-01-22-01, LCJR, LHC, summarized in *LHQ* 23(1940): 603; Manumission of Mimi, April 8, 1762.

29. "Surgeon Antoine Meuillion grants freedom to his female slave" (1746), *LHQ* 15 (1932): 133–134.

30. Several reenslavements of properly manumitted slaves are noted in Superior Council Records. Jean-Baptiste was reenslaved for theft of clothes, for example, Fabry v. Jean-Baptiste, 19–14 August, September 1743, cited in Thomas N. Ingersoll, *Mammon and Manon in Early New Orleans: The First Slave Society in the Deep South, 1718–1819* (Knoxville, TN: University of Tennessee Press, 1999), 79. Shannon Lee Dawdy, *Building the Devil's Empire: French Colonial New Orleans* (Chicago: University of Chicago Press, 2008), 181, argues that unsanctioned manumissions were common, but her assertion rests on limited evidence.

31. Rebecca Scott and Jean Hébrard, *Freedom Papers: An Atlantic Odyssey in the Age of Emancipation* (Cambridge, MA: Harvard University Press, 2012), 19; Manumission of Louis Connard et al., March 6, 1739.

32. Will of A. Vanga, A. Leon Higginbotham Jr., *In the Matter of Color. Race and the American Legal Process: The Colonial Period* (New York: Oxford University Press, 1978), 47; H. R. McIlwaine, ed., *Minutes of the Council and General Court of Colonial Virginia*, 2nd ed. (Richmond: Virginia State Library, 1979), 477 (minutes from March 31, 1641); ibid., 513 (minutes from September 24, 1668); ibid., 316 (minutes from October 5, 1672).

33. See *Northampton County, Virginia, Record Book: Orders, Deeds, Wills &c*, ed. Howard Mackey and Marlene E. Groves, 17 vols. (Rockport, ME: Picton Press, 1999–2006): *Northampton County Deeds and Wills 1645–1651*, folder 75, 237; *Northampton County Orders, Deeds, Wills 1651–1654*, 123 (January 10, 1647) and 226 (February 28, 1652); *Northampton County Deeds and Wills 1654–1655*, folder 10, 35 (March 8, 1655); *Northampton County Orders Wills 1655–1657*, 10; Manumission of Black Jacke and Nese, in *Northampton County Orders 1654–1655*; Manumission of Bashaw Fernando (1659), in *Northampton County Deeds, Wills 1657–1666*, folder 106, 57. For more detail, see Paul Heinegg, *Free African Americans of North Carolina, Virginia, and South Carolina*, vol. 2 (Baltimore: Clearfield, 2005), 705–707; J. Douglas Deal, *Race and Class in Colonial Virginia* (New York: Garland, 1993), 219–221.

34. *Northampton County Deeds, Wills 1645–1651*, 39, folder 217; *Northampton County Deeds, Wills 1654–1655*, folder 25, 54; *Northampton County Deeds, Wills 1651–1654*, 33, folder 33; Heinegg, *Free African Americans*, 839–840.

35. Nell Marion Nugent, *Cavaliers and Pioneers: Abstracts of Virginia Land Patents and Grants, 1623–1800* (Richmond, VA: Dietz Printing Co., 1934), 1:74; *Northampton County Deeds, Wills 1651–1654*, folders 118, 174; see also Deal, *Race and Class in Colonial Virginia*, 398–412.

36. Ira Berlin, *Generations of Captivity: A History of African-American Slaves* (Cambridge, MA: Harvard University Press, 2004). According to April Lee Hatfield, Francisco and Mingo were probably former Barbadians who had acquired Iberian names in Brazil, where Dutch traders purchased many of the slaves they took to Barbados in that period. April Lee Hatfield, *Atlantic Virginia: Intercolonial Relations in the Seventeenth Century* (Philadelphia: University of Pennsylvania Press, 2004), 166–167.

37. *Northampton County Deeds, Wills 1657–1666*, 70, 74; Deal, *Race and Class in Colonial Virginia*, 337–338; JoAnn Riley McKey, ed., *Accomack County, Virginia, Court Order Abstracts, Volume 3: 1671–1673* (Westminster, MD: Heritage Books, 2012), 94 (September 17, 1672); York County Deeds, Orders, Wills (6) 67, February 24, 1678/9, and 117, August 25, 1679, available at Virtual Jamestown, Institute for Advanced Technology in the Humanities, University of Virginia, accessed March 22, 2019, www.virtualjamestown.org/yorkfreedomsuits1685_1715.html.

38. Rebecca A. Goetz, *The Baptism of Early Virginia: How Christianity Created Race* (Baltimore: Johns Hopkins University Press, 2012), 102–103.

39. Northumberland Record Book, 1652–1658, 66–67, 85, reprinted in Warren M. Billings, ed., *The Old Dominion in the Seventeenth Century: A Documentary History of Virginia, 1606–1700*, rev. ed. (Chapel Hill: University of North Carolina Press, 2007), 195–197; Goetz, *The Baptism of Early Virginia*, 101–102; Warren M. Billings, "The Cases of

Fernando and Elizabeth Key: A Note on the Status of Blacks in Seventeenth-Century Virginia," *William and Mary Quarterly* 30 (1973): 468.

40. McIlwaine, *Minutes,* 477 (minutes from March 31, 1641); "An Act to Free Will, a Negro Belonging to Robert Ruffin," 1667.

41. Goetz, *The Baptism of Early Virginia,* 108; York County Deeds, Orders, and Wills (10) 137, April 6, 1695, judgment confirmed in ibid., (10) 230, Virtual Jamestown, Institute for Advanced Technology in the Humanities, accessed March 22, 2019, www .virtualjamestown.org/yorkfreedomsuits1685_1715.html; Heinegg, *Free African Americans,* 707.

42. Manumission of Jeane, 1672, in McKey, *Accomack County Court Order Abstracts, 1671–1673;* Manumission of Bashaw Fernando, 1659, in *Northampton County Deeds, Wills 1657–1666,* folder 106; Petition of Henry Jackson to William Sterling, in Frank V. Walczyk, ed., *Northampton County, Virginia, Orders & Wills* (Coram, NY: Peter's Row, 2000), pp. 62, 64–65; also in Northampton Wills & Orders, Book 13, 1689–1698, microfilm no. 27a, LVA.

43. Edmund S. Morgan, *American Slavery, American Freedom: The Ordeal of Colonial Virginia* (New York: Norton, 1975), 328.

44. John C. Coombs, "The Phases of Conversion: A New Chronology for the Rise of Slavery in Early Virginia," *William and Mary Quarterly* 68, no. 3 (July 2011): 332–360.

45. Act for the Better Ordering of Negroes, 1661. The act's preamble explains that Africans were a "heathenish brutish and an uncertain dangerous pride of people" requiring "punishionary Laws for the benefit and good" of the colony. Barbados and Jamaica never restricted a master's right to free a slave, and Barbados continued to allow free people of color many civil rights well into the eighteenth century, imposing only a ban on courtroom testimony in the second half of the eighteenth century. Not until 1739 did Barbados impose manumission fees on slave owners, and some have argued that these were easy to circumvent; when the fees were increased in 1801, the law was overturned within a few years because of public opposition. See Jerome S. Handler, *The Unappropriated People: Freedmen in the Slave Society of Barbados* (Baltimore: Johns Hopkins University Press, 1974), 60–83; Bradley J. Nicholson, "Legal Borrowing and the Origins of Slave Law in the British Colonies," *American Journal of Legal History* 38, no. 1 (1994), 38–54; Jerome S. Handler, "Custom and Law: The Status of Enslaved Africans in Seventeenth-Century Barbados," *Slavery & Abolition* 37, no. 2 (2016); 233–255; Edward B. Rugemer, "The Development of Mastery and Race in the Comprehensive Slave Codes of the Greater Caribbean during the Seventeenth Century," *William and Mary Quarterly* 70, no. 3 (2013): 429–458; Melanie J. Newton, *The Children of Africa in the Colonies: Free People of Color in Barbados in the Age of Emancipation* (Baton Rouge: Louisiana State University Press, 2008), 36–39; David Barry Gaspar, "'Rigid and Inclement': Origins of the Jamaica Slave Laws of the Seventeenth Century," in *The Many Legalities of Early America,* ed. Christopher L. Tomlins and Bruce H. Mann (Chapel Hill: University of North Carolina Press, 2001), 78–96; Elsa Goveia, *The West Indian Slave Laws of the Eighteenth Century* (Barbados: Caribbean Universities Press, 1970); Hatfield, *Atlantic Virginia,* 154.

46. "An Act for suppressing outlying slaves" (1691), in Hening, *The Statutes at Large*, 3:86–88; Henry R. Mc Ilwaine, ed., *Executive Journals of the Council of Colonial Virginia*, 6 vols. (Richmond: Virginia State Library, 1925–1967), 3:332; "An Act Directing the Trial of Slaves" (1723), in Hening, *The Statutes at Large*, 4:132.

47. Michael L. Nicholls, "Strangers Setting among Us: The Sources and Challenge of the Urban Free Black Population of Early Virginia," *Virginia Magazine of History and Biography* 118 (2000): 155.

48. Karl Offen, "Environment, Space, and Place: Cultural Geographies of Afro-Latin America," in *Afro-Latin American Studies: An Introduction*, ed. Alejandro de la Fuente and George Reid Andrews (New York: Cambridge University Press, 2018), 486–533; McIlwaine, *Executive Journals*, 3:199, 217.

49. McIlwaine, *Executive Journals*, 4:315, 366; 5:60.

50. McIlwaine, *Executive Journals*, 5:298; two of these cases are mentioned by Linda Rowe in "After 1723, Manumission Takes Careful Planning and Plenty of Savvy," *Colonial Williamsburg Interpreter* 25 (2004): 2, accessed March 23, 2019, www.history.org/history/teaching/enewsletter/volume3/february05/manumission.cfm.

51. McIlwaine, *Executive Journals*, 5:196, 215.

52. Ibid., 3:277–278, 442.

53. Petition of Thomas Ferrell, Folder 1, Pk. 5, April 1723, Northampton County Free Negro and Slave Records [NCFNSR], 1723–1808, Barcode 1168313, LVA; Petition of Nanny Bandy, alias Judea, Folder 1, Pk. 18, August 1732, NCFNSR, LVA; "Will, mulatto, held illegally in slavery," Folder 1, Pk. 33, September 1747, NCFNSR, LVA; "Indian Will illegally held as a slave," Folder 1, Pk. 33, September 1747, NCFNSR, LVA.

54. Webb v. Savage, Northampton County Chancery Court Records, 1721 (Northampton County Chancery Court, 1726), LVA.

55. Ibid.

56. King vs. Abimeleck Webb, "a free negro," Northampton County Criminal Causes, 1735–1759, Barcode 1168308, Folder 3, Pk. 36 (September 1750), LVA.

57. De la Fuente, *Havana and the Atlantic*, 165–167.

58. Jennifer M. Spear, *Race, Sex, and Social Order in Early New Orleans* (Baltimore: Johns Hopkins University Press, 2009), 50–51.

59. *Le Code Noir ou recueil des reglements rendus jusqu'a present* (Paris: Prault, 1767).

60. Spear, *Race, Sex, and Social Order*, 79–80; Cécile Vidal, "Caribbean Louisiana: Church, *Métissage*, and the Language of Race in the Mississippi Colony during the French Period," in *Louisiana: Crossroads of the Atlantic World*, ed. Cécile Vidale (Philadelphia: University of Pennsylvania Press, 2014), 125–146.

61. Vidal, "Caribbean Louisiana," 131, 132–135, 138.

62. Emily Clark, *The Strange History of the American Quadroon* (Chapel Hill: University of North Carolina Press, 2013), 166–167.

63. Catherine Clinton and Michele Gillespie, *The Devil's Lane: Sex and Race in the Early South* (New York: Oxford University Press, 1997), 124.

64. Marriage of William Greensted and Elizabeth Key, in Billings, *Old Dominion*, 199; for Philip Mongom, Martha Merris, and Margery Tyer, see Heinegg, *Free African Americans*,

2:840; for Francis Payne and Aymey, see Morgan, *American Slavery, American Freedom*, 334; for Emanuel Driggus, Richard Johnson, and Anthony Longo, see Parent, *Foul Means*, 116. Terri L. Snyder, "Marriage on the Margins: Free Wives, Enslaved Husbands, and the Law in Early Virginia," *Law and History Review* 30, no. 1 (February 2012): 141–171, also includes several cases of free white wives with enslaved husbands (although most of Snyder's cases involve free women of color).

65. John Johnson and Hannah Leach, in JoAnn Riley McKey, ed., *Accomack County, Virginia, Court Order Abstracts, Volume 1: 1663–1666* (Westminster, MD: Heritage Books, 2012), February 17, 1664/65, 115, and March 14, 1664/65, 117; Elizabeth Lang and Indian Father, in McKey, *Accomack County Court Order Abstracts, 1671–1673*, January 17, 1671/72, 37; Dorothy Bestick, in McKey, ed., *Accomack County, Virginia, Court Order Abstracts, Volume 7: 1682–1690* (Westminster, MD: Heritage Books, 2012), 315 (September 17, 1690). See, generally, McKey, ed., *Accomack County, Virginia, Court Order Abstracts, Volume 10: 1703–1710* (Westminster, MD: Heritage Books, 2012), including, e.g., Easter Rae, October 6, 1703, 15; Jane Salmond, October 4, 1704, 46; Mary Newman, October 6, 1704, 47.

66. "Negro womens children to serve according to the condition of the mother," Act 12 (December 1662), in Hening, *The Statutes at Large*, 2:170; T. H. Breen and Stephen Innes, *"Myne Owne Ground": Race and Freedom on Virginia's Eastern Shore, 1640–1676* (New York: Oxford University Press, 2004), 89–90; Hening, *The Statutes at Large*, 3: 87, 453–454; Northampton County Criminal Causes, 1735–1739, Barcode 1168308, Folder 1, Pk. 24, November 1738, LVA; King v. Hitchens, for intermarrying or cohabiting with mulattoes, in John M. Mihalyka, *Northampton County Loose Papers and Sundry Court Cases* [*NCLPSCC*], vol. 2 (Eastville, VA: Hickory House, 1997), 16.

67. Northampton County Criminal Causes, 1722–1734, Barcode 1168307, Pk. 2 (1721), Pk. 9 (1725), Pk. 37 (1751), LVA; for Anne Toyer, see *NCLPSCC*, 19 (in June 1733 packet); Elisha Pitts, see *NCLPSCC*, 16; Mary Newman, see McKey, *Accomack County Court Order Abstracts, 1703–1710*, October 6, 1704, 47, 50; Elizabeth Lang and Rachell Wood, see Goetz, *The Baptism of Early Virginia*, 81–85. In Westmoreland County, see Mary Lawler, "free Christian white woman" with "mulatto bastard child," July 30, 1707, *Westmoreland County, Virginia Court Orders, 1705–1757*, microfilm reel nos. 55–61, LVA, at 64 (transcript available at www.freeafricanamericans.com/westmore.htm, accessed April 24, 2019); Mary Hipsley (same description), July 31, 1707, ibid., 69; Sara Bryan (same description), January 26, 1708/9, ibid., 108a; Elizabeth Crane, November 28, 1712, ibid., 203a; Mary Fullam, July 27, 1719/20, ibid., 392a.

68. The important concept of "critical mass" comes from Kimberly Hanger, *Bounded Lives, Bounded Places: Free Black Society in Colonial New Orleans, 1769–1803* (Durham, NC: Duke University Press, 1997), 17–18.

69. Northampton County Tithable Lists, in Breen and Innes, *"Myne Owne Ground,"* 68–69.

70. Gwendolyn Midlo Hall, *Afro-Louisiana History and Genealogy, 1719–1820*, accessed March 24, 2019; Dawdy, *Building the Devil's Empire*, 178–179.

71. NCFNSR, 1723–1808; *NCLPSCC*, 1744–1761; Northampton County Criminal Causes, 1722–1799; McKey, *Accomack County, Virginia, Court Orders*, see volumes for the years 1703–1799; Breen and Innes, *"Myne Owne Ground,"* 92–94.

72. Breen and Innes, *"Myne Owne Ground,"* 5–6.

73. Deal, *Race and Class in Colonial Virginia*; Nicholls, *Strangers Setting among Us*, 151; Heinegg, *Free African Americans*.

74. Thomas Ingersoll, "Slave Codes and Judicial Practice in New Orleans, 1718–1807," *Law and History Review*, 13 (1995): 39.

75. Gayarré, *History of Louisiana*, 2:363–364; "Judgment Rendered by the Superior Council, 1743," *LHQ* 12 (1929): 147.

76. Leví Marrero, "Article 53 of the Ordinances," *Cuba: Economía y sociedad*, 15 vols. (Madrid: Editorial Playor, 1971–1992), 2:437; ANC, PNH, ER, 1600, fol. 83; ibid., 1605, fol. 810; ibid., 1601, fol. 635; ibid., 1609, fol. 385v.; ANC, PNH, Escribania Fornaris, 1640, fol. 27; ANC, PNH, ER, 1604, fol. 557v; ibid., 1606, fol. 515v.; Bishop Geronimo de Lara to the King, n.d., 1635, Archivo General de Indias, Santo Domingo, leg. 150, ramo 3; "Relación del Obispado de Cuba," 1636, Biblioteca Nacional, Madrid, Ms. 3000; Juan Garcia de Palacios, *Sinodo de Santiago de Cuba de 1681* (Madrid: CSIC, 1982), 11.

77. Diego Fernández de Quiñones to the king, December 12, 1582, ANC, Academia de la Historia, leg. 82, no. 110; ACAHT, September 3, 1630, vol. 1630–1639, fol. 7; ANC, PNH, Escribania Fornaris, 1694, fol. 422; Marrero, *Cuba*, 8:163, 165; José Martín Félix de Arrate y Acosta, *Llave del Nuevo Mundo, antemural de las Indias Occidentales: La Habana descripta* (Mexico: Fondo de Cultura Económica, 1949), 95.

78. *Actas Capitulares del Ayuntamiento de la Habana* (Havana: Municipio de la Habana, 1937), 1(2):150, 297 (November 26, 1565); ibid., 3:172 (November 22, 1577); Irene A. Wright, *Historia documentada de San Cristobal de la Habana en el siglo XVI*, 2 vols. (Havana: Imp. El Siglo XX, 1927), 1: 73; Marrero, *Cuba*, 8:164.

CHAPTER 3 "THE NATURAL RIGHT OF ALL MANKIND"

1. Keila Grinberg, "Freedom Suits and Civil Law in Brazil and the United States," *Slavery & Abolition* 22, no. 3 (2001): 66; Peter Blanchard, *Under the Flags of Freedom: Slave Soldiers and the Wars of Independence in Spanish South America* (Pittsburgh: University of Pittsburgh Press, 2008); James Sanders, *Contentious Republicans: Popular Politics, Race, and Class in Nineteenth-Century Colombia* (Durham, NC: Duke University Press, 2004); Marixa Lasso, *Myths of Harmony: Race and Republicans during the Age of Revolution, Colombia, 1795–1831* (Pittsburgh: University of Pittsburgh Press, 2007); George Reid Andrews, *Afro-Latin America, 1800–2000* (New York: Oxford University Press, 2004); Marcela Echeverri, *Indian and Slave Royalists in the Age of Revolution: Reform, Revolution, and Royalism in the Northern Andes, 1780–1825* (New York: Cambridge University Press, 2016).

2. Daniel E. Walker, *No More, No More: Slavery and Cultural Resistance in Havana and New Orleans* (Minneapolis: University of Minnesota Press, 2004), 113; Ada Ferrer, *Freedom's Mirror: Cuba and Haiti in the Age of Revolution* (New York: Cambridge University Press, 2014), 71–328; Matt Childs, *The 1812 Aponte Rebellion in Cuba and the Struggle against Atlantic Slavery* (Chapel Hill: University of North Carolina Press, 2006), 162–171; Ada Ferrer, "Speaking of Haiti: Slavery, Revolution, and Freedom in Cuban Slave

Testimony," in David Patrick Geggus and Norman Fiering, eds., *The World of the Haitian Revolution* (Bloomington: Indiana University Press, 2009), 228; Caryn Cossé Bell, *Revolution, Romanticism, and the Afro-Creole Protest Tradition in Louisiana, 1718–1868* (Baton Rouge: Louisana State University Press, 1997), 30.

3. Manuel M. Fraginals, *The Sugarmill: The Socioeconomic Complex of Sugar in Cuba* (New York: Monthly Review Press, 1976), 28; Anthony E. Kaye, "The Second Slavery: Modernity in the Nineteenth-Century South and the Atlantic World," *Journal of Southern History* 75, no. 3 (2009): 627–650; Ferrer, "Speaking of Haiti," 223.

4. James H. Dormon, "The Persistent Specter: Slave Rebellion in Territorial Louisiana," *Louisiana History: The Journal of the Louisiana Historical Association* 18, no. 4 (1977): 389–404, quote on 393; Ferrer, "Speaking of Haiti," 228, 234–237.

5. Ferrer, *Freedom's Mirror*, 186, 189; Bell, *Revolution, Romanticism, and the Afro-Creole Protest Tradition*, 46; for freedom suits by Saint-Domingue refugees, see Rebecca Scott and Jean M. Hébrard, *Freedom Papers: An Atlantic Odyssey in the Age of Emancipation* (Cambridge, MA: Harvard University Press, 2012).

6. Grinberg, "Freedom Suits and Civil Law"; Bianca Premo, *The Enlightenment on Trial: Ordinary Litigants and Colonialism in the Spanish Empire* (New York: Oxford University Press, 2017).

7. Rashauna Johnson, *Slavery's Metropolis: Unfree Labor in New Orleans during the Age of Revolutions* (New York: Cambridge University Press, 2016), 13.

8. "Jefferson's 'original Rough draught' of the Declaration of Independence," accessed March 25, 2019, http://www.loc.gov/exhibits/declara/ruffdrft.html.

9. "An Act for Preventing the Further Importation of Slaves, Laws of Virginia, October 1778 – 3d of Commonwealth," in *Hening's Statutes at Large*, vol. 9: *1775–1778*, (Richmond, VA, 1821), 471; "An Act to amend an act, intituled, 'An act to reduce into one the several acts concerning slaves, free negroes and mulattoes, and for other purposes (1795),'" in Samuel Shepherd, ed., *The Statutes at Large of Virginia, From October Session 1792, to December Session 1806, Inclusive, in Three Volumes, (New Series,) Being a Continuation of Hening* (Richmond, VA: Samuel Shepherd, 1835), 1:363–365; "An Act to Authorize the Manumission of Slaves, Laws of Virginia, May 1782 – 6th of Commonwealth," in William Waller Hening, ed., *The Statutes at Large: Being a Collection of All the Laws of Virginia*, 13 vols. (New York: R. & W. & G. Bartow, 1819–1823), 11:39. See also A. Leon Higginbotham and F. Michael Higginbotham, "'Yaearning to Breathe Free': Legal Barriers against and Options in Favor of Liberty in Antebellum Virginia," *New York University Law Review* 68, no. 6 (1993): 1213–1271.

10. Eva Sheppard Wolf, *Race and Liberty in the New Nation: Emancipation in Virginia from the Revolution to Nat Turner's Rebellion* (Baton Rouge: Louisiana State University Press, 2009), 21–25, 25.

11. Wolf, *Race and Liberty in the New Nation*, 35.

12. Accomack Petition, June 3, 1782, Accession No. 36121, Box 1, Folder 10, Legislative Petitions of the General Assembly [LPGA], 1776–1785, LVA-LPDC, pid 1327233.

13. Hanover County Petition, November 16, 1784, Box 105, Folder 128, LPGA, LVA-LPDC, pid 708535; Henrico Petition, November 16, 1784, Box 116, Folder 24, LPGA, LVA-LPDC, pid 712311.

14. Wolf, *Race and Liberty in the New Nation*, 97.

15. Amelia County Petition, November 10, 1785, Accession No. 36121, Box 3, Folder 22, LPGA, LVA-LPDC, pid 150451. For abstracts of the other counties' petitions, see the Race and Slavery Petitions Project, Petition Number 11678502 (Halifax), 11678503 (Pittsylvania), 11678504 (Brunswick), 11678508 (Mecklenburg), November 10, 1785, University Libraries, University of North Carolina at Greensboro, accessed March 25, 2019, https://library.uncg.edu/slavery/petitions/index.aspx?s=1.

16. Wolf, *Race and Liberty in the New Nation*, 121.

17. Michael L. Nicholls, "Strangers Setting among Us: The Sources and Challenge of the Urban Free Black Population of Early Virginia," *Virginia Magazine of History and Biography* 108, no. 2 (2000): 172.

18. Wolf, *Race and Liberty in the New Nation*, 123–125; Kirt von Daacke, *Freedom Has a Face: Race, Identity, and Community in Jefferson's Virginia* (Charlottesville: University of Virginia Press, 2012); Ted Maris-Wolf, *Family Bonds: Free Blacks and Re-Enslavement Law in Antebellum Virginia* (Chapel Hill: University of North Carolina Press, 2015).

19. Thomas D. Morris, *Southern Slavery and the Law, 1619–1860* (Chapel Hill: University of North Carolina Press, 1999), 372.

20. Art Budros, "Social Shocks and Slave Social Mobility: Manumission in Brunswick County, Virginia, 1782–1862," *American Journal of Sociology* 110, no. 3 (2004): 539–579; Howard Bodenhorn, "Manumission in Nineteenth-Century Virginia," *Cliometrica: Journal of Historical Economics and Econometric History* 5, no. 2 (2011): 145–164. In Brunswick County, Budros shows the free black population doubling between 1790 and 1800, growing by 40 percent in 1800–1810, doubling again in 1810–1820, and then leveling off or shrinking slightly in the remaining decades before the Civil War. In surrounding Piedmont counties, Budros found a significant drop in manumission numbers after 1830, which he attributes to the "social shock" of Nat Turner's rebellion; Bodenhorn corroborates this finding across a wider sample of Virginia counties.

21. "Wills Manumitting Slaves, Accomack Co, VA," in *Accomack County, Virginia, Free Negro Records: Register of Free Negroes, 1807–1863, and List of Free Negroes, 1804*, ed. Richard H. Smith (Accomack County, VA: Firewood Treasures, 2007), 8; Accomack County Deeds, vol. 6, 1783–1788, microfilm reel 14, LVA, at 496.

22. Accomack County Deeds, vol. 7, 1788–1793, microfilm reel 15, LVA, at 45; *Accomack County, Virginia, Free Negro Records*, 8.

23. See, e.g., Samuel Hargrave, Charles City County Deed Book 4, 1789–1802, reel 2, LVA, 33, 211, 260; John Crew Jr., ibid., 375; Martha Charles, ibid., 451. John West, Charles City County Deed Book 5, 1803–1816, reel 2, LVA, 120; Robert Evans, ibid.

24. See, e.g., Samuel Landrum, Chesterfield County Deed Book 11, 1779–1791, reel 4, LVA, 517; Martin Baker, ibid., 639; John Anderson, ibid.: "seeing such an Inconsistancy betwixt our Declaration of Independence viz. that all men are equally born free and our Practice in holding a great number of our fellow Men in the most abject Slavery

especially those born since that Declaration and also seeing our Youths supported thereby instead of becoming useful Members of Society in our Commonwealth are rather become a mere Nuisance and Scandal thereto"; Wolf, *Race and Liberty in the New Nation*, 53.

25. Thomas v. Edward Roberts (October 1794) and Mary v. Edward Roberts (May 1795), 0007573136, Accomack County Judgments (Freedom Suits), 1790–1808, LVA.

26. Wolf, *Race and Liberty in the New Nation*, 63–64.

27. Deeds of Emancipation, Will of J. Peterfield, Box 1, Folder 16, Chesterfield County Free Negro and Slave Records, LVA; Eady Cary alias Idy Cary v. Stith E. Burton (1824), Box 1, 007520827, Petersburg County District Court Judgments (Freedom Suits), 1824–1852, LVA.

28. See, e.g., Mary v. Andrews, October 1804, Accomack County Judgments (Freedom Suits), 1790–1808, LVA.

29. Maria v. Robert Saunders, 1845, Accomack County Judgments (Freedom Suits), 1818–1860, LVA.

30. Harry v. Representative of Samuel Trader, November 1812, record contained on page 5 of Mary Bagwell v. William Elliott, Accomack County Judgments (Freedom Suits), 1790–1808, LVA. Often, the petition and the lawyer's statement are the only records that remain of a freedom suit, with no record of the jury verdict or other disposition of the case. It is possible that many of these cases were settled before going to a jury, or that the enslaved person escaped, was sold, or otherwise became unable to pursue the claim.

31. Honor Sachs, "Slaves and Lawyers: Freedom Suits and Legal Representation in Revolutionary and Early National Virginia," unpublished manuscript on file with the authors.

32. Sachs, "Slaves and Lawyers," 22–29.

33. Bazil alias Bazil Thomas v. James Kenneday, Jr. (Arlington County Court Records, 1805, LVA), and "July Term, jury sworn & verdict for plff 1c damges. Subject to the opinion of the Court upon the case agrred & cont. for argument. On hearing the case agreed it is the opinion of the Court that the Law is for the Deft &find accordingly." Silvia alias Sylvia v. George Coryell, Arlington County Circuit Court Records, July 1801, LVA.

34. Peter Wallenstein, "Indian Foremothers: Race, Sex, Slavery, and Freedom in Early Virginia," in *The Devil's Lane: Sex and Race in the Early South*, ed. Catherine Clinton and Michele Gillespie (New York: Oxford University Press, 1997), 57–73. See also advertisement for Sam Howell, *Virginia Gazette* (Williamsburg), May 2, 1766 ("His pretence for going away was to apply to some lawyer at Williamsburg to try to get his freedom"), quoted in Sachs, "Slaves and Lawyers"; Gregory Ablvasky, "Making Indians 'White': The Judicial Abolition of Native Slavery in Revolutionary Virginia and Its Racial Legacy," *University of Pennsylvania Law Review* 159 (2011): 1457–1531.

35. Robin v. Hardaway, Jeff 109 (Va. 1772); Jenkins v. Tom, 1 Va. 123 (1792); Coleman v. Dick & Pat, 1 Va. 233 (1793); Pallas v. Hill, 12 Va. 149 (1807); Honor Sachs, "'Freedom by a Judgment': The Legal History of an Afro-Indian," *Law and History Review* 30, no. 1 (2012): 173–203.

36. George v. John Walker, Jr., May 1796; Major v. Ann Maria Andrews, May 1801; Mary v. Robert Andrews, Ibby v. William S. Roberts, October 1805; Lydia v. John Mears, May 1806, 0007573136, Accomack County District Court Judgments (Freedom Suits), 1790–1808, LVA.

37. Ibby v. William S. Roberts, Accomack County Judgments (Freedom Suits); Wells v. Lewis, November 1824, Arlington County District Court Judgments, LVA.

38. Nicolas Hudson, "From 'Nation' to 'Race': The Origin of Racial Classification in Eighteenth-Century Thought," *Eighteenth Century Studies* 247, no. 3 (1996): 247–264; Robert G. Parkinson, *The Common Cause: Creating Race and Nation in the American Revolution* (Chapel Hill: University of North Carolina Press, 2016); Ariela J. Gross, *What Blood Won't Tell: A History of Race on Trial in America* (Cambridge, MA: Harvard University Press, 2008), ch. 1. See also Ablavsky, "Making Indians 'White,'" 1510–1512 ("Indian freedom reinforced African bondage . . . . Although they never regarded Natives as their equals, elite Virginians made Indians 'white' to maintain their racial ideology and strengthen African enslavement").

39. Hudgins v. Wright, 11 Va. 134 (1806); Gross, *What Blood Won't Tell*, 20–27; Adrienne Davis, "The Sexual Economy of Slavery," in Sharon Harley et al., eds., *Sister Circle: Black Women and Work* (New Brunswick, NJ: Rutgers University Press, 2002), 108–109.

40. Gregory v. Baugh, Virginia Supreme Court manuscript records (Library of Virginia, 1826), appeal reported in 4 Rand. 611 (Va. 1827); Negro John Davis v. Wood, 14 U.S. 6 (1816). See also Gross, *What Blood Won't Tell*, ch. 1.

41. Petition of John Rivers vs. John Luckett (July 1795), Box 1, Barcode 0007339659, Arlington County District Court Judgments (Freedom Suits) [ACDCFS] LVA; see also, e.g., Jenny v. Nicholas Lowe (August 1795), ACDCFS, LVA; Milly v. John Muir (August 1795), ACDCFS, LVA; Rose v. James Kennedy (July 1801), ACDCFS, LVA.

42. Silvia v. Coryell, July 1801, ACDCFS, LVA.

43. Michael L. Nicholls, "'The Squint of Freedom': African-American Freedom Suits in Post-Revolutionary Virginia," *Slavery & Abolition* 20, no. 2 (2008): 47–62.

44. See, e.g., Minter v. Moore, 1809, Rockbridge County Judgments (Freedom Suits), 1809–1854, Box 1, Barcode 0007347552, LVA; Darky v. Ritchie, 1821, ibid.; London v. Scott, 1808, ACDCFS, LVA; James v. Campbell, 1809, ACDCFS, LVA; Glenn v. Jim, 1817, ACDCFS, LVA; Nace v. Swann, 1818, ACDCFS, LVA; Winny v. Moore, 1820, ACDCFS, LVA.

45. 1790 Census, Social Explorer, U.S. Census Bureau, Michael R. Haines, *Historical, Demographic, Economic and Social Data: The United States, 1790–2000*, accessed March 25, 2019, http://www.socialexplorer.com; Thomas Morris, *Southern Slavery and the Law: 1619–1860* (Chapel Hill: University of North Carolina Press, 1996), 9; Tommy L. Bogger, *Free Blacks in Norfolk, Virginia, 1790–1860: The Darker Side of Freedom* (Charlottesville: University of Virginia Press, 1997), 8, 53; James Sidbury, *Ploughshares into Swords: Race, Rebellion, and Identity in Gabriel's Virginia, 1730–1810* (New York: Cambridge University Press, 1997), 279; 1810 Census, Social Explorer, U.S. Census

Bureau, Haines, Historical, Demographic, Economic and Social Data, accessed March 25, 2019, http://www.socialexplorer.com.

46. Representación del Síndico Procurador General Andrés de Jauregui, October 30, 1802, ACAHO, vol. 59, fols. 149–156; Moreno Fraginals, *The Sugarmill.*

47. Klein, *Slavery in the Americas,* 217–218; Kenneth Kiple, *Blacks in Colonial Cuba 1774–1899* (Gainesville: University Presses of Florida, 1976). On black participation in the militias, see Pedro Deschamps Chapeaux, *Los batallones de pardos y morenos libres* (Havana: Editorial Arte y Literatura, 1976); Francisco Castillo Meléndez, *La defensa de la isla de Cuba en la segunda mitad del siglo XVII* (Seville: Disputación Provincial, 1986), 194–201.

48. Francisco de Arango y Parreño, "Discurso sobre la agricultura de la Habana y medio de fomentarla," in *Obras* (Havana: Imprenta de Howson y Heinen, 1888), 1:97.

49. "Bando del Gobernador Diego José Navarro," May 4, 1779, in Leví Marrero, *Cuba: Economía y sociedad,* 15 vols. (Madrid: Editorial Playor, 1971–1992), 13:207.

50. Representación del Síndico Procurador General Andrés de Jauregui.

51. El síndico del ayuntamiento contra Da. Francisca Lorinak sobre livertad de sus cuatro esclavos, 1819, ANC, Escribanías (Junco), leg. 141, no. 2100. This case is examined in detail in Rebecca J. Scott and Carlos Venegas, "Adjudicating Status in a Time of Slavery: Luisa Coleta and the Capuchin Friar (Havana, 1817)," Robert R. Wilson Lecture, Duke University Law School, March 6, 2017.

52. Allan J. Kuethe and Kenneth J. Andrien, *The Spanish Atlantic World in the Eighteenth Century: War and the Bourbon Reforms, 1713–1796* (New York: Cambridge University Press, 2014), 3.

53. Allan J. Kuethe and G. Douglas Inglis, "Absolutism and Enlightened Reform: Charles III, the Establishment of the 'Alcabala' and Commercial Reorganization in Cuba," *Past and Present* 109 (1985): 118–143.

54. Marrero, *Cuba,* 13:64; Manuel Lucena Samoral, "El derecho de coartación del esclavo en la América Española," *Revista de Indias* 59, no. 216 (1999): 357–374; Alejandro de la Fuente, "Slaves and the Creation of Legal Rights in Cuba: *Coartación* and *Papel,*" *Hispanic American Historical Review* 87, no. 4 (2007): 659–692.

55. José Serapio Mojarrieta, *Esposición sobre el origen, utilidad prerogativas, derechos y deberes de los síndicos procuradores generales de los pueblos* (Puerto Príncipe: Imprenta del Gobierno, 1830). For the *síndicos*' functions in the *cédula real* of 1789, see articles 9, 11, and 13 in Ortiz, *Los negros esclavos,* 412–414. See also Klein, *Slavery in the Americas,* 78–84; Ley 1, Tit. 18, Libro 7 of *Novísima Recopilación de las Leyes de España,* 6 vols. (Madrid, 1805); Mojarrieta, *Esposición,* 16–17.

56. Gloria García Rodríguez, *Voices of the Enslaved: A Documentary History* (Chapel Hill: University of North Carolina Press, 2011), 57. According to most scholars, the RC of 1789 was never implemented or "even read" in the colonies. However, some judicial cases during the nineteenth century continued to invoke this regulation and some judges passed sentence based on it. For scholarly opinions, see Franklin Knight, *Slave Society in Cuba during the Nineteenth Century* (Madison: University of Wisconsin Press, 1970), 125; Ortiz, *Los negros esclavos,* 329–335. For an example in which a sentence is based on the RC, see "Diligencias promovidas por el síndico procurador general contra

Luis Gerbet por el cruel castigo que dio a su esclava Luisa Montoro," 1811, ANC, Audiencia de Santiago de Cuba, leg. 606, no. 13897.

57. Fernando de Armas Medina, "La Audiencia de Puerto Príncipe (1775–1853)," *Anuario de Estudios Americanos* 15 (1958): 273–370; Camilla Townsend, "'Half My Body Free, the Other Half Enslaved': The Politics of the Slaves of Guayaquil at the End of the Colonial Era," *Colonial Latin American Review* 7, no. 1 (1998): 108; Grinberg, "Freedom Suits and Civil Law," 78.

58. Real Academia Española, *Diccionario de la Lengua Castellana* (Madrid: Imprenta de Francisco del Hierro, 1729), 626. Reference to the case of Francisco Josef appears in "Primer cuaderno de autos de la residencia del señor Marqués de Casa Cagigal," 1770, AHN, Consejos (Indias), leg. 28898, pieza 1, fol. 161v.

59. Marrero, *Cuba*, 13:164; Lucena Samoral, "El derecho," 364; Juan Miguel de Arozarena a Bucareli, Trinidad, October 29, 1768. AGI, Cuba, leg. 1079, no. 53; El síndico procurador general del común a nombre del moreno Santiago, 1826, ANC, Escribanías (Salinas), leg. 676/7858.

60. Antonio de Camba al Capitán General, Trinidad, April 20, 1778, AGI, Cuba, leg. 1257, no. 128.

61. El negro Jose Maria esclavo de la ciudad sobre qe se declare la cantidad que debe exivir por su libertad, March 6, 1800, ACAHO, vol. 58, fol. 27.

62. Lucena Samoral, "El derecho," 366.

63. Martin Arostegui negro contra Dn. José Maria Alfonso sobre su livertad, 1818, ANC, Escribanías (Daumy), leg. 334, no. 8.

64. See the RCs of June 21, 1768, and April 8, 1778, in Lucena Samoral, "El derecho," 366, and Mojarrieta, *Esposición*, 21; Promovido por Juana Josefa de la Torre, morena esclava contra don Nicolas Aguado sobre su livertad, 1802, ANC, Escribanías (Daumy), leg. 693, no. 22.

65. Lucena Samoral, "El derecho," 358; Martin Arostegui negro contra Dn. José Maria Alfonso.

66. ANC, PNH, Escribanía Fornaris, 1690, fol. 44.

67. El síndico contra Francisco Prado sobre la coartación del pardo José Genaro, 1826, ANC, Escribanías (Galleta), leg. 814, no. 7; Mojarrieta, *Esposición*, 19. We used here Richard Madden's translation as it appears in Edward J. Mullen, *The Life and Poems of Juan Francisco Manzano, 1797–1854* (New York: Palgrave, 2014), 184. Marrero, *Cuba*, 13:166; Declaración del síndico José Morales Lemus, 1861, ANC, Intendencia, leg. 760, no. 3.

68. Don Francisco de Ponce de León y Maroto con don Manuel Dueñas, AHN, Consejos, leg. 20839, cited in de la Fuente, "Slaves and the Creation of Legal Rights in Cuba," 673–674; Expediente en que el moreno Cristóbal del Castillo solicita carta de libertad, 1836, ANC, GSC, leg. 937, no. 33080.

69. Micaela O'Farrill al Capitán General, 1835, ANC, GSC, Correspondencia sobre esclavitud, 1834–1842, leg. 937, no. 33052; El síndico procurador solicita que Da. Felicia Jauregui le de papel al moreno Pedro López, 1835, ANC, GSC, leg. 937, no. 33057; Incidente a la testamentaría de Pedro Santo, 1837, ANC, Escribanías (Junco), leg. 309/ 4743.

70. Bernardo Lucumí sobre su coartación y venta, 1820, ANC, Escribanías (Daumy), leg. 778, no. 3. El síndico sobre que el Marqués de Campo Florido le otorgue escritura de venta a su esclavo Francisco, 1833, ANC, Escribanías (Salinas), leg. 672, no. 7776. It is interesting to note that in this last case, the judge nonetheless mediated to persuade the marquis to sell the slave, an arrangement to which he agreed.

71. Expediente en que el moreno Cristóbal del Castillo solicita carta de libertad, 1836, ANC, GSC, leg. 937, no. 33080.

72. Mojarrieta, *Esposición*, 20–21, as translated by Madden, in Mullen, *The Life and Poems*, 184; Diario de las causas despachadas por esta Real Audiencia, 1800, AGI, Ultramar, leg. 92. For a similar gap between appellate court opinions and lower-court practice in the United States, see Laura F. Edwards, *The People and Their Peace: Legal Culture and the Transformation of Inequality in the Post-Revolutionary South* (Chapel Hill, NC: University of North Carolina Press, 2009), and Ariela J. Gross, *Double Character: Slavery and Mastery in the Antebellum Southern Courtroom* (Princeton, NJ: Princeton University Press, 2000).

73. El moreno Pedro Pascasio sobre su libertad, 1835, ANC, GSC, leg. 937, no. 33074.

74. Mojarrieta, *Esposición*, 23; Lucena Samoral, "El derecho de coartación," 367–370; Marrero, *Cuba*, 13:165.

75. Johnson, *Slavery's Metropolis*, 9; Jennifer M. Spear, *Race, Sex, and Social Order in Colonial New Orleans* (Baltimore: Johns Hopkins University Press, 2009), 110.

76. Kimberly Hanger, *Bounded Lives, Bounded Places: Free Black Society in Colonial New Orleans, 1769–1803* (Durham, NC: Duke University Press, 1997), 42–47; Hans Baade, "The Law of Slavery in Spanish Louisiana," in *Louisiana's Legal Heritage*, ed. Edward F. Haas (Pennsacola, FL: Perdido Bay Press, 1983), 48, 76; Vernon V. Palmer, *Through the Codes Darkly* (Clark, NJ: Lawbook Exchange, Ltd., 2012), 98–99; Ira Berlin, *Many Thousands Gone: The First Two Centuries of Slavery in North America* (Cambridge, MA: Harvard University Press, 1998), 331–332.

77. Paul F. Lachance, "The 1809 Immigration of Saint-Domingue Refugees," *Louisiana History: The Journal of the Lousiana Historical Association* 29, no. 2 (1988): 112, offers detailed figures for Orleans Parish, which we used for our calculations in the table in Chapter 4 (table 2). For other estimates, see Gilbert C. Din, *Spaniards, Planters, and Slaves: The Spanish Regulation of Slavery in Louisiana, 1763–1803* (College Station: Texas A&M Press, 1999), 235; Amy R. Sumpter, "Segregation of the Free People of Color and the Construction of Race in Antebellum New Orleans," *Southeastern Geographer* 48, no. 1 (May 2008): 23; Jennifer M. Spear, review of Gilbert C. Din, *Spaniards, Planters, and Slaves: The Spanish Regulation of Slavery in Louisiana, 1763–1803*, in *William and Mary Quarterly* 58 (January 2001): 276. For 1810, we used the U.S. Census for Louisiana Territory, although the territory was larger than what would become the state of Louisiana in 1812.

78. Palmer, *Through the Codes Darkly*, 100.

79. Maria Juana, a Negress Slave v. Juan Suriray de la Rue, February 23, 1776, Document 1776-02-28-02, Box 33, LCJR, LHC, summarized in *LHQ* 11 (1928): 338–340.

80. Maria Luisa Saly v. Matheo Parin called Canon, her Owner, January 23, 1781, Document 1781-01-23-01, p. 3, LCJR, LHC, summarized in *LHQ* 15 (1932): 546–548.

81. Maria Theresa v. Marie-Françoise Girardy Veuve Desruisseau, September 4, 1782, Document 1782-09-04-03, LCJR, LHC, summarized in *LHQ* 19 (1936): 512–515. See also Bernarda Arciny v. Francisco Daniel Dupain, January 14, 1783, Document 1783-01-15-01, Box 41, LCJR, LHC, summarized in *LHQ* 20 (1937): 266–268 (appraiser for "negress" appraises her at 600 pesos, appraiser for owner at 800; court-appointed appraiser agrees on 800, and Bernarda Arciny comes up with 800 pesos); Nicolas v. Mercier, October 27, 1780, Document 1780-10-27-01, LCJR, LHC, summarized in *LHQ* 15 (1932): 164–165 (he claims they agreed on 400 pesos because his owner "found no one to buy a man without a trade and with frequent stomach pain," but he is appraised at 800 pesos).

82. Antonio, Mulato v. Deshotel Succession, March 7, 1774, Document 1774-03-07-012, Box 31, p. 35, Louisiana Judicial Court Records, Louisiana Historical Center, New Orleans, summarized in *LHQ* 10 (1927): 300–301; regarding the importance of papers, see, generally, Scott and Hébrard, *Freedom Papers*.

83. For typical, nonadversarial notarial proceedings, see, e.g., Hardy, Magdalena, free negress v. Luis Forneret re: petition of emancipation of her son Bautista, mulatto, August 26, 1790, doc. 3, pp. 86–150, in Francisco Broutin, *Notary – Acts – Court Proceedings*, vol. 1, New Orleans Notarial Archives (NONA); Liberta Francisco Aime a Roseta Mulata, May 5, 1792, p. 139, in ibid., vol. 15; Letter of freedom of Maria Juana Lebouef, a Negress, October 2, 1797, p. 217, in ibid., vol. 46.

84. Elena v. Henrique Desprez, August 12, 1780, Document 1780-08-12-01, Box 37, pp. 12–13, LCJR, LHC, summarized in *LHQ* 14 (1931): 619–621.

85. See Gwendolyn Midlo Hall, *Africans in Colonial Louisiana: The Development of Afro-Creole Culture in the Eighteenth-Century* (Baton Rouge: Lousiana State University Press, 1992); Spear, *Race, Sex, and Social Order*, 163; Marguerite v. Chouteau, July 1825, Saint Louis County, Missouri Circuit Court Records, Missouri State Archives, St. Louis Circuit Court Collection Online, accessed April 18, 2019, http://repository.wustl.edu/concern/texts/b2773w92s.

86. Spear, *Race, Sex, and Social Order*, 166–167; Hall, *Africans in Colonial Louisiana*, 336–337; Seville v. Chretien, no. 34 (September 1817), LSCA, UNO, appeal reported in 5 Mart. (O.S.) 275 (La. 1817).

87. Hall, *Africans in Colonial Louisiana*, 305–306; Din, *Spaniards, Planters, and Slaves*, 64; Letter from Villiers to Unzaga, April 6, 1773, quoted in Hall, *Africans in Colonial Louisiana*, 305; see also Palmer, *Through the Codes Darkly*, 95–96.

88. Hall, *Africans in Colonial Louisiana*, 103; Bell, *Revolution, Romanticism, and the Afro-Creole Protest Tradition*, 18.

89. Bell, *Revolution, Romanticism, and the Afro-Creole Protest Tradition*, 19, 25–28.

90. Bell, *Revolution, Romanticism, and the Afro-Creole Protest Tradition*, 9, 57, 79; Donald E. Everett, "Emigrés and Militiamen: Free Persons of Color in New Orleans, 1803–1815," *Journal of Negro History* 38, no. 4 (1953): 390–391, 397–399; Claiborne to Smith, January 4, 1811, quoted in ibid., 394; *Acts Passed at the First Session of the First General Assembly of the State of Louisiana* (New Orleans: W. Van Benthuysen & P. Besancon Jr., State Printers, n.d.), ch. 23 (July 27, 1812), 72–73.

91. "An Act Prescribing the Rules and Conduct to Be Observed with Respect to Negroes and Other Slaves of This Territory," Act of June 7, 1806, *Acts Passed at the First Session of the First Legislature of the Territory of Orleans* (New Orleans: Bradford and Anderson, 1806), 150–190. See also Palmer, *Through the Codes Darkly*, 118–222.

92. Cottin v. Cottin, 5 Mart. (O.S.) 93 (La. 1817); "An Act Providing for the Promulgation of the Digest of the Civil Laws Now in Force in the Territory of Orleans," *Acts passed at the first session of the second Legislature of the Territory of Orleans* (New Orleans: Bradford and Anderson, 1808), 120–128; *Civil Code of the State of Louisiana: With the statutory amendments from 1825 to 1853 inclusive* (New Orleans: Bloomfield and Steel, 1861).

93. Lachance, "The 1809 Immigration of Saint-Domingue Refugees," 116. The Digest of 1808, which represented itself as a compilation of "all the law now in force in the territory," left in force the 1806 Black Code, which was inspired by the Code Noir. Regardless of the exact proportion of French to Spanish influence, Louisiana jurists continued to draw on French, Spanish, and Roman law, in addition to the 1808 Digest, and the 1825 Civil Code that remained in force until 1870 drew heavily on the French Civil Code.

    See Robert Pascal, "Sources of the Digest of 1808: A Reply to Professor Batiza," *Tulane Law Review* 46 (1972): 603; Rodolfo Batiza, "The Louisiana Civil Code of 1808: Its Actual Sources and Present Relevance," *Tulane Law Review* 46 (1971): 4; Rodolfo Batiza, "Sources of the Civil Code of 1808, Facts and Speculation: A Rejoinder," *Tulane Law Review* 46 (1971): 628. For guidance on this debate, see Vernon V. Palmer, *The Louisiana Civilian Experience: Critiques of Codification in a Mixed Jurisdiction* (Durham, NC: Carolina Academic Press, 2005); Richard Holcombe Kilbourne Jr., *A History of the Louisiana Civil Code: The Formative Years, 1803–1839* (Baton Rouge: Louisiana State University, 1987); Hans Baade, "The Bifurcated Romanist Tradition of Slavery in Louisiana," *Tulane Law Review* 70 (1996): 1481; A. N. Yiannopoulos, "The Early Sources of Louisiana Law: Critical Appraisal of a Controversy," in *Louisiana's Legal Heritage*, ed. Edward F. Haas (Pensacola, FL: Perdido Bay Press, 1983), 87, 96–100. For Louisiana law, see Warren M. Billings and Mark F. Fernandez, eds., *A Law unto Itself? Essays in the New Louisiana History* (Baton Rouge: Louisiana State University Press, 2001); George Dargo, *Jefferson's Louisiana: Politics and the Clash of Legal Traditions* (Cambridge, MA: Harvard University Press, 1975).

94. Adele vs. Beauregard, 1 Mart. (O.S.) 183–184 (La. 1810).

95. Seville v. Chretien, ("non seulement la loi, mais la coutume et l'usage d'acheter et vendre les sauvages, femmes commes hommes comme esclaves ... de meme que les nègres."); appeal reported in 5 Mart. (O.S.) 275 (La. 1817).

96. *Acts Passed at the First Session of the First Legislature of the Territory of Orleans* (New Orleans: Bradford & Anderson, 1807), 82.

97. Judith Schafer, *Slavery, the Civil Law, and the Supreme Court of Louisiana* (Baton Rouge: Louisiana State University Press: 1997), 220, 224.

98. Cuffy v. Castillon, no. 255, May 1818, p. 10, LSCA, UNO ("Yo estoy convenido con Cofy mi negro liberto de darle la libertad a Pedro, Honore, Maria, y J. Baptiste, mis negros esclavos y sus hijos por el precio de dos mil quarto cientos pesos luego que me satisfaga

la dicha cantidad y entonces le pasare la carta de libertad y para que ... le doy el presento resguardo. En la Nueva Orleans en 4 de Julio de 1789. Andrew almonaster y Roxas"), appeal in 5 Mart. (O.S.) 494 (La. 1818).

99. Doubrere v. Grillier's Syndics, no. 860 (February 1824), LSCA, UNO, appeal in 2 Mart. (N.S.) 171 (La. 1824); Prince Mathews v. Michael Boland & William Smith, no. 5119 (June 1843), LSCA, UNO, at 15, appeal in 5 Rob. 200 (La. 1843); Marie v. Avart, no. 255 (May 1818), LSCA, UNO, appeal in 6 Mart. (O.S.) 731 (La. 1819); Victoire v. Dussau (1816); Beard v. Poydras, no. 72 (December 1814), LSCA, UNO, appeal in 4 Mart. (O.S.) 348 (La. 1816).

100. Metayer v. Noret, no. 288 (June 1818), appeal in 5 Mart. (O.S.) 566 (La. 1818), LSCA, UNO, and Metayer v. Metayer, no. 318 (January 1819), appeal reported in 6 Mart. (O.S.) 16 (La. 1819), LSCA, UNO. See Rebecca Scott, "Paper Thin: Freedom and Re-enslavement in the Diaspora of the Haitian Revolution," *Law and History Review* 29, no. 4 (2011): 1061–1087, on Adelaide Metayer. See also, e.g., Verdun v. Splane, 6 Rob. 530 (La. 1844), and Eulalie v. Long and Mabry, no. 3237 (January 1854), appeal in 9 La. Ann. 9 (1854).

101. Laurence J. Kotlikoff and Anton J. Rupert, "The Manumission of Slaves in New Orleans, 1827–1846," *Southern Studies* 19, no. 2 (1980): 172–181; for a summary of Louisiana freedom cases, see Schafer, *Slavery, the Civil Law, and the Supreme Court of Louisiana*, 180–288; Sue Peabody and Keila Grinberg, "Free Soil: The Generation and Circulation of an Atlantic Legal Principle," *Slavery & Abolition* 32, no. 3 (2011): 331–339; Lunsford v. Coquillon, no. 815, LASC, UNO, appeal in 2 Mart. (N.S.) 401 (La. 1824).

CHAPTER 4 "RULES ... FOR THEIR EXPULSION"

1. Citizens: Petition, Northampton County, December 6, 1831, LVA-LPDC.
2. Charles Gayarré, *History of Louisiana: The French Domination*, 4 vols. (New Orleans: Armand Hawkins, 1867), 4:683.
3. Cabildo ordinario de 8 de noviembre de 1805, ACAHO, vol. 60, fol. 328; Sesión del Consejo de Indias, 14 de Abril 1825. AHN, Ultramar, leg. 3549/1; Cabildo ordinario de 4 de marzo de 1841, ACAHO vol. 125, fol. 414v.
4. El Ayuntamiento de la Habana pidiendo la reforma del artículo 7º del Reglamento de las Comisiones Mixtas sobre el tráfico de negros [1826–1833], AHN, Ultramar, leg. 3547, no. 2.
5. James Madison, "Answers to Questions Concerning Slavery 1823," in *Writings of James Madison, Comprising His Public Papers and His Private Correspondence, including Numerous Letters and Documents Now for the First Time Printed*, ed. Gaillard Hunt (New York: G. P. Putnam's Sons, 1900–1910), 9–134; Citizens: Petition, Northampton County, December 6, 1831.
6. Richard J. Follett, "The Sugar Masters: Slavery, Economic Development, and Modernization on Louisiana Sugar Plantations, 1820–1860," PhD diss., Louisiana State University, 1997, 64; Steven Deyle, *Carry Me Back: The Domestic Slave Trade in American Life*

(New York: Oxford University Press, 2005); Walter Johnson, ed. *The Chattel Principle: Internal Slave Trades in the Americas* (New Haven: Yale University Press, 2004).

7. On free black people's claims to citizenship, see Martha S. Jones, *Birthright Citizens: A History of Race and Rights in Antebellum America* (New York: Cambridge University Press, 2018); quotation in "Un interrogatorio absuelto por el Capitán General don Francisco Dionisio Vives," 1832, in José Antonio Saco, *Historia de la Esclavitud*, 5 vols. (Havana: Imagen Contemporánea, 2006), 5:283, 288–290.

8. "Un interrogatorio."

9. David Walker, *Walker's Appeal in Four Articles; Together with a Preamble to the Coloured Citizens of the World* (Boston: Revised and Published by David Walker, 1830).

10. Ibid., 30.

11. Ibid., 19.

12. Ibid., 62, 52.

13. William Lloyd Garrison, "To the Public," *The Liberator*, January 1, 1831.

14. Lacy K. Ford, *Deliver Us from Evil: The Slavery Question in the Old South* (New York: Oxford University Press, 2009), 338.

15. *The Bee*, September 15, 1831; see also Judith K. Schafer, "The Immediate Impact of Nat Turner's Insurrection on New Orleans," *Louisiana History* 21, no. 4 (1980): 361–376.

16. James E. Alexander, *Transatlantic Sketches Comprising Visits to the Most Interesting Scenes in North and South America and the West Indies* (London: Richard Bentley, 1833), 227; Schafer, "The Immediate Impact of Nat Turner's Insurrection," 363–364.

17. *The Bee*, November 19, 1831; Levi Peirce et al., *The Consolidation and Revision of the Statutes of the State* (New Orleans: Printed at The Bee Office, 1852), 534; Schafer, "The Immediate Impact of Nat Turner's Insurrection," 367–368.

18. Alexander, *Transatlantic Sketches*, 230; William Lloyd Garrison, "New Orleans," *The Liberator*, June 27, 1835, 104.

19. Matt D. Childs, *The 1812 Aponte Rebellion in Cuba and the Struggle against Slavery* (Chapel Hill: University of North Carolina Press, 2006); Fernando Ortiz, *Los Negros Esclavos* (Havana: Editorial de Ciencias Sociales, 1975), 385–394; Manuel Barcia, *Seeds of Insurrection: Domination and Resistance on Western Cuban Plantations, 1808–1848* (Baton Rouge: Louisiana State University Press, 2008); Robert Paquette, *Sugar Is Made with Blood: The Conspiracy of La Escalera and the Conflict between Empires over Slavery in Cuba* (Middletown, CT: Wesleyan University Press, 1988); Aisha K. Finch, *Rethinking Slave Rebellion in Cuba: La Escalera and the End of Insurgencies, 1841–1844* (Chapel Hill: University of North Carolina Press, 2015).

20. Manuel Barcia, *The Great African Slave Revolt of 1825: Cuba and the Fight for Freedom in Matanzas* (Baton Rouge: Louisiana State University Press, 2012), 151; Finch, *Rethinking Slave Rebellion in Cuba*, 92; William Lloyd Garrison, "The Late Servile Insurrection in Cuba," *The Liberator*, May 5, 1843, 71.

21. Gabino La Rosa Corzo, "Cuba: Resistencia esclava y represión esclavista, 1796–1868," *Debate y Perspectivas* 4 (2004): 105–126; Leví Marrero, *Cuba: Economía y sociedad*, 15 vols. (Madrid: Editorial Playor, 1971–1992), 13:212–213.

22. Levantamiento de Negros en El Cafetal de Fouquier, 1825, AHN, Ultramar, leg. 1603, no. 21; Finch, *Rethinking Slave Rebellion in Cuba*, 89; Barcia, *Seeds of Insurrection*, 40–41.
23. "José Luis Alfonso to Domingo del Monte, Havana, December 22, 1843," in Domingo del Monte, *Centón Epistolario*, 4 vols. (Havana: Imagen Contemporánea, 2002), 3:215; "Miguel de Aldama to Domingo del Monte, Havana, June 29, 1844," in del Monte, *Centón Epistolario*, 3:xviii, 289.
24. Quoted in Barcia, *Seeds of Insurrection*, 28–29.
25. Mariano Torrente, *Slavery in the Island of Cuba* (London: Printed by C. Wood, 1853), 7; "Informe Reservado del Real Consulado, September 28, 1841," in José Antonio Saco, *Historia de la esclavitud*, 5 vols. (Havana: Imagen Contemporánea, 2006), 5:179; Finch, *Rethinking Slave Rebellion in Cuba*, 115–118; Jonathan Curry-Machado, "How Cuba Burned with the Ghosts of British Slavery: Race, Abolition and the Escalera," *Slavery & Abolition* 25, no.1 (2004): 71–93.
26. Excerpts from Governor John Floyd's Message to the General Assembly, (December 6, 1831), *Niles' Weekly Register* 41, no. 1,059 (January 7, 1832): 350–351, accessed April 29, 2019, www.encyclopediavirginia.org/Excerpts_from_Governor_John_Floyd_s_Message_to_the_General_Assembly_December_6_1831; William Lloyd Garrison, "Matanzas," *The Liberator*, July 1, 1844; "The Negro Troubles," *New York Times*, February 1, 1857.
27. Ford, *Deliver Us from Evil*, 330, 334; Peirce et al., *Statutes of the State*, 208, 551–552, 554; Erik S. Root, *Sons of the Fathers: The Virginia Slavery Debate of 1831–32* (New York: Rowman and Littlefield, 2012).
28. Kenneth S. Greenberg, *Nat Turner: A Slave Rebellion in History and Memory* (New York: Oxford University Press, 2003); Tommy L. Bogger, *Free Blacks in Norfolk, Virginia, 1790–1860* (Charlottesville: University of Virginia Press, 1997), 39–40; Root, *Sons of the Fathers*; Ford, *Deliver Us from Evil*, 378–379, 380–381.
29. Ford, *Deliver Us from Evil*, 360, 380.
30. Andres de Jáuregui y Rafael de Quesada al Secretario de Estado, Havana, April 28, 1825, AHN, Ultramar, leg. 3547/1; El capitan general Leopoldo O'Donnell al Secretario de Estado, Havana, February 15, 1845, AHN, Ultramar, leg. 3547/13.
31. Cabildo Ordinario de 4 de Marzo de 1841, ACAHO, vol. 126, fol. 414v.; Tribunal de Comercio de La Habana, "A la Regencia Provisional del Reyno," March 30, 1841, AHN, Ultramar, leg. 3547/9; Comunicación del Capitán General, Havana, August 9, 1831, AHN, Ultramar, leg. 3547/3; Esfuerzos Ocultos y Maquinaciones de Las Sociedades Antiesclavistas, AHN, Ultramar, leg. 3547/7; El Gobernador al Secretario de Estado, Havana, October 24, 1839, AHN, Ultramar, leg. 3547/8; Expediente instruido con el objeto de vencer los inconvenientes que resultan de la legislación sobre la trata, 1851, AHN, Ultramar, leg. 3547/13; El Conde de Alcoy al Secretario de Estado, Havana, November 7, 1848, AHN, Ultramar, leg. 3547/13
32. Esfuerzos ocultos y maquinaciones de las sociedades antiesclavistas, AHN, Ultramar, leg. 3547/7.
33. William Lloyd Garrison, "Refuge of Oppression," *The Liberator*, June 11, 1847; "Reply to Abolition Objections of Slavery," *De Bow's Review* 20 (1856): 647.

34. Thomas R. R. Cobb, *Inquiry into the Law of Negro Slavery* (Philadelphia: T. & J. W. Johnson & Co., 1858), 51.

35. Josiah C. Nott, *Two Lectures on the Connection between the Biblical and Physical History of Man* (New York: Bartlett and Welford, 1849), 20; Root, *Sons of the Fathers*, 43–56; *Dictamen del Ministerio de Estado, Madrid,* December 22, 1846, AHN, Ultramar, leg. 3547/13. On the discourse of benevolent slavery in Cuba, see Jaime Holeman, "'A Peculiar Character of Mildness': The Image of a Humane Slavery in Nineteenth-Century Cuba," in *Francisco Arango y la invención de la Cuba azucarera,* Maria Dolores González-Ripoll and Izaskun Àlvarez Cuartero, eds. (Madrid: CSIC, 2010), 41–54.

36. June Purcell Guild, *Black Laws of Virginia* (Richmond, VA: Whittet and Shepperson, 1936), 95, 109, 113, 117; Art Budros, "Social Shocks and Slave Social Mobility: Manumission in Brunswick County, Virginia, 1782–1862," *American Journal of Sociology* 110, no. 3 (2004): 558; Tommy Bogger, *Free Blacks in Norfolk, 1790–1860* (Charlottesville: University of Virginia Press, 1970), 25; Robert C. Reinders, "The Decline of the New Orleans Free Negro 1850–1860," *Louisiana History* 6, no. 3 (1965): 273–285; Richard Tansey, "Out-of-State Free Blacks in Late Antebellum New Orleans," *Louisiana History: The Journal of the Louisiana Historical Association* 22, no. 4 (1981): 372–375; H. E. Sterkx, *The Free Negro in Ante-Bellum Louisiana* (Rutherford, NJ: Fairleigh Dickinson University Press, 1972), 303.

37. Peirce et al., *Statutes of the State,* 287; Ada Ferrer, *Freedom's Mirror: Cuba and Haiti in the Age of Revolution* (New York: Cambridge University Press, 2014), 131–137, 175–176; Childs, *The 1812 Aponte Rebellion,* 38–40; David Turnbull, *Travels in the West; With Notices of Porto Rico, and the Slave Trade* (London: Longman, Orme, Greens and Longmans, 1840), 69–70; El Gobernador Leopoldo O'Donnell a las Autoridades Locales, May 31, 1844, ANC, GSC, leg. 138/7. Turnbull mentions that the practice of imprisoning black sailors and visitors followed "the example of the slave-holding states of the North American Union"; Peirce et al., *Statutes of the State,* 287; Circular del Gobernador Gerónimo Valdés, December 7, 1842, ANC, Asuntos Politicos, leg. 37/13.

38. "Un interrogatorio absuelto por el capitán general don Francisco Dionisio Vives," 1832, in Saco, *Historia de la esclavitud,* 5:283, 288–290.

39. José Antonio Saco, "La estadística criminal de Cuba en 1862," in *Colección póstuma de papeles científicos, históricos, políticos* (Havana: Editor Miguel de Villa, 1881), 148–49.

40. Ford, *Deliver Us from Evil,* 380; Root, *Sons of the Fathers,* 43–56, 317–318; newspapers quoted in Alison Goodyear Freehling, *Drift toward Dissolution: The Virginia Slavery Debate of 1831–32* (Baton Rouge: Louisiana State University Press, 1982), 85; Nott, *Two Lectures,* 18. A somewhat similar view was articulated by a group of Havana slaveholders; see Tribunal de Comercio de La Habana, "A la Regencia Provisional del Reyno."

41. Nott, *Two Lectures,* 18; Tribunal de Comercio de La Habana, "A la Regencia Provisional del Reyno."

42. Nicholas Guyatt, "'The Outskirts of Our Happiness': Race and the Lure of Colonization in the Early Republic," *Journal of American History* 95, no. 4 (March 2009): 986–1011; Eric Burin, *Slavery and the Peculiar Solution: A History of the American Colonization Society* (Gainesville: University Press of Florida, 2005); Bogger, *Free Blacks in Norfolk, 1790–1860,*

32–41; Guild, *Black Laws of Virginia*, 119, 139; Manisha Sinha, *The Slave's Cause: A History of Abolition* (New Haven, CT: Yale University Press, 2016), 164.

43. Richmond and Manchester Auxiliary Society for Colonizing in Africa: Petition, Richmond City, January 20, 1825, Accession No. 36121, Box 278, Folder 69, LVA-LPDC, pid 1049480.

44. Richmond and Manchester Colonization Society: Petition, Richmond City, December 20, 1827, Accession No. 36121, Box 279, Folder 7, LVA-LPDC, pid 1049509.

45. Ibid.; Board of Managers of the Lynchburg Colonization Society: Petition, Lynchburg City, January 12, 1828, Accession No. 36121, Box 265, Folder 10, LVA-LPDC, pid 986110; Colonization Society of Virginia: Petition, Petersburg City, December 17, 1828, Accession No. 36121, Box 272, Folder 75, LVA-LPDC, pid 814873.

46. Citizens: Petition, James City County, December 27, 1831, Accession No. 36121, Box 3, Folder 106, LVA-LPDC, pid 540034; Citizens: Petition, Amelia County, December 20, 1831, Accession No. 36121, Box 3, Folder 106, LVA-LPDC, pid 150526; Colonization Society of Virginia: Petition, Richmond (City), December 20, 1831, Accession No. 36121, Box 279, Folder 46, LVA-LPDC, pid 1049548; Citizens: Petition, Northampton County, December 6, 1831, Accession No. 36121, Box 184, Folder 51, LVA-LPDC, pid 718043; Auxiliary Colonization Society of Frederick County: Petition, Frederick County, January 3, 1832, Accession No. 36121, Box 324, Folder 11, LVA-LPDC, pid 1061085; Citizens of Fredericksburg: Petition, Spotsylvania County, January 27, 1837, Accession No. 36121, Box 236, Folder 43, LVA-LPDC, pid 1473067; Citizens: Petition, Bedford County, January 25, 1838, Accession No. 36121, Box 21, Folder 80, LVA-LPDC, pid 331300; William Lloyd Garrison, "American Colonization Society: Mr. Garrison's Second Lecture," *The Liberator*, October 19, 1833.

47. Sinha, *The Slave's Cause*, 165; Thomas Price, "American Colonization Society," *The Liberator*, November 2, 1833.

48. Jones, *Birthright Citizens*, 124; "Meeting of the Coloured People in Baltimore," *Genius of Universal Emancipation*, March 1831, quoted in ibid., 126; Garrison, "American Colonization Society: Mr. Garrison's Second Lecture."

49. American Colonization Society, *Twenty-Fifth Annual Report of the American Colonization Society: With the Abridged Proceedings of the Annual Meeting and of the Board of Directors, at Washington, January 18, 1842* (Washington, DC: A. & G. S. Gideon, 1842), 9, 12, 22.

50. Judith K. Schafer, *Becoming Free, Remaining Free: Manumission and Enslavement in New Orleans, 1846–1862* (Baton Rouge: Louisiana State University Press, 2003), 12. The immediate response to the law was a deluge of requests from slaveholders for exceptions. Many freed slaves were allowed to stay in Louisiana.

51. American Colonization Society, *Forty-First Annual Report of the American Colonization Society: With the Proceedings of the Board of Directors and of the Society: January 19, 1858* (Washington, DC: C. Alexander, 1858), 22.

52. James T. Edwards, *Some Interesting Papers of John McDonogh* (McDonogh, MD: Library of Congress, 1898), 48, 52; Annie Lee West Stahl, "The Free Negro in Ante-Bellum

Louisiana," *Louisiana Historical Quarterly* 25, no. 2 (1942); 340–346; Schafer, *Becoming Free, Remaining Free*, 46.

53. El capitan general Francisco Dionisio Vives al Secretario de Estado, Havana, January 6, 1825, AHN, Ultramar, leg. 3547/1; Andres de Jáuregui y Rafael de Quesada al Secretario de Estado, Havana, April 28, 1825, AHN, Ultramar, leg. 3547/1; Arthur F. Corwin, Spain and the Abolition of Slavery in Cuba (Austin: University of Texas Press, 1967).

54. El Ayuntamiento de la Habana pidiendo la reforma del artículo 7° del Reglamento de las Comisiones Mixtas sobre el tráfico de negros (1826–1833), AHN, Ultramar, leg. 3547/2; Henry B. Lovejoy, "The Registers of Liberated Africans of the Havana Slave Trade Commission: Implementation and Policy, 1824–1841," *Slavery & Abolition* 37, no. 1 (2016): 23–44; Inés Roldán de Montaud, "En los borrosos confines de la libertad: El caso de los negros emancipados en Cuba, 1817–1870," *Revista de Indias* 71, no. 251 (2011): 159–192; Leslie Bethell, "The Mixed Commissions for the Suppression of the Transatlantic Slave Trade in the Nineteenth Century," *Journal of African History* 7, no. 1 (1966): 79–93; Rodolfo Sarracino, *Los que volvieron a África* (Havana: Editorial de Ciencias Sociales, 1988).

55. Consuelo Naranjo Orovio, "La amenaza haitiana, un miedo interesado: Poder y fomento de la población blanca en Cuba," in María D. González-Ripoll et al., *El rumor de Haití en Cuba: Temor, raza y rebeldía, 1789–1844* (Madrid: CSIC, 2004), 83–178; Junta de Fomento, *Real Cédula de 21 de Octubre de 1817, Sobre Aumentar La Población Blanca de la Isla de Cuba* (Havana: Oficina de Arazoza y Soler, 1818).

56. El Consejo de Indias, April 14, 1825, AHN, Ultramar, leg. 3549/1.

57. Historian Marial Iglesias Utset has found several examples of free blacks who left Havana for Senegal in 1818 and 1822. These individuals may have tried to escape what was a rapidly deteriorating social and racial environment. She discussed these findings in "La travesía intermedia al revés: La diáspora africana en Cuba y los proyectos de retorno a África," Afro-Latin American Research Institute Seminar Series, Harvard University, (October 26, 2018).

58. Quoted by A. Leon Higginbotham Jr. and Barbara Kopytoff, "Racial Purity and Interracial Sex in the Law of Colonial and Antebellum Virginia," *Georgetown Law Journal*, 77, no. 6 (August 1989): 1985.

59. Ira Berlin, *Many Thousands Gone: The First Two Centuries of Slavery in North America* (Cambridge, MA: Harvard University Press, 1998), 282; Loren Schweninger, "The Underside of Slavery: The Internal Economy, Self-Hire, and Quasi-Freedom in Virginia, 1780–1865," *Slavery & Abolition* 12, no. 2 (1991): 1–22, 15; Bogger, *Free Blacks in Norfolk, 1790–1860*, 27; Joseph Logsdon and Caryn Cossé Bell, "The Americanization of Black New Orleans," in *Creole New Orleans: Race and Americanization*, ed. Arnold R. Hirsch and Joseph Logsdon (Baton Rouge: Louisiana State University Press, 1992), 210; La Rosa Corzo, "Cuba: Resistencia esclava."

60. Philip J. Schwarz, "Emancipators, Protectors, and Anomalies: Free Black Slaveowners in Virginia," *Virginia Magazine of History and Biography* 95, no. 3 (July 1987): 317–338; Laurence J. Kotlikoff and Anton J. Rupert, "The Manumission of Slaves in New

Orleans, 1827–1846," *Southern Studies* 19, no. 2 (1980): 172–181; Aisnara Perera Díaz and María de Los Angeles Meriño Fuentes, "La manumisión en Cuba: Aproximaciones desde San Felipe y Santiago de Bejucal (1800–1881)," *Especiaria: Cadernos de Ciências Humanas* 10, no. 18 (2017): 533–564; Howard Bodenhorn, "Manumission in Nineteenth Century Virginia," NBER Working Paper Series, National Bureau of Economic Research, Cambridge, MA (2010); Luther Porter Jackson, *Free Negro Labor and Property Holding in Virginia, 1830–1860* (New York: D. Appleton-Century Company, 1942), 181; Thomas D. Morris, *Southern Slavery and the Law, 1619–1860* (Chapel Hill: University of North Carolina Press, 1996), 396–397.

61. Maria del Carmen Barcia Zequeira, *La otra familia: Parientes, redes y descendencia de los esclavos en Cuba* (Havana: Casa de las Américas, 2003); Pedro Deschamps Chapeaux, *El negro en la economía habanera del siglo XIX* (Havana: UNEAC, 1971), 49–55; Childs, *The 1812 Aponte Rebellion*, 116; Philip A. Howard, *Changing History: Afro-Cuban Cabildos and Societies of Color in the Nineteenth Century* (Baton Rouge: Louisiana State University Press, 1998), 49.

62. Bodenhorn, "Manumission in Nineteenth Century Virginia," 19, argues that women were a minority in manumissions in Virginia, but Bogger, *Free Blacks in Norfolk*, 13, 53, shows that women outnumbered men among free blacks and benefited from higher manumission rates as well. For New Orleans, see Kotlikoff and Rupert, "The Manumission of Slaves," 176. For Cuba, Aisnara Perera Díaz and María de los Angeles Meriño Fuentes, *Estrategias de libertad: Un acercamiento a las acciones legales de los esclavos en Cuba (1762–1872)*, 2 vols. (Havana: Editorial de Ciencias Sociales, 2015), 1:316–17.

63. Andrés Pletch, "Isle of Exceptions: Slavery, Law, and Counter-Revolutionary Governance in Cuba, 1825–1856," PhD diss., University of Michigan, 2017, 209–211; Curry-Machado, "How Cuba Burned with the Ghosts of British Slavery," 87.

64. Arthur: Petition, Chesterfield County, February 15, 1848, Accession No. 36121, Box 56, Folder 86, LVA-LPDC, pid 515093.

65. Butler, George: Petition, Washington County, December 9, 1813, Accession No. 36121, Box 249, Folder 88, LVA-LPDC, pid 971276; Sterling: Petition, Chesterfield County, October 12, 1814, Accession No. 36121, Box 316, Folder 15, LVA-LPDC, pid 514972.

66. James M. Campbell, *Slavery on Trial: Race, Class, and Criminal Justice in Antebellum Richmond, Virginia* (Gainesville, FL: University Press of Florida, 2007), 156, 153–157; Ted Maris-Wolf, *Family Bonds: Free Blacks and Re-Enslavement Law in Antebellum Virginia* (Chapel Hill: University of North Carolina Press, 2015), 14.

67. See, for example, Accomack County, where eighty-six slaves were freed by deed in the years 1831–1860, and a significantly larger number by will. "Unlike with deeds, the number of manumission wills remained modestly high throughout the period 1831–1853," with significant decrease 1853–1860. *Manumission Wills of Accomack County, Virginia*, compiled by Richard H. Smith Jr. (http://AccomacRoots.com, 2012), LVA, 9; ibid., 8.

68. See, e.g., Smith v. Owens, November 1852, Arlington County Judgments (Freedom Suits) [ACJFS], Box 2 (1823–1858), Barcode 0007451842, LVA; Graham v. Swann,

March 1845, ACJFS, Box 2, LVA; Blue v. Kephart, October 1843, ACJFS, Box 2, LVA; Rustin v. Stromatt, May 1846, ACJFS, Box 2, LVA.

69. This is according to our sample of cases from Accomack County, Arlington County, Westmoreland County, Rockridge County, Frederick County, Northampton County, LVA. These samples mirror the findings of Loren Schweninger's much larger sample of several thousand freedom suits files across the South, in which litigation rates remained steady throughout the antebellum period, and plaintiffs won a sizable majority of their suits during each decade. Loren Schweninger, *Appealing for Liberty: Freedom Suits in the South* (New York: Oxford University Press, 2018).

70. Catherine Wisnosky, "The Will of the Master: Testamentary Manumission in Virginia, 1800–1858," PhD diss., University of Las Vegas, 2015, 256.

71. Samuel alias Samuel Peyton v. Executors of John Peyton, Index No. 1831-005, Fluvanna County, Virginia Chancery Records, LVA; Sarah (Sally) Savage ("All my Negroes & their increase to be FREE at my decease [naming each] & to all whom I give the family name of Savage & $100 amongst them to obtain their FREE papers . . . . To man Bowen my house & lot during his life & then to George S. Savage . . . "), Elizabeth Garrison, and William Walters, in *Manumission Wills of Accomack County, Virginia*, 69, 74; Peggy, alias Peggy Gordan and Peggy Henley v. Arthur Smith, trustee, Index No. 1844-086, Isle of Wight County, Virginia Chancery Records, LVA.

72. Revell Twiford, Walter Bayne, and Mary Stran, in *Manumission Wills of Accomack, Virginia*, 68, 69, 83.

73. Judge Thomas Bayly, Sallie Parsons, in *Manumission Wills of Accomack County, Virginia*, 96, 106; Jarret v. Executor of William A. Bragg, Index No. 1846-016, Amelia County, Virginia Chancery Court Records, LVA.

74. Lucy v. Parish's executors, Index No. 1832-011, Petersburg City, Virginia Chancery Records, LVA; Edy etc. v. Administrator of Noah Meund, Index No. 1835-011, Norfolk County, Virginia Chancery Court Records, LVA; Moses &c. v. Executors of John Stockdell, Index No. 1837-007, Madison County, Virginia Chancery Court Records, LVA. Likewise, John M. Watson freed five slaves by deed in 1833, either if "permitted to remain in state, or if remove[d] to Liberia or other provided place but must serve longer to pay for transport unless funds provided by state or the Colonization Soc." Dosha v. Executors of John Watson, Index No. 1873-001, Prince Edward County, Virginia Chancery Records, LVA.

75. Billy &c. v. Administrator of Thomas Blankenship, Index No. 1847-003, Amelia County, Virginia Chancery Records, LVA; Dicey v. Executor of Craddock Vaughn, Index No. 1853-030, Halifax County, Virginia Chancery Records, LVA.

76. Guild, *Black Laws of Virginia*, 106, 209; Maris-Wolf, *Family Bonds*, 30–32.

77. Guild, *Black Laws of Virginia*, 100–101; Jacob &c. v. Executor of Philip E. Vass, Index No. 1841-010, Halifax County, Virginia Chancery Court Records, LVA; Loren Schweninger, "The Vass Slaves: County Courts, State Laws and Slavery in Virginia, 1831–1861," *Virginia Magazine of History and Biography* 114, no. 4 (2006): 477–478.

78. Schweninger, "The Vass Slaves," 466–472.

79. Morris, *Southern Slavery*, 32; Bogger, *Free Blacks in Norfolk*, 43, 157; Guild, *Black Laws of Virginia*, 107, 120; Schwarz, "Free Black Slaveowners in Virginia," 322–335; Jackson, *Free Negro*, 187–189.
80. Bodenhorn, "Manumission in Nineteenth Century Virginia," 7; Schweninger, "The Vass Slaves," 486; Guild, *Black Laws of Virginia*, 104, 106; Maris-Wolf, *Family Bonds*, 33.
81. Guild, *Black Laws of Virginia*, 95; Art Budros, "Social Shocks and Slave Social Mobility: Manumission in Brunswick County, Virginia, 1782–1862," *American Journal of Sociology* 100, no. 3 (November 2004): 558; Bogger, *Free Blacks in Norfolk*, 25.
82. Budros, "Manumission in Brunswick County," 544; Bodenhorn, "Manumission in Nineteenth Century Virginia," 3; Jackson, *Free Negro*, 174–175; figures from "Free Blacks during the Civil War," Encyclopedia Virginia, accessed April 5, 2019, www .encyclopediavirginia.org/Free_Blacks_during_the_Civil_War.
83. William Sumner Jenkins, *Pro-Slavery Thought in the Old South* (Chapel Hill: University of North Carolina Press, 1935), 246; Guild, *Black Laws of Virginia*, 209; "absurdity," quoted in Morris, *Southern Slavery*, 31.
84. Schwarz, "Free Black Slaveowners in Virginia," 324–325; Stahl, "The Free Negro in Ante-Bellum Louisiana," 319–326; Laura Foner, "The Free People of Color in Louisiana and St. Domingue: A Comparative Portrait of Two Three-Caste Slave Societies," *Journal of Social History* 3, no. 4 (Summer 1970): 407; Logsdon and Bell, "The Americanization of Black New Orleans," 207; Amy R. Sumpter, "Segregation of the Free People of Color and the Construction of Race in Antebellum New Orleans," *Southeastern Geographer* 48, no. 1 (May 2008): 24; Tansey, "Out-of-State Free Blacks," 372; Logsdon and Bell, "The Americanization of Black New Orleans," 209–210.
85. Schafer, *Becoming Free, Remaining Free*, 149–151; Reinders, "The Decline of the New Orleans Free Negro," 95–96.
86. Peirce et al., *Statutes of the State*, 549; Kotlikoff and Rupert, "The Manumission of Slaves in New Orleans, 1827–1846"; Schafer, *Becoming Free, Remaining Free*, 7. Three emancipation courts were established in New Orleans in 1836.
87. Schafer, *Becoming Free, Remaining Free*, 73–82; Reinders, "The Decline of the New Orleans Free Negro," 97.
88. Duhulcod v. Philippe, no. 447 (March 1848); Zabelle v. adm'r of Otis, no. 1201 (June 1848); Baptiste v. Mix, no. 3347 (April 1850); Leocarde v. Blanc, no. 2889 (May 1850); Dowd v. Stream, no. 9921 (May 1856); Bracy v. Lombard, no. 10968 (May 1856); Elizabeth v. Pellandini, no. 11321 (January 1857); Claude v. Lombard, no. 11344 (June 1858), all discussed in Schafer, *Becoming Free, Remaining Free*, 47–55.
89. Ibid., 32–33.
90. See, e.g., Adams v. Routh, no. 3009 (April 1853), LSCA, UNO, appeal in 8 La. Ann. 121 (1853); Marie and Angel v. Destrehan, no. 2228 (March 1832), LSCA, UNO, appeal in 3 La. 434 (1832).
91. Gaudet v. Gourdain, no. 364 (February 1848), LSCA, UNO, appeal in 3 La. Ann. 136 (1848); Eulalie v. Long no. 3979 (June 1856), LSCA, UNO, appeal in 11 La. Ann. 463 (1856); Francois v. Lobrano, no. 5347 (April 1845), LSCA, UNO, at 50 (Arguments and Authorities in Plaintiff's Favour), appeal in 10 Rob. 450 (La. 1845).

92. *Acts Passed by the Fourth Legislature of the State of Louisiana 1852* (New Orleans: Bee Office, 1852), 200, 122; "Manumission," *The Liberator*, April 21, 1848; *Acts Passed by the Fourth Legislature of the State of Louisiana 1859* (Baton Rouge: J. M. Taylor, State Printer, 1859), 214.

93. Adelus, "New Orleans," *New York Times*, April 3, 1853; Tansey, "Out-of-State Free Blacks," 381, 386; Logsdon and Bell, "The Americanization of Black New Orleans," 208.

94. Stahl, "The Free Negro in Ante-Bellum Louisiana," 349. Bitaud's petition is reproduced in the digital archive of the Gilder Lehrman Center for the Study of Slavery, Resistance, and Abolition, Yale University, accessed April 19, 2019, https://glc .yale.edu/VoicesFromTheArchive/WhatdidFreedomMean/LifeAfterFreedom/ MarieLouiseBitian.

95. Adelus, "New Orleans"; De Rocheville, "New Orleans: Worship among the Negroes," *New York Times*, May 25, 1858; "Manumission of Slaves," *The Liberator*, July 29, 1859; "Free Negroes," *De Bow's Review* 1, no. 1 (January 1859), fol. 114.

96. Representación del Ayuntamiento de la Habana, September 22, 1837, AHN, Ultramar, leg. 3547/7; El gobernador al Secretario de Estado, Havana, October 24, 1839, AHN, Ultramar, leg. 3547/8; Noticias referentes al estado de decadencia en que se encuentra la Jamaica desde la emancipación de los negros, 1844, AHN, Ultramar, leg. 3547/10; Expediente instruido con el objeto de vencer los inconvenientes que resultan de la legislación sobre la trata, 1851, AHN, Ultramar, leg. 3547/13; El Conde de Alcoy al Secretario de Estado, Havana, November 7, 1848, AHN, Ultramar, leg. 3547/13; Louis A. Pérez Jr., *Cuba and the United States: Ties of Singular Intimacy* (Athens: University of Georgia Press, 2003); Josef Opatrny, *U.S. Expansionism and Cuban Annexationism in the 1850s* (Prague: Charles University, 1990); Christopher Schmidt-Nowara, *Empire and Antislavery: Spain, Cuba, and Puerto Rico, 1833–1874* (Pittsburgh, PA: University of Pittsburgh Press, 1999).

97. El Ayuntamiento de la Habana pidiendo la reforma del articulo 7° del Reglamento de las Comisiones Mixtas sobre el trafico de negros [1826–1833], AHN, Ultramar, leg. 3547/2.

98. Saco came close to proposing as much in one of his writings in 1864; see Saco, "La estadística criminal," 149.

99. El Consejo de Administración al Gobernador Superior Civil, October 27, 1862, ANC, Intendencia, leg. 960/3.

100. Alejandro de la Fuente, "Slaves and the Creation of Legal Rights in Cuba: *Coartación* and *Papel*," *Hispanic American Historical Review* 87, no. 4 (2007): 659–692.

101. Gerónimo de Valdés, *Bando de gobernación y policía de la Isla de Cuba* (Havana: Imprenta del Gobierno, 1842), 4. On the conflicts surrounding the Reglamento, see Jean-Pierre Tardieu, *"Morir o dominar": En torno al Reglamento de Esclavos de Cuba (1841–1866)* (Madrid: Iberoamericana, 2003); Manuel Barcia Paz, *Con el látigo de la ira: Legislación, represión y control en las plantaciones cubanas, 1790–1870* (Havana: Editorial de Ciencias Sociales, 2000); Franklin W. Knight, *Slave Society in Cuba during the Nineteenth Century* (Madison: Univ. of Wisconsin Press, 1970), 126–132; Manuel

Lucena Salmoral, *Los códigos negros de la América española* (Madrid: Ediciones UNESCO, 1996), 140–59.

102. José I. Rodríguez, "La coartación y sus efectos," *Revista de Jurisprudencia* 1 (1856): 353–362, quote on 355; Nicolás Azcárate, untitled entry, ibid., 363; Expediente sobre la queja del negro José Casanova, 1846, ANC, GSC, leg. 944/33306.

103. Expediente en el que el negro Filomeno Lula pide licencia para buscar nuevo amo, 1852, ANC, GSC, leg. 947/33417; Gloria García Rodríguez, *Voices of the Enslaved: A Documentary History* (Chapel Hill: University of North Carolina Press, 2011), 140; Expediente promovido por el moreno libre Felipe Herrera, 1864, ANC, Miscelánea de Expedientes, leg. 4105/Ñ; Máximo Arozarena to the Captain General, March 8, 1859, ANC, Intendencia, leg. 960/3.

104. Alexander von Humboldt, *Ensayo político sobre la isla de Cuba* (Paris: J. Renouard, 1827), 279; Robert F. Jameson, *Letters from the Havana during the Year 1820* (London: J. Miller, 1821), 41; Edward Mullen, ed., *The Life and Poems of a Cuban Slave: Juan Francisco Manzano, 1797–1854* (Hamden, CT: Archon Books, 1981), 98; Cirilo Villaverde, *Cecilia Valdés, or El Angel Hill* (New York: Oxford University Press, 2005), 428.

105. Laird W. Bergad, Fe Iglesias García, and María del Carmen Barcia, *The Cuban Slave Market, 1790–1880* (New York: Cambridge University Press, 1995), 122–142.

106. Richard Henry Dana Jr., *To Cuba and Back* (Boston: Ticknor and Fields, 1859), 252.

107. A point that David Turnbull makes in his *Travels in the West*, 148.

108. The quote concerning "discipline" comes from the New Orleans *Picayune*, as quoted in "The Negro Troubles," *New York Times*, February 1, 1857; Rodríguez, "La coartación y sus efectos," 355.

109. This statement appears in a marginal note that Bachiller wrote on Máximo Arozarena, letter to the captain general, March 8, 1859, Expediente sobre la coartación, 1853–1862, ANC, Intendencia, leg. 960/3. The text was reproduced with some variation in Bachiller y Morales, *Los negros* (Barcelona: Gorgas y Compañía Editores, [1887]), 156–157.

110. Perera Díaz and Meriño Fuentes, "La manumisión en Cuba."

111. There were exceptions, such as the proslavery tract of José Ferrer de Couto, *Los negros en sus diversos estados y condiciones* (New York: Imprenta de Hellet, 1864). But it is probably not a coincidence that this book was written in New York, in direct response to the challenges to slavery in Cuba posed by Northern abolitionism and the Civil War in the United States.

CHAPTER 5 "NOT OF THE SAME BLOOD"

1. William H. Tucker, *The Science and Politics of Racial Research* (Urbana: University of Illinois Press, 1994), 12–17; Josiah C. Nott, *Two Lectures on the Connection between the Biblical and Physical History of Man* (New York: Batlett and Welford, 1849), 36; Samuel A. Cartwright, "Philosophy of the Negro Constitution," in *Cotton Is King, and Pro-Slavery Arguments*, ed. E. N. Elliot (Augusta, GA: Pritchard, Abbott and Loomis, 1860), 691–706, quotation on 701; "Free Negroes in Hayti," *De Bow's Review* 2, no. 5 (November 1859): 549; Juan

Bernardo O'Gavan, *Observaciones sobre la suerte de los negros del Africa, considerados en su propia patria, y trasplantados á las Antillas españolas: Y Reclamación contra el tratado celebrado con los ingleses el año de 1817* (Madrid: Imprenta del Universal, 1821), 9; Albert Taylor Bledsoe, *An Essay on Liberty and Slavery* (Philadelphia: J. P. Lippincott, 1856), 299.

2. Quoted in William Sumner Jenkins, *Pro-Slavery Thought in the Old South* (Chapel Hill: University of North Carolina Press, 1935), 243.

3. George M. Fredrickson, *White Supremacy: A Comparative Study in American and South African History* (New York: Oxford University Press, 1981), 154–155; John C. Calhoun, "Slavery a Positive Good, February 06, 1837," accessed December 22, 2018, http://tea chingamericanhistory.org/library/document/slavery-a-positive-good/.

4. Francis Pendleton Gaines Jr., "The Virginia Constitutional Convention of 1850–1851: A Study in Sectionalism," PhD diss., University of Virginia, 1950, 252; Virginia Constitutional Convention, *Journal, Acts and Proceedings of a General Convention of the State of Virginia, Assembled at Richmond, on Monday: The Fourteenth Day of October, Eighteen Hundred and Fifty* (W. Culley, printer, 1850), accessed April 2, 2019, http://hdl .handle.net/2027/mdp.35112105105821.

5. Quoted in Ted Maris-Wolf, *Family Bonds: Free Blacks and Re-enslavement Law in Antebellum Virginia* (Chapel Hill: University of North Carolina Press, 2015), 72.

6. This argument is articulated by Robert J. Cottrol, *The Long Lingering Shadow: Slavery, Race, and Law in the American Hemisphere* (Athens: University of Georgia Press, 2013).

7. Cuba, Comité Estatal de Estadística, *Los censos de población y vivienda en Cuba* (Havana: Instituto de Investigaciones Estadísticas, 1988).

8. Ariela J. Gross, "Litigating Whiteness: Trials of Racial Determination in the Nineteenth-Century South," *Yale Law Journal* 108, no. 1 (October 1998): 152.

9. Ibid., 152–153.

10. Ariela J. Gross, *What Blood Won't Tell: A History of Race on Trial in America* (Cambridge, MA: Harvard University Press, 2008), 11; Cottrol, *The Long Lingering Shadow*, 102.

11. Act of March 15, 1832, ch. 22, 1831 Va. Acts 20–22.

12. Ira Berlin, *Slaves without Masters: The Free Negro in the Antebellum South* (New York: Pantheon Books, 1974), 129–130; Emily West, "Family or Freedom: People of Color in the Antebellum South," *American Historical Review* 119, no. 2 (2013): 38.

13. Kimberly M. Welch, *Black Litigants in the Antebellum American South* (Chapel Hill: University of North Carolina Press, 2018), 134–160; Gary B. Mills, *The Forgotten People: Cane River's Creoles of Color* (Baton Rouge: Louisiana State University Press, 2013); Carl A. Brasseaux, Keith P. Fontenot, and Claude F. Oubre, *Creoles of Color in the Bayou Country* (Jackson: University Press of Mississippi, 1994); H. E. Sterkx, *The Free Negro in Ante-Bellum Louisiana* (Rutherford, NJ: Fairleigh Dickinson University Press, 1972); Loren Schweninger, "Antebellum Free Persons of Color in Postbellum Louisiana," *Louisiana History* 30, no. 4 (Autumn 1989): 353–354.

14. Martha S. Jones, *Birthright Citizens: A History of Race and Rights in Antebellum America* (New York: Cambridge University Press, 2018); Welch, *Black Litigants*.

15. Gerónimo de Valdés, Bando de gobernación y policía de la Isla de Cuba (Havana: Imprenta del Gobierno, 1842), 28, 36 (articles 102 and 143); Herbert S. Klein, "The Colored Militia of Cuba, 1568–1868," *Caribbean Studies* 6, no. 2 (1966): 20–24; Leví Marrero, *Cuba: Economía y sociedad*, 15 vols. (Madrid: Editorial Playor, 1971–1992), 13:134–142; David A. Sartorius, *Ever Faithful: Race, Loyalty, and the Ends of Empire in Spanish Cuba* (Durham, NC: Duke University Press, 2013), 85–89.

16. Circular del Gobernador Leopoldo O'Donnell, May 31, 1844, ANC, Asuntos Políticos, leg. 138, no. 7; El Gobernador Leopoldo O'Donnell a las autoridades locales, May 31, 1844, ANC, GSC, leg. 138, no. 7.

17. June Purcell Guild, *Black Laws of Virginia* (Westminster, MD: Heritage Books, 2011), 96, 107, 113; Tommy Bogger, *Free Blacks in Norfolk, Virginia, 1790–1860* (Charlottesville: University of Virginia Press, 1997), 162; Donald E. Everett, "Emigrés and Militiamen: Free Persons of Color in New Orleans, 1803–1815," *Journal of Negro History* 38, no. 4 (October 1953): 394–398; Levi Peirce et al., *The Consolidation and Revision of the Statutes of the State* (New Orleans: Printed at The Bee Office, 1852), 32, 284, 397, 527; Annie Stahl, "The Free Negro in Ante-Bellum Louisiana," *Louisiana Historical Quarterly* 25, no. 2 (April 1942): 318.

18. Guild, *Black Laws of Virginia*, 112, 117, 167, 175, 179. These punishments were increased in the criminal code of 1848 to a larger fine and up to six months in prison.

19. Janet Duitsman Cornelius, *When I Can Read My Title Clear: Literacy, Slavery and Religion in the Antebellum South* (Columbia: University of South Carolina Press, 1992), 33, 80; Heather Andrea Williams, *Self-Taught: African American Education in Slavery and Freedom* (Chapel Hill: University of North Carolina Press, 2005), 19.

20. Margaret Douglass, *Educational Laws of Virginia: The Personal Narrative of a Southern Woman* (Boston: John P. Jewett and Co., 1854), 21–22; ibid., 44–45, 48.

21. Laura Foner, "The Free People of Color in Louisiana and St. Domingue: A Comparative Portrait of Two Three-Caste Slave Societies," *Journal of Social History* 3, no. 4 (1970): 414; Stahl, "The Free Negro in Ante-Bellum Louisiana," 359–365, 392; Peirce et al., *Statutes of the State*, 290; Robert C. Reinders, "The Decline of the New Orleans Free Negro in the Decade before the Civil War," *Journal of Mississippi History* 24 (April 1962): 89.

22. The best study of Couvent and the school is Elizabeth Clark Neidenbach's, "The Life and Legacy of Marie Couvent: Social Networks, Property Ownership, and the Making of a Free People of Color Community in New Orleans," PhD diss., College of William and Mary, 2005, especially ch. 6. Despite its title, Alphonse Desdunes, *Nos hommes et notre histoire* (Montreal: Aurbur and Dupont, 1911), includes a section on Couvent, and Desdunes writes hagiographically about the school and its teaching staff. See also Walter C. Stern, *Race and Education in New Orleans: Creating the Segregated City, 1764–1960* (Baton Rouge: Louisiana State University Press, 2018).

23. On the law of 1847, see Peirce et al., *Statutes of the State*, 228. On the creation of public education system in New Orleans, see Sarah L. Hyde, *Schooling in the Antebellum South: The Rise of Public and Private Education in Louisiana, Mississippi, and Alabama* (Baton Rouge: Louisiana State University Press, 2016), and Raleigh A. Suarez, "Chronicle of

a Failure: Public Education in Antebellum Louisiana," *Louisiana History: The Journal of the Louisiana Historical Association* 12, no. 2 (Spring 1971): 109–122; Neidenbach, "The Life and Legacy of Marie Couvent," 411; Reinders, "The Decline of the New Orleans Free Negro," 89.

24. "From the Anti-Slavery Bugle: Abolitionism in New Orleans," *The Liberator*, September 16, 1853. The little information available on the Cook Jr. case comes from testimonies gathered by Alice Dunbar-Nelson, "People of Color in Louisiana, Part II," *Journal of Negro History* 2, no. 1 (January 1917): 66. See also Willard B. Gatewood Jr., "John Francis Cook, Antebellum Black Presbyterian," *American Presbyterians* 67, no. 3 (Fall 1989): 221–229.

25. José Antonio Saco, *Colección póstuma de papeles científicos, históricos, políticos* (Havana: Editor Miguel de Villa, 1881), 60–78, quotation on 70; Marrero, *Cuba*, 14:90–95.

26. Official correspondence between Juan José Benites, José Policeto Gómez, and Francisco Dionisio Vives concerning a license to establish a primary school, 1828, Houghton Library, Harvard University, José Augusto Escoto Cuban History and Literature Collection, item 921.

27. Juan Justo Reyes, *Consideraciones sobre la educación doméstica y la instrucción pública en la Isla de Cuba* (Havana: Imprenta del Gobierno, 1832), 83; Antonio Bachiller y Morales, *Apuntes para la historia y de la instrucción pública de la Isla de Cuba*, 3 vols. (Havana: Imprenta de P. Massana, 1859), 1:7.

28. Saco, *Colección póstuma*, 95–96, 101; Jacobo de la Pezuela, *Diccionario geográfico, estadístico, histórico de la Isla de Cuba*, 4 vols. (Madrid: Imprenta del establecimiento de Mellado, 1863), 3:16–17, 438–439. Pezuela's figures differ slightly in these two entries, but that difference does not alter the trends discussed in the text.

29. José María Zamora y Coronado, *Biblioteca de legislación ultramarina*, 6 vols. (Madrid: Imprenta de J. Martin Alegria, 1846), 6:117; Pezuela, *Diccionario*, 3:449.

30. Pedro Deschamps Chapeaux, *El negro en la economía habanera del siglo XIX* (Havana: UNEAC, 1971), 126; Saco, *Colección póstuma*, 74.

31. Bachiller y Morales, *Apuntes para la historia*, 1:19; Zamora y Coronado, *Biblioteca de legislación ultramarina*, 6:119; *Cuadro estadístico de la siempre fiel Isla de Cuba* (Havana: Imprenta del Gobierno y Capitanía General por S.M., 1847); Pezuela, *Diccionario*, 3:363; Deschamps Chapeaux, *El negro*, 129–131; Marrero, *Cuba*, 14:99.

32. This report is cited by Michele Reid-Vazquez, "Tensions of Race, Gender and Midwifery in Colonial Cuba," in *Africans to Spanish America: Expanding the Diaspora*, ed. Sherwin K. Bryant and Rachel Sarah O'Toole (Champaign: University of Illinois Press, 2012), 203n36.

33. Nicholas May, "Holy Rebellion: Religious Assembly Laws in Antebellum South Carolina and Virginia," *American Journal of Legal History* 49 (July 2007): 237–256; Guild, *Black Laws of Virginia*, 107, 167.

34. Albert Raboteau, *Slave Religion: The "Invisible Institution" in the Antebellum South* (New York: Oxford University Press, 2004), 130, 135, 137; Robert C. Reinders, "The Churches and the Negro in New Orleans, 1850–1860," *Phylon* 22 no. 3 (1961): 242, 246.

35. Raboteau, *Slave Religion*, 133; Caryn Cossé Bell, *Revolution, Romanticism, and the Afro-Creole Protest Tradition in Louisiana, 1718–1868* (Baton Rouge: Louisiana State University Press, 1997), 90; Joseph Logsdon and Caryn Cossé Bell, "The Americanization of Black New Orleans, 1850–1900," in *Creole New Orleans: Race and Americanization*, ed. Arnold R. Hirsch and Joseph Logsdon (Baton Rouge: Louisiana State University Press, 1992), 215.

36. Reinders, "The Churches and the Negro in New Orleans," 246; African Methodist Episcopal Church v. City of New Orleans, 15 La. Ann. 441, 441–446 (1860).

37. On the regulatory regime of the cabildos, see Valdés, *Bando de gobernación y policía de la Isla de Cuba*, 25, 40, 78 (articles 87, 88 and 159 of the Bando, plus article 21 of the "Instrucción de Pedáneos"). See also Maria del Carmen Barcia Zequeira, *La otra familia: Parientes, redes y descendencia de los esclavos en Cuba* (Havana: Casa de las Américas, 2003), 121–136; Philip A. Howard, *Changing History: Afro-Cuban Cabildos and Societies of Color in the Nineteenth Century* (Baton Rouge: Louisiana State University Press, 1998), 49–99; Barcia Zequeira, *La otra familia*, 331–344.

38. Byron Curti Martyn, "Racism in the United States: A History of Anti-Miscegenation Legislation and Litigation," PhD diss., University of Southern California, 1979, 488; Verena Martínez-Alier, *Marriage, Class and Colour in Nineteenth-Century Cuba: A Study of Racial Attitudes and Sexual Values in a Slave Society* (Ann Arbor: University of Michigan Press, 1989), 46.

39. Richard Konetzke, *Colección de documentos para la historia de la formación social de Hispanoamérica, 1493–1810*, 3 vols. (Madrid: CSIC, 1953–1958), 3(1): 406–413; Patricia Seed, *To Love, Honor and Obey in Colonial Mexico: Conflicts over Marriage Choice, 1574–1821* (Stanford: Stanford University Press, 1998).

40. Issued for Cuba, this royal decree reiterated a previous instruction to the viceroy of Buenos Aires, ordering that in marriages of individuals of "known nobility and notorious purity of blood" with members of the lower castes, official authorization was required even if the partners were of legal age and did not need parental consent. See "Real Cédula de 15 de octubre de 1805 acerca de los matrimonios, que personas de conocida nobleza pretendan contraer con las de castas de negros y mulatos," in Zamora y Coronado, *Biblioteca de legislación ultramarina*, 4:236–238.

41. Don Joaquin Vazquez solicitando contraer matrimonio con la parda libre Catalina Guerrero, 1820, ANC, GSC, leg. 893, no. 30472.

42. Martínez-Alier, *Marriage, Class and Colour*, 13.

43. Promovido por Jorge Barrera, blanco y del Estrado Mayor, pidiendo se le permita contraer matrimonio con Justina María Serrano, mestiza libre, 1875, ANC, GSC, leg. 932, no. 32673.

44. Of all the cases studied by Martínez-Alier, only twenty-one were initiated by priests who refused to proceed with requests for mixed marriages.

45. Martínez-Alier, *Marriage, Class and Colour*, 48; Zamora y Coronado, *Biblioteca de legislación ultramarina*, 4:237; Valdés, *Bando de gobernación y policía*, 92 (article 44 of the "Instrucción de Pedáneos"); Mariano Aguilar, *Vida admirable del siervo de Dios P. Antonio María Claret*, 2 vols. (Madrid: Establecimiento Tipográfico de San Francisco de Sales,

1894), 1:456–70; Miguel Estorch, *Apuntes para la historia de la administración del Marqués de la Pezuela en la Isla de Cuba* (Madrid: Imprenta de M. Galiano, 1856), 29–33; Diligencias para evacuar el informe acerca de los matrimonios celebrados en esta jurisdicción de raza distinta, 1853, ANC, GSC, leg. 916, no. 31858. The *Gaceta* report is reproduced in "Letter from Havana," *Daily Picayune*, July 23, 1854.

46. This suggestion would contradict the findings of Martínez-Alier, *Marriage, Class and Colour*, 63, who perceived these marriages as "exceptional." But as she noted, additional empirical research on the parish registries is needed to clarify this point. Since parochial books were kept according to race, it is not obvious where such marriages would be recorded.

47. Mary Williams, "Private Lives and Public Orders: Regulating Sex, Marriage, and Legitimacy in Spanish Colonial America," in *Louisiana: Crossroads of the Atlantic World*, ed. Cécile Vidale (Philadelphia: University of Pennsylvania Press, 2014), 147–164.

48. La. Civ. Code art. 95 (1825); on interracial marriage, see generally Diana Williams, "They Call It Marriage: The Interracial Louisiana Family and the Making of American Legitimacy," PhD diss., Harvard University, 2007; Emily Clark, "Atlantic Alliances: Marriage among People of African Descent in New Orleans," in *Louisiana: Crossroads of the Atlantic World*, ed. Cécile Vidale (Philadelphia: University of Pennsylvania Press, 2014), 165–183; Virginia M. Gould, *Chained to the Rock of Adversity: To Be Free, Black and Female in the Old South* (Athens: University of Georgia Press, 1998), 7; Brasseaux, Fontenot, and Oubre, *Creoles of Color*. See also the following cases involving "concubinage": Adams v. Routh, no. 3009 (April 1853), LSCA, UNO, appeal reported in 8 La. Ann. 121 (1853); Turner v. Smith, no. 5076 (June 1857), LSCA, UNO, appeal reported in 12 La. Ann. 417 (1857); Bird v. Vail, no. 3454 (March 1854), LSCA, UNO, appeal reported in 9 La. Ann. 176 (1854).

49. Armand Lanusse, "Un mariage de conscience," and "Progress of Amalgamation," cited in Williams, "They Call It Marriage," 103, 148. On free women of color as concubines, see Williams, "They Call it Marriage," 231–241. On vigilantes targeting interracial couples, see Alexandre Barde, *Histoire des comités de vigilance aux Attakapas* (Saint-Jean-Baptiste: Impr. du Meschacébé et de l'Avant-coureur, 1861), 219; Sterkx, *Free Negro*, 255; Brasseaux, Fontenot, and Oubre, *Creoles of Color*, 82–84.

50. Act of Dec. 22, 1792, ch. 42, sec. 17–18, 1792 Va. Acts 130, 134–135; Peter Wallenstein, "Race, Marriage, and the Law of Freedom: Alabama and Virginia, 1860s–1960s," *Chicago-Kent Law Review* 70, no. 2 (1994): 393; Act of 1848, ch. 8, sec. 4–5, 1848 Va. Acts 110, 111; Wallenstein, "Race, Marriage, and the Law of Freedom," 394; Joshua D. Rothman, *Notorious in the Neighborhood: Sex and Families across the Color Line in Virginia, 1787–1861* (Chapel Hill: University of North Carolina Press, 2003), 8; ibid., 263.

51. Dean v. Commonwealth, 45 Va. 541 (Va. Gen. Ct. 1847); Gross, *What Blood Won't Tell*, 56; Gross, "Litigating Whiteness," 165; Rothman, *Notorious in the Neighborhood*, 220.

52. Petition to General Assembly from Stafford County, Accession No. 36121, Box 239, Folder 35, LVA.

53. Act of 1833, ch. 243, 1832 Va. Acts 198; Rothman, *Notorious in the Neighborhood*, 215.

54. Act of 1833, ch. 80, sec. 1, 1832 Va. Acts 51; Rothman, *Notorious in the Neighborhood*, 210; A. Leon Higginbotham and Barbara K. Kopytoff, "Racial Purity and Interracial Sex in the Law of Colonial and Antebellum Virginia," *Georgetown Law Journal* 77, no. 6 (August 1989): 1984–1985n78; Berlin, *Slaves without Masters*, 162; Norfolk City Free Negro and Slave Records, Box 1, Accession No. 115577, July 15, 1833, Affidavit/ Certification re Indian Descent of Asa Price, etc., LVA; City of Petersburg Free Negro and Slave Records, 1809–1865, Box 1, Accession No. 1152180, 1841, Certification of Lavinia Sampson, LVA.

55. Rothman, *Notorious in the Neighborhood*, 227.

56. Bailey received his certificate despite this testimony about Indian ancestry. Ex parte John Scott Bailey, 1852, Henrico County FNSR, Box 2, Accession No. 1186850, LVA. Certificates were also issued to Mary Blount and Julia Simmons, and to James Howell, 1851, Norfolk City FNSR, Box 1, Accession No. 115577, LVA; to William Turner and Martha Ann Turner, 1851, Norfolk County FNSR, Box 2, Accession No. 1188995, LVA; to Sylvia Jeffers, and to William Freeman, 1853, Petersburg City Court FNSR, 1809–1865, Box 1, Accession No. 1152180, LVA; to Amanda Perkins, and to Pastora Bissell and Oliver Bissell, 1855, Norfolk County FNSR, Box 2, Accession No. 1188995, LVA. Braxton Smith, January 3, 1853, was refused by the court, Henrico County FNSR, Box 2, Accession No. 1186850, LVA.

57. Petition of Eleanor Vaughan et al., Halifax County, January 15, 1851, Accession No. 36121, Box 99, Folder 63, LVA. No act was passed on their behalf.

58. Quoted in Rothman, *Notorious in the Neighborhood*, 235.

59. Petition from Citizens of Lancaster County to General Assembly, February 25, 1858, Accession No. 36121, Box 136, Folder 74, LVA; Rothman, *Notorious in the Neighborhood*, 324.

60. Transcript of Trial, Boullemet v. Phillips, no. 4219, June 1837, LSCA, UNO, 9, 11, 12, 14, 24–29, 31–32, 36, rev'd, 2 Rob. 365 (La. 1842); Gross, "Litigating Whiteness," 148.

61. Transcript of Trial, Boullemet v. Phillips, 9–36, 12, 24 (testimony of Jean Chaillot), 14, 26 (testimony of Jean Fauchet), 31–32 (testimony of Mrs. Lavigne), 28–29 (testimony of Herzamu Mouchon), 36–38 (testimony of Mrs. Piquery); Gross, "Litigating Whiteness," 148.

62. Transcript of Trial, Boullemet v. Phillips, 18–69; 2 Rob. La. 365, 366–367 (1842).

63. Transcript of Trial, Cauchoix v. Dupuy, no. 2125, July 1831, LSCA, UNO, aff'd, 3 La. 206, 207 (1831).

64. Transcript of Trial, Dobard v. Nunez, no. 1944, April 1851, LSCA, UNO, 17, 301, 303, 305, aff'd, 6 La. Ann. 294, (1851). See also Transcript of Trial, Williamson v. Norton, no. 2417, June 1852, LSCA, UNO, 48–50, aff'd, 7 La. Ann. 393 (1852), rev'd on reh'g, 7 La. Ann. 394 (1852) (Robert "had more the appearance of the gentleman than the plebeian" and his "dress was genteel, his deportment was quiet and retiring, and his appearance that of a modest and unassuming gentleman").

65. Transcript of Trial, Miller v. Belmonti, no. 5623, May 1845, LSCA, UNO (notes by plaintiff's counsel on the rule for a new trial), rev'd, 11 Rob. 339 (La. 1845); Gross, "Litigating Whiteness," 166–168.

66. Transcript of Trial, Morrison v. White, no. 442, Sept. 1858, LSCA, UNO, 24–35, rev'd, 16 La. Ann. 100 (1861).

67. Seed, *To Love, Honor and Obey*, 205; Martínez-Alier, *Marriage, Class and Colour*, 18; Estorch, *Apuntes para la historia*, 29.

68. Don Nicolás Rondón solicita contraer matrimonio con la parda ingenua Maria Irene Valdespino, 1821, ANC, GSC, leg. 895, no. 30520; Don Florencio José Curbelo solicitando contraer matrimonio con la parda Nicolasa Josefa Camacho, 1827, ANC, GSC, leg. 900, no. 30881; Don Francisco Camejo solicitando contraer matrimonio con Juana Francisca Izquierdo, 1818, ANC, GSC, leg. 893, no. 30297.

69. Manuel de Jesus solicitando contraer matrimonio con Maria de la O, 1813, ANC, GSC, leg. 888, no. 29871; Don Jose Telles solicitando contraer matrimonio con la parda Luisa Martinez, 1813, ANC, GSC, leg. 888, no. 29890.

70. Félix Varela y Morales, "Proyecto y memoria para la extinción de la esclavitud en la Isla de Cuba," in *Obras*, 3 vols. (Havana: Imagen Contemporánea, 2001), 2:196.

71. Autos promovidos por D. Francisco Fernández, D. Juan Bautista Angeli y D. Mariano Tabasco; en solicitud de contraer matrimonio con tres mulatas, 1855, ANC, GSC, leg. 917, no. 31914; Mathias Maruny solicitando contraer matrimonio con Josepha Estrada, 1826, ANC, GSC, leg. 989, no. 30819; Don Simón José de Jesus Barcañela solicitando contraer matrimonio con la parda Feliciana Pascuala Soler, 1828, ANC, GSC, leg. 897, no. 30698; Don José Cárdenas solicitando contraer matrimonio [con] Juana Francisca Vazquez, 1820, ANC, GSC, leg. 895, no. 30522.

72. Don Joaquin Vazquez solicitando contraer matrimonio con la parda libre Catalina Guerrero, 1820, ANC, GSC, leg. 893, no. 30472; Don Florencio José Curbelo solicitando contraer matrimonio con la parda Nicolasa Josefa Camacho, 1827, ANC, GSC, leg. 900, no. 30881.

73. Cited in Martínez-Alier, *Marriage, Class and Colour*, 23.

74. Don Florencio José Curbelo solicitando contraer matrimonio con la parda Nicolasa Josefa Camacho, 1827, ANC, GSC, leg. 900, no. 30881; Don Luis Luaces pidiendo se le permita contraer matrimonio con la parda María de la Luz García, 1824, ANC, GSC, leg. 897, no. 30724.

75. See additional examples in Martínez-Alier, *Marriage, Class and Colour*, 24.

76. Vicente Vázquez Queipo, *Informe fiscal sobre fomento de la población blanca en la Isla de Cuba* (Madrid: Imprenta de J. Martín Alegría, 1845), 33; Documents concerning marriage licenses for esclavos y libres de color, 1856, Houghton Library, Harvard University, Collection of Cuban Slavery Documents, MS Span 170 (26). See also Certification of "solteria y buenas costumbres" for a "moreno libre," Manuel Acosta, 1853, Houghton Library, Harvard University, Collection of Cuban Slavery Documents, MS Span 170 (24). On the reproduction of patriarchy in Cuban slave society, see Sarah L. Franklin, *Women and Slavery in Nineteenth-Century Cuba* (Rochester, NY: University of Rochester Press, 2012).

77. Zamora y Coronado, *Biblioteca de legislación ultramarina*, 4:237. The case of Graverán and Dau is discussed in Deschamps Chapeaux, *El negro*, 191; Don Juan Tenreyro solicitando

licencia para contraer matrimonio con Da. Catalina Valdes por negársela su madre, 1849, ANC, GSC, leg. 912, no. 31658.

78. Martínez-Alier, *Marriage, Class and Colour*, 24; Konetzke, *Colección de documentos*, 3-(2):695–697. On the stain associated with sacrilegious children, see Isabel dos Guimarães Sá, "Up and Out: Children in Portugal and the Empire (1500–1800)," in *Raising an Empire: Children in Early Modern Iberia and Colonial Latin America*, ed. Ondina E. González and Bianca Premo (Albuquerque: University of New Mexico Press, 2007), 17–40.

79. Martínez-Alier, *Marriage, Class and Colour*, 16; D. Tomás Alvarez contra el matrimonio de su hermana Da. María Diniosia Alvarez, viuda, con el pardo Pedro Vargas, 1822, ANC, GSC, leg. 896, no. 30630. This case is mentioned in Deschamps Chapeaux, *El negro*, 194.

80. Documents concerning marriage licenses for esclavos y morenos libres, 1856, Houghton Library, Harvard University, Collection of Cuban Slavery Documents, MS Span 170 (27).

81. Martínez-Alier, *Marriage, Class and Colour*, 16, 37, 39; Don Juan Tenreyro solicitando licencia para contraer matrimonio con Da. Catalina Valdes por negársela su madre, 1849, ANC, GSC, leg. 912, no. 31658; Promovida por Don Joaquín Calderón y Gómez en solicitud de licencia para contraer matrimonio con la parda Antonia Cano, 1853, ANC, GSC, leg. 916, no. 91839.

82. Don Enrique Severino Carvajal sobre matrimonio con Lusila Maria de la Caridad Castillo, 1882, ANC, Gobierno General, leg. 450, no. 21492.

CONCLUSION

1. The term comes from William Watkins, "For the Genius of Universal Emancipation," quoted in Martha S. Jones, *Birthright Citizens: A History of Race and Rights in Antebellum America* (New York: Cambridge University Press, 2018), 40.

Index

abolitionists, 134–53, 167, 171, 173, 176–77, 179–82. *See also* emancipation movements; manumission

Accomack County, xii, 54, 57–58, 70–71, 90, 93, 95–96, 100, 161, 163, 257n67. *See also* Virginia

Act for the Better Ordering of Slaves, 229n17

Adèle (enslaved person), 125–26

Africa (and Africans). *See* blacks and blackness; colonization movements; emancipation movements; free people of color; Liberia; slavery

African Methodist Episcopal (AME) churches, 193

Agassiz, Louis, 178

Akyeampong, Emmanuel, xiii

Albemarle County, 199

Alexander, James E., 138–39

Alvarez, Tomás, 215–16

Amelia County, 161–62

American Colonization Society (ACS), 148, 150–52, 161–62

American Revolution, 60–61

American Slavery, American Freedom (Morgan), 58

Andrews, George Reid, xi, xiii

Antonio of Pointe Coupée, 118–19

Aponte, José Antonio, 80, 82, 100–101, 139

Appeal to the Coloured Citizens of the World (Walker), 135–37, *136*, 137–39, 142

Aram, Marie, 39–41, 51

Arango y Parreño, Francisco, 80, 102, 130

Arostegui, Martin, 108–10

Arozarena, Máximo, 175, 261n109

Arthur (freedman from Chesterfield County), 158–59

Asbury, Francis, 88

Audiencia de Santo Domingo, 77, 105

Bachiller y Morales, Antonio, 176, 190, 261n109

Bacon, Izar, 163

Bacon's Rebellion, 36, 58–59, 74–75

Bailey, John Scott, 204

Bandy, Nanny, 63

Bañon, Juan, 14

Baptists, 88, 90, 191, 193

Barbados, 19, 60, 229n17, 238n45

Barcañela, Simón de Jesús, 213

Barcia, Manuel, x

Barker, Eliza, 169

Barrios, Esteban, 48–49

bastardy cases, 8, 42, 63–65, 69–71. *See also* fornication; sexuality

Battalion of Pardos, 194

Battle of New Orleans, 124, 185–86

Battle of Santo Domingo, 82

Baugh, James, 97–98

Bayly, Thomas H., 161

Bayne, Walter D., 161

The Bee, 138–39

Belen Convent, 189

Bell, Sarah, 164

Belmonti, Louis, 209

Bennett, James, xiii

Bergad, Laird, 175

Berlin, Ira, 56, 73–74

Bernard, Raphael, 50

Bestick, Dorothy, 70

Bienville (Governor), 52

Billy v. Blankenship, 162

birthright citizenship, 135–36
Bitaud, Marie Louise, 170
Black Code (1806), 83, 125, 127, 250n93
Black Jacke (enslaved person), 54
blacks and blackness: citizenship's
    curtailment and, 15, 21–38, 130–31,
    135–41, 146–48, 158–71, 178–82, 193;
    colonization movement and, 7, 11,
    142–53, 156, 161–63, 169; free
    communities of color and, 2, 5–7, 11–17,
    38, 42–43, 45, 49–53, 71–78, 101–2,
    129–33, 146, 153–88, 219, 221; Indian
    ancestry and, 1–2, 6, 11, 31, 94–98,
    200–201, 204–6, 245n38; military service
    and, 7, 51, 76, 87, 102, 122–25, 184–86,
    194, 206, 222; passing and, 200, 209–10,
    267n64; presumption of enslavement
    and, 4–6, 9, 11, 15–17, 21–44, 50–64,
    74–75, 78–80, 97–98, 127, 130–31,
    153–77, 181–82, 217, 219; property
    ownership and, 14–15, 74, 183–86;
    reenslavement and, 25–26, 82, 140–41,
    159, 166–67, 169, 222, 223, 236n30;
    religious institutions of, 31–33, 182–85,
    191–94; residency appeals and, 158–66;
    sexuality and, 8–10, 34–35, 38, 42–48,
    64–66, 69–71, 194–218; slavery's defenses
    and, 6, 145–46, 157–58, 179–80; state
    determinations of racial categories and,
    178–82, 199–218; weapons ownership
    and, 29, 31, 185–86. See also Cuba; free
    people of color; Louisiana; race; slavery;
    Virginia
Blanco, Catalina, 194
Bledsoe, Albert Taylor, 179
Bodenhorn, Howard, 165
Body of Liberties (Ward), 229n17
Booth, Margrett, 57
Borroto, Melchor, 41
borrowings (legal), 228n15, 229n17
Boullemet, Stephen, 206–7
Boullemet v. Phillips, 207
Bourbon Reforms, 11, 82, 103–4
Bragg, William, 161–62
branding, 29
British Honduras, 152
British Slavery Abolition Act (1833), 144
Broutin, Francisco, xii
Brown, Rebecca and John, 92
Brunswick County, 165, 243n20
Bucarelli, Antonio Maria, 24, 109
Budros, Art, 243n20

Burcareli, José María, 103, 108
Burton, Sarah and Francis, 204
Burton, Stith, 92
Butler, George, 159
Butterwood Nan, 97

cabildos, 17, 23, 25, 193–94
Cáceres Ordinances, 75
Calhoun, John C., 179–80
Camacho, Nicolasa Josefa, 211, 213
Cantillon, Bernard, 50
Caribbean. See slavery; specific colonies
Carondelet, Francisco, 121
Carter, Hannah, 71
Cary, Eady, 92
Casanova, José, 174–75
Casor, John, 14–15
Castilla, William, 57
Castillo, Antonio Maria del, 194
Castor, John, 54
Cauchoix family, 207–8
Cauchoix v. Dupuy, 207
Cecilia Valdés, 175
César, Jean-Baptiste, 50, 236n30
Chaillot, Jean, 207
Charles City County, 91
Chesterfield County, 91–92, 98, 158
children. See bastardy cases; fornication;
    free people of color; inheritance rights;
    intermarriage; race
churches, 182–85, 191–94, 222. See also
    religion; specific denominations and
    institutions
cimarrones, 140, 155. See also running away
citizenship, 6–7; birthright, 135–36;
    colonization movements and, 7, 11,
    132–35, 142–53, 156, 161–63, 169; race
    and, 15, 17, 26–33, 130–31, 146–48,
    153–84, 193, 206; religion and, 26, 45;
    vecinidad and, 13–14, 21–27, 48, 75, 182,
    184; voting and, 180–81, 224; whiteness
    and, 5–7, 11, 78, 157–58, 181–82, 200,
    203, 206, 221–24
civic acts (as evidence of whiteness), 5, 201,
    206–8, 217
Civil Code of Louisiana (1825), 125,
    127–28, 197–98, 250n93
Civil War (U.S.), 157–58, 170–71, 217,
    224
Claiborne, Herbert A., 202
Claiborne, William C. C., 123–24
Clarisse (enslaved person), 168

coartación: ambiguous status of, 48–49, 105, 111, 176–77; definition of, 105–6; *entero* status and, 104; in Louisiana, 116–22, 125, 127–28; mother's status and, 113–14; *papel* and, 1, 111–13, 117, *120, 128,* 173–74, *174;* regulation of, 171–73; slaves' rights and, 6, 103–12, 130–31, 175–76, 221; taxation and, 103–4
Cobb, Thomas Reade, 145
Code Noir (1685), 19, 44, 53, 67
Code Noir (1724), 19, 21, 33–35, 44, 50, 67, 75, 78, 122, 125
Coke, Thomas, 88
Coleman, Francis, Sr., 95
Coleman v. Dick and Pat, 95
Coleta, Maria, 102–3
Coliseum Place Baptist Church, 193
colonization movements, 7, 11, 132–35, 142–53, 156, 161–63, 169
Colonization Society of the State of Virginia, 161
Company of the Indes (French), 36–37
comparative history, x–xi
concubinage, 34–35, 66–67, 123, 197–98, 215. *See also* fornication; marriage
Conga, Catalina, 14
Congo, Manuel, 14
Connard, Louis and Catherine, 52
Consejo de Administración, 171–72
Consejo de Indias, 106, 109, 111, 113–14, 173
Constitution (U.S.), 11, 84, 130, 150, 193, 217
Cook, John Francis, Jr., 188
Cook, Mary, 96
Cooke, John, 201
Cookson, Richard, 29
Coomee, John, 62–63
Cope, Tabitha, 71
Corsey, James, 205
Cortes de Cadiz, 143–44
Cottin v. Cottin, 125
Couto, José Ferrer de, 261n111
Couvent, Marie Justine Sirnir, 187, 263n22
Cruzat, Francisco de, 121
Cuba: annexation movement and, 171–72; *coartación* in, 1, 6, 39–43, 221; colonization movements and, 134, 152–53, 256n57; emancipation efforts in, 143–45; free communities of color in, 5–7, 11–17, 38, 49, 71–78, 101–2, 129–31, 133, 146, 153, 155–58, 171–77, 219, 221;

freedom suits in, 102–14; Haitian Revolution and, 80–82, 100–105; Iberian slavery laws and, 6, 8, 10–12, 16, 21–27, 41–49, 65, 89–90, 218, 220; manumission regulation in, 10, 38–44, 65, 77–78, 89–90, 101–2; maps of, *22, 101;* marriage laws in, 5, 65–67, 181–82, 195–96, 210–16, 224, 265n40; mutual-aid societies in, 187, 193–94; *pardo* designation and, 7, 16, 47–48, 76–77, 122, 181, 188, 194, 199–218; racial distinctions legally codified in, 13–17, 21–27, 66–67, 72–73, 141–42, 146–47, 157–58, 184–85, 209–11, 216–17, 219, 223–24; Reglamento de Esclavos (1842) in, 134; runaways and, 36; schooling in, 188–91; slave revolts in, 80–82, 100–101, 133, 139–40, 144; slave trade in, 143–44, 152–53, 175; whiteness of, 79–80, 181. *See also* free people of color; law; marriage; race; slavery
Cuban National Archives, 196
Cuffy, Maria, 127
Curbelo, Florencio José, 211–12
Cuszens, William, 95

Daily Picayune, 141
Dana, Richard Henry, 175–76
Daniel, Patsey, 163–64
Daniel, Terry, 163
Darby, Jonathas, 50
Dau, Margarita, 215
David (enslaved person), 95
De Bow's Review, 171, 179
Declaration of Independence, 84, 136–37, 243n24
De Coustillas, Captain, 53
Demerea, John, 62
Deposit of Runaway Slaves (Havana), 154–55
Depres, Henrique, 120–21
Desdunes, Alphones, 188, 263n22
Deslondes, Charles, 82, 124
Dew, Thomas Roderick, 142, 165
Diago, Clara, 175
Dicy (enslaved person), 162
Digest of the Civil Laws (1808), 125
Dobard v. Nunez, 208
Dolores Abileyra, Maria de los, 107
Doubrère, Louis, 128
Douglass, Mary, 186–87
Driggus, Emanuel, 70

Dunn-Haley, Karen, xiii
Du Tertre, Jean-Baptiste, 19

Edgg, William, 71
Edsall, Magret, 71
Eleanor (enslaved person), 162
Elizabeth City County, 62
Eltonhead, William, 55
emancipados, 152–53
emancipation movements, 84–89, 132–41, 143–44, 148–53
Emanuel the Negro, 29
Engerman, Stanley, xi
entero status, 104, 111, 176. *See also* coartación
Epes, Travis, 204–5
Epiphany, 193, *194*
Erman, Sam, xiii
Essay on Liberty and Slavery (Bledsoe), 179
Estelle, Samuel, 169
Estrada, Josepha, 213
Estrada, Pedro, 215
Exchanging Our Country Marks (Gomez), 227n7
Ezpeleta, José de, 114

families. *See* bastardy cases; fornication; free people of color; inheritance rights; marriage; race; slavery
Fassin, Eric, xiii
Fauchet, Jean, 207
Fernández, Anna Josefa, 215
Fernando (enslaved person), 18
Fernando, Bashaw, 54
Ferrer, Ada, x, 80
First African Baptist Church, 193
First African Church, 192, *192*
fornication, 30, 42, 63–65, 70–71. *See also* bastardy cases; sexuality
Foster, John, 54
Francisco Josef (enslaved person), 106
François (enslaved person), 168
Frank (enslaved person), 161
Fredrickson, George, x, 179
Freedom's Journal, 135
Freedom Suit Act (1795), 86, 93
freedom suits: abusive masters and, 92–93, 109, 112–13, 174–75; *coartación* and, 48–49; Cuban context and, 100–114, 171–77; equality ideals and, 83–84; gender and, 7–8; Iberian customs of, 46–49; illegal importation and, 11, 86,

98–100, 139, 152–53, 200; Indian ancestry and, 11, 94–97; juries in, 94–95, 167–68, 244n30; Louisiana's regulations of, 50–53, 114–31; racial determinations and, 181–82, 200, 203–4, 209–10, 267n64; records of, xii, *107*, 244n30; reenslavement and, 169–71; regulation of, 4–5, 39–43, 103–4; testamentary claims and, 45, 52–54, 86–87, 91–94, 129, 160–62; testimony in, 2, 14–15, 57, 86–87, 118–19; Virginia's role in, 54–57, 85–86, 92–100, 159–61, 221–22. *See also specific cases*
free people of color: citizenship demands and, 135–37, 180–81, 238n45; communities of, 2, 4–7, 11–17, 38, 49, 71–78, 101–2, 129–33, 146, 153–58, 171–90, 219, 221; Indian ancestry and, 1, 6, 58–59, 61–63, 200–201, 204–6; legal claims of, xi; marriage and, 8, 65–71, 181–82, 194–99; military service and, 7, 76, 87, 102, 122–25, 184–86, 194, 206, 222; passing and, 200, 209–10, 267n64; populations of, 6, 26–33, 38, 49–53, 65–66, 71–78, 82–86, 101–2, 129–33, 146–48, 153–77, 182–84, 219–21, 243n20, 255n50; property ownership and, 14–15, 74, 183–86, 224; regulations regarding, 4–5, 33–35, 73–78, 89, 114–15, 134–35, 141–48, 153–77, 192–93, 223–24; religious institutions and, 75–76, 182–85, 191–94, 222; removal of, 7, 11, 132–35, 142–53, 156, 161–63, 169; residency requirements and, 2, 53–66, 86, 146–48; revolutionary participation of, 139–42; schooling for, 184–91; segregation and, 14, 123; sexuality and, 8–10, 34–35, 38, 42–48, 64–71, 194–218; slave ownership by, 14–15, 155, 164, 183–84; the state's racial determinations and, 199–218; white man's democracy and, 7, 180–81, 219. *See also* blacks and blackness; manumission; race; slavery; *specific jurisdictions*
French and Indian War. *See* Seven Years' War

Gabriel's Rebellion, 88–89, 185
Gaceta de la Habana, 197
Garcia, Juan, 41
Garcia, Juana, 26

Garcia, Marcos Jose, 216
García y Sanabria, Leandro, 112
Garrison, Elizabeth, 161
Garrison, William Lloyd, 136–37, 150
Garzés, Rafael, 214
Gaspart, Marie, 67
Gaudet, Azela, 168
Genaro, José, 110
gender: manumission and, 7–8, 43; mothers as reproducers of freedom, 7–8, 18, 26–33, 43, 47, 54, 62–65, 70–71, 98, 113–14, 168, 203; racial performances and, 208–10; white womanhood's status and, 42. *See also* citizenship; marriage; race; sexuality
George (enslaved person), 86, 96
George III, 84–85
Gershenowitz, Debbie, xiii
Gholson, James, 147
Gillfield Baptist Church, 191
Girardy, Marie-Françoise, 118
Godsey, Mary, 199
Goldman, Jon, xiii
Gomez, Michael, 227n7
Gonzalez, Juan Junco, 1
Gonzalez, Patricia, xiii
Gordon, Bob, x, xiii
Graverán, Jorge, 215
Graweere, John, 54, 57
Grenada, 152
Griggs, John, 56
Grinberg, Keila, x
Grinsted, William, 69
Guadeloupe, 18, 21, 44
Guerrero, Catalina, 196, 213
Gwyn, Hugh, 29

Haitian Revolution, 6–7, 10–11, 79–80, 88–90, 100–105, 123–24, 140, 167. *See also* New Orleans; Saint-Domingue; Virginia
Halifax County, 162–63
Hall, Gwendolyn Midlo, 51, 73
Hannah (enslaved person), 97
Hanover County, 88
Harman, William, 56
Harriet (enslaved person), 161
Harris, Leslie, xiii
Hartog, Dirk, xiii
Hatfield, April Lee, 237n36
Havana: *coartación* in, 10, 12, 117, 175; fears of revolts in, 80–82, 100–101, 133,

139–40, 144; free communities of color in, 13–14, 26–27, 38, 65–66, 72–73, 75–77, 100–103, 128–31, 133, 141, 152, 154–58, 165, 175–76, 188, 191, 200, 208, 211, 221; images of, *101, 154, 194*; manumission regulations in, 1–3, 13–14, 41, 46–49, 52, 61, 83, 103, 108–14, 116, 171, 176–77; marriage in, 65–66, 195–97; municipal regulations in, 21–25, 36–37, 188–89, 191, 208; New Orleans and, 9–10; racial certification procedures in, 208, 211; removal proposals in, for free people of color, 147–48; slave trade in, 21, 139–40
Hawley, William, 54
hearsay, 97–98
Hébard, Jean, x, xiii, 53
Helena (enslaved person), 119–21
Henley, William, 161
Henrico County, 88, 163
Hernandez, Rafael, 194
Herrera, Felipe, 175
Higginson, Humphrey, 57
Hispaniola, 125
historiography, x–xi, 5, 8–9
Hitchens, Edward, 71
Hôpital des Pauvres de la Chartié, 39–40
Howard, Reuben, 163
Hudgins v. Wright, 97, 127, 225n1

Ibby (enslaved person), 96
Iglesias Utset, Marial, 256n57
illegal importation laws, 11, 86, 98–100, 139, 152–53, 200
Importation Act (1778), 86, 139
indentured servants, 14–15, 70–71
Indian ancestry, 1, 58–59, 61–63, 66–69, 94–96, 121–22, 202–6; racial regimes and, 6, 204–7. *See also* blacks and blackness; freedom suits; race; *specific jurisdictions*
Indian Will, 63
inheritance rights, 195–99. *See also* bastardy cases; fornication; free people of color; marriage
intermarriage, 8–10, 34–35, 38, 42–48, 64–66, 69–71, 194–218. *See also* marriage; race
involuntary sales, 111–13, 173
Isaacs, David, 199

Jackson, Henry, 58

Jamaica, 144, 152, 238n45
"A Japan-Based Global Study of Racial
  Reparations" (symposium), xiii
Jeane (enslaved person), 58
Jefferson, Thomas, 84, 88, 143, 148
Jenkins v. Tom, 95
Jesus, Manuel de, 212
Jim (enslaved person), 95
Johnson, Anthony, 14–15, 54, 55, 70
Johnson, John, 15, 57
Johnson, Priscilla, 96
Johnson, Richard, 70
Johnson, Susanna, 70
Johnson, Walter, ix
Jones, Martha, ix, x, xiii
Jose Maria (enslaved person), 108
Joynes, Thomas R., 93–94
Juana (enslaved person), 1–2, 6
Junta de Fomento, 80
juries, 94–95, 167–68,
  244n30

Kendall, P. R., 96
Kendall, William, 56, 58
Key, Elizabeth, 57, 69
Key, Thomas, 57
King and Queen County, 88–89
Kitt, Oni, 71
Klein, Herbert, xi, 228n13
Kotlikoff, Laurence J., 129
Ku Klux Klan, 198

Ladd, James, 87
La Escalera, 139–42, 157, 184–85
Lang, Elizabeth, 70–71
Lara, Silvia Hunold, x
Leach, Hannah, 70
Leigh, Benjamin Watkins, 142
Lewis, Thomas, 142
The Liberator, 136–37, 142, 145
Liberia, 4, 148–52, 161–62, 167, 169
"The Life and Legacy of Marie Couvent"
  (Neidenbach), 263n22
Lilly (enslaved person), 62
limpieza de sangre, 17, 191, 211
L'Institution Catholique des Orphelins
  Indigents, 187–88
Lisbon, 45
Loa, Francisco Manuel de, 41
Long, Daniel, 2
Longo, Anthony, 70
Lorignac, Francisca, 102–3

Lorinak, Francisca, 246n51
Los negros en sus diversos estados y condiciones
  (Couto), 261n111
Louis, Jean, 39
Louisiana: Black Code (1806), 83, 126–27,
  250n93; Civil Code (1825) of, 125–28,
  197–98, 250n93; *coartación* in, 116–22,
  125, 127–28; Code Noir of 1724, 19, 21,
  33–35, 44, 50, 67, 75, 78, 122, 125;
  concubinage in, 34–35, 66–67, 123,
  197–98, 215; Constitutional Convention
  of 1852 and, 184; Constitution of, 184,
  186; as destination for free people of
  color, 6–7, 72–73, 80–82, 115–16, 124–25,
  132–33, 166, 183–84; fears of revolt in,
  81–82, 123, 137–38; freedom suits in, 44,
  50–53, 114–31; free people of color in,
  49–53, 71–78, 129–33, 155–58, 166–71,
  182–84, 255n50; hybrid legal system of,
  9–11; Iberian slavery laws in, 79–84,
  116–18, 120–21, 125, 127, 168–69;
  Indians' racial position in, 66–68, 121–22;
  legal borrowings of, 19–21, 33–38;
  manumission regulations in, 10, 39–43,
  50–53, 65, 75, 77–78, 116, 130–31,
  166–71; maps of, 20, 115, 124; marriage
  regulations in, 10, 65, 197–98; as part of
  United States, 4, 116, 124–26; racial
  identity in, 206–7, 219; racialization of
  laws in, 83–84, 142, 146–47, 157–58,
  183–85, 206; religious institutions of,
  192–94; residency requirements and, 11,
  134–35, 166–71; runaways and, 36–37;
  schooling restrictions in, 186–88; slave
  trade in, 2, 6, 10; Spanish colonialism in,
  6, 35, 79–80, 114–15, 117
Louisiana Historical Center, xii
Louisiana State Colonization Society, 151
Louisiana Supreme Court, 2–3, 126–29,
  168–69, 206–8, 217
L'Ouverture, Toussaint, 79–80
Lucy v. Parish, 258n74
Ludwell, Philip, 61
Lula, Filomeno, 175
Luz García, María de la, 214

Mabry, Zachariah, 2
Madison, James, 84, 133
Magloire (enslaved person), 119–21
Magnimara, D. Patricio, 119–21
Major, Peter, 96
Malemba, Juan, 14

manumission: black slave owners and, 155; citizenship demands and, 135–37, 159–60, 170–71; colonization movement's connection to, 7, 11, 132–35, 142–53, 161, 163, 169; Cuban restrictions on, 171–77; definition of, 1; free communities of color and, 2, 5–7, 11–17, 38, 49, 71–78, 101–2, 129–33, 146, 153–88, 219, 221; freedom suits as bargaining chip for, 98–99; gender and, 7–8, 42–43, 46–47; Iberian customs and, 41–49, 79–84, 101–4, 116, 220; justifications for, 61, 87–88; masters' property rights and, 38, 41, 51–53, 59–60; military service and, 51; as private affair, 78, 89, 127–29; proofs of, 40–41, 45, 60–61, 91–92, 118–19, 126–27; regulation of, 4–5, 10, 41–63, 65, 75, 87, 167–68, 222; self-purchase rights and, 48–49, 52, 77–78, 100, 106–8, 121–22, 126–27, 156, 168–69, 220–21, 250n98; testamentary, 45, 52, 54, 86–87, 91–92, 94, 129, 160–62, 257n67; Virginia's codes and, 53–64, 84–91, 126–27, 130–31. *See also* self-purchasing; *specific jurisdictions*
Manumission Act (1782), 86–89
Manzano, Juan Francisco, 175
Maria Juana (enslaved person), 117
Maria Theresa (enslaved person), 118
Maria v. Robert Saunders, 93
Marie (free person of color), 50
maroons. *See* running away
marriage: class restrictions on, 195–96, 200, 210–16, 265n40; manumission and, 40; racial restrictions on, 5, 8, 10, 34–35, 42, 47–48, 53–71, 75, 181–82, 194–99, 207–8, 216–17, 220, 224. *See also* concubinage; fornication; free people of color; gender; sexuality; slavery; *specific jurisdictions*
Marriage, Class and Colour (Martínez-Alier), 266n46
Martin, Angelina, 26
Martínez-Alier, Verena, 196, 266n46
Martinique, 18, 21, 44, 50, 67, 229n18
Martinsburg Gazette, 147
Maruny, Mason Mathias, 212
Mason, Thomson, 95
Mathews, Morris, 70
McDonogh, John, 151
Melendez, Lorenzo, 188
Mercedes Suarez, Maria Josefa de las, 216
Mercer, Charles Fenton, 148–49

meritorious service, 61, 88
Merris, Martha, 69
Metayer, Adelaide, 128–29
Methodists, 88–90, 144–45
Meullion, Antoine, 52
Meund, Noah, 162
Michaux, Paul, 95
Michel, Johann, xiii
microhistories, 8–9
military service, 7, 51, 76, 87, 102, 122–25, 184–86, 194, 206, 222
militias. *See* military service
Miller, Christopher, 29
Miller, John F., 209
Miller, Sally, 208–9
Miller v. Belmonti, 208–9
Mina, Cristobal, 41, 49, 52
Mina, Jose, 41, 49, 52
Mingo, John, 50
Mingo, Thérèse, 50
Minor, John, 89
Miró, Esteban, 121, 123
Missouri Compromise, 137
Mitchell, William, 99
Mojarrieta, José, 113
Mongom, Philip, 54, 69
Morelli, Frederica, xiii
Moreno Fraginals, Manuel, xi
Morgan, Edmund, 58–59
Morrison, Alexina, 209
Morrison v. White, 209
Morton, Samuel, 178
Mozingo, Edward, 54
mulatto designation, 2, 7, 15, 25–42, 56–71, 74–77, 89, 95, 101–2, 110, 141–47, 181–86, 195–200
Murdaugh, John, 203
mutual-aid associations, 187, 193

Nanny Pegee v. Hook, 3
Nata, Andres, 119–20
Natchez war, 40, 122
Ndiaye, Pap, xiii
Negro John Davis v. Wood, 97–98
Nese (enslaved person), 54
Newman, Mary, 71
New Orleans: colonization movement in, 150–52; fears of revolt in, 81–82, 123, 137–38; freedom suits in, 2, 51, 83, 115–16, 119–23, 127–28, 155, 170, 208; free people of color in, 6, 35, 49–50, 72–78, 129–31, 154–58, 165, 176, 184–85,

187, 190, 193, 200, 221, Havana and,
9–10; images of, *115*; marriage in, 68, 197,
198, 207; racial regulations in, 123–24,
127, 132, 141–42, 145–46, 183–84; slave
trade in, 9, 137–39, 178
New Orlean Semi-Weekly Creole, 132–33
Newton, Abram, 62
New York Times, 170
Nieidenbach, Elizabeth Clark, 263n22
Nizardo, Beatriz, 13–14, 38
Norfolk and Portsmouth Herald, 147
Norfolk County, 60, 99
Northampton County, xii, 14–15, 54–55, 64,
70–71, 73, 100, 149
Nos hommes et notre histoire (Desdunes),
263n22
notaries, 1, 119, *120*
Notes on the State of Virginia (Jefferson), 88
Nott, Josiah, 146–48, 178
Noxe, Andrew, 29

O, Maria de la, 212
O'Donnell, Leopoldo, 185
O'Gavan, Juan Bernardo, 179
Oliveau, Eulalie, 2–4, 168
Oliveau, Henri, 2
Ordenanzas de los negros, 21–22
O'Reilly, Alejandro, 73, 116–17, 121–22
Organization of Creole Free Men of Color
Militia Act, 124

Palmer, Vernon Valentine, 229n18
Pamunky Tribe, *202, 203*
Pantalon (enslaved person), 52
Papaw (enslaved person), 61
papeles, 112, 117, 119, *120*, 128, 173
pardo designation, 7, 16, 47–48, 76–77, 122,
181, 188, 194, 199–218
Parin, Mateo, 117–18
Parish, Mary, 161–62
Parker, George, 15
Parsons, Sallie, 161
partus sequitur ventrem, 7, 18, 30–31, 33, 65,
69, 113–14. *See also* bastardy cases
Pascasio, Pedro, 113
passing, 200, 209–10, 267n64
Paulino (enslaved person), 175
Payne, Francis, 55–56, 69–70
Peake, Mary, 186
Pease, Jonathan, 61
Pegee, Nanny, 1–2, 5–8, 169
Pegram v. Isbell, 95

Peñalver, Maria Faustina, 191
Perez, Isabel, 14
Perez, Matias and Diego, 14
performativity (of race), 201, 206–8, 217
Peterfield, J., 92
petitions to legistlature: for manumission,
4–5, 10, 41–63, 65, 75, 87, 167–68, 222;
"not a negro" certification and, 82,
140–41, 159, 166–69, 222, 236n30; for
reenslavement, 25–26, 82, 140–41, 159,
166–69, 222, 236n30; to remain in state,
1–2, 5, 11, 41, 49, 71–78, 132–35, 156–66,
188; for removal of free people of color,
7, 11, 132–35, 142–53, 156, 161–63, 169.
See also manumission; race;
reenslavement; *specific jurisdictions*
Peyton, John, 161
Phillips, Alexander, 206
phrenology, 178. *See also* scientific racism
Pierce, William, 29
Pitts, Elisha, 71
plaçage, 69
Pointe Coupée Parish, 2, 4
Ponce, Francisco, 76
Porche, Magdelaine Oliveau, 2
Pott, Francis, 58
Powhatan County, 165
Prado, Francisco, 110
Pragmatic on Marriage (Cuba), 66, 182
Premo, Bianca, xiii
prescription (principle), 168
Price, Thomas, 150
Prince George County, 86
Prosser, Gabriel, 80–81
Puerto Príncipe, 105, 113
purity of blood. *See limpieza de sangre*

Quakers, 2, 84–85, 87, 90

race: blood quantum ideas and, 17, 66–68,
191, 211; certifications of, 201–3;
citizenship and, 11–12, 17, 21–27, 78,
130–31, 135–36, 158–66, 193, 221–22;
class and (in Cuba), 195–96, 200, 210–17,
221–22, 265n40; fluid categories of,
26–33, 69; Iberian codifications of, 6–12,
15–27, 42–49, 79–80, 89–90, 220; legal
determinations of, 2, 5, 7, 9, 15–17,
21–27, 43–44, 53–71, 97–98, 178–82, 191,
193, 199–218, 267n64; marriage and, 5, 8,
10, 34–35, 53–71, 75, 181–82, 194–99,
207–8, 210–16, 220, 224; mother's status

and, 7, 54, 65, 70–71, 98, 203; mulatto category's ambiguity and, 2, 7, 15, 25–26, 31–38, 42, 56–71, 74–77, 89, 95, 101–2, 110, 141–47, 181–86, 195–218; passing and, 200, 209–10, 267n64; performance of, 201, 209–10, 217, 267n64; presumption of enslavement and, 5–7, 15–17, 21–44, 50–65, 74–75, 78–80, 97–98, 127, 130–31, 153–77, 181–82, 217, 219; property ownership and, 14–15, 74, 183–86; religious institutions and, 5, 75–76, 184–85, 191–94, 221–22; residency requirements and, 3–5, 146–47, 156, 158–66; schooling and, 5, 184–91; scientific racism and, 178–82, 189; segregation and, 123, 188–90; sexuality and, 8–10, 34–35, 38, 42–48, 64–66, 69–71, 194–218; slavery's role in white solidarity and, 142–48, 157–58, 178–82; state or colonial regulation of, 4–5; testimony and, 57–58, 74, 200–201, 204; white man's democracy and, 141–53, 161–71, 179–80. See also bastardy cases; blacks and blackness; concubinage; free people of color; gender; Indian ancestry; manumission; scientific racism; whiteness
Randolph, Thomas Jefferson, 143
Raphael, Jean-Baptiste, 67
real cédula (1577), 230n29
real cédula (1768), 108
real cédula (1789), 104–5, 246n56
real cédula (1805), 195–96
Real Consulado de Agricultura y Comercio, 17
reenslavement, 25–26, 82, 140–41, 159, 166–69, 222, *223*, 236n30. See also free people of color; gender
Reglamento de Esclavos (1842), 134, 173
Regla Travieso, María Josefa de, 214
religion: citizenship proof and, 26, 45; colonization movements and, 148–53; race and, 75–76, 182–84; schooling and, 187–88; sexuality and, 65–66; slavery's compatibility with, 16, 19, 26–27, 31, 33, 49, 89–92, 220–21. See also specific *denominations and institutions*
removal efforts, 7, 11, 132–35, 142–53, 161, 167, 169. See also citizenship; colonization movements; free people of color; manumission
Revell, Randall, 14–15

revolts (against slave system): Cuban contexts and, 80–82, 100–101, 133, 139–40, 144; Louisiana context and, 81–82, 123, 137–38; Virginian context and, 79–83, 88–89, 102–3, 137–41, 185, 191, 222, 243n20
Richmond: colonization efforts and, 147, 149, 163, 180, 202; free people of color in, 83, 99, 142, 154, 159, 165, 202–5; Haitian Revolution and, 80–81; religious institutions in, *192*; slave markets of, 133–34. See also Virginia
Richmond Dispatch, 203
Richmond Enquirer, 147, 180, 204–5
Riter, Ann, *223*
Rivero Valdés, Orlando, xii
Roberts, Ann and Humphreys, 91
Roberts, William, 96
Robin (enslaved person), 61
Robin v. Hardaway, 95
Rodriguez, Catalina, 26
Rodríguez, José Ignacio, 176
Rodriguez, Juan, 48
Rodriguez de la Soledad, Luis, 76
Rojas, Diego de, 13
Rojas, Hernán Manrique de, 48
Roman law, 4, 8, 33, 44, 65, 125–28, 135–36, 228n15
Romano, Renee, xiii
Rosario, Juan del, 26
Royal Pragmatic on Marriage (1776), 66, 182
Ruffin, Robert, 40
Ruffner, William Henry, 186
running away, 29–30, 36–38, 140, 153–55, 201–2, 221
Rupert, Anton J., 129

Sachs, Honor, 95
Saco, José Antonio, 147
Saint Augustine's Cathedral, 192–93
Saint-Domingue, 6–7, 10–11, 21, 79–83, 89–90, 100–105, 115–16, 123–25, 140, 187, 229n18. See also Haitian Revolution
Saint Landry Parish, 184
Salazar, Diego de, 13–14
Saly, Maria Luisa, 117–19
Sampson, Lavinia, *202*, 203
Sampson, Sally, 203
Samuel (enslaved person), 161
Santiago v. Antonion Moreira, 107
Santo Domingo, 21, 46, 141, 207

Savage, Sally, 161
Savage, Thomas, 63
Scarbrough, Edmund, 96
Schaub, Jean-Fred, xiii
schools, 182–91
Schor, Hilary, xiii
Schor, Paul, xiii
Schweninger, Loren, 258n69
scientific racism, 178–82, 189
Scott, Rebecca J., ix, x, xiii, 53
Sebastiani, Silvia, xiii
"second slavery,"80
Seed, Patricia, 210–11
self-purchase, 42–43, 92, 100, 106–7;
    Bourbon expansions of, 82–83; *coartación*
    and, 48–49, 107–11; colonization
    movement and, 151–52; Iberian customs
    regarding, 11, 42–49, 77–78, 220–21;
    Indian slavery and,
    121–22; involuntary sales and, 111–13,
    173; lawsuits regarding, 4; Louisiana's
    jurisdictional change and, 115–31; loved
    ones and, 39–41, 50–51, 92, 164; notaries
    and, 1, 119, *120*; regulations of, 39–43,
    156, 164. *See also coartación*; gender;
    manumission
Seven Years' War, 79,
    103
Seville, 45
Seville v. Chrétien, 127
sexuality: bastardy cases and, 8, 42, 63–65,
    69–71; concubinage and, 34–35, 66–67,
    123, 197–98, 215; fornication and, 30, 42,
    63–65, 70–71. *See also* gender; marriage
Siete Partidas, 16, 46, 117, 125–26, 128. *See
    also* law; slavery
Silvia (enslaved person), 98–99
síndico, 104, 108–10, 112, 174
Slave Law in the Americas (Watson), 228n15
slavery: agency within, xi, 6, 11, 17–21,
    115–22, 130–31, 160–62,
    220, 227n7; British colonial laws and, 5, 8,
    16, 19, 26–33; comparative
    methodologies and, x–xi; as criminal
    sanction for people of color, 183–84;
    emancipation movements and, 84–85,
    87–89, 132–41, 143–44; gender and, 7–8,
    168; historians of, ix; illegal importation
    laws and, 11, 86, 98–100, 139, 152–53,
    200; indentured servitude and, 14–15, 58,
    70–71; Indian ancestry and, 1, 31, 58–59,
    95–98, 121, 245n38; legal borrowings

and, 17–21, 102–5; mother's status and, 7,
    18, 26–33, 43, 47, 62–65, 68–71, 98,
    113–14, 203; positive good defenses of, 6,
    145–46, 157–58, 179–80; race and, x–xi,
    15, 21–33, 53–64, 74–78, 146–77, 219–24,
    225n1; religion and, 16, 19, 26, 31–33, 49,
    89–92, 220–21; revolts and, 79–84, 88–89,
    100–103, 133, 135–41, 144, 185, 191, 222,
    243n20; running away and, 29, 36–38,
    140, 153–55, 201–2, 221; self-purchasing
    and, 1, 4, 77–78, 82–83, 92, 151–52,
    168–69; slaves' rights and, 1, 5–6, 17–21,
    48–49, 82–84, 100, 104–6, 112, 117–18,
    121–23, 130–31, 159–61, 171–74, 218,
    220; Southerners' moral defenses of,
    145–46, 157–58, 179–80; terms of service
    and, 44–53; U.S. commitment to, 130–31,
    133–34; weapons prohibitions and,
    185–86; whiteness as criterion of freedom
    and, 181–82, 208–10. *See also*
    concubinage; free people of color;
    gender; manumission; marriage;
    reenslavement; whiteness; *specific
    jurisdictions*
Smith, John, 61
Smith, Tamar, 71
Smith, William "Extra Billy,"165
Sociedad Económica de Amigos del País,
    189–91
Southampton County, 137,
    164
South Carolina, 19, 125, 229n17
Stafford County, 201
statu liberi (Louisiana), 125
Stephan, Dame, 119
Sterling (enslaved person), 159
Sterling, William, 58
Stockdell, John, 162
Stockly, Charles, 90–91
Stolzenberg, Nomi, xiii
Strader v. Graham, 168
Stran, Mary P., 161
Superior Council (Louisiana), 50–53, 75

Takezawa, Yasuko, xiii
Taney, Roger, 195, 222
Taylor, George Keith, 94
Taylor, Philip, 55
Teackle, Levin, 91
Tenreyro, Juan, 215
Terry (enslaved person), 99
testaments. *See* wills

Thibeaud, Clément, xiii
Tiocon, Fançois, 39–41, 51
Tolet y Vargnes, Feliciana Pascuala, 213
Tomlins, Christopher, 229n17
Torre, Juana Josefa de la, 109–10
Toyer, Anne, 71
Trader, Samuel, 93–94
Trinidad, 152
Trinidad, Manuel de la, 112–13
Trouin, Andrew, 99
Turits, Richard, x
Turnbull, David, 141, 254n37
Turner, Nat, 79, 137–38, 138, 139, 141, 148–49, 162–63, 182–83, 191, 222, 243n20
Twiford, Revell, Sr., 161–62
Tyer, Margery, 69–70

unequal marriage (Cuba), 195–96, 200, 210–17, 265n40. See also Royal Pragmatic on Marriage (1776)
Unzaga, Luis de, 119, 122
Ursuline nuns, 187

Valdés, Gerónimo, 173, 185, 197
Valencia, 45
Vanon, Simon, 50
Varela, Felix, 212
Vargas, Pedro, 215–16
Varinas (Marquis of), 25
Vaughan, Eleanor, 204
Vaughn, Craddock, 162, 204
Vaundry, Norbert, 207
Vázquez, Joaquín, 196, 211, 213
Vazquez, Sebastian, 14
Vázquez de Espinosa, Antonio, 26
Velazco, Matías, 191
Villaverde, Cirilo, 175
Villeinage, 19
Virginia: citizenship's curtailment and, 179–81, 221–22; colonization society movement and, 132–35, 148–51, 156, 161; Constitution of, 180; emancipation efforts and, 143–44; equality ideals and, 84–100; freedom suits in, 11, 44, 91–100; free people of color and, 6, 26–33, 65–66, 82–83, 86, 89, 129–31, 146–48, 153–56, 158–66, 182–83, 243n20; illegal importation laws and, 11, 86, 98–100, 139, 152–53, 200; Indian ancestry and, 1–2, 31, 69, 245n38; legal borrowings of, 19–21; manumission regulations in, 10,

39–43, 53–64, 77–78, 90–91, 126–27, 130–31, 222; maps of, 28, 85; marriage regulations in, 10, 65, 195–96, 198–99; racial regulations in, 5, 10, 26–33, 141–48, 157–66, 204–6, 219, 263n18; Reform Convention of, 180; residency requirements of, 1–2, 5, 11, 41, 49, 71–78, 132–35, 156, 158–66, 188; runaways and, 36–37; schooling restrictions in, 186–87; slave revolt possibilities in, 79–80, 82–83, 88–89, 102–3, 137–41, 185, 191, 222, 243n20; slave trade in, 6, 16, 33, 56, 74–75, 84–86, 98, 139, 200
Virginia Importation Act (1778), 86, 139
Virginia Manumission Act, 86–89
Virginia Supreme Court, 2, 86, 95, 98, 160, 201

Walker, David, 135–39, 142
Walker, John, Jr., 96
Wall, Wendy, xiii
Walters, William, 161
Walthum, Elisabeth, 57–58
Ward, Nathaniel, 229n17
Warren, Henry, 63
Warwick, Hannah, 31
Washington, George, 84
Watson, Alan, 228n15
Watson, John M., 258n74
Webb, Abimeleck, 64
Webb, Jane, 63–64
Webb, Thomas, 56
Weeks, Esther, 71
Wells v. Lewis, 96
West, John, 56
West, Nancy, 199
Whartons (family), 201–2
Wheeler, Stephen B., 180
whipping, 29, 32, 36
White, James, 209
white man's democracy, 7, 180–81, 219. See also citizenship; free people of color; race; Virginia
whiteness: certifications of, 201–4, 208–10; citizenship and, 5–7, 11, 15, 31, 78, 181–82, 200–201, 203, 206, 219, 223–24; Cuba's colonial settlement efforts and, 152–53, 216; emancipation claims based on, 181–82; gender and, 8; Haitian Revolution and, 6–7; passing and, 200, 209–10, 267n64; privilege and, ix; schooling and, 191; slavery's

reinforcement of, 142–43, 145, 167–71,
179–80
Wickliffe, Robert C., 132–33
Wilcocke, Peter, 29
Wilkinson, James, 80
Will (enslaved person), 40–41
Williams, John, 29
Williamsburg Church, 191
wills, 45, 52–54, 86–87, 91–94, 129, 160–62

witnesses, 2, 118–19, 200–201, 206–8. *See
also* freedom suits; race
Wood, Rachell, 71
Wythe, George, 94

Yang, Alice, xiii
Young, Elizabeth, 61–62

Zeuske, Michael, x